The Good Retirement Guide 2020

34th Edition

The Good Retirement Guide 2020

Everything you need to know about health, property, investment, leisure, work, pensions and tax

Edited by Jonquil Lowe

KoganPage

Thirty-fourth edition published in Great Britain and the United States in 2020 by Kogan Page Limited

2nd Floor, 45 Gee Street
London
EC1V 3RS
United Kingdom

122 W 27th St, 10th Floor
New York, NY 10001
USA

4737/23 Ansari Road
Daryaganj
New Delhi 110002
India

www.koganpage.com

© Kogan Page Limited, 2013, 2014, 2015, 2016, 2017, 2018, 2019, 2020

ISBNs

Hardback   978 1 78966 067 8
Paperback   978 1 78966 065 4
eBook   978 1 78966 066 1
ISSN   2397-1967

British Library Cataloguing-in-Publication Data

A CIP record for this book is available from the British Library.

Typeset by Integra Software Services, Pondicherry
Print production managed by Jellyfish
Printed and bound by CPI Group (UK) Ltd, Croydon CR0 4YY

CONTENTS

14   No-one is immortal 349

Additionally, a directory of useful organizations and contacts is available online at:

www.koganpage.com/GRG2020

01
Are you looking forward to retirement?

It's official... old age has been postponed! The age at which we consider ourselves to be old is steadily moving upwards, and even at 80 years old, 20 per cent of us say we do not feel old according to the European Social Survey. So maybe 60 years old is the new 40, and 80 years old the new 60?

Whatever you think, over the last century, retirement has changed dramatically. Not so long ago, life expectancy was shorter and many people who stopped working at 65 enjoyed a retirement of less than 10 years. Now it is very different. According to the Office for National Statistics, one in three of today's babies in the UK will live until they are 100. And it's not just the young who can expect to live longer: one in 14 men aged 65 today will become centenarians, and even more women (one in nine).

This situation has been described by the International Longevity Centre as 'a huge societal success', but it comes at a price. Indeed there is a real risk that increased longevity could generate serious intergenerational tensions between workers and pensioners over how resources should be shared. One response has been a shift towards people staying in work longer.

But what about those of us approaching retirement now? Since it can last 25 years or even more, perhaps we should embark on some radical rethinking when planning for the future to ensure it is a positive experience. Work–life balance is important at any age, and whether we intend to carry on working to some extent or enjoy our retirement in a leisurely way, we need to give it serious thought. If we do not spend time now concentrating on 'the work of growing old', we won't have the right things in place when we need them. It is a fact: pensioners are becoming harder to recognize, and retirement now means different things to different people. Planning for a meaningful life after work ends cannot start too soon, and there is far more to it than putting together a financial portfolio.

How to use this book

The Good Retirement Guide is packed with information, suggestions and advice on every aspect of retirement and beyond. It aims to inspire you to do things you've never thought of, and help you to sort out the practicalities should you have not already explored the opportunities available. It is an invaluable resource book which will help you enjoy your retirement to the full.

Whichever aspect of retirement concerns you most, the first step is of course to do some figure work. It is vital, when planning to retire, that you know how to make the most of what you've got. Chapter 2 deals with money in general and contains a very practical budget planner. Working through this is time well spent, if you haven't already carried out such a financial exercise. It will help you to have a clear idea of how much you spend and on what, how much you will need to live comfortably in retirement, and whether you have a shortfall that you'd like to try to fill.

The main way to ensure you have enough income in retirement is to save while you are working, so Chapter 3 is all about pensions, first building up your savings and then understanding your options when you want to start drawing money out. It also deals with the various tax angles relating to pension schemes. The wider picture of tax is discussed in Chapter 4, which looks at the calculation and collection of income tax and capital gains tax, ceasing to pay National Insurance contributions once you reach State Pension age, and how inheritance tax affects what you leave to your heirs, while Chapter 14 looks at issues such as making a will.

In the course of your preparation, you will want to assess your likely savings, including lump sums from your pension and any insurance policies you may have. The more accurate the picture, the more detailed the plan can be of how to maximize the value of your assets. Chapter 5 deals with investments and the many types on offer, why you might consider buying an annuity, and investment strategies if you opt to draw a pension direct from your invested funds (called 'drawdown'). These decisions can get quite complex, so you may decide to get professional advice – and in some situations, you will have to. In each chapter, you will find recommendations for sources of financial advice, and how to find a reputable person to assist you in this complex field.

Around seven in 10 retirees own their own home, according to the Department for Work and Pensions. If that includes you, it is probably your most valuable asset alongside your pension savings. It may be that downsizing is the answer, but Chapter 6, *Your home*, will help you weigh it against other options, such as equity release or home improvements, before taking the plunge.

When it comes to leisure activities, there are opportunities throughout the country for almost every kind of sport and hobby, many with over-55s especially welcome. There are hundreds of specialist bodies, and although the lists are by no means exhaustive, Chapters 7 and 12 give details.

For some, retirement offers the opportunity to start a new career. Some individuals turn their talents to something entirely new, while others go freelance or become consultants in their existing area of expertise. Should you be interested in becoming a mature entrepreneur, Chapter 8, *Starting your own business*, provides good advice to help you decide whether this course of action is right for you. Despite legislation outlawing age discrimination at work, finding paid work over the age of 55 may not be easy, but it is worth considering. There are a growing number of recruitment websites designed especially for retirees. Chapter 9 has suggestions for looking for paid work.

More than any other group in society, older people are the social glue of most communities. They are often the linchpins of local clubs and societies. Millions of over-65s make valuable contributions to many different types of work. Giving back to society increases feelings of self-worth, and adds greatly to a sense of fellowship. Whether you can spare only the occasional day or can help on a regular basis, Chapter 10, *Voluntary work*, has an abundance of suggestions. If you feel like devoting some of your energy to local good causes, there are scores of opportunities for retired people.

Your health is the subject of Chapter 11, which contains information and advice on how to keep well. The key ingredient to a happy and fulfilling retirement is good health. Without it, energy is lacking and many activities are restricted. Notwithstanding unexpected illness, good health as you grow older is largely in your own hands. In real terms, there is a big gap between those who look after themselves and those who make little or no attempt to follow a healthy lifestyle.

If you are caring for elderly parents, the range of organizations that can provide you with backup is far more extensive than you might realize. These are listed in Chapter 13, *Caring for elderly parents*.

Pre-retirement courses

If, as previously suggested, 60 is the new 40, then 80 is the new 60. Whatever age you are due to retire, taking a pre-retirement course will help you plan well for the next stage in your life. Some companies run in-house courses, but if your organization doesn't offer such help, or if you are self-employed, there are a number of independent organizations that can help you. When would be the best time to attend such a course? One or two years before retirement, or earlier? Some people like to prepare for retirement in stages. It is important that some financial decisions, such as those affecting company or personal pension planning, are taken as early as possible. Others, like whether or not to move house, could wait till much later on.

Pre-retirement courses are designed to address the main subjects: finances, health, activity, leisure, housing and the implications and adjustments needed to be made when you retire. The usefulness of such courses can be measured less by the amount of factual information it contains, and more by the extent to which it helps to focus your own thoughts on the issues ahead for you and your family. If your course stimulates discussion with your partner and others in similar situations, it will have achieved its objective.

Here are some websites with loads of information and advice to those planning retirement. They offer good pre-retirement courses, including some online courses:

- **Experience Matters** is aimed at people aged 50 and over. It offers one-to-one coaching either face-to-face or by phone, as well as workshops on topics ranging from relationships to managing elderly parents. See experiencematters.org.uk/about-experience-matters/.

- **LaterLife Learning** provides the most comprehensive approach to retirement in the UK. Pre-retirement and mid-life planning courses are available across the UK. See laterlife.com and retirement-courses.co.uk.

- **PRIME Cymru** (The Prince's Initiative for Mature Enterprise) is a charity dedicated to providing people in Wales over the age of 50 with support to find employment or set up their own business. There used to be a national version of this organization, but sadly it closed down. See primecymru.co.uk.

- **Retirement Education Services** hosts regular one- and two-day retirement planning open courses at venues throughout the country, open to all individuals and couples approaching retirement, covering money, pensions and lifestyle issues. It also offers online learning about retirement. See res-ltd.net/index.php.

New focus for the retired

There are many organizations and websites representing the interests of retired people. The over-50s are an increasingly large and important section of the population, so it is not surprising to find numerous local and national sources of advice and information on issues that affect their lives. Here are some useful websites:

- **Age UK** is the largest charitable organization providing information, advice, products and services to people to improve later life. See ageuk.org.uk.
- **GOV.UK** is the UK government's website for all issues relating to the government, including State Pensions and tax. See gov.uk/browse/working.
- **National Pensioners Convention** is the campaigning voice for UK pensioners – for dignity, financial security and fulfilment for all older people. See npcuk.org.
- **Pension Wise** is another government site which focuses on your private (non-state) pension options as you approach retirement. See pensionwise.gov.uk.
- **Retirement Expert** offers expert advice and information on all issues related to retirement. See retirementexpert.co.uk.

Financial advice

There are many aspects of retirement, such as planning how much income you'll need, pension choices, and investment decisions, where you may want the help of a professional financial adviser. There are a number of organizations that supply directories you can use to find an adviser near you, such as:

- **Chartered Institute for Securities and Investment** (CISI): financialplanning.org.uk/wayfinder;
- **My Local Adviser:** mylocaladviser.co.uk;
- **Personal Finance Society** (PFS): thepfs.org/yourmoney/find-an-adviser;
- **Personal Investment Management and Financial Advice Association** (PIMFA): pimfa.co.uk/managing-your-money;
- **Society of Later Life Advisers** (SOLLA): societyoflaterlifeadvisers.co.uk;
- **Unbiased:** unbiased.co.uk.

Check that any adviser is genuine and properly regulated by checking a firm's entry on the Financial Services Register before doing business: fca.org.uk/firms/financial-services-register. Pensions and investments are fertile areas for scams and fraud. If you are approached out of the blue by anyone claiming they can give you investment or pension advice and/or offering you deals that sound too good to be true, do not do business and report the scam to Action Fraud: 0300 123 2040, actionfraud.police.uk.

Additional resources

Throughout this guide, you will find many signposts to places where you can get relevant and helpful additional support and information. You can download a directory of these resources from www.koganpage.com/GRG2020.

02
Money and budgeting

Retirement is the reward for a hard-working life – but while you may be ceasing work, you should not allow your money to retire as well. It is important that it continues to work hard for you, so that you've got the financial flexibility you need. There are many money-related decisions to be made when you retire: get them right, and your income could increase year by year. If you fail to plan, you might be faced with making personal cutbacks at a time when you should be relaxing and enjoying yourself.

With people living longer, secure pensions from salary-related pension schemes fading fast and new pension freedoms that have reduced the use of annuities, more pensioners are directly exposed to the three great risks of retirement: longevity risk (outliving your savings), inflation risk (the buying power of your money falling over time), and investment risk (being exposed to the ups and downs of the stock market). Chapters 3 and 5 look at the pension and investment choices you can make to help to ensure the income you have coming in is guarded against these risks. But here and throughout this guide, you should try to be aware of inflation in all aspects of your retirement and planning for it.

Inflation means a sustained rise in prices – not just a temporary hike in the cost of coffee or petrol, but the relentless upward drift of prices over time that means your money buys less today than it did in the past. Even low rates of inflation have a big impact on prices over a long period: for example, if inflation averaged 2 per cent a year (the official target for the UK), £100 after 25 years would buy only the same as £61 today, meaning you'd have to cut your spending by over a third. Aviva (an insurance and pensions provider) suggests that over three-quarters of pensioners are worried about the rising cost of living and having to continue working to make ends meet. Obviously one way of increasing the problem is to bury your head in your hands and do nothing. Failing to work out how much you are actually worth and what you can really afford to buy will simply postpone facing reality.

So, what steps can you take to avoid being strapped for cash once you leave your job? Whether you are close to giving up work or are several years away from retirement, the most important thing to do is carry out a serious review of your retirement plans. This will help you work out what options there are for maximizing your future income.

There are many ideas on what makes a good financial plan, but the core elements are the same. In order of priority, a typical person should normally aim to:

1 Sort out any problem debts.

2 Stay in your workplace pension scheme. (Since your employer must contribute on your behalf, opting out is like turning down part of your pay!) If you are not an employee, save through your own pension plan.

3 Get term life assurance if anyone is financially dependent on you.

4 Build up at least three months' worth of outgoings in accessible savings, such as a cash Individual Savings Account (ISA) to cover emergencies.

5 Buy a home if you are ready to settle somewhere.

6 Save and invest to achieve other goals.

Everyone's circumstances and resources are different, so you may have a slightly different plan and, if you're already retired, maintaining a stable income from your pensions will often be your second highest problem after sorting out problem debts. In some situations, you may need to get professional advice to help you. If you have problem debts, you should urgently consult one of the free, independent money advice agencies, such as Citizens Advice, nationaldebtline. co.uk or stepchange.org. These impartial, non-judgemental organizations can efficiently help you deal with your creditors, without stigma, and identify any additional sources of income you may be eligible for. Debt problems get worse if you ignore them, so be honest with yourself that there is a problem. Warning signs include borrowing to buy day-to-day essentials, and taking out new loans to pay off old ones.

To ensure you have a comfortable retirement, you will need to carry out a full financial health check. If you are still pre-retirement, this involves looking ahead to your income and likely spending in retirement. If you are already retired, you should be repeating this health check on an annual basis to get a clear view of your current financial position and how it may change in future. For pre-retirement planning, you should get a State Pension statement (which says how much State Pension you are currently entitled to once you reach State Pension age and whether there is any scope to improve this), and check the benefit statements you receive from pension schemes you belong to now and have done in the past. If you don't have recent statements, contact the employer or pension provider concerned to ask for one. The government is backing an industry initiative to introduce 'pension dashboards' – online apps that will let you automatically see all your pensions in one place. Once that's up and running (maybe in 2020), it will take a lot of the legwork out of this part of doing a financial health check. But until then, you will have to rather laboriously gather up all these pension statements for yourself. If you've lost track of old pensions, there is a free government service, the Pension Tracing Service, gov.uk/find-pension-contact-details, which can help. (Be aware that commercial firms with a similar name charge.)

Factor in any other sources of retirement income, for example, from non-pension savings you have built up, to give you a complete picture of your budget from the income side. Once you've done that, work out how much you are likely to need to spend in retirement. Bear in mind that, if your income is high enough, some of it will go in income tax. Be as realistic as you can about your spending – for example, how much you are likely to save once you are not travelling to and from work. Remember to factor in holidays and repayments on any debts you might have.

Doing the sums – budgeting

With the current economic climate causing difficulties for so many, the ability to manage your money and know how to budget is important. Knowing how much you spend, and on what, is essential. While you have records of formal bills, it's very easy to overlook casual and ad hoc purchases. A tip some people recommend is keeping track of your expenditure by means of a 'spending diary'. Whether you use a notebook, a spreadsheet or an app on your phone, the result is the same. Put down everything you spend over a period of, say, one month, so you can see what you are spending on and how much; it's then quite easy to see if these are essentials and/or whether they are costing too much. Don't forget that there are some 'retirement freebies' which are well worth taking advantage of: various things you become entitled to once you've passed a certain age. These include travel and entertainment concessions, some health benefits and help with fuel bills. It's surprising how much these small things add up.

Once you have gathered objective data about your income and spending, you are armed to analyse and improve your finances. One sensible way to do this is to draw up a budget showing your income and outgoings. To make a proper assessment, you need to draw up several lists:

- expected sources of income on retirement;
- essential outgoings;
- normal additional spending (such as holidays and other luxuries).

And, for improving your current finances and planning ahead, the following should also be considered:

- possible ways to boost your retirement income;
- spending now for saving later, or vice versa.

If retirement is imminent, then doing the arithmetic in as much detail as possible will not only reassure you, but also help you plan your future life with greater confidence. You'll feel better knowing how you stand financially. Don't forget that there are probably a number of options open to you. Examining the figures written down will highlight the areas of greatest flexibility. One tip, offered by one of the retirement magazines, is to start living on your retirement income some six months before you retire. Not only will you see if your budget estimates are broadly correct, but since most people err on the cautious side when they first retire you will have the bonus of all the extra money you will have saved.

If retirement is still some years ahead, there will be more unknowns and more opportunities. When assessing the figures, you should take account of your future earnings. Perhaps you should also consider what steps you might be able to take under the pension rules to maximize your pension savings. You could also consider whether you should be putting money aside now into other savings plans and investments. Imprecise as they will be, the estimates you make in the various income and expenditure columns should indicate whether, unless you take action now, you could be at risk of having to make serious adjustments in your standard of living later on. To be on the safe side, assume an increase in inflation – the official Bank of England target is 2 per cent a year, but actual inflation can of course be more or less. Everyone should, if they possibly can, budget for a rainy-day fund to help cover the cost of any emergencies or special events that may come along.

Let's look at some things it is worth thinking about in preparation for planning your budget.

Possible savings

Once you stop working, you could save quite a lot because there will be expenses you no longer have. These include travelling costs to and from work, meals out, business clothes, and other work-related incidentals such as drinks with colleagues, staff collections and entertainment. Other costs like National Insurance contributions cease once you reach State Pension age, and unless you choose to invest in a private plan, your pension contributions will also stop. It is important to check (once you retire) what your tax coding is, because you may well move to a lower tax bracket (Chapter 4 has details).

If your children are no longer financially dependent on you and your mortgage is almost paid off, you could begin to feel quite good about things. On top of that, there are some concessions that come with retirement. Some, such as a free bus pass, are linked to reaching State Pension age. This has been equalized for men and women, and is currently rising to reach 66 for all by 2020. Many other retirement concessions kick in somewhat arbitrarily from age 60, including concessionary travel on trains and coaches, free NHS prescriptions, cheaper theatre and cinema tickets (usually matinees), reduced entrance charges for exhibitions, historic properties and a wide choice of special holiday offers.

At present, if you're 75 or over, you qualify for a free TV licence. However, the government passed funding of this particular concession to the BBC, which has announced that from June 2020 onwards the free licence will be means-tested. This means that only people aged 75 and over who are getting Pension Credit will qualify for the free licence.

In addition, many insurance companies give discounts to mature drivers, some of which apply from age 50+. Discounts typically range from 10 to 15 per cent. However, premiums may rise from, say, age 75 onwards because statistics gathered by insurance companies show the risk of making claims increases at higher ages. There are considerable extra savings for drivers who have five or more years claim-free so, if this applies to you, you might consider paying a bit extra to protect your no-claims discount. That said, to get the best prices you may need to shop around each year and switch insurer – though, if you do find a cheaper deal elsewhere, talk to your current insurer. They may be willing to reduce your renewal quote to something closer to the new quote you've found. The easiest way to shop around is to use an online price comparison website (the downloadable directory that comes with this guide lists a few), but if you prefer non-digital methods, consider using an insurance broker.

Extra outgoings

If you are spending more time at home once you retire, your utility bills will increase. You may also find you spend more on outings, hobbies and holidays. Looking ahead, home comforts become increasingly important and you may want to think about paying other people to do some of the jobs that you previously managed yourself. Anticipating such areas of additional expenditure is the surest way of avoiding future money worries. Once you've worked out your retirement income and expenditure in detail, you should be able to manage well. However, if you are mainly dependent on the State Pension and benefits (as is the case for almost a quarter of pensioners, according to GOV.UK), you may find you're managing on a tight income. This has become tougher as a result of austerity policies, and leaves little if anything to spare for extras.

Expected sources of income on retirement

Your list will include at least some of the following. Once you have added up the figures in the budget planner later in the chapter, you will have to deduct income tax to arrive at the net spending amount available to you:

- your State Pension (if you reached State Pension age before 6 April 2016, this may be made up of a basic pension, graduated pension, SERPS and state second pension; otherwise you get the new single-tier State Pension – Chapter 3 has details);
- one or more occupational pension(s);
- one or more personal pension(s), which may be workplace schemes or ones you arranged for yourself;
- earnings or profits from continuing to do some work at least in the early part of retirement;
- state benefits.

Additionally, you may receive income or a capital sum from some of the following:

- a company share option scheme;
- sale of business or personal assets;
- investments (stocks and shares, unit trusts, etc);
- other existing income (from a trust, property or family business);

- bank/building society savings;
- National Savings & Investments bonds or certificates;
- endowments or other investment-type life insurance policies;
- rent, if you let out a property.

Unavoidable outgoings

No one will have the same list as another, since one person's priority is another's luxury. For this reason, the divide between 'unavoidable outgoings' and 'normal additional expenditure' (see section following) is likely to vary considerably with each individual. For example, pet owners would consider pet food and veterinary bills an essential item of expenditure. If you do not have, or intend to get, a pet, such costs can be disregarded. Almost everyone will want to juggle some of the items between the two lists or add their own particular requisites or special enthusiasms.

Whatever your own essentials, some of the following items will certainly feature on your list of unavoidable expenses:

- food;
- rent or mortgage repayments;
- council tax or (in Northern Ireland) rates;
- repair and maintenance costs eg emergency call-out costs, appliance servicing, gardening or window cleaning;
- water bills;
- heating, lighting and other energy;
- TV licence;
- telephone/mobile, internet connection and entertainment packages;
- postage (including Christmas cards);
- household insurance;
- clothes, shoes, shoe repairs;
- domestic cleaning products, laundry products and dry cleaning;
- your car, including road tax, fuel, insurance, roadside assistance (RAC/ AA or similar) and servicing;
- other transport;
- outgoings on health, such as the dentist, chiropractor, non-prescription medicines and products;

- regular savings and (if you have dependents) life assurance;
- credit card and other loan repayments (though don't double-count if this covers spending that is already itemized above).

Although the above items may all be considered essential, it does not necessarily mean they cannot be pared back. It's often possible to save money by switching to cheaper providers, brands or other alternatives (such as cheaper seasonal fruit and veg). You might also be able to save money in the long run by buying foodstuffs in bulk provided they store well, or tailoring what you buy to any available coupons or special offers.

Normal additional expenditure

This could include:

- gifts;
- holidays;
- newspapers/books/magazines/CDs/DVDs;
- computer expenses (including broadband);
- drink;
- hairdressing;
- toiletries/cosmetics;
- entertainment (hobbies, outings);
- miscellaneous subscriptions/club membership fees;
- charitable donations;
- expenditure on pets;
- garden purchases.

Work out the figures against these lists. Then, to compare your expenditure against likely income, jot them down on the budget planner below.

Budget planner

It's not possible to cover absolutely everything here, but the main things are listed. Once you've an idea of what you will need money for, the next thing is to make what you've got go as far as possible. Drawing up a budget – a record of where your income comes from and how you spend it – will help you keep track of your money and manage your finances. While this will be no more than a draft, the closer you are to retirement, the more sensible it is to do this exercise. Repeat it as often as necessary, and certainly update it each time you obtain more facts and information.

Before you move on to draw up a complete budget, the tables that follow are designed to help you think about the outgoings you might save and the extra costs you might incur when you stop or cut back on work or simply reach the threshold age for age-related concessions.

Table 2.1 looks at potential savings on retirement. You should also take into account reduced running costs if you move to a smaller home, any expenses for dependent children that may cease, other costs such as mortgage payments that may end around the time you retire, and the fact that you may be in a lower tax bracket. You may not be liable for National Insurance contributions either (either because you have passed State Pension age or because your income is lower).

Table 2.1   Potential savings on retirement

Items	Estimated monthly savings
National Insurance contributions	....
Pension payments	....
Travel expenses to work	....
Bought lunches	....
Incidentals at work, eg drinks with colleagues, collections for presents	....
Special work clothes	....
Concessionary travel	....
NHS prescriptions	....
Eye tests	....
Mature drivers' insurance policy	....
Retired householders' insurance policy	....
Life assurance payments and/or possible endowment policy premiums	....
Other	....
TOTAL	....

Table 2.2 covers potential additional costs when you retire. Looking ahead, you will need to make provision for any extra home comforts you might want and also, at some point, for having to pay other people to do

Table 2.2 Potential additional costs when you retire

Items	Estimated monthly extra costs
Extra heating and lighting bills	....
Extra spending on hobbies and other entertainment	....
Replacement of company car	....
Private healthcare insurance	....
Longer or more frequent holidays	....
Life and permanent health insurance	....
Cost of substituting other perks, eg expense account lunches	....
Out-of-pocket expenses for voluntary work activities	....
Other	....
TOTAL	....

some of the jobs that you normally manage yourself. If you intend to make regular donations to a charity or perhaps help with your grandchildren's education, these too should be included in the list. The same applies to any new private pension or savings plan that you might want to invest in to boost your long-term retirement income.

Creating a budget

Now you've thought about how spending might change with retirement, you're ready to start creating a budget. The first step is to record all the income (Table 2.3) and outgoings (Table 2.4) you expect to have. This is your cash flow statement. If the result is spending that exceeds income, or a surplus that is smaller than the sum you would ideally like to save each month, then you need to go through a process of adjusting your spending, and possibly your income, until you get to a budget that will work for you.

NB: Before adding up the total in Table 2.4, you should look at the list in Table 2.5, as you may well want to juggle some items between the two.

Table 2.5 deals with normal additional expenditure. For some items, such as holidays and gifts, you may tend to think in terms of annual expenditure.

Table 2.3   Calculating your total net income

A. Income received before tax	
State Pension	....
Occupational pension(s)	....
Personal pension (annuity or drawdown income)	....
State benefits	....
Income from savings and investments	....
Earnings (before tax) from any continuing work	....
Other incomes (eg rental income)	....
TOTAL before tax	....
Less: income tax and (if any) National Insurance	....
	....
	....
TOTAL NET INCOME	....

However, for the purpose of comparing monthly income and outgoings, it is probably easier if you itemize all expenditure in the same way. Also, if you need to save for a special event, such as a holiday, it helps if you get into the habit of putting so much aside every month (or even weekly).

Finally, Table 2.6 asks you to consider: does your budget work? If you have a budget deficit, your income and spending plans are not currently viable. Look for ways you can save on spending, starting with the items in Table 2.5. You may also be able to save on some items in Table 2.4, for example, by shopping around and switching to cheaper suppliers, brands, and so on. Consider whether you could boost your income – see some suggestions in the following section.

In this age of digital innovation, there are a growing number of online and phone apps that will help you draw up a budget based on your current spending, and this can be automated to some degree if you allow the app to link directly to your bank account, credit card and any other financial accounts. If you prefer, there are online budget templates where you simply

Table 2.4   Your normal regular expenditure

Normal regular expenditure	
Items	*Estimated monthly cost*
Food	....
Rent or mortgage repayments	....
Council tax (or rates in Northern Ireland)	....
Repair and maintenance costs	....
Heating, lighting and other energy	....
Telephone/mobile/internet/digital entertainment subscriptions	....
TV licence	....
Postage (including Christmas cards)	....
Household insurance	....
Clothes	....
Laundry, cleaner's bills, shoe repair	....
Domestic cleaning products	....
Miscellaneous services, eg plumber and window cleaner	....
Car (including licence, petrol, etc)	....
Other transport	....
Regular savings and (if still required) life assurance	....
Loan repayments (Personal Contract Purchase, HP, credit card, other)	....
Outgoings on health	....
Other	....
TOTAL REGULAR SPENDING	....

enter your own figures. For example, you could use the Budget Planner from the Money Advice Service at moneyadviceservice.org.uk/en/tools/budget-planner, as well as a dedicated tool for checking whether you might have a budget shortfall in retirement: moneyadviceservice.org.uk/en/tools/pension-calculator.

Table 2.5   Your normal additional expenditure

Normal additional expenditure	
Items	*Estimated monthly cost*
Gifts	....
Holidays	....
Newspapers/books/CDs/DVDs	....
Computer (including broadband)	....
Drink	....
Cigarettes/tobacco	....
Hairdressing	....
Toiletries/cosmetics	....
Entertainment (hobbies, outings, home entertaining, etc)	....
Miscellaneous subscriptions/ membership fees	....
Gifts, charitable donations	....
Expenditure on pets	....
Garden purchases	....
Other	....
TOTAL ADDITIONAL SPENDING	....

Table 2.6   Does your budget work?

Items	Estimated monthly cost
Total net income (from Table 2.3)	....
Less Total regular spending (from Table 2.4)	....
Less Total additional spending (from Table 2.5)	....
BUDGET SURPLUS/DEFICIT	....

Possible ways of boosting your retirement income

Unless you're expecting to win millions on the lottery, or inherit untold wealth from a relative, a bit more money is always useful. Few people can afford to turn away extra income these days, yet there are really only three main ways to give your retirement finances a boost: your home, work and investments. There is a fourth possibility, but it applies only if your income and savings are low, or particular circumstances apply to you, such as having a disability or being a carer. In those cases, you should check whether you are eligible for any state benefits.

Your home

Nearly three-quarters of people aged 65 and over own their home outright, and a further 4 per cent are homeowners with a mortgage, according to the government's Family Resources Survey. Your home is not just a place to live and offers several different options for boosting your income: moving somewhere smaller, taking in lodgers or raising money on your home. All the possibilities are explored in greater detail in Chapter 6, *Your home*.

Work

How about continuing to work? There is plenty of scope here for earning money, and it's important to realize that work can also be an important source of social contact, identity and self-esteem. Since age discrimination legislation was introduced, in most jobs there is no compulsory retirement age, so it's up to you to decide when you want to stop. However, you might want to talk to your employer to see what options there are for you to remain with your present organization, but working reduced or more flexible hours. Lots of people now choose this way of boosting their income by easing down to part-time work. Your workplace pension usually has a normal pension age at which you can start the full pension you have built up. If your scheme rules allow this, you might want to start drawing this alongside your earnings for work, though check you are happy with the amount of tax you'll pay on this combined income. (Chapter 4 has information about tax.) Another option might be to defer your pension, and this might increase the amount you eventually get – check the rules for your scheme. Similarly, if you have reached State Pension age but don't need it yet, you can opt to defer it and receive a higher sum later (see Chapter 3).

Retirement for you may offer the chance of a job switch or setting up on your own. When you do the figures, it is as well to err on the side of caution with regard to any additional income this will provide: there is a lot more information on work, and how to get it, in Chapters 8 and 9.

Investment

Investing is not just the preserve of the rich. Everyone has to start somewhere and, for many, arriving at retirement with a sizeable pension pot provides the opportunity. There is a mind-boggling array of financial products, and if managing your own investments is something you haven't done before, it can be fascinating and rewarding. You will learn in Chapter 5 the various forms investment can take.

State benefits

In addition to the State Pension, there are a number of other state benefits that you may be entitled to. Some are aimed at people on a low income and with a low level of savings (excluding the value of their home). The principal of these 'means-tested' benefits for older people is Pension Credit, which tops up your income to at least a minimum level. There are details in Chapter 3. Pension Credit can be claimed only once you've reached State Pension age.

Before that, you might instead be able to claim Universal Credit, which is the main means-tested benefit for people of working age (replacing Working Tax Credit and several other benefits). For new claims since 15 May 2019, mixed-age couples where one partner is under State Pension age can no longer claim Pension Credit, only Universal Credit (which will often be a lot less generous). Entitlement to some other state benefits depends not on your means, but on your circumstances. For example, if you are caring for someone for at least 35 hours a week, you may be able to claim Carer's Allowance. If you need help looking after yourself because of frailty or a disability, you may be entitled to Attendance Allowance (if you are aged 65 or over) or Personal Independence Payment if younger. These benefits are not intended to top up your income, but rather to help you with the extra costs you face because of your circumstances.

The number of state benefits and allowances available to help pensioners that are not claimed is staggering. Many pensioners live on low to middle incomes and have been hit hard by falling interest rates, the rising cost of living and public spending cuts. Despite just under half of all pensioners being entitled to Pension Credit, a third of people don't claim it; Age UK warn that 2 million pensioners live in poverty, yet millions of pounds of pensioner benefits go unclaimed each year.

For further advice and information on benefits, see the following websites, some of which include benefits calculators that are free and anonymous to use:

- **GOV.UK**: gov.uk/browse/benefits.
- **Age UK**: ageuk.org.uk/information-advice/money-legal/benefits-entitlements/. There is also a Benefits Calculator: benefitscheck.ageuk.org.uk/Home/Start/.
- **Citizens Advice Bureau**: citizensadvice.org.uk/benefits/.
- **entitledto** (benefits calculator): entitledto.co.uk.
- **Policy in Practice**: (benefits calculator which can be combined with budgeting tools): betteroffcalculator.co.uk.
- **Turn2Us** (benefits calculator): benefits-calculator.turn2us.org.uk.

Spending now for saving later

Do you enjoy spending your hard-earned money? Perhaps you consider very carefully before committing yourself? You may be surprised to know that many people when making retirement plans find they need, or want, to make certain purchases. These could, for example, include paying off all outstanding commitments. Most people's basic list – at least to think about – includes one or more of the following:

- expenditure on their home;
- the purchase of a new car;
- paying off any credit cards and loans.

In addition, there might be some general domestic or luxury items that you have been promising yourself for some time. The question is simply one of timing. Ask yourself these questions: Can I afford it more easily now – or in the future? By paying now rather than waiting, will I be saving money in the long run? This is something you will need to work out before you can complete the figures for your retirement planning.

Though it involves a few minutes' paperwork, a worthwhile exercise is to jot down your own personal list of pros and cons under the headings 'spending now' and 'spending later'. If still in doubt, waiting is normally the more prudent course.

Home improvements

With a Brexit cloud of uncertainty hanging over the housing market, many people have taken the view: 'Don't move, improve'. If you plan to remain in the same property, would making some changes or improvements be sensible now? These could include installing double glazing, insulating the loft, modernizing the kitchen, installing a downstairs shower room or converting part of the house to a granny flat. Any significant expenditure on your home is best undertaken when you can most easily afford it. Some people find it easier, and more reassuring, to pay major household bills while they are still earning. Others specifically plan to use part of the lump sum from their pension to create a dream home. What would make best financial sense for you?

Of course, if you intend to stay in your present home for a long time, investing in your property is fine. But should plans change and you need to move after a couple of years, you will be lucky to recoup your expenditure on a property you've modified to your own taste.

Purchasing a car

Would buying a new car cheer you up? If so, there are two reasons for getting one ahead of your retirement. Perhaps you have a company car that you are about to lose, or your existing vehicle is getting old and is beginning (or will probably soon start) to give you trouble. Or maybe the kind of journeys you plan to do after retirement can be done with a smaller, more economical car than the one you use for work. Should any of these apply, then it probably makes sense to buy a replacement vehicle sooner rather than later.

Company car owners should first check whether they are entitled to purchase their present car on favourable terms. A number of employers are quite happy to allow this. Also, in terms of reducing carbon footprints, two-car families should think seriously about reducing to one vehicle come retirement, when it is possible that having two vehicles is no longer necessary. A further complication is whether to stick with traditional fuels or switch to an electric car. While electric vehicles and hybrids are costly to buy, recent research from the International Council for Clean Transportation suggests that they are cheaper to run than petrol and diesel cars. Perhaps the biggest factor holding many people back is a lack of a sufficient nationwide infrastructure to support long journeys in electric vehicles, though this is likely to improve.

Paying off credit cards and loans

This is, generally speaking, a good idea, since delay is unlikely to save you money. However, one precaution is to check the small print of your agreement for any charge on early repayment, which is common with fixed-term personal loans. Similarly, if you have a mortgage, particularly one with a fixed or discounted interest rate or that came with a cashback deal, there may be a charge for paying off the mortgage before the period of the special deal has finished. So you may want to hold off paying it off for a while. After that, there is normally just a 'sealing fee' (also called a 'deeds fee') to cover the lender's legal costs involved in the mortgage coming to an end. At this point, you'll receive any deeds to your property that your lender had in its keeping. If your ownership of the property is recorded in the Land Registry, you might think the deeds are unimportant. However, they often contain additional information that is not held by the Land Registry, such as covenants about how the property may be used, who is responsible for boundaries, and so on. So keep your deeds in a safe place.

Saving now for spending later

Having spent a lifetime saving for retirement, surely now is the time to let go and spend to your heart's content? Well, not quite. There are two major reasons why you might want to carry on setting aside some of your income for saving or earmarking some of your wealth as strictly for future use. These are: inflation, and care.

Inflation

At retirement, there are two ways to turn pensions savings into income: buy an annuity (which provides a secure income for life) or use drawdown (where you leave your savings invested and cash in part of them each time you want to take some income or a lump sum). Whichever you choose, over time, even low rates of annual inflation can severely reduce how much your money can buy. Despite this, before 2015 when most people reaching retirement with a pension pot used it to buy an annuity, the most popular choice was a level annuity that paid the same, fixed income year after year. Other types of annuity where the income increases each year either at a set rate or in line with inflation have always been available, but are not a popular choice (and often wisely so since, while the concept of an inflation-proofed annuity is a good one, the ones on offer are often uncompetitive and poor value for money). If you opt for a level annuity, you should consider saving some of the income you receive now to top up your income later on, and so compensate for the loss of buying power caused by inflation. That will help you to maintain the same standard of living as retirement progresses.

Since 2015, you have greater choice over how to use your pension savings, and only one pension pot in eight that is accessed for the first time is used to buy an annuity. Drawdown is nearly three times more popular than annuities (and the rest of the access is in the form of partially or fully cashing in the savings), according to the Financial Conduct Authority. The value of your drawdown fund and the income you can afford to draw out will vary as the value of the stock market investments in the fund goes up and down. This means you should ideally review the situation on, say, an annual basis to determine how much income you can draw out now, while protecting your ability to draw future sums that will increase in line with inflation.

Care

Increasingly, people are fit and well when they reach retirement and with luck that will continue for a long time. However, the reality is that the chance of developing health conditions does increase with age. Not all health conditions mean you need help with day-to-day living and, where you do, this will often be provided unpaid by your partner (if you have one) or other family members. Where you need substantial help, though, you may need at some stage to move into a care home. In theory, your local authority might fund some or all of the cost. In practice, you will pay all or a substantial part, unless your income and assets are low or if you want the freedom to choose which care home you live in.

A government report estimated that around one in 10 people now aged 65 will face future long-term care costs of more than £100,000. On the other hand, a quarter of this age group will end up spending little or nothing on care. It is a total lottery and you have no real way of knowing if you will be one of the lucky ones. Therefore, it makes sense to plan ahead for how you might meet care costs later on if the worst does happen. Your plan might be to set aside some savings now. Alternatively, for people who own their home, you might plan on selling it or using equity release to fund care. There is more information in Chapter 6.

Money – if you are made redundant

The prolonged uncertainty over Brexit is taking its toll, contributing to the financial difficulties of firms such as British Steel. Many people fear being made redundant, and much of the information in the earlier part of this chapter is equally valid whether you become redundant or retire in the normal way. However, there are several key points with regard to redundancy that it could be to your advantage to check.

From your employment

You may be entitled to statutory redundancy pay

Your employer is obliged to pay the legal minimum, which is calculated on your age, length of service and weekly pay. To qualify, you will need to have worked for the organization for at least two years, with no age restriction. Redundancy pay is 1.5 weeks' pay for each year worked if you are 41 or older, based on pay up to a maximum of £525 a week (£547 in Northern Ireland) and a maximum of 20 years. There is a calculator on GOV.UK to help you work out your entitlement: gov.uk/calculate-your-redundancy-pay.

Ex gratia payments

Many employers are prepared to be more generous and will pay you more than just the statutory amount. As long as it's not more than £30,000, redundancy pay is not taxable. Any payment over this limit is subject to tax and National Insurance. Redundancy pay means genuine compensation for loss of your job. It does not include, for example, pay in lieu of notice or holiday pay, which will be taxed just like any other earnings (see Chapter 4).

Benefits that are not part of your pay

Redundancy may mean the loss of several valuable benefits such as a company car, life assurance and health insurance. Your employer might agree to include your company car as part of your redundancy pay. Some insurance companies allow preferential rates to individuals who were previously insured with them under a company scheme.

Holiday entitlement

You could be owed holiday entitlement, for which you should be paid.

Workplace pension

There are different types of workplace pension. If yours is a personal pension (see Chapter 3), it will continue even though you leave your employer, though any contributions your employer was paying into it on your behalf will stop and your own contributions can of course no longer be deducted direct from your pay packet. Contact your pension provider if you want to arrange another way to pay into it.

If you belong to a company pension, you will cease to be an active member when you leave, but will usually have what is called a 'deferred pension' that you will be able to claim when you reach retirement. However, if you are already close to retiring, your employer might offer an early or enhanced pension to encourage employees to opt for voluntary redundancy. Check the redundancy terms being offered with your firm's human resources department.

Your mortgage

If you have a mortgage and are worried about keeping up the repayments, you should contact your mortgage lender as soon as possible. It may agree to a more flexible repayment system and, if you do fall into arrears, must explore ways to help you pay – this is called the Mortgage Protocol. Read more at www.justice.gov.uk/courts/procedure-rules/civil/protocol/prot_mha. Repossession of your home must be treated by your lender as the last resort.

Check whether your mortgage package includes insurance against redundancy. Called Mortgage Payment Protection Insurance (MPPI), this will typically cover your mortgage interest (but not capital) payments for a maximum of one, occasionally two, years. There is help (called Support for Mortgage Interest or SMI) available from the state if you are claiming means-tested benefits, such as Universal Credit, Income Support or income-based Jobseeker's Allowance. Those claiming these benefits could have their interest payments on up to £200,000 of mortgage covered. However, you have to wait nine months after you claim before the help kicks in. SMI used to be in the form of benefit payments, but since April 2018 it takes the form of a loan secured against your home. The loan is repaid to the government when your home is eventually sold or if you choose to pay off the debt earlier.

Other creditors/debts

Any creditors that you may have difficulty in paying (electricity, gas, a bank overdraft) should be informed as early as possible in the hope of agreeing easier payment terms. There could be an argument for paying off credit card bills immediately, even if this means using some of your redundancy pay.

Jobseeker's Allowance (JSA)

Even if you are hoping to get another job very soon, you should sign on without delay. Your National Insurance contributions will normally be credited to you. This is important to protect your State Pension. To qualify for JSA, you need to be under State Pension age and must have paid sufficient Class 1 National Insurance contributions. You must also be both available for and actively seeking work. You can get JSA for a maximum of 182 days (around six months). After that, if your income and savings are low, you may be eligible for Universal Credit, a means-tested benefit for people of working age.

Current information about JSA, Universal Credit and other possible benefits can be found at gov.uk.

Further information about redundancy

The **Money Advice Service** publishes a useful guide to all aspects of redundancy, both online at moneyadviceservice.org.uk/en/categories/redundancy and as a printed guide which you can order from 0800 138 7777. Another useful agency is the **Citizens Advice Bureau**: see citizensadvice.org.uk.

Money left unclaimed

Experian estimates that there are £15 to £20 billion of unclaimed assets in the UK. During the course of this year millions of pounds of unclaimed money will be handed over to the Treasury because there are no clues as to who it belongs to. That means there are hundreds of thousands of people who do not even know the money is theirs. Some funds are in unclaimed benefits and entitlements, others are unclaimed lottery prizes, the remainder is money such as legacies from wills, funds from pensions and insurance policies where there is no next of kin to claim them. (The beneficiaries are possibly no longer alive, or have moved and are difficult to trace.) More than one in 10 people think they may have forgotten assets, and many people do not know how to begin to trace their money.

There are a number of useful websites to help you. Experian's Unclaimed Assets Register has lots of helpful information: uar.co.uk. For lost building society, bank and National Savings & Investments accounts, use mylostaccount. org.uk. If you are looking for a lost pension, use the government's Pension Tracing Service: gov.uk/find-pension-contact-details.

Be alert to scams! The websites listed above are free, independent services set up by the relevant financial sector to help repatriate people with their accounts. Be wary of other sites and do not respond to unsolicited e-mails or texts claiming to reunite you with missing money.

More money information

If you enjoy browsing the internet and this chapter has whetted your appetite for research on the matter of retirement planning, the following websites cover a broad range of topics relating to your finances and retirement:

- citizensadvice.org.uk;
- financingretirement.co.uk;
- litrg.org.uk;
- moneyadviceservice.org.uk;
- moneyweek.com;
- thisismoney.co.uk;
- which.co.uk.

Useful reading

The following publications are especially for those coming up to retirement and the recently retired.

The Money Advice Service, which is part of the Money and Pensions Service, a government initiative to ensure that everyone has access to guidance about money matters, has a number of printed guides available through moneyadviceservice.org.uk, including:

- *Your Pension – It's Time to Choose*
- *Personal Pensions*
- *Releasing Equity from Your Home*
- *The Redundancy Handbook*
- *Problems Paying Your Mortgage*

03
Pensions

You may be enrolled in, have access to, or wish to consider a variety of pension schemes.

The State Pension

First, let's consider the State Pension. The earliest you can claim it is at State Pension age. You do not have to stop work when you reach State Pension age or to claim your State Pension.

For some time, women's State Pension age has been increasing and, in November 2018, reached equality with men at age 65. Now the pension age for both men and women is gradually increasing to reach age 66 by September 2020. If you are a man or woman born between 6 December 1953 and 5 September 1954, your State Pension age is between 65 and 66. If you were born between 6 September 1954 and 5 April 1960, your State Pension age is 66. After that, there is a further gradual rise to age 67 and possibly 68 (though this last increase has still to be made law). Any further rises will depend on whether life expectancy increases. You can check your State Pension age and date online at gov.uk/state-pension-age.

Many workplace pension schemes align their normal pension age with State Pension age, so you may have to wait longer for these pensions too. Pension age is not the same as retirement age. Since October 2011 the default retirement age (which used to be 65) has been scrapped. Employers are no longer allowed to dismiss staff just because they are 65.

Because some people retire and start a workplace pension early, they can mistakenly assume it is possible to get an early State Pension. This is not correct – State Pension is never payable before State Pension age. However, if you're retiring early because of, say, ill health or the need to care for someone, you might be eligible to claim other state benefits (see Chapters 11 and 13).

Getting your State Pension

Your State Pension is not paid automatically; you need to claim it. You'll usually get a letter two months before your State Pension birthday inviting you to make a claim and telling you how to do this. If you don't receive a letter, you can still claim online at gov.uk/get-state-pension, or by post or phone by contacting the Pension Service.

All State Pensions are taxable, even though they are paid without any tax deducted. Chapter 4 explains how tax is collected on State Pensions if your income is high enough for you to pay tax. State Pensioners also get a bonus paid shortly before Christmas, and this is tax-free. Since it was introduced in 1972, the amount has been unchanged at £10. Back then it would have bought a handsome family Christmas dinner! The bonus is automatically added to your normal pension payment for the first week in December.

State Pensions are increased in April each year – but if you retire abroad, you only get these increases if you live in a European Economic Area (EEA) country, Switzerland or a country with which the UK has a reciprocal agreement that includes State Pensions. At the time of writing, whether Brexit would go ahead and on what terms was still undecided, but would potentially affect these reciprocal agreements.

When you reach State Pension age, you decide whether or not to start drawing the State Pension. Retirement does not have to start on any particular date or a single day. Many people prefer to stop working gradually by reducing hours or shifting to part-time work, so you might not need your entire pension straight away. By deferring your State Pension, you can have a bigger pension when it does start or, if you are covered by the old state scheme rules (see below), alternatively a lump sum.

How your State Pension can be paid

Pensions are usually paid every four weeks direct into a bank account. This can be a bank or building society account, credit union account or, if you prefer, a Post Office Card Account (POCA). The government has said that the option to use a POCA will remain until at least 2021. Individuals who genuinely cannot use a bank account can ask the Pension Service to pay them by cheque, which can be cashed, for example, at the post office.

Other situations

Pensions can be paid to an overseas address if you are going abroad for six months or more. See gov.uk (see section 'State Pension if you retire abroad').

If you are in hospital, your pension can still be paid to you, and you will receive your pension in full for the duration of your stay, regardless of how long you have to remain in hospital. For advice contact either the Pension Service or the Citizens Advice Bureau.

Your right to a State Pension

You build up your right to claim a State Pension by paying, or being credited with, National Insurance contributions (NICs). Each year that counts is called a 'qualifying year'. How many qualifying years you need during your working life (defined as the years from age 16 up to State Pension age) depends on when you reached or will reach State Pension age.

If you reached State Pension age before 6 April 2016, you will be in the old State Pension scheme. There were two types of State Pension – basic and additional. From 6 April 2010, the number of qualifying years needed to get a full basic State Pension was reduced to 30 years for women and men (before this it was normally 39 and 44 years respectively). If you reach(ed) State Pension age on or after 6 April 2016, you will be in the new single-tier State Pension system, and need 35 years to get the full amount and at least 10 qualifying years to get any State Pension at all. You can check your National Insurance record at gov.uk/check-national-insurance-record.

Anyone trying to decide whether they can afford to retire should get a statement of their State Pension from the Pension Service. It is worth getting an early estimate of what your pension will be, as there may be steps you can take to improve your NIC record as described below.

Under current rules, you stop paying National Insurance once you reach State Pension age.

Paying National Insurance contributions

If you are an employee, your employer will have automatically deducted Class 1 NICs from your salary, provided your earnings were above a certain limit (2019/20: £166 a week – the 'primary threshold'). Your employer pays these contributions to the government, which keeps a record of your qualifying years.

If you are self-employed, you will have been paying flat-rate Class 2 NICs, currently £3 every week. These count towards your State Pension. If your profits are less than a given threshold (2019/20: £6,365), you can opt out of paying Class 2 contributions, but if you don't yet have enough qualifying years for the full pension it's usually better to pay these NICs if you can afford it. As a self-employed person, you may also be paying Class 4

NICs. These are purely a tax on your profits (between limits) and do not count towards the State Pension at all.

If you have gaps in your NICs record – for example, because you have been studying at university or taken some time out to travel – you can go back up to six years to fill the gaps by paying Class 3 voluntary contributions. Exceptionally, some people can fill gaps from longer ago – see Table 3.1. In 2019/20, Class 3 NICs cost £15 a week. It will only be worth paying these if you don't already have enough qualifying years for a full State Pension. You can check whether it is worth your while paying them by contacting the government's Future Pensions Centre at gov.uk/future-pension-centre.

Lived or worked outside Great Britain?

If you have lived in Northern Ireland or the Isle of Man, any contributions paid there will count towards your pension. The same should also apply in most cases if you have lived or worked in an EU country, or any country whose social security is linked to Britain's by a reciprocal arrangement. However, there have sometimes been problems with certain countries, so, if you have any doubts, you should enquire what your position is by contacting the government's International Pension Centre: gov.uk/international-pension-centre.

Caring for children or adults

If you were a carer for a child or a disabled person throughout any tax year after 1978 up until 5 April 2010, and you were not doing any paid work, or had low earnings and did not get credits, you may have got Home Responsibilities Protection. HRP reduced the number of qualifying years you needed for a full basic State Pension. HRP was awarded automatically

Table 3.1   Who can pay voluntary Class 3 contributions?

Who is eligible?	Time limit for paying them
Anyone	Six years after the year with the gap
A man born between 6 April 1945 and 5 April 1950, or a woman born between 6 April 1950 and 5 October 1952	Six years after reaching State Pension age for years going back to 1975
A man born after 5 April 1951, or a woman born after 5 April 1953	Until 5 April 2023 to make up gaps between April 2006 and April 2016

if you got Child Benefit for a child under 16, but if you were caring for a disabled person or you were a foster carer, you usually had to complete an application form for it. HRP was available only for complete tax years; for example, it could not turn a year in which you were earning and paying NICs for part of the year into a qualifying year.

Since 6 April 2010, Home Responsibilities Protection has been replaced with weekly credits for parents and carers, called Carer's Credit. You can receive these credits for any weeks you are getting Child Benefit for a child under 12, you are an approved foster carer, or you are caring for one or more sick or disabled people for at least 20 hours a week. If you reach State Pension age on or after 6 April 2010, any years of HRP you have been awarded before April 2010 will have been converted to qualifying years of credits, up to a maximum of 22 years.

Carer's Credits are awarded automatically if you are claiming Child Benefit, even if this is a 'nil claim'. You may want to make a nil claim because of the interaction between Child Benefit and the income tax system. Since April 2013, if you are getting Child Benefit and you or your partner (if you have one) have taxable income of £50,000 or more, the higher earner has to pay extra income tax called a High Income Child Benefit Tax Charge. The effect is to claw back some or all of the Child Benefit. If you or your partner are caught by this tax charge, you'll have to declare it by completing a tax return each year. That can be inconvenient and you may have decided it's simpler just to stop getting the Child Benefit. In that case, though, you should still register for Child Benefit, but on the form put 'no' at the question that asks if you want to be paid the benefit. That way, you will still get Carer's Credits towards your State Pension.

Since 2011, the Carer's Credit that goes with Child Benefit can be transferred to someone else if they are caring for the child or children. For example, if you are a grandparent looking after your daughter's children, you could apply to have your daughter's Carer's Credit transferred to you to help you build up your State Pension. To do this, complete the application form for Specified Adult Childcare Credit at gov.uk.

Other situations when you may get credits

If you have been in any of the following situations you will have been credited with contributions (instead of having to pay them):

- You were sick or unemployed (provided you sent in sick notes to your social security office, signed on at the unemployment benefit office or were in receipt of Jobseeker's Allowance).

- You were a man over the women's State Pension age, but under 65 and not working, during the period when women's State Pension age was lower than men's.
- You were entitled to maternity allowance, invalid care allowance or unemployability supplement.
- You were taking an approved course of training.
- You had left education but had not yet started working.
- (post-April 2000) Your earnings were between what is known as the lower earnings limit and the primary threshold. These change each year, and in 2019/20 are £118 and £166 a week, respectively.

Married women and widows

Under the old State Pension system, married women and widows who do not qualify for a basic pension in their own right or have built up a relatively low State Pension may be entitled to a basic pension based on their husband's NICs record, at about 60 per cent of the level to which he is entitled.

Reduced-rate contributions note: a dwindling number of women retiring today may have paid a reduced-rate NICs (sometimes called the 'small stamp') under a scheme that was abolished in 1978. Women who were already paying reduced-rate contributions were, however, allowed to continue doing so (although the right automatically ceased on divorce). These reduced-rate contributions do not count towards your pension, and you will not have had any NICs credited to you. If you and/or your husband reach State Pension age on or after 6 April 2016, special rules mean you may still be able to claim a pension based on your husband's NICs record. Contact the Pension Service for more information.

How the old State Pension is worked out

If you reached your State Pension age before 6 April 2016, your State Pension is paid under the old rules described in this section. Your pension may have two parts: a basic pension that most people get, and an additional pension mainly built up during periods when you worked as an employee. (You might also get some 'graduated pension' under an even older state scheme, but the amount will be small.)

Basic State Pension

The full basic State Pension for a man or woman (April 2019/20) is £129.20 a week, and £206.65 for a married couple. These are the maximum amounts available. If you do not have enough qualifying years for the full basic State Pension, you will be entitled to a lower amount based on the number of qualifying years in your NICs record. The rules have changed, and the number of qualifying years you need for a full basic State Pension depends on when you reached State Pension age. Those who reached State Pension age on or after 6 April 2010 require 30 qualifying years to get a full basic State Pension and just one year to qualify for any pension. Each qualifying year of paid or credited contributions is therefore worth 1/30th of the full basic State Pension, up to a maximum of 30/30ths.

Since April 2011, the basic pension is increased annually by the highest of price inflation, earnings or 2.5 per cent (sometimes called the 'triple lock').

Additional State Pension

If you spent some or all of your working years as an employee, you may have been building up an additional State Pension. (This was formerly known as SERPS – the State Earnings Related Pensions Scheme – but was replaced by the State Second Pension in April 2002.) The amount of additional pension you get depends on your earnings, your NICs record and whether you were 'contracted out' of the additional pension. Contracting out means that you were covered by a pension scheme at work or a personal pension that you arranged yourself which was designed to provide a pension that would replace your state additional pension. In return, you either paid a lower rate of NICs or part of the NICs you had paid were given back by paying them into your pension scheme. It's common for people to have been contracted out for just part of their working life. So, at retirement, you may still get some additional pension, as well as the replacement pensions from the workplace and personal schemes.

In theory, the additional pension can be a substantial amount – over £170 a week (2019/20) on top of the basic pension. In practice, because of low earnings and contracting out, the average amount is much lower, at around £20 to £30 a week.

There were other means of entitlement to some State Second Pension: for example if you earned below a certain amount set by the government, if you could not work through long-term illness or disability, or if you were a carer.

You could not build up any additional pension during periods when you were self-employed.

The additional pension is increased each year in line with price inflation. (The 'triple lock' does not apply to this part of your pension.)

Deferring the old State Pension

If you decide not to start your pension straight away on reaching your State Pension age, your State Pension is increased by 1 per cent for each five weeks you defer it, ie an increase of 10.4 per cent a year for each year you defer. Ignoring tax, you would need to survive just over 9½ years to get back as much in extra pension as you give up during the delay until it starts.

You can continue deferring your pension for as long as you like. The extra money will be paid to you when you eventually decide to claim your pension. Alternatively, you can opt for a lump sum. This is worked out as if your deferred pension had been invested and earned a return of 2 per cent more than the Bank of England base rate.

There is no upper limit on the extra State Pension or lump sum you can have. You have to defer your State Pension for at least five weeks to qualify for extra pension or at least one year for a lump sum. The resulting extra pension is increased each year in line with prices, and is taxable in the usual way.

If you opt to receive a lump sum, this also counts as taxable income, but special rules limit the tax due. However large, the whole amount is taxed at the top rate of tax you were paying before the lump sum was added. For example, if your top rate was 20 per cent, the whole lump sum is taxed at 20 per cent and cannot push you into a higher tax bracket. You can start your pension, but put off receiving the lump sum until the next tax year. This is useful if your tax rate will be lower in the next year – for example, because you will have stopped work.

More information can be found at gov.uk/deferring-state-pension.

Adult Dependency Increase

This is an increase in the old State Pension for a husband, wife or someone who is looking after your children, as long as certain conditions are met. Since 6 April 2010, you are no longer entitled to claim an Adult Dependency Increase. If you were already entitled to this increase on 5 April 2010 you will be able to keep it until you no longer meet the conditions for the increase, or 5 April 2020, whichever is the first.

How the new State Pension is worked out

If you reach your State Pension age on or after 6 April 2016, your State Pension is paid under the new rules described in this section. So this section applies to you if you are a woman born on or after 6 April 1953 or a man born on or after 6 April 1951. Eventually, everyone will get just the single-tier State Pension. However, there are rules to protect your rights to the amount of pension you may already have built up under the old state scheme, so for a long time many people will get a transitional amount of State Pension that is higher than the single-tier pension.

Single-tier State Pension

The full-rate single-tier pension for a man or woman (April 2019/20) is £168.60 a week. Each person builds up their own entitlement, so – unlike the old state system – there is no rate for couples. This is the maximum available. If you do not have enough qualifying years for the full single-tier pension, you will be entitled to a lower amount based on the number of qualifying years in your NICs record.

The number of qualifying years you need for a full single-tier State Pension is 35, though you need 10 years to qualify for any pension. Once the new system is fully operational, provided the 10-year threshold is met, each qualifying year of paid or credited contributions is worth 1/35th of the full basic State Pension up to a maximum of 35/35ths. (However, the calculation is a little different if you had also built up pension rights under the old state system – see below).

The single-tier pension up to the full rate is increased annually by the highest of price inflation, earnings or 2.5 per cent (sometimes called the 'triple lock').

The full-rate single-tier pension is higher than the old basic-rate State Pension. However, under the single-tier system, there is no additional pension. The full rate for the single-tier pension has been set at broadly the amount that the average person under the old system receives from their combined basic and additional pensions. The new State Pension is particularly generous for self-employed people, since they were not eligible for any additional pension under the old system and – so far – still pay lower NICs than employees.

Protecting your old State Pension rights

Most people now covered by the new single-tier State Pension will have built up some pension under the old state scheme. To ensure they did not lose out under the switch to the new system, there are transitional rules. Broadly they work as follows. On 6 April 2016, two calculations were made: firstly, the pension you had built up so far under the old system was worked out using the old system rules, and secondly, your qualifying years so far were used to calculate what your pension would have been if the new system had applied all along. In both cases, the calculation includes a deduction if you had been contracted out of the additional State Pension under the old system. You were then credited with the higher of the two amounts, and this is called your 'starting amount'.

If your starting amount on 6 April 2016 was higher than the full-rate of the single-tier pension, your State Pension will be this higher amount. This amount is increased both up to the time you reach State Pension age, and then once it starts to be paid. To do this, your starting amount is divided into two parts: the full-rate single-tier pension which currently increases each year in line with the triple lock. The excess is your 'protected payment' and it increases each year in line with price inflation. You cannot build up any more State Pension because you are already over the maximum full rate.

If your starting amount on 6 April 2016 is less than the full rate of the single-tier pension, you can continue to build up more State Pension until you reach the full rate. The whole of your pension increases each year by the triple lock.

These transitional rules particularly benefit people who had been contracted out of the old state additional pension, because this means their starting amount is likely to be low. Thus, as well as having a workplace or personal pension that replaces some of their old State Pension, they can still build up more new State Pension until they reach the full rate. By contrast, an employee who had never been contracted out is likely to have a starting amount that already exceeds the full single-tier rate.

CASE STUDY

On 16 April 2016, under the old state system rules Roshni, then aged 58, had built up a combined state basic and additional pension of £166.22 a week. On that date, based on her NICs to date but the new state system rules, she would already have been entitled to the full-rate single-tier pension, which was then £155.65. This means her starting amount was £166.22 and, since it was higher than the full single-tier rate, she cannot build up any more State Pension. Since then, £155.65 of Roshni's State Pension has been increasing each year in line with the triple lock, and the excess – her protected payment of £10.57 a week – in line with price inflation. With these increases, by 2019/20, her expected weekly State Pension stood at £179.86.

Deferring the new State Pension

If you decide not to start your pension straight away on reaching your State Pension age, your State Pension is increased by 1 per cent for each nine weeks you defer it, ie an increase of 5.8 per cent a year for each year you defer. Ignoring tax, you would need to survive just over 17 years to get back as much in extra pension as you give up during the delay until it starts. However, especially if you are still working at State Pension age and would lose a lot of the pension in tax, it could be worth delaying its start.

You can continue deferring your pension for as long as you like. The extra money will be paid to you when you eventually decide to claim your pension.

There is no upper limit on the extra State Pension you can have. You have to defer your State Pension for at least nine weeks to qualify for extra pension. The resulting extra pension is increased each year in line with prices and is taxable in the usual way. More information can be found at gov.uk/deferring-state-pension.

Other state benefits for pensioners

If your income is low, you might qualify for some means-tested state benefits to top up your income and possibly help with your housing costs and council tax bills (or rates bills in Northern Ireland). 'Means-tested' means that your eligibility and how much you get depend on your income and savings. These benefits do not depend on paying NICs. There is additional state help that you can claim in particular circumstances: if you are getting a means-tested benefit, you can also apply for a Budgeting Loan to help with exceptional expenses if you are facing financial difficulties; and there are a range of non-means-tested benefits to help with the extra costs of living with a disability (discussed in Chapter 11).

Pension Credit

Pension Credit is the main means-tested benefit for those who have reached State Pension age. There are two parts to Pension Credit, both of which are tax-free.

Guarantee Credit tops up your income to a guaranteed minimum level. For the year 2019/20, the standard amount is £167.25 if you are single, or £255.25 if you have a partner. It may be increased if you have a disability or you are a carer. It can also be increased to cover some housing costs, such as service charges, but not rent or mortgage interest – see the following section for help you might get with these.

Savings Credit is available only to people aged 65 and over who reached State Pension age before 6 April 2016. It is for those who have saved some money of their own towards their retirement. The maximum amount of Savings Credit (for the year 2019/20) is £13.73 a week if you are single, or £15.35 a week if you have a partner. You may be able to get Savings Credit as well as Guarantee Credit.

If you wish to apply for Pension Credit, you do this by contacting the Pension Credit Claim Line (0800 99 1234). You can make a claim up to four months before the date from which you want to start getting Pension Credit. The longest claims can be backdated is three months. Where one member of a couple is under State Pension age, the couple can get Pension Credit provided their claim started before 15 May 2019; but, for new claims effective from (or backdated to) that date onwards, both members of a couple must have reached State Pension age. Such couples may instead be able to claim Universal Credit, which is a means-tested benefit for working-age people and is usually a lot less than Pension Credit. You must normally apply for Universal Credit online at gov.uk/apply-universal-credit.

Help with housing costs and council tax

If you are getting Pension Credit or Universal Credit and still have a mortgage, you may be able to get help paying some or all of your mortgage through a scheme called Support for Mortgage Interest (SMI). This help used to be given as an increase in your benefit payments. However, since 6 April 2018, that arrangement has been replaced. Now, if you opt for SMI, the help is treated as a loan which has eventually to be repaid to the government with interest, usually when you sell your home. When you apply for Pension Credit or Universal Credit, you'll also be offered an SMI loan if you are eligible.

If you rent your home, you may be able to get Housing Benefit. This can help people on a low income pay some or all of their rent. In Northern Ireland, Housing Benefit can also help you pay your rates bill.

Council Tax Reduction (also called Council Tax Support) is to help people on a low income pay some or all of their council tax. The help is given as a reduction in your council tax bill. Each local council sets up its own scheme, so the amount of help you get varies not just with your income and savings, but also where you live. You can claim this even if you don't get other benefits. Contact your local council to make a claim – find details at gov.uk/apply-council-tax-reduction.

Advice about State Pensions and benefits

Information about all types of State Pensions and benefits is available at gov.uk.

The Pension Service – part of the Department for Work and Pensions (DWP), the government department responsible for State Pensions and many state benefits – handles claiming and payments, and will explain what the state will provide when you retire and let you know what pension-related benefits you may be entitled to.

If you have any queries or think you may not be obtaining your full pension entitlement, you should contact the Pension Service as soon as possible. You will need to quote either your National Insurance number (or your spouse's) or your pension number if you have already started receiving your pension. If you think a mistake has been made, you can ask DWP to reconsider the Pension Service decision and, if you are still not satisfied, you then have the right to appeal and have your claim looked at by an independent tribunal. This is a formal process and you may want the help of a trained representative from, say, Citizens Advice Bureau or another benefits advice agency.

Private pensions

'Private pensions' means any pension schemes you have apart from a State Pension. They may be schemes you join through your workplace, or schemes that you arrange for yourself.

How much you can save

Private pension schemes are one of the most tax-efficient ways to save, because you get tax relief on the money you pay in, your savings build up tax-free, and you can take out a quarter of those savings tax-free (the rest counts as taxable income). In fact, the tax reliefs on pension schemes cost the government nearly £39 billion a year. To contain that cost, there are limits on the amount that you can save through pension schemes. These work in several ways.

First, tax relief on contributions is given only on contributions up to a maximum of £3,600 a year or an amount equal to 100 per cent of your UK earnings for the year, whichever is higher. This tax relief is given in one of two ways: *at source* or through the *net pay* method. With the at-source method, you deduct tax relief at the basic rate (2019/20: 20 per cent) from your contribution before handing it over to your pension provider. The provider then claims the same amount from HM Revenue & Customs (HMRC) and adds it direct to your pension savings. For example, suppose you want to pay £3,600 into your pension scheme. 20 per cent of £3,600 is £720. You deduct this from the £3,600 and hand over just £2,880 to your pension provider. The provider claims £720 from HMRC and adds it to your savings. The upshot is that £3,600 in total has gone into your scheme at a cost to you of £2,880. Under the at-source method – used for many workplace schemes and all schemes you arrange for yourself – you get this tax relief even if you are a non-taxpayer. If your top rate of tax is higher than the basic rate, you can claim extra tax relief by filling in a tax return (see Chapter 4 for how to do this).

The net-pay method is used by some workplace schemes. Your employer subtracts your pension contributions from your pay before working out how much income tax to deduct from your pay packet. This method is convenient because it automatically gives you all the tax relief you are due, without the need to complete a tax return. But, tax-wise, this method is not great if your earnings are too low to have to pay tax, because you don't get any tax relief at all, unlike the at-source method. Since it is a workplace scheme, you do still benefit from contributions paid in for you by your employer, so for most people it will usually still be worth saving through a net-pay scheme.

The second way that the government limits the amount you save through pension schemes is to set an Annual Allowance, which is the maximum amount by which your savings can increase each year. With a defined-contribution scheme (the sort where you build up your own personal pot of savings), the amount it grows each year is measured as the sum (before tax relief) of the contributions that you, your employer and anyone else pay in. With a defined-benefit scheme (the sort that promises you a given level of pension usually linked to your pre-retirement pay), the increase is deemed to be 16 times any rise in your promised pension compared with the previous year. Don't worry, you don't have to work this out for yourself – you can ask each pension scheme you have to tell you how much of your Annual Allowance has been used. The standard amount of the allowance has been £40,000 a year since 6 April 2016 and, if you want to make a bigger increase to your savings, you can carry forward unused allowance from the previous three years. But the standard allowance is reduced in some circumstances to £10,000 (affects high earners) or even £4,000 (if you withdraw your savings early or flexibly) – see *Pension questions* later in this chapter. If your savings increase by more than your Annual Allowance, you have to pay a tax charge that, in effect, claws back the tax relief you've had on the 'excess' savings.

The last way the government limits the amount you can save through pension schemes is by setting a Lifetime Allowance. This is a maximum value of benefits you can have from private pension schemes over your whole life. The standard limit has been changed a number of times (in 2019/20 it stands at £1.055 million), and is increased each year in line with inflation. Some people have kept an earlier higher limit under transitional rules. A check is made each time a pension or other benefit starts to be paid (and in some circumstances at age 75) and, if you're over the limit, there is a tax charge to pay on the 'excess'. Again, each pension scheme you are in can tell you how much of your Lifetime Allowance it is using up.

The Annual Allowance and Lifetime Allowance are high compared with the amount most people can afford to save for retirement, so you might not need to worry about them. However, the Annual Allowance can cause unwelcome tax bills, especially as you reach the peak of your career, if you are in work that pays you £110,000 a year or more. For example, a prominent item in the news during 2019 concerned NHS doctors turning down extra work because the increased earnings cause high pension-related tax bills. If you think you might be affected, you can find out more at gov.uk/guidance/pension-schemes-work-out-your-tapered-annual-allowance. It's also important to be aware that, if you do draw out some or all of your pension savings early, your Annual Allowance can fall sharply, making it harder to rebuild your savings – for more about this, see *Drawing your savings early* later in this chapter.

Workplace pension schemes

Between 2012 and 2018 a system of automatic enrolment was rolled out, and now nearly every employee will find themselves by default belonging to a pension scheme at work. Although you can opt out if you want to, it's usually a good idea to stay in the scheme as not only does your employer contribute, but you often get other benefits as well as a pension and tax-free lump sum when you retire. These could include life insurance, which pays a lump sum and/or a pension to your dependents if you die while working for that employer. It could also include a pension if you have to retire early because of ill health, and a pension for your spouse and other dependents when you die.

There are several different types of workplace scheme. You might find yourself in a company scheme set up by your employer, or in some type of group personal pension plan arranged by your employer but provided by another organization, usually an insurance company. You could be enrolled into a multi-employer scheme that is like a company scheme but has members from many different firms, or you might be in NEST (the National Employment Savings Trust), a multi-employer scheme set up by government to ensure there was at least one scheme suitable for automatic enrolment available to everyone. The key difference when thinking about your retirement is whether the scheme promises you a certain level of pension (a defined-benefit scheme) or you are simply building up a personal pot of savings (a defined-contribution scheme).

Defined-benefit schemes

These are the Rolls-Royce of pension schemes because they promise a known proportion of your pay when you retire. They are always company schemes set up by your employer. Defined-benefit schemes used to be quite common, and are still the norm if you work in the public sector, but are becoming rare in the private sector.

How much you get is worked out from how many years you're in the scheme and your annual salary while working. You build up a pension at a certain rate – 1/60th or 1/80th is quite common – so for each year you've been a scheme member, you receive, say, 1/60th of your final salary. For example, if you were in the scheme for 10 years and your salary was £30,000, you'd receive a £5,000 a year pension – that is, 10/60ths of £30,000.

How your salary is defined depends on the scheme rules. In the past, it typically meant your pay shortly before retiring (or at the time you left the scheme if earlier) and these are known as *final salary schemes*. These days it is more common for 'salary' to mean your average pay during all the years you've been a member of the scheme. Pay in the earlier years will have been lower because the cost of living was lower, so usually your pay from previous years is revalued in line with price inflation before the average is worked out. For this reason, such schemes are often called *career average revalued earnings (CARE) schemes*.

Defined-benefit schemes are costly for employers to run. A combination of people living longer, statutory improvements to benefits and increased regulation have made these schemes safer and more generous over time for employees, but have pushed up the costs and uncertainties for employers, to the point at which many have pulled back from this type of scheme. Typical changes are to switch from a final salary to a CARE basis, close the defined-benefit scheme to new members, stop existing members building up future defined-benefit pensions, and to offer some form of defined-contribution scheme to employees instead. These changes are not usually backdated, so when you reach retirement you may find you have a pension with several parts, for example, a bit that's worked out on a final-salary basis, another bit on a CARE basis and some on a defined-contribution basis.

Another way that some employers have been trying to cut the costs of defined-benefit schemes is to buy out your pension rights. You may be offered an eye-watering sum that you can transfer into a defined-contribution scheme (and then perhaps cash it in – see below). For example, someone might be promised a pension of £20,000 a year when they retire (increasing yearly) and offered a sum of £600,000 to give that up. That may seem like winning the lottery, but to replace that £20,000 pension would cost about £690,000 and any of the sum taken out as cash today reduces the eventual pension.

Defined-contribution schemes

All other workplace pension schemes are defined-contribution schemes. These can be company schemes set up by your employer, but are often some type of personal pension scheme – see *Pensions you arrange for yourself* later in this chapter – or multi-employer schemes, such as NEST. The money paid in by you and your employer is invested and builds up a fund that buys you an income when you retire. Since April 2019, the minimum amount paid in must be 8 per cent of your salary between a lower and upper limit, with at least 3 per cent of that coming from your employer. You typically pay 4 per cent, and tax relief adds the final 1 per cent. With defined-contribution schemes, you don't know the amount of pension you'll get at retirement. This will depend on how much you and your employer pay into the fund, how well your invested contributions perform, the charges taken out of your fund by your pension provider, how much you take out as a tax-free lump sum at retirement (or cash in before then), and the terms on which you eventually convert your savings into pension.

It helps to think of money-purchase pensions as having two stages:

1 *Accumulation.* The fund is invested, usually in stocks and shares and other investments, with the aim of growing it over the years before you retire. Most schemes offer a choice of investment funds, but have a default fund that you are invested in if you don't make an active choice. You can find information about choosing investments in Chapter 5, but broadly speaking, for savings that you will not be cashing in within the next 10 years, it usually makes sense to invest mainly in shares. For savings you do intend to cash in or use to buy an annuity, it is common to gradually shift your savings towards safer investments such as cash and bonds (a process sometimes called 'lifestyling').

2 *Decumulation.* When you retire, you can take a tax-free lump sum from your fund and use the rest to provide an income – either in the form of a lifetime annuity or through drawdown (leaving your savings invested and just cashing in amounts as you need them).

Annuities

A lifetime annuity is an income you buy with part or all of your pension fund. It provides a secure income for the rest of your life, however long you live, so is best thought of as insurance against living longer than your savings would otherwise last. While the average 65-year-old today can expect to survive to age 86 (man) or 89 (woman), you'd be unwise to plan your retirement on an average, since you might well be in the half of the population that lives longer – often much longer. According to the Office for National Statistics, a man aged 65 has a one in four chance of reaching age 94, and a one in 14 chance of surviving to age 100. For women, there's a one in four chance of reaching age 96 and one woman in nine can expect to survive to 100.

On the other hand, many people worry that, having handed over a large chunk of their savings for an annuity, they might die within a few years and not get value from the annuity. But some types of annuity can help you guard against that either by guaranteeing to pay the income for a minimum number of years even if you die before that, or paying out any remaining balance of the sum you paid to your heirs. And, if you might be expected to die younger than average because of poor health, smoking or other lifestyle factors, you may qualify for an 'enhanced annuity' which pays you a higher-than-average income each year.

Lifetime annuities can be bought to pay an income just for your own life, or until your partner (if you have one) dies as well. You can choose whether to receive a level income or one that increases each year, for example, in line with inflation.

If you are buying an annuity, it's important to shop around for the type that's most suitable for you and the best deals on the market. The Money Advice Service has a free tool to help you do this: moneyadviceservice.org.uk/en/tools/annuities.

Drawdown

Don't confuse drawdown with taking cash out of your pension savings before retirement (discussed below). Drawdown lets you choose the point at which you want to start drawing some kind of retirement income. First, you take any tax-free lump sum, and what remains goes into your drawdown fund. These savings are invested, usually with quite a high proportion still in shares because your fund may have to support you for several decades. This means the value of your drawdown fund will go up and down with the stock market.

Drawdown is very flexible. You don't have to draw out anything and, if you do, you choose how much to draw out and when. You might opt to draw out sums regularly to create an income. You might draw out lump sums to cover one-off expenses. You can even cash in the whole lot! Whatever you do draw out, the whole sum counts as income for that year and is taxed in the normal way (as explained in Chapter 4). Any unused amount left in your fund on death can be left as a pension or lump sum to anyone you choose – there is more information about this in the section *Divorce, separation and bereavement* later in this chapter.

A challenge with drawdown is that you do not know how long your savings will have to last. You might want to draw out a steady income each year, rising just enough to keep pace with inflation, but there is a risk that your savings will run dry part way through retirement. To guard against this, some advisers suggest you draw off a set percentage of your savings each year, say 4 per cent. The drawback with doing that is that in years when the value of your investments falls, your income will also fall.

Opting for drawdown affects your Annual Allowance (described in *How much you can save* earlier in this chapter.) The limit on the amount you can save in future each year through defined-contribution pension schemes is capped at £4,000 – see *Pension questions* later in this chapter for more details.

Striking a balance

Annuities and drawdown each have advantages and disadvantages, and many experts suggest you use both.

One strategy is to work out the minimum income you would be prepared to live on. Check whether your State Pension plus any defined-benefit pensions from work provides that minimum. If not, consider buying an annuity to top up your income to the minimum. This ensures you have secure sources of income up to that level. You could then use any remaining pension savings for drawdown.

Another strategy is to rely on drawdown during the early part of your retirement, but use part or all of the remaining drawdown fund to buy an annuity once you reach, say, age 85. The annuity then covers the remaining risk that you might continue to need an income until a very old age. This strategy is helped by the fact that annuities get cheaper as you get older (because the income they provide is expected to be paid out for a shorter period than buying the same income when you are younger).

Pensions you arrange for yourself

Pension schemes you arrange for yourself are always defined-contribution pensions, so all of the information in the relevant earlier sections applies.

Anyone can have a pension scheme, and anyone else can pay into it for you – for example, if you're caring for children or doing other unpaid work, your partner could pay into a scheme for you; and grandparents, say, could pay into a pension scheme for grandchildren even from the day they are born. But usually people arrange their own scheme in order to top up the savings they are building up through their workplace scheme or because they are self-employed. Saving for retirement is especially tough if you work for yourself, because there is no automatic enrolment and no employer to contribute to your scheme. It's up to you to motivate yourself to start saving, decide how much you can afford to pay in and choose a provider.

There are several types of personal pension scheme:

- *Stakeholder pensions* must have certain features, including limited charges, low minimum contributions, flexible contributions, penalty-free transfers and a default investment fund – ie a fund your money will be invested in if you don't want to choose one yourself.

- Standard *personal pensions* are similar to stakeholder pensions, but they usually offer a wider range of investment funds. Personal pension charges may be similar to stakeholder pension charges, but some are higher. High charges deducted from your fund by the pension provider can reduce the growth of your fund (and high charges do not necessarily mean better performance).

- A *self-invested personal pension (SIPP)* gives you an even wider choice of investments, including for example property, direct investment in stocks and shares, as well as a huge range of investment funds. The charges for SIPPs are usually higher than for other types of personal pension, so you should make sure you really do want the greater range of options that they offer.

Stakeholder schemes and standard personal pensions are typically provided by insurance companies, while SIPPs tend to be offered by stockbrokers and investment firms, often through online platforms.

Another option if you are self-employed is to join NEST. Although this scheme was set up especially to support the automatic enrolment of employees, it is also open to self-employed people. It has been designed with relatively low charges in order to offer good value pensions, but has only a limited range of investment choices. For more information, visit nestpensions.org.uk and search for 'Joining as self-employed'.

Starting your pension

A company pension scheme usually has a normal pension age which is the earliest age at which you can start to draw your full pension. With a personal pension scheme, you choose the age at which you want to start drawing a pension.

You can often choose to start your pension earlier but, in that case, the amount of pension you get from a company defined-benefit scheme will be lower and stay at that lower level throughout your retirement. Similarly, with a company defined-contribution scheme or any personal pension scheme, the pension pot you've built up (and so the amount of pension it can provide) will be permanently lower if you retire early. Some company schemes pay a higher amount of pension for a few years to bridge the gap between your retiring early and your State Pension starting. The extra amount is called a 'bridging pension' and the whole arrangement is sometimes called a 'step-down pension'. It's important to understand this arrangement if it applies to you so you are not taken by surprise when your company pension falls at State Pension age.

The earliest you can normally start drawing a pension is currently age 55. This is due to rise to 57 in 2028 when State Pension age reaches 67. You can start your pension at any age if you have to retire early because of ill health. Starting your pension later may mean you get a larger pension.

Some employers have rules that prevent you continuing to work for them after starting your pension or limit the number of hours you can work – check your scheme rules to see if this applies. But there is no general rule stopping you working and drawing pensions, so you could take work elsewhere or start your own business. It is now increasingly common for people to gradually phase into retirement, spending many years combining work and pension.

Drawing your savings early

Since April 2015, with many defined-contribution schemes, provided you have reached at least age 55, you can draw out some or all of your savings before retirement to use in any way you choose. Your pension provider can tell you if it offers this option; if not, you might consider transferring your savings to another scheme that does.

These early withdrawals go by the ungainly name of 'uncrystallised funds pension lump sums' (UFPLS). 'Uncrystallised' means that you have not yet turned your pension pot into an annuity or drawdown fund, so your savings are still in that first (accumulation) stage.

A quarter of any sum you draw out in this way is tax-free, but the rest counts as taxable income for the year you make the withdrawal. This can come as a shock, especially if it tips you into a higher tax bracket, as in the case study following. You might pay less tax if you take several smaller lump sums spread over several years.

Tax on an UFPLS withdrawal is usually deducted automatically by the provider using the PAYE system (which is explained in Chapter 4). The system is designed to cope with regular payments rather than large one-off lump sums and can result in the wrong amount of tax being deducted. You would then need to claim some tax back (or, less usually, have extra tax to pay) – how to do this varies with circumstances. You can find out more using the tool at gov.uk/claim-tax-refund.

CASE STUDY

John is normally a basic-rate taxpayer (paying a top rate in 2019/20 of 20 per cent), and his income is £5,000 below the threshold at which higher-rate tax starts. He decides to draw £50,000 out of his pension savings. A quarter of this (£12,500) is tax-free. The remaining £37,500 is added to his income for the year and taxed in the normal way. £5,000 uses up his remaining basic-rate band, but the rest is taxed at 40 per cent. The total tax bill on his UFPLS withdrawal is £14,000. After tax, his £50,000 withdrawal has shrunk to £36,000.

You cannot make UFPLS withdrawals from a defined-benefit scheme. However, if the scheme is run by a private-sector employer, you could transfer your pension rights out of that scheme and into a personal pension scheme that does allow early withdrawals. You should think carefully before doing this, because you will be giving up a secure promised pension that you might need in retirement. If the value of the pension rights you are transferring comes to more than £30,000, you will in any case have to take professional financial advice.

If you belong to a public-sector defined-benefit scheme, you are not allowed to transfer your pension rights to a defined-contribution scheme.

Drawing your savings early affects your Annual Allowance (described in *How much you can save* earlier in this chapter). The limit on the amount you can save in future each year through defined-contribution pension schemes is capped at £4,000 – see *Pension questions* later in this chapter for more details.

How safe is your pension?

Pensions seem constantly to be in the news, usually making bad headlines. Scandals are typically of two types: defined-benefit schemes breaking their pension promises, and individual savers in all types of scheme being scammed out of their money.

Although big news when it happens, most defined-benefit schemes do not fail and, where they do, there is a compensation scheme to help. The Pension Protection Fund (PPF) may take over a scheme where the employer running it has become insolvent. Pensions are protected up to a cap that varies with age (just over £40,000 at age 65 in 2019/20). Members below their scheme's normal pension age will at retirement receive 90 per cent of the pension they've built up subject to the relevant cap. Members already drawing their pension receive 100 per cent of their pension up to the relevant cap. In both cases, when pension payments start, pensions built up since 1997 are increased each year in line with inflation up to a maximum of 2.5 per cent a year, but any part of the pension built up during earlier years does not increase. See ppf.co.uk.

There is also a Fraud Compensation Fund that may take over pensions where company scheme members lose out because of fraud or negligence. This applies to both defined-benefit and defined-contribution company schemes. See ppf.co.uk/fraud-compensation-fund.

Personal pension schemes and annuities are covered by a different compensation scheme, the Financial Services Compensation Scheme (FSCS). This can help where the provider has become insolvent owing you money, provided the firm is authorized to operate. You can check a firm's authorization by consulting the FCA Register: register.fca.org.uk/. Compensation is generally up to a maximum of £85,000. This limit is low relative to the amount you may have saved, but pension savings should in any case be ring-fenced and kept separate from the provider's own finances to keep your money safe. Where you are receiving income from an annuity, the compensation is unlimited.

While pension scams have been around for decades, they have increased significantly since April 2015 when, if you're aged 55 and over, you started to be able to withdraw money from your pension savings before retirement (see *Drawing your savings early* earlier in this chapter). The Pensions Regulator and Financial Conduct Authority (FCA) carried out a joint survey in 2018, and found that the average person scammed loses £91,000. Often whole life savings vanish and the chances of getting your money back are low. Both regulators publish guidance on their websites on how to protect yourself against being scammed: thepensionsregulator.gov.uk/pension-scams and fca.org.uk/scamsmart/how-avoid-pension-scams. They highlight five common tactics that should set your alarm bells ringing: contact out of the blue (whether by phone, e-mail or other means); promises of high and/or guaranteed returns; free pension reviews; access to your savings before age 55; and pressure to act quickly.

Since January 2019, it has become illegal for firms to cold-call you about pensions. The only pension calls that are legitimate are from authorized firms where you have specifically given your consent to be contacted. If you are contacted in any other circumstances, treat it as a scam call and hang up. Scammers will seem very plausible, and their websites and paperwork will typically look genuine. To protect yourself, reject any unexpected offers, check the FCA Register to make sure the firm is legally authorized to operate, refuse to be pressured into quick decisions, and seek out impartial information and guidance or advice.

Information, guidance and advice about private pensions

If you find it difficult to understand how your pension scheme works, you are not alone! Pensions are notoriously complicated and governments do like to keep changing the rules. However, your pension is a valuable asset, especially as you approach retirement, and it is important that you should know the main essentials, including any options that may still be available to you.

If you have a query or if you are concerned in some way about a workplace pension, you should approach whoever is responsible for the scheme in your organization. If the company is large, there may be a special person to look after the scheme on a day-to-day basis. This could be the pensions manager or, quite often, it is someone in the human resources department. In a smaller company, the pension scheme may be looked after by the company secretary or managing director.

With a pension you've arranged for yourself, your first port of call for any queries or concern should be your pension provider. If you need more general information or you are confused by the response from your company scheme or pension provider, The Pensions Advisory Service (TPAS) has a wealth of information at pensionsadvisoryservice.org.uk, and can provide guidance through its telephone helpline. There is information about your options at retirement at pensionwise.gov.uk and, if you are aged 50 or over, you can book a free phone or face-to-face session to guide you through the options.

Guidance is not the same as advice. If you do not feel confident making pension decisions on your own, consider paying for professional financial advice (see Chapter 1).

Other help and advice

Making a complaint

If you are unhappy with the way a personal pension scheme has been marketed or sold to you, you should first complain to the firm involved. Authorized firms are required to have a complaints procedure that you can use. The firm should reply within eight weeks. If it doesn't, or if you're unhappy with its response, you can take your complaint to the Financial Ombudsman Service (FOS). This is an independent, free-to-use service. It can order the firm to put matters right, which may include compensation up to a maximum of £350,000 (since 1 April 2019; £150,000 before that).

In most other cases, whether your complaint concerns a workplace pension or a personal pension scheme you've arranged for yourself, you should again give the scheme provider a chance to resolve the matter first. If you don't get a reply or you are not happy with the response, you can take your complaint to the Pension Ombudsman, which can order the scheme to put matters right.

Keeping track of your pensions

In addition to understanding your current pension scheme, you may also need to chase up any previous schemes of which you were a member. This is well worth pursuing, as you could be owed money from one or more schemes, which will all add to your pension on retirement day. According to research by the Pensions Policy Institute, there could be as many as 1.6 million 'lost' pension pots potentially worth over £19 billion, with an average lost pot size of £12,670. These lost pots are left behind when workers move between jobs, particularly at the start of their careers. As retirement approaches, many face problems tracking down small-sized funds, or simply don't think to look for them at all.

However, there is a free, government service, the Pension Tracing Service, which can help you trace your old pensions. It deals with some 170,000 requests a year. You can use the service by phone, post or online at gov.uk/find-pension-contact-details.

With government encouragement, the pensions industry is working on creating a 'pensions dashboard' which will let you view all your pensions in one place. This should make it easier to keep track of your pensions, spot if an old pension is missing and estimate how much income you may have in retirement. Many different organizations will offer you this dashboard service – for example, your bank, your employer, your pension providers, advice agencies or an app you download to a smartphone. Pension dashboards were due to start rolling out in 2019, but the project has previously been delayed several times. To learn more and keep track of progress, visit pensionsdashboardproject.uk.

Divorce, separation and bereavement

Events like divorce, separation and bereavement typically mean that you shift from living in a shared household to living alone, and may become newly eligible to claim state benefits if your income is low – see *Other state benefits for pensioners* earlier in this chapter.

These life events can have a big impact on your financial situation. Pension savings and pensions built up by you and your partner are a major part of those finances, so it's important to think about how they are affected and what you can do to make sure they give you the best support.

Divorce

On divorce or the dissolution of a civil partnership, the couple's assets have to split between them. Often, the two most valuable assets will be a property if the couple have bought their home, and any private pensions each has built up. Because women still traditionally take on most of the unpaid work of caring and looking after the home, it is common for the husband to have built up the bulk of the couple's private pensions, with the original intention that they would share the income in retirement. There are three ways in which pension savings can be dealt with on divorce:

- Offsetting. This means one person might keep the pensions, but the other get a similarly valuable asset, such as the home.

- A pension attachment order (earmarking in Scotland). There is no immediate change to the pension arrangements, but it is agreed that, once the pension starts to be paid, part of it will be transferred to the former partner. Similarly, benefits might be due to be paid to you if your ex-partner dies.

- Sharing. Part of the pension savings are transferred to the former partner, so this part becomes their own savings and will provide their own pension in retirement.

You can agree to offsetting without involving a court, but a court order is needed for pension attachment, earmarking or pension sharing.

Offsetting and pension sharing are both commonly used and have the advantage of creating a clean break between the couple. Pension attachment orders or earmarking are less popular. There is no clean break, and they have several other drawbacks. For example, the partner with the pension scheme might die, stop paying into the scheme or delay their retirement, all of which affect the amount of pension the other person may get. If you are due to receive part or all of any death benefits, you might not be aware if your ex-partner dies. If there is a possibility that they may have died but that you have not been informed, you can check by contacting the General Register Office at gov.uk/general-register-office. The indexes to all birth, marriage and death entries in England and Wales are available from the National Archives website at nationalarchives.gov.uk.

If either or both of the couple have already started to draw pensions, this income will be taken into account as part of the divorce settlement.

How to split pension savings is particularly complex, and a subject to raise with your solicitor if you are in the process of divorce proceedings. For a free and less formal discussion of your options, contact The Pensions Advisory Service or Pension Wise.

The old state basic pension could not be shared, but for divorced people reaching State Pension age before 6 April 2016, they could use their ex-partner's NICs record to increase their own State Pension as high as the full rate. A court could order that any additional pension be shared.

Under the new single-tier State Pension, each person builds up their own pension and there are no arrangements for sharing either State Pension or NICs. However, for many years to come, people reaching State Pension age on or after 6 April 2016 will be covered by transitional rules because they spent time in both the old and new State Pension systems. Under these rules, you might have a 'protected payment' which is an amount over and above the full single-tier rate (see *How the new State Pension is worked out* earlier in this chapter). A court can order that this protected payment be shared with your ex-partner on divorce. Contact the Pension Service for help understanding which rules may apply to you and how.

Separation

If you separate without getting divorced or going through any other formal proceeding, there is usually no change to your pensions. You may, however, want to check that in the event of death any survivor pension from a company scheme could still be paid to your separated partner if that is what you want to happen.

You might consider getting a judicial separation (where a court formally recognizes your separation and can make orders about your finances). In that case, the court can make an order for a pensions attachment order or offsetting (but not pension sharing).

Bereavement

You may get some help from the state if your spouse or civil partner dies. If you are under State Pension age, you may qualify for Bereavement Support Payment. To qualify, your late partner must have paid NICs for at least 25 weeks, or their death must have been work-related. There are two parts to the payment – if you are not caring for children, these are a lump sum of £2,500, and then £100 a month paid for up to 18 months (in 2019/20). (If you are getting Child Benefit the amounts are higher.) Both parts are tax-free. To claim, complete form BSP1 available from www.gov.uk/bereavement-support-payment/how-to-claim or order it from your local Jobcentre Plus. In Northern Ireland, download an application form from nidirect.gov.uk, or contact the Bereavement Service on 0800 085 2463.

If you are over State Pension age at the time of your partner's death, your own State Pension may increase. If you reached State Pension age before 6 April 2016, you can use your late partner's NICs record to increase your basic pension up to the full amount and you may inherit up to half of their additional pension. If you reached State Pension age on or after 6 April 2016, you may inherit half their 'protected payment' if any (see *How the new State Pension is worked out* earlier in this chapter). Contact the Pension Service to check what you are entitled to and to make a claim.

Your spouse or civil partner may have had one or more private pensions. These may pay a variety of death benefits. Your late partner will usually have been asked to complete an 'expression of wish' form saying who should receive these benefits. The scheme will normally follow these wishes, but in some circumstances might consider making payments to other people – for example, to a former spouse if they had been financially dependent on your late partner.

Pension savings are normally passed on free of inheritance tax, but income tax might apply. If your spouse or civil partner belonged to a defined-benefit scheme, you will usually be entitled to a lump sum and/or a survivor pension from this. Any lump sum you receive is usually tax-free. If your income is high enough, though, you will pay tax on the pension income in the normal way (see Chapter 4). You also normally pay tax on any pension you get from a defined-contribution company scheme that your late partner had, if that pension is paid direct from the scheme.

Where your late partner had any other sort of defined-contribution scheme, in general, lump sums, annuity payments or drawdown withdrawals that you receive from the scheme are tax-free if your late partner died before age 75 and you're paid within two years of their death. If they were over 75 or the payments are made more than two years later, the payments will count towards your taxable income. Be aware that if all the benefits paid out from your late partner's pension schemes, including the death benefits now being paid, come to more than their Lifetime Allowance, there will be a tax bill on the excess amount (see *How much you can save* earlier in this chapter).

To claim a lump sum, the savings pot or a pension from your late partner's pension arrangements, contact each scheme for advice.

Pension questions

There is no doubt that pensions are complex, and there is often no one-size-fits-all answer to the questions you have. So much depends on your particular circumstances. Nevertheless, here are some pointers to the answers for some common pension questions.

What is 'freedom and choice'?

This is the name given to the change in government policy from April 2015 that allows you to draw out your pension savings for any purpose – not just to provide yourself with a retirement income – provided you have reached age 55 (rising to 57 from 2028). You may recall pensions minister Steve Webb saying that if you want to blow your pension on a Lamborghini, that's fine. The policy also changed the way defined-contribution pension savings can be passed on at death – where death occurs before age 75, they can usually be passed on tax-free generation after generation.

Is cash I take out of my savings tax-free?

That depends. The general principle is that overall you can have a quarter of your pension savings tax-free. However, there are three different times when you may want to draw out cash from your pension savings – before retirement (accumulation stage), at retirement (when you shift from the accumulation to the decumulation stage), and after retirement (decumulation stage) – and the tax treatment is different in each case.

Starting with at retirement, you can take up to a quarter of your savings tax-free. This is a one-off opportunity: if you decide to take less than a quarter of your savings as a tax-free lump sum, you cannot come back later for more. The remainder of your savings provides you with a pension, buys an annuity or goes into a drawdown fund.

You can only draw out cash sums after retirement if your savings are now in a drawdown fund. That being the case, the whole of any lump sum drawn out is taxable. This is because you've already had all the tax-free cash you're allowed at retirement.

Provided you've reached age 55, you can also draw out cash while you are still in the accumulation stage of saving for a pension, but only from defined-contribution schemes, and only if the provider offers that option. In this case, a quarter of the cash you draw out is tax-free, but the rest is taxable.

If I cash in my savings now, I can build them back up again – right?

Up to a point. You can cash in savings from many defined-contribution schemes before retirement. But, if you do that, your Annual Allowance (see *How much you can save* earlier in this chapter) is reduced. Basically the allowance is split in two. Part, which is called the Money Purchase Annual Allowance (MPAA) is reduced to £4,000 ('money purchase' is another name for 'defined contribution'). It means that you, and anyone else, can only pay up to £4,000 a year into your defined-contribution schemes in future, instead of the normal £40,000. Moreover, you can no longer carry forward any unused Annual Allowance from the previous three years to cover bigger contributions to defined-contribution schemes. That might be too low for you to be able to fully replace the savings you drew out early. But, if you also belong to a defined-benefit scheme, you still have £36,000 of Annual Allowance for saving that way.

In what other situations do I need to worry about the MPAA?

Your MPAA is reduced to £4,000 whenever you withdraw money from your savings flexibly. This can mean cashing in savings before retirement as already described, but also opting for a drawdown arrangement under the rules that apply from April 2015 onwards. You might also be affected if you have an earlier style of drawdown arrangement called 'capped drawdown'. This is where you can draw money out of your drawdown fund, but only up to a certain amount each year (the cap was intended to guard against you running out of money part way through retirement). If you go over the cap, your MPAA is reduced to £4,000.

Lifetime Individual Savings Accounts (LISAs)

Individual Savings Accounts (ISAs) are a tax-efficient way to save or invest for all sorts of purposes and there's information about them in Chapter 5. However, from April 2017, a new Lifetime ISA (LISA) became available specifically designed as a way for younger people to save for retirement. A LISA can be taken out by anyone aged between 18 and 40. The maximum amount you can save is £4,000 a year, but the government adds a bonus of 25 per cent to this (so a maximum government bonus of £1,000 a year). The money grows tax-free within the LISA and, from age 60 onwards, can be withdrawn tax-free and used for any purpose.

Savings in a LISA can also be drawn out early, and will be tax-free if used as a deposit to buy a home. Otherwise, on early withdrawal, the government bonus is taken back and there is also a 5 per cent penalty charge. If you are a non-taxpayer or pay tax at no more than the basic rate (20 per cent in 2019/20), a LISA is a more tax-efficient way to save for retirement than a pension scheme. However, bear in mind that workplace pension schemes also benefit from money paid in by your employer. LISAs are offered by a range of providers, including some banks, building societies and investment firms. For a list of providers, see which.co.uk (search for 'Lifetime ISAs').

04
Tax

There is no doubt that your tax position is likely to change once you start to take retirement, and it is vital that everyone reaching retirement age should invest some time in understanding how the tax system applies to them. If you are new to retirement, now is a perfect time to consider a money make-over, and check up on what the current taxation rules mean for you.

The most common types of tax (and we are familiar with most of them) are income tax, National Insurance contributions, capital gains tax (CGT) and inheritance tax (IHT). While you were employed you may have been contributing many thousands of pounds to HM Revenue & Customs (HMRC), but in practice you may have had very little direct contact with the tax system. The accounts department would have automatically deducted – and accounted for – the PAYE on your earnings as a salaried employee. If you were self-employed, or had other money unconnected with your job, you may have had more dealings with HMRC. On reaching retirement you should be able to calculate how much money (after deduction of tax) you will have available to spend: the equivalent, if you like, of your take-home pay. Understanding the broad principles could help you save money, by not paying more in tax than you need.

The purpose of this chapter is not to give you tax planning advice. If your affairs are complex, you may want to hire a professional tax adviser to help you do that. The aim here is simply to remind you of the basics and to draw your attention to some of the latest variations that could have a bearing on your immediate or longer-term plans. The following information is based on our understanding, as at May 2019, of current taxation, legislation and HMRC practice, all of which are liable to change from one year to the next. The impact of taxation (and any tax relief) depends on individual circumstances.

Since 1990, the UK has had 'independent taxation', meaning that taxes normally apply to each person separately. However, this principle has been breached in the case of the high-income child benefit tax charge (described in Chapter 3), where one person in a family may have to pay extra tax be-cause another is receiving child benefit.

Income tax – the basics

This is calculated on all (or nearly all) of your income, after deduction of the personal allowance (which most people get). The reason for saying 'nearly all' is that some income you may receive is tax free; types of income on which you do not have to pay tax are listed a little further on. Having deducted the personal allowance, what remains is called your 'taxable income'.

Most income counts. You will be assessed for income tax on your pensions (including your State Pension), interest you receive from most types of savings, dividends from investments, any earnings from a job (even if these are only from casual work), profits from being self-employed, plus rent from any lodgers, should the amount you receive exceed £7,500 a year. However, there are other allowances that may reduce or eliminate the tax you pay on savings income, dividends and very small business ventures. Many social security benefits are also taxable.

You may pay less income tax if you have some types of expenditure that qualify for tax relief – these are sometimes called 'outgoings'. The most common outgoings that qualify for relief are payments you make to a pension scheme, and donations to charity.

Income tax is an annual tax. The tax year runs from 6 April to the following 5 April, so the amount of tax you pay in any one year is calculated on the income you receive (or are deemed to have received) between these two dates.

Personal allowance

You don't pay tax on every single penny of your money. Most people are allowed to retain a certain amount before income tax becomes applicable. This is known as your personal allowance. When calculating how much tax you will have to pay in any one year, first deduct from your total income the amount represented by your personal allowance. It does not matter where the income comes from, whether from earnings, an investment, a pension or another source. The personal allowance is given automatically; you do not have to claim it.

In the past, many people aged 65 and over received a higher personal allowance often called the 'age allowance'. This was phased out, and since 2016/17 all older people get the same allowance as everyone else. The good news is that the government has been increasing the personal allowance by more than inflation for the past few years in order to honour a manifesto pledge to increase the allowance to £12,500 by 2020. In the event, the increase has been brought forward by one year, so that the personal allowance for 2019/20 is £12,500. It will be frozen at this level during 2020/21, and then increased in line with inflation in subsequent years.

Not everyone gets the personal allowance. For people with a total income of more than £100,000, their personal allowance is reduced: £1 of allowance is lost for every £2 by which their income exceeds £100,000. This means that in 2019/20, someone earning £125,000 or more does not get any personal allowance.

Rates of income tax

Your taxable income (what's left after subtracting your personal allowance) is divided into slices, called tax bands, and different rates of tax apply to each band. Scotland has different tax bands and rates from the rest of the UK. Wales also has the power to set its own Welsh income tax rates, but in 2019/20 has chosen to set these at the same level as the rates for England and Northern Ireland. The four different rates of income tax for 2019/20 for the UK apart from Scotland are:

1 The 0 per cent savings rate, which applies to the first £5,000 of any savings income. However, if an individual's taxable non-savings income exceeds the savings rate limit, then the 0 per cent rate for savings will not be available for savings income.

2 The 20 per cent basic rate for income up to £37,500.

3 The 40 per cent higher rate, which is levied on all taxable income from £37,501 up to £150,000.

4 The top rate of 45 per cent on income in excess of £150,000.

Different tax rates apply to dividend income, and these are described later in the chapter.

Scottish income tax

Scotland has the power to set its own tax bands and rates of tax for all types of income, except savings income and dividends – for these, the UK rates described later in this chapter apply. Scotland must also have the same personal allowance as the rest of the UK. Scottish income tax applies if your only or main home is in Scotland. Your tax is still collected by HMRC on behalf of the Scottish tax authority, Revenue Scotland.

Scotland charges less tax than the rest of the UK on lower incomes, but more on higher incomes. In 2019/20, it does this through a system of five tax bands:

1 a 19 per cent starter rate on the first £2,049 of income from pensions, earnings, rents, and so on;

2 a 20 per cent basic rate on taxable income from £2,050 to £12,444;

3 a 21 per cent intermediate rate on taxable income from £12,445 to £30,930;

4 a 41 per cent higher rate on taxable income from £30,931 to £150,000;

5 a 46 per cent top rate on taxable income over £150,000.

Welsh income tax

Since April 2019, Wales can set its own Welsh income tax rate for all types of income, except savings income and dividends – for these, the UK rates described later in this chapter apply. Wales must also have the same personal allowance as the rest of the UK. If you live in Wales, you count as a Welsh taxpayer (even if you work over the border in England or elsewhere).

The way Welsh income tax works is that the normal UK rates are reduced by 10 per cent – so the UK basic rate becomes 10 per cent instead of 20 per cent, the higher rate becomes 30 per cent instead of 40 per cent, and the additional rate becomes 35 per cent instead of 45 per cent. The Welsh Assembly can then add a Welsh income tax rate on top of these reduced UK rates. For 2019/20, the Welsh rate has been set at 10 per cent for all the tax bands. This means you pay the same total tax rate as taxpayers in the rest of the UK except Scotland. Your tax is still collected by HMRC, and the Welsh part is then passed across to the Welsh Revenue Authority.

Other allowances

In addition to your personal allowance, there are some other tax allowances that can reduce the amount of tax you have to pay. Tax relief is given in different ways, depending on the allowance.

Blind person's allowance

Registered blind people can claim an allowance of £2,450 in 2019/20. This reduces your tax bill by being deducted from your total income before tax is worked out (in the same way as the personal allowance).

If both husband and wife are registered as blind, they can each claim the allowance. If you think you would be eligible, you should contact the HMRC helpline, 0300 200 3301, with relevant details of your situation. If you were entitled to receive the allowance earlier but for some reason missed out on doing so, you may be able to backdate your claim and obtain a tax rebate for up to four earlier years.

Marriage allowance

Marriage allowance is not really an extra allowance; rather, it is the ability to transfer some of your personal allowance to your partner. If you are married or in a civil partnership, you may be able to do this. To be eligible, neither you nor your partner must be paying tax at more than the basic rate (or no more than the intermediate rate in Scotland). The most common situation where the transfer is worthwhile is if your income is too low to use your full personal allowance, but your partner has a bigger income on which they are paying tax.

The amount you can transfer is one-tenth of your personal allowance, so a fixed amount of £1,250 in 2019/20. The way your partner then gets tax relief is different from the personal allowance. Tax relief is worked out as 20 per cent of the £1,250 marriage allowance, which comes to £250. This amount is deducted from your partner's tax bill, but cannot reduce the bill to less than zero. This means the amount of tax relief they get could be any amount up to a maximum of £250.

You have to claim Marriage Allowance, and should normally do this online at gov.uk/apply-marriage-allowance. The person with the lowest income should make the claim, and you will need your own and your partner's National Insurance number and proof of your identity. If you cannot claim online, phone the HMRC general enquiries helpline on 0300 200 3300.

If you or your partner were born before 6 April 1935, consider claiming Married Couple's Allowance instead as this is more generous.

Married couple's allowance

This is an extra allowance for older couples where one or both of them were born before 6 April 1935. In 2019/20, the full allowance is £8,915. Tax relief is 10 per cent of this – £891.50 – and given as a reduction in your tax bill. But the allowance cannot reduce your tax bill to less than zero. For example, if your tax bill was only £200 in 2019/20, the benefit you'd get from the married couple's allowance is £200, enough to reduce your tax bill to £0.

However, that's not the end of the story. The amount of married couple's allowance you can get also depends on your income. In 2019/20, if your income is more than £29,600, the married couple's allowance is reduced by £1 for every £2 of 'excess income'. But the married couple's allowance is only ever reduced to a minimum amount of £3,450 (2019/20). That means the tax relief you get will be somewhere between £345 and £891.50, assuming your original tax bill is at least that much. To work out what you might get, there's a calculator at gov.uk/calculate-married-couples-allowance.

Since the amount varies with your income, you are probably asking: whose income? Mine or my partner's? For marriages before 5 December 2005, married couple's allowance is given initially to the husband to set against his income. For marriages and civil partnerships on or after that date, it goes to whichever of you has the higher income. But, in either case, you can arrange to transfer the whole allowance to the other person, agree to split it equally between you, or transfer any unused part. You'll need to fill in form 18, which is available online at gov.uk/married-couples-allowance/further-information or you can get a copy posted to you by calling the HMRC general helpline: 0300 200 3300. This is also the number to call to claim married couple's allowance unless you fill in a tax return each year, in which case you can claim there.

Tax relief on 'outgoings'

Separate from any personal allowances, you can obtain tax relief on the following:

- a donation to charity under the Gift Aid scheme or through a payroll giving scheme at work;
- contributions to occupational pensions, self-employed pension plans and other personal pensions;
- some maintenance payments, if you are divorced or separated and you or your partner were born before 6 April 1935;
- for some older borrowers only, mortgage interest on a loan taken out to provide you with extra income.

Donations to charity

You can get tax relief on a donation to charity if you make a Gift Aid declaration. Usually the charity provides you with a form to fill in to do this. Donating this way means that the charity can claim a top-up from HMRC equal to 25 per cent of whatever you give. For example, if you give £8, the charity gets £10 once the HMRC top-up is added on. The top-up the government gives to the charity is equivalent to giving you tax relief at the basic rate (20 per cent in 2019/20) on your donation. For example, when your £8 donation is topped up to £10, the extra £2 is 20 per cent of the total £10 received by the charity.

If you are a higher-rate or additional-rate taxpayer, you can claim extra tax relief. To do this, you need to fill in a tax return or ask HMRC to adjust your tax code (see below for information about this). Beware of using Gift Aid if you are a non-taxpayer or pay very little tax. If you do not already pay at least as much tax as the top-up, HMRC can ask you to pay the difference.

Some employers run payroll giving schemes that let you make donations to charity direct from your pay. Your employer deducts the donations from your pay before working out how much tax to collect (through the PAYE system described below). This means you automatically get tax relief up to your highest rate, and there is no need to fill in a tax return.

Pension contributions

The tax rules surrounding pension contributions are quite complex, and you can read about them in Chapter 3.

Maintenance payments

In general, maintenance payments you receive are not taxable, and you cannot claim tax relief on any maintenance payments you make to a partner following separation, divorce or the dissolution of a civil partnership. An exception has been made in cases where one (or both) of the divorced or separated partners was born before 6 April 1935. Those paying maintenance are still able to claim tax relief, but only at a rate of 10 per cent and only on payments up to £3,450 (2019/20). This gives maximum tax relief of £345, which you get as a reduction in your tax bill. (However, your tax bill cannot be reduced to less than zero.)

Tax relief on mortgage interest

Mortgage interest relief was abolished on 6 April 2000. The only purpose for which relief is still available is in respect of loans secured on an older person's home to purchase a life annuity (a home income scheme). However, to qualify, the loan must have been taken out (or at least processed and confirmed in writing) by 9 March 1999. Borrowers in this situation can continue to benefit from the relief for the duration of their loan. The relief applies to interest on only the first £30,000 of the loan, and is given at a rate of 10 per cent. You get the relief by making reduced payments to your lender, who then claims the relief back from HMRC.

Tax-free income

Some income you may receive is entirely free of tax. It is important to know what income is non-taxable and can be ignored for tax purposes. If you receive any of the following, you can forget about the tax aspect altogether (for a full list see litrg.org.uk/tax-guides/tax-basics/what-income-taxable):

Non-taxable state benefits include:

- Attendance Allowances;
- bereavement support payments;
- Child Benefit, unless you or your partner have income over £50,000 a year – see *Caring for children or adults* in Chapter 3 for details;
- Child Tax Credit;
- Council Tax Reduction (also called Council Tax Support);
- Disability Living Allowance;
- Housing Benefit;
- Industrial Injuries Benefit;
- Income-related Employment and Support Allowance;
- Income Support (unless you are involved in a strike);
- Pension Credit;
- Personal Independence Payment;
- Severe Disablement Allowance;
- a free TV licence for over-75s (though the BBC which is now responsible for this benefit is considering abolishing it);
- Universal Credit;
- War Widow's Pension;
- the £10 Christmas bonus paid to pensioners;
- Winter Fuel Payments;
- Working Tax Credit.

For a complete list of the tax treatment of different state benefits, see litrg. org.uk/tax-guides/tax-credits-and-benefits/state-benefits.

Non-taxable savings and investments include:

- National Savings & Investments (NS&I) Premium Bond prizes;
- interest on NS&I Savings Certificates (fixed-income and index-linked);

- interest on NS&I Children's Bonus Bonds;
- all income and dividends received from savings in Individual Savings Accounts (ISAs);
- your Personal Savings Allowance – the first amount of interest from savings if you are a basic-rate taxpayer (£1,000) or higher-rate taxpayer (£500);
- your Dividend Allowance – the first £2,000 of dividends (income from shares);
- interest and bonuses from Save As You Earn (SAYE) schemes;
- dividend income from investments in venture capital trusts (VCTs).

There is more information about the Personal Savings Allowance and Dividend Allowance in the section *Income tax on savings and investments* later in this chapter.

Some types of insurance can be used as investments. The return you get may be tax-free in your hands, although this is because the insurance company has already paid tax on this money and you cannot reclaim what the company has paid.

Other non-taxable income includes:

- Up to a quarter of lump sums drawn out of your pension savings either before or at retirement (see Chapter 3).
- Winnings on the National Lottery and other forms of betting.
- Rental income of up to £7,500 a year from letting out rooms in your home (called Rent-a-Room Relief).
- Up to £1,000 a year of income, since 2017/18, from using your home (called Property Allowance). This could cover, for example, renting out your home for short periods through an internet platform or renting out your drive as a parking space. You cannot combine this with Rent-a-Room-Relief.
- Up to £1,000 a year of income, since 2017/18, from trading if you are self-employed (called Trading Allowance). This could cover, say, selling things you make or own at craft fairs or online. You claim the allowance instead of expenses. There is more information about the Trading Allowance in Chapter 8.
- Income received from certain insurance policies (mortgage payment protection, permanent health insurance, creditor insurance for loans and utility bills, various approved long-term care policies) if the recipient is sick, disabled or unemployed at the time the benefits become payable.
- Up to £30,000 of compensation for being made redundant.

- Gallantry awards.
- Pensions paid to victims of Nazism.
- Maintenance payments following separation, divorce or dissolution of a civil partnership.
- Part of compensation money paid to people who were mis-sold payment protection insurance (PPI) (but some of the interest component is usually taxable).

There are some other forms of money you may get that do not count as income. These include, for example, loans you receive and gifts from somebody (see *Inheritance tax (IHT)* later in this chapter for how tax works if you are the giver). Similarly, if you sell something for a profit, that does not count as income, but you might have to pay CGT on the profit (see *Capital gains tax* later in this chapter).

Income tax on savings and investments

Savings

Savings income means interest from bank and building society accounts, National Savings & Investments (NS&I) products, credit union accounts, peer-to-peer lending, government bonds (gilts), corporate bonds and investment funds that invest in similar assets. In general, savings income is taxable. However, there are several reasons why in fact you might not have to pay any tax on it.

Firstly, some types of savings income is specifically tax-free (see the list above). In particular, each year you can put up to a certain amount (£20,000 in 2019/20) into ISAs. If you don't use your full annual ISA allowance, you cannot carry it forward – so use it or lose it! There are several different types of ISA: cash ISAs, which take the form of bank, building society or NS&I accounts; stocks and shares ISAs, through which you can invest in shares, gilts, corporate bonds and investment funds, and Innovative Finance ISAs, through which you can invest in peer-to-peer lending and other forms of crowdfunding. There are also some special types of ISA aimed mainly at younger people to help them save for a home or retirement, and Junior ISAs for children (with their own separate annual limit of £4,368 in 2019/20). The most popular type of ISA is the cash ISA, accounting for about seven out of every 10 ISAs taken out each year according to HMRC.

If your income including taxable savings income is no more than £17,500 in 2019/20, you might benefit from the savings-rate band. As explained above, you have a personal allowance (£12,500 in 2019/20), and the first tax band after that is the savings-rate band (£5,000 in 2019/20 with a 0 per cent tax rate but only on savings income). The personal allowance and savings rate band are set first against any income you have from sources like pensions, earnings and rental income. Whatever is left is next set against any savings income (and any left after that against dividend income). This is most easily understood by looking at a couple of case studies.

CASE STUDY

In 2019/20, Adrian's income is made up of £9,000 pension, £3,000 earnings and £6,000 of interest from savings. His personal allowance (£12,500) is set against the pension, the earnings and £500 of the interest. The savings-rate band is then set against £5,000 of the remaining interest. So at least £5,500 of the interest from his savings is tax-free. (And, in fact, the remaining £500 is also tax-free, as we will see shortly.)

CASE STUDY

In 2019/20, Gemma has income as follows: £16,000 pension and £6,000 of interest from savings. Her personal allowance (£12,500) is set against the pension. That leaves £3,500 of pension which falls into the savings-rate band, but because it is not savings income, it is taxed at the normal basic rate (20 per cent in 2019/20). But there is £1,500 of the savings-rate band left to set against part of the interest she gets, so that £1,500 of interest will be tax-free. (And, in fact, another £1,000 of the interest will also be tax-free, as we will see shortly.)

Finally, since 2016/17, basic-rate taxpayers and higher-rate taxpayers have a Personal Savings Allowance (PSA). The allowance is £1,000 for basic-rate taxpayers and £500 for higher-rate taxpayers. Additional-rate taxpayers don't get any PSA. This allowance is set against the first chunk of savings income that would otherwise be taxed at your top rate. In the case studies above, both

Adrian and Gemma are basic-rate taxpayers. The last £500 of Adrian's income is savings income that falls into the basic-rate band, but he pays no tax on it because he can set his PSA against that interest. In Gemma's case, she has £6,000 of interest. The first £1,500 is covered by her savings-rate band; another £1,000 is tax-free because it's covered by her PSA; that leaves just £3,500 of the interest in the basic-rate band to be taxed at the normal 20 per cent rate.

If a substantial part of your income comes from savings, you could have up to £18,500 of tax-free income by combining your personal allowance, the savings-rate band and your PSA.

Since 2016/17, savings income is paid to you without any tax deducted (in other words, this income is paid 'gross'). Because of the PSA and the current low level of interest rates, most savers don't have any tax to pay. If you do, you'll usually have to fill in a tax return to ensure you pay the correct amount of tax.

Before April 2016, savings income was often paid 'net', meaning with tax at the basic rate already deducted. If you were a non-taxpayer, you could either register to receive your interest gross or claim back the tax that had been deducted. You have four years to claim this tax back, so if you think you overpaid tax on your savings in the 2015/16 tax year, you have until 5 April 2020 to get the tax back. To make a claim, use form R40, which you get from HMRC either online or by phone.

Investments

'Investments' usually means assets whose value can go up and down: mainly shares and bonds quoted on the stock exchange. For tax purposes, income from bonds counts as savings income and is taxed as described above. This section describes the tax treatment of income from shares – called 'dividends' – and investment funds that invest in them.

In some circumstances, dividend income may be tax-free. This is most commonly where you have invested through an ISA. You can invest up to £20,000 in ISAs in 2019/20 as outlined in *Savings* earlier in this chapter. Since 2016/17, the following rules apply to taxable dividend income:

- no tax on dividends covered by your personal allowance;
- the first £2,000 (2019/20) of dividends that fall into the basic-rate, higher-rate or additional-rate bands are tax-free because they are covered by your Dividend Allowance;
- remaining dividends that fall into the basic-rate band are taxed at a rate of 7.5 per cent;

- remaining dividends that fall into the higher-rate band are taxed at a rate of 32.5 per cent;
- remaining dividends that fall into the additional-rate band are taxed at a rate of 38.1 per cent.

Dividends are paid without any tax deducted. If you have tax to pay, you will normally have to fill in a tax return.

Paying and reclaiming income tax

Nobody wants to pay more tax than they have to. However, underpaying tax can be equally problematic because you may face a sudden bill for back taxes later on that would be hard to manage. Therefore, it's important to understand how tax is collected and check that you're paying the right amount. Tax is collected in two main ways: through Pay As You Earn (PAYE) and Self-Assessment.

Pay As You Earn (PAYE)

Income tax on earnings and private pensions is collected through the PAYE system. This means your employer or pension provider acts as tax collector. They deduct the tax you owe from your pay or pension before you get it, and hand the tax direct to HMRC. PAYE does not simply collect the tax due on those particular earnings or that particular pension. The system is designed so that it can collect all the tax you owe on your income from all sources and also collect or refund tax relating to earlier tax years. In particular, PAYE on a private pension may be used to collect tax due on your State Pension (since State Pensions are taxable, but paid gross).

CASE STUDY

In 2019/20, Masud gets a State Pension of £9,000 and a private pension of £7,000, giving him a total income of £16,000. The first £12,500 is covered by his personal allowance and so is tax-free. Basic-rate tax at 20 per cent is due on the remaining £3,500, which comes to £700. The whole £700 tax is deducted through PAYE from his private pension. This means he receives £9,000 pension from the state and £6,300 from his pension provider.

Your employer or pension provider knows how much tax to deduct because each year HMRC provides them and you with a coding notice, detailing how much tax-free pay or pension you are entitled to, and a tax code that tells your employer or pension provider what tax rates to apply. If you have both a job and a pension or more than one job or pension, you will have a separate tax code for each. Usually your personal allowance is set against whichever source of PAYE income seems to be your main one. Your tax code is made up of a number and one or two letters. The number is your tax-free pay or pension divided by 10, and the letter says something about your tax circumstances – for example, if you just get the full personal allowance of £12,500, the number in your code will be 1250L. An M in your code means you get Marriage Allowance and an N that you've given Marriage Allowance to your partner. An S means you pay Scottish income tax, a C that you pay Welsh income tax, and so on. HMRC do sometimes make mistakes, so it's important to check your code and tell HMRC if it's wrong. The HMRC website has a tool to help you check that you have been given the correct tax code: gov.uk/check-income-tax-current-year. This tool also lets you inform HMRC if your code is wrong. You will need to register to create an account in order to use this tool. If you cannot use the online tool, contact HMRC.

Income tax is an annual tax, based on your income for the whole year. If you change job part way through the year, or you stop work and start a pension, your old employer will give you a P45 form which details the income you've had so far. You hand this to your new employer or pension provider so that they can seamlessly deduct the correct amount of tax from your new income source. Sometimes the system is not quite so seamless, in which case you may be put on a 'Month 1' (or similar weekly) basis, sometimes called an 'emergency tax code'. This means you pay tax as if what you receive this month is the same as what you get every month of the tax year, regardless of whether the amount was/will be more or less in previous or subsequent months. Once your correct code is issued, you'll get a refund or have to pay extra normally through PAYE. This emergency tax code may in particular apply if you take a lump sum out of your pension savings before retirement (an UFPLS, as described in Chapter 3), so make sure to check the tax deducted and claim a refund if necessary.

HMRC cross-checks the income on which you pay tax and, if it thinks you have under- or over-paid tax through PAYE, you may get a P800 form. This shows the income HMRC thinks you have, and you should check this carefully. If HMRC reckons you have paid too little tax and the amount is under £3,000, this can be collected through an adjustment to your PAYE code. If the tax owed is £3,000 or more, you'll normally be expected to pay it in a single lump sum. If you have paid too much tax, you will get a refund either by cheque or by claiming through your online account.

Self-Assessment

If you have non-PAYE income, such as profits from self-employment or rental income, or you have made a capital gain (see later in this chapter), you will usually have to fill in a tax return each year and pay tax through a system called Self-Assessment.

However, since 2016/17, HMRC has been rolling out a system of Simple Assessment which aims ultimately to reduce the number of people who have to complete a tax return. Under Simple Assessment, you may receive a letter from HMRC detailing the income it thinks you have and the tax you owe. If the details are wrong, you have 60 days to get in touch with HMRC to ask them to put it right. Once the Simple Assessment is finalized, the amount due has to be paid by a set date, normally 31 January after the tax year to which the assessment applies.

Tax returns

Tax returns normally have to be submitted by a set 'filing date', which is 31 October following the end of the tax year if you use a paper tax return or 31 January if you submit online (as most people do these days). There is an automatic £100 fine if you miss the January deadline. If you are not already completing a tax return each year and have some untaxed income or gains, you must let HMRC know within six months of the end of the tax year (so by 5 October 2020 for income or gains received in the 2019/20 tax year). HMRC will then arrange for you to receive a tax return (or notice to file online) and you may be given a bit longer than the normal deadline to do this.

If you fill in a tax return, you will need to supply details of all your income and any taxable capital gains, giving details of any tax already paid through PAYE or other means if that applies. So the tax return asks you about:

- your earnings plus any bonus, expenses and benefits in kind received;
- bank and building society interest;
- dividends and other income from investments;
- pension payments from state, occupational and private pensions;
- miscellaneous income, such as freelance earnings, maintenance payments and taxable social security benefits;
- payments against which tax relief can be claimed (eg charitable donations or contributions to a personal pension);
- profits from self-employment;

- rents received and other income from property;
- foreign income, for example from foreign investments or renting out a holiday home abroad;
- income from trusts and estates;
- capital gains;
- details about your domicile and residence if you are non-resident in the UK.

If you want to file your tax return online, you can use commercial software if you want to, but HMRC provides its own free online service and that's what most people use. You need to register in advance and activate your account using a code sent to you by post, so allow enough time for this.

Keeping records

HMRC advises that taxpayers are obliged to keep the records on which the information in their tax return is based for 12 months after the filing date (normally 22 months after the end of the tax year to which they relate). However, if you are self-employed or a partner in a business, you need to keep these records for five years after the filing date. You can be fined £3,000 if you cannot produce your records.

Calculating and paying the tax

For the 2019/20 tax year, Self-Assessment tax (due for example on self-employment profits or rental income) is due in instalments on 31 January 2020 and 31 July 2020, with a final balancing charge or refund on 31 January 2021; tax on a capital gain is paid in a single lump sum by the deadline of 31 January 2021. But if you owe less than £3,000 tax and have a source of PAYE income, you can ask for the tax to be deducted from that income through PAYE.

If you send in a paper tax return, HMRC will send you a calculation of the tax you owe, based on the information in your return. If you file online, the software will calculate your tax bill, but will not usually take into account any instalments you have already paid for the year.

Sorting out problems

As the 'self' in the name suggests, under Self-Assessment, it's your responsibility to declare all your taxable income correctly and pay the right amount of tax. Even if HMRC calculates your tax bill for you, it's still your responsibility to make sure the calculation is correct. You might think that Self-Assessment opens the way for people to forget some of their income, either by accident or design. However, HMRC may check what you're doing and can impose hefty fines if you are found to have negligently or deliberately under-declared your income or gains.

If you make a mistake on your tax return, you have a year to correct it without too much fuss – in the case of an online return, just go back online to make the changes and then refile your return. For the tax return covering the 2019/20 tax year, this means you can make corrections up to 31 January 2022. If you filed a paper return, you'll need to contact HMRC.

If, say, you find you have failed to claim a tax relief or allowance in the past, you can go back up to four years to put matters right. For example, providing you claim by 5 April 2020, you can go back to the 2015/16 tax year to claim an allowance or relief and get a refund of the tax you paid. You need to write to HMRC to do this.

If you pay tax late, you will be charged interest (in addition to any fines). You normally get (tax-free) interest on tax refunds, though the rate of interest is currently low. In 2019/20, interest is charged on tax paid late at 3.25 per cent a year, but paid on refunds at just 0.5 per cent a year.

An independent Adjudicator's Office can examine taxpayers' complaints about their dealings with HMRC and, if considered valid, determine what action would be fair. Complaints appropriate to the Adjudicator are mainly limited to the way HMRC has handled someone's tax affairs, for example excessive delay, errors, discourtesy or how discretion has been exercised. In deciding fair treatment, the Adjudicator has power to recommend the waiving of a payment or even the award of compensation if, as a result of error by HMRC, the complainant had incurred professional fees or other expenses. Before approaching the Adjudicator, taxpayers must have tried to resolve the matter first with HMRC.

Getting a tax refund

When you retire, you may be due for a tax rebate. If you are, this would normally be paid automatically, especially if you are getting a pension from your last employer. The matter could conceivably be overlooked, either if you are due to get a pension from an earlier employer (instead of from your last employer) or if you will be receiving only a State Pension and not a company pension in addition.

In either case, you should ask your employer for a P45 form. Then either send it – care of your earlier employer – to the pension fund trustees or, in the event of your receiving only a State Pension, to the tax office together with details of your age and the date you retired. Ask your employer for the address of the tax office to which you should write.

A note of caution: of course everyone likes a tax rebate and HMRC processes tens of thousands per year after checking Self-Assessment returns. But however welcome a cash payment may seem, don't believe any e-mail promising a refund. These are 'phishing' scams, designed to get your financial details. HMRC says it never sends notifications of a tax rebate by e-mail, or asks you to disclose personal or payment information by e-mail. For more advice see hmrc.gov.uk/security.

National Insurance contributions (NICs)

Getting older has some benefits and one is that, once you reach State Pension age, you no longer pay National Insurance contributions (NICs) even if you carry on working. There are different classes of National Insurance: Class 1 is paid by employees; self-employed people pay Classes 2 and 4. If you are the owner-director of your own company, you are technically an employee and pay Class 1 contributions.

If you work for an employer, once you reach your State Pension birthday, you need to show your employer proof of your age – usually your birth certificate or passport, if you have one. However, if you do not want your employer to see your documents, you can ask HMRC to provide you with a letter confirming that you've reached State Pension age. You might have a 'certificate of age exemption' issued some time ago. HMRC no longer issues these, but, if you have one, you can show that to your employer as proof. Class 1 contributions stop as soon as you reach State Pension age. If you've paid any NICs since then, you can get a refund provided the error is put right before the end of the tax year.

If you're self-employed, you stop paying Class 2 NICs from the week in which you reach State Pension age. Class 4 contributions continue a bit longer, and you stop paying them from 6 April following the tax year in which you reached State Pension age.

Although, under current rules, people over State Pension age do not pay NICs, there have been suggestions that this should change in order to fund the increasing costs of care for an ageing population. But, as at May 2019, there had been no official statement that this might happen.

Capital gains tax

You may have to pay CGT if you make a profit (or, to use the proper term, 'taxable gain') on the sale or other disposal (for example, gift) of a capital asset – for example, stocks and shares, jewellery, any property that is not your main home (and, in some cases, part of the profit from selling your main home), and other items of value. CGT applies only to the actual gain you make, so if you buy shares to the value of £100,000 and sell them later for £125,000, the tax office will be interested only in the £25,000 profit you have made.

Not all your gains are taxable. Some types of gain are always tax-free (see the next section). In working out your gain, you may be able to deduct various expenses, such as buying and selling costs, and the cost of changes that enhance the value of the asset (but not maintenance costs). You can deduct losses you have made in the same tax year, as well as losses carried forward from earlier years. Then, the first slice of otherwise taxable gains is tax-free, because you have an annual exempt amount of £12,000 in 2019/20, which usually rises each year in line with inflation. If you are still left with a taxable gain, CGT is charged at the following rates:

- 18 per cent and 28 per cent in the case of residential property;
- 10 per cent and 20 per cent in other cases (for example, shares and other investments).

Now comes the complicated bit! To work out which of the rates applies, you add the taxable gain to your taxable income. Any part of the gain that falls into the basic-rate income tax band is taxed at the lower rate; anything more is taxed at the higher rate.

CASE STUDY

Arif inherited a house when his father died. The value of the house at that time was £200,000. The value had risen by the time Arif sold the home. He had never lived there, and, after deducting various expenses and his annual exempt amount, he had a taxable gain of £10,000. His income that year used up all of his basic-rate income tax band except the last £1,000. This means that when the gain was added to his income, £1,000 of the gain fell into the basic-rate band and was taxed at 18 per cent. The remaining £9,000 of gain was taxed at 28 per cent. Therefore, his CGT bill was £2,700, leaving him with a net gain after tax of £7,300.

CASE STUDY

After all deductions, Angela has made a taxable gain of £5,000 on some shares she sold. Her income is high enough that she is a higher-rate taxpayer. Therefore the whole of the gain is taxed at 20 per cent. Her CGT bill is £1,000, leaving her with a net gain after tax of £4,000.

Free of CGT

The following assets are not subject to CGT and do not count towards the gains that may be taxed:

- your only or main home (but see below);
- your car;
- wasting assets, meaning those with an expected life of 50 years or less (such as a caravan or boat);
- personal belongings up to the value of £6,000 each (sets of things count as one asset);
- British money, which includes gold sovereigns from 1837 onwards;
- foreign currency for your personal use abroad;
- gains from assets held in an ISA;
- proceeds of a life assurance policy (in most circumstances);
- profits on UK government stocks (gilts);
- profits on qualifying corporate bonds;
- futures and options in gilts and qualifying corporate bonds;
- National Savings & Investments products;
- Premium Bond winnings;
- terminal bonuses from SAYE contracts;
- building society mortgage cashbacks;
- betting and lottery winnings;
- gains on the disposal of qualifying shares in a Venture Capital Trust (VCT) or within the Enterprise Investment Scheme (EIS), provided these have been held for the necessary holding period.

Some types of transaction (regardless of the assets involved) are also free of CGT. These include:

- gifts to registered charities and community amateur sports clubs;
- gifts between husbands and wives or civil partners (but be aware that any gain or loss does not disappear, but is taken over by the recipient and may be taxed when they eventually sell or give it away);
- gains made during your lifetime on whatever you leave at death.

Your home

Any gain you make when you sell your only or main home is usually exempt from CGT. This exemption is called 'private residence relief' or PRR. However, there are certain 'ifs and buts' that could be important. If you convert part of your home into an office or into self-contained accommodation on which you charge rent, the part of your home that is deemed to be a business may be separately assessed – and CGT may be payable on that part when you come to sell it.

There may also be a CGT bill on part of the gain if you do not live in your home for prolonged periods. Some periods of absence are usually still exempt – for example, if you have to live away because of work – and living somewhere else during the first year of ownership is ignored for CGT if you are doing the place up. The last 18 months of ownership (2019/20) is also always free of CGT regardless of whether you still live in the home or not. However, this final period is due to be reduced to just 9 months from 2020/21 (a longer 36-month period applies for people moving into a care home, and this will not be reduced).

If you let out part or all of your home, in general CGT applies to that part of any gain you make when you dispose of the home. However, tax may be reduced if you are eligible for 'letting relief'. To qualify, the property must have been your home at some stage. The amount of letting relief is the lowest of: the value of PRR you are getting on the rest of the home; the amount of the gain associated with the letting; or £40,000. This relief has been useful, for example, if you've needed to move elsewhere and decided to rent out your former home rather than sell it. However, the government has said that, from 2020/21, letting relief will be available only if you live in the home at the same time as your tenant(s).

CGT normally does not apply if you simply take in one lodger who is treated as family, in the sense of sharing your kitchen or bathroom.

If you leave your home to someone else who later decides to sell it, then he or she may be liable for CGT when the property is sold, but only on the gain since the date of death. (There may also be IHT implications – see the following section.)

If you own two or more homes, only one of them at a time can count as your main residence and so be exempt from CGT. Each time the number of homes you have changes, you have a two-year window in which you can nominate which home is your main home. Having made the nomination, you can switch it to a different home at any time. Husbands and wives, and civil partners, can only have one main home between them, but unmarried partners can each have a different main home.

Inheritance tax (IHT)

Income tax and CGT are annual taxes (charged on the income or gains you receive each tax year). IHT is quite different – it is based on the gifts and bequests that you've made over the last seven years. Although gifts you make in your lifetime are within the scope of IHT, there are many exemptions and other rules that mean they are usually tax-free. Therefore, most people come across IHT as the tax that may be payable on your 'estate'. Broadly speaking, this is everything you own at the time of your death, less any debts you have. For example, assets included in your estate include property, possessions, money and investments. If you own assets jointly with someone else, just your share counts as part of your estate. Note, though, that savings in a pension scheme and the pay-out from any life insurance policies usually go direct to whoever you nominated to receive these amounts, bypassing your estate, and so are normally free of IHT.

Tax at the time of death

People worry a lot about IHT but, in practice, only around one in 20 deaths trigger an IHT bill. Most estates are too small or can make use of various exemptions. For example, anything you leave to your husband, wife or civil partner is free of IHT, as are bequests you make to charity. Common taxable bequests are things you leave to your children or a brother or sister, and bequests to your partner if you are an unmarried couple.

The estate you leave is treated as the final gift you make in the seven years up to death. All taxable gifts over the seven years are added together, but the first slice of the total, called your 'nil-rate band' (NRB) is tax-free. Your NRB is set against the earliest gifts first, and lastly against your estate. These rules may seem rather odd, but essentially they are making sure you do not avoid IHT by giving away all your possessions in the last few years before death.

Anything you leave that is not either tax-free or covered by your NRB is taxed at an IHT rate of 40 per cent (2019/20). However, if you leave at least 10 per cent of your taxable estate to charity, the rate is reduced to 36 per cent.

Your nil-rate band

Since 2017/18, there have been two parts to your nil-rate band: the standard part which is £325,000, and a main-residence nil-rate band, which stands at £150,000 in 2019/20.

The standard part of the NRB has been unchanged at £325,000 since 2009/10. Before then, it used to increase each year in line with inflation. Successive chancellors have frozen it at this level, originally to help pay for state spending on long-term care. However, repeated delays to new care policies mean that link has now been lost in the mists of time. A result of freezing the NRB for so long has been that more estates have been pulled into the IHT net, mainly because of the rise in house prices over the years. To counter this, in 2017/18, the government introduced the main-residence NRB. From the start it was planned to rise year by year until it reaches its maximum level of £175,000 by 2020/21. At that point, a single homeowner could leave an estate of up to £500,000 free of IHT and couples £1 million. There are some conditions, mainly that the home has to be left to your children, their children or others in that direct line of descent. But, if you downsize (move to a cheaper home) or cease to own a property, the main-residence NRB can cover an equivalent amount of assets. Also, the main-residence nil-rate band is tapered away at a rate of £1 for each £2 by which the value of a person's estate exceeds £2 million. If you rent your home, you cannot qualify for the main-residence NRB, so the maximum you can leave tax-free is just the standard £325,000.

Each person has their own NRB and, if applicable, main-residence NRB. However, since 2007/08, married couples and civil partners can leave any used part of their NRB to their partner. This also applies to the main-residence NRB. Unmarried couples cannot do this, so any part of their NRB unused on their own death is lost.

CASE STUDY

Jim and Emma were married and jointly owned their home. When Jim died in 2019/20, he left an estate, including his share of the home, worth £600,000. He left everything to Emma, so the whole amount was exempt from IHT. That meant Jim's estate didn't use any of his £325,000 NRB or £150,000 main-residence NRB. Sadly Emma died later the same year. With what she had inherited from Jim, her estate was worth £900,000 and she left this entirely to their children. The people sorting out her estate (her 'executors') were able to claim Jim's unused NRBs of £475,000. Combined with Emma's own NRBs of the same amount, this meant there was no tax to pay on Emma's estate.

CASE STUDY

Hattie and Xiang are unmarried. When Hattie died in 2019/20, she left an estate of £600,000 including her share of their home, with everything going to Xiang. Since they were unmarried, the bequest to Xiang was not tax-free and, since she left her share of the home to him and not their children, her estate did not qualify for main-residence NRB. Her standard NRB of £325,000 was deducted from what she left, meaning there was IHT to pay on the remaining £275,000 of what she left. At a rate of 40 per cent, the tax bill came to £110,000. Therefore Xiang inherited £490,000.

Lifetime gifts

The case studies above assumed that each person had not made any taxable gifts during the seven years before they died. That's a common situation, because many lifetime gifts are free of IHT. These include, for example:

- Gifts to your husband, wife or civil partner (though limited to a lifetime amount of £325,000 if their permanent home is not in the UK).
- Gifts to charity.
- Gifts up to £250 a year to any number of people. This covers things like birthday and Christmas gifts.
- Gifts when someone marries – parents can each make tax-free gifts to the couple of £5,000, grandparents £2,500 and anyone else £1,000.

- Gifts of any amount to one or more people if the gifts form a regular pattern, are given out of your income and do not reduce your normal standard of living. This is quite a flexible exemption. It could cover, for example, paying regular sums into a pension scheme or insurance policy for the benefit of someone else. But equally it could cover regularly giving each of your grandchildren a gift on reaching age 25.

- Gifts of any amount that are for the maintenance of your children, your current partner or a former partner. This includes children still in full-time education, so could cover gifts to help your son or daughter through university.

- Up to £3,000 a year of any other gifts. If you do not use the full £3,000, you can carry forward the unused bit, but only for one year. After that it's lost.

While the gifts above are definitely exempt from IHT, most other lifetime gifts that you make are potentially exempt and so are called Potentially Exempt Transfers (PETs). This means that they are treated as if they are exempt at the time you make them and, if you survive for seven years after making a PET, it actually becomes exempt. However, if you die within the seven years, it is instead reclassified as a taxable gift. This may have two effects: firstly, there might be tax to pay on the gift itself; secondly, it may use up part of your NRB, causing more tax to be payable on your estate.

CASE STUDY

Shivani died in 2019/20, leaving an estate of £400,000. Five years earlier, she made a gift of £13,000 to her niece. £3,000 of this gift was exempt. At the time, the remaining £10,000 was a PET, but because Shivani did not survive seven years it is now a taxable gift. The first £10,000 of Shivani's standard NRB is set against this failed PET. That leaves £315,000 of NRB to set against her estate.

Making lifetime gifts can be used to reduce the value of your estate, and so to minimize the IHT payable. However, make sure not to give away more than you can afford. You need to leave yourself with enough to live on and to cope with unexpected expenses. Be aware too that your gifts must be genuine. If, say, you give away your home but continue living in it, the home will still count as part of your estate for IHT (or alternatively you might have to pay extra income tax each year). A nasty sting in the tail is that, while the gift would not be effective for IHT, it would nevertheless count as a genuine gift for CGT purposes so the recipient would lose the benefit of gifts on death being free of CGT. Be wary, too, of contrived schemes designed to save IHT – often HMRC decides later that they do not work. If you are thinking of ways to save IHT that go beyond the simple exemptions and PETs outlined above, get professional advice (see *Information and advice about tax* later in this chapter).

Just a few lifetime gifts are taxable at the time you make them. These are mainly gifts you make to a company or to a trust. A trust is a separate legal entity where one or more people (the trustees) are the legal owners of assets, but must use them for the benefit of other people (the beneficiaries). The person who gives assets to a trust is called the settlor, and you can set up trusts either during your lifetime or in your will.

Trusts must be carefully worded to achieve your aims, and the way they are taxed can be complicated – you will need to consider CGT and income tax, as well as IHT – so this is another area where you are strongly recommended to get professional advice. HMRC is fairly hostile towards trusts because they are sometimes used as part of IHT avoidance schemes, but they can be useful. For example, if you and your spouse or civil partner have been previously married, you might want to set up a trust in your will so that your current spouse could continue using your assets during their lifetime but, on their death, the assets would go to your children from your first marriage. Trusts can also be a way to provide for your adult children where you are unsure that they will all use an inheritance wisely. In that case, you could specify that the trustees have discretion over how the assets are used and paid out, according to the circumstances.

Retiring abroad

There are many examples of people who retired abroad in the expectation of being able to afford a higher standard of living and who returned home a few years later, thoroughly disillusioned. As with other important decisions, this is where it is essential to research your options thoroughly. It is crucial to investigate property prices, as well as the cost of healthcare. As anyone who has ever needed a doctor or dentist abroad knows, the term 'free health service' does not always mean what it says. While these and other risks, such as how exchange rates may affect your pension income, are perhaps obvious, a vital question that is often overlooked is the tax effects of living overseas. If you are thinking of retiring abroad, do look into the effect this will have on your finances before you go and factor in that tax agreements that exist now between the UK and other European countries might change if or when Brexit goes ahead.

Taxation abroad

Tax rates vary from one country to another: a prime example is VAT, which varies considerably in Europe. Additionally, many countries levy taxes that don't apply in the UK. Wealth tax exists in quite a few parts of the world. Estate duty on property left by one spouse to another is also fairly widespread. There are all sorts of property taxes, different from those in the UK, which – however described – are variously assessable as income or capital. Sometimes a special tax is imposed on foreign residents. Some countries charge income tax on an individual's worldwide income, without the exemptions that apply in the UK.

Apart from the essential of getting first-class legal advice when buying property overseas, if you are thinking of retiring abroad the golden rule must be to investigate the situation thoroughly before you take an irrevocable step, such as selling your home in the UK. A common mistake is for people to misunderstand their UK tax liabilities after their departure.

Your UK tax position if you retire overseas

Many intending emigrants cheerfully imagine that, once they have settled themselves in a dream villa overseas, they are safely out of the clutches of the UK tax office. This is not so. You first have to acquire non-resident status. If you have severed all your ties, including selling your home, to take up a permanent job overseas, this is normally granted fairly quickly. But for most retirees, acquiring unconditional non-resident status can take up to three years. The purpose is to check that you are not just having a prolonged holiday, but are actually living as a resident abroad. During the check period, HMRC may allow you conditional non-resident status and, if it is satisfied, full status will be granted retrospectively.

Rules

The rules for non-residency changed in 2013 and are pretty stringent. You are automatically resident if you spend 183 days or more in the UK in any one tax year, or you spend at least one continuous period of 91 days in the UK and have a UK home in which you live for at least 30 days in a tax year.

Even if these automatic tests do not apply, you may be considered UK resident if you have had sufficient ties with the UK during the past three years, such as family, a UK home or UK work, and spend a specified number of days in the UK which varies according to the number of ties you have. You can find detailed information in the HMRC guidance note RDR3 available at gov.uk/government/publications/rdr3-statutory-residence-test-srt.

Even if you are not resident in the UK, your income will still normally be liable for UK taxation.

UK income tax

If you are non-resident, all overseas income (provided it is not remitted to the UK) is exempt from UK tax liability. Income deriving from a UK source is, however, normally liable for UK tax. This includes any director's or consultant's fees you may still be receiving, as well as more obvious income such as pensions, rent from a property you still own, and interest on UK savings. However, interest paid on certain British government securities is not subject to tax and some former colonial pensions are also exempt. If you are living in a country that belongs to the European Economic Area (EEA) (the European Union plus Iceland, Liechtenstein and Norway) or spent part of the tax year working for the UK government, you will be able to claim the personal allowance to set against your UK income.

It's possible that your income may be taxed twice, both in the UK and in the country where you reside. In that case, you can usually claim some of the tax back. Alternatively, the country in which you have taken up residency may have a double taxation agreement with the United Kingdom (see the following section). If this is the case, you may be taxed on the income just in your new residence – and not in the UK, or vice versa.

Double taxation agreement

A person who is a resident of a country with which the UK has a double taxation agreement may be entitled to exemption or partial relief from UK income tax on certain kinds of income from UK sources, and may also be exempt from UK tax on the disposal of assets. The conditions of exemption or relief vary from agreement to agreement. It may be a condition of the relief that the income is subject to tax in the other country. It's important to check, before you decide on retiring abroad, if there is such an agreement and how it will affect you. You can find details of all the UK's double taxation agreements at gov.uk/government/collections/tax-treaties.

NB: if, as sometimes happens, the foreign tax authority later makes an adjustment and the income ceases to be taxed in that country, you have an obligation under the Self-Assessment rules to notify HMRC.

Double taxation agreements do not cover any gain you make on selling your UK home or other UK property.

CGT

From the 2019/20 tax year onwards, you have to tell HMRC about the disposal of UK land or property and may have to pay CGT, even if you are non-resident. You have only 30 days from the date the property sale completes to do this. On other assets, CGT is charged only if you are resident or ordinarily resident in the UK; so if you are in the position of being able to realize a gain, it is advisable to wait until you acquire non-resident status. However, to escape CGT you must wait to dispose of any assets until after the tax year of your departure and must remain non-resident (and not ordinarily resident) in the UK for five full tax years after your departure. Different rules apply to gains made from the disposal of assets in a UK company; these are subject to normal CGT.

IHT

IHT generally applies to all your UK and worldwide assets. You escape IHT on overseas assets only if you are no longer domiciled in the UK. Broadly speaking, domicile is the country you consider as your permanent home. This is distinct from nationality or residence. A person may be resident in more than one country, but at any given time he or she can be domiciled in only one. Regardless of your intentions, for IHT, you will be considered domiciled in the UK if:

- you have lived in the UK for 15 of the last 20 years; or
- you had a permanent UK home at any time during the last three years before death.

If you count as domiciled abroad, only your UK assets will be subject to IHT. Even if you have been resident overseas for many years, if you do not have an overseas domicile, your estate will have to pay IHT on your worldwide assets as if you lived in the UK and the same assets may also be subject to the equivalent taxes in the country where you lived, unless a double taxation agreement specifies otherwise.

UK pensions paid abroad

Both state and occupational pensions may be paid to you in any country. However, there are some pitfalls to be aware of. If you live in the UK, your State Pension increases each year at least in line with inflation. This is also the case if you retire to an EEA country (though this may change with Brexit), Gibraltar, Switzerland or some other countries with which the UK has a social security agreement. Outside these countries, your State Pension is frozen at the rate you received when you left the UK (though if later you come back to live permanently in the UK, it will be increased up to the current rate). In some fairly popular retirement destinations, such as Australia, Canada, New Zealand or South Africa, you will not receive any annual increases. Your frozen State Pension will, therefore, tend to buy less and less as time goes by.

You should also factor in the impact of changing exchange rates. According to government data, despite getting the annual pension increases, people who retire to European destinations have seen the value of the full State Pension in local currency vary over recent years, from a high of €164 a week in 2015 to a low of €138 in 2017. Exchange rate fluctuations will also affect the buying power of any UK company and personal pensions paid to you abroad.

Any queries about your State Pension should be addressed to the International Pension Centre. For contact details see gov.uk/international-pension-centre.

UK tax will normally be payable on your UK pensions, including your State Pension. However, as discussed above, if you retire to an EEA country, you will be able to claim the UK personal allowance which will reduce or even eliminate UK tax. You may also have to pay foreign tax on the same income, unless there is a double taxation agreement (see earlier in this chapter). Even then, be aware that tax treatment you take for granted in the UK – such as taking a quarter of your pension savings tax-free and drawing money from ISAs tax-free – may not apply under the foreign tax rules. Therefore, you may want to consider taking any tax-free cash before you make the move. Your pension providers will not necessarily be willing to pay your pension into a foreign bank account, so you may need to retain a UK bank account and either access you money using a debit card abroad or transfer it to your foreign account. An alternative strategy would be to transfer your private UK pensions to a pension provider in the country where you intend to live. Pension transfers are fertile ground for fraudsters, so take care: if you do fall into the hands of scammers, not only are you likely to irretrievably lose your pension savings, but you may well have to pay a hefty tax bill to HMRC as well for making an 'unauthorized payment' from your pension scheme. So make sure that you transfer only to a genuine qualifying recognized overseas pension scheme (QROPS), recognized by HMRC to receive transfers from UK schemes. Provided you and the new pension provider are based in the same country, the transfer should not trigger any tax charge. If not, there could be an immediate overseas tax charge (25 per cent in 2019/20).

Healthcare overseas

People retiring to another EEA country are entitled to the same state healthcare as other residents of that country if they receive any sort of pension from that country. If they do not have a local pension, they can apply for a form S1 (formerly E106, E109 and E121), which will entitle them to state healthcare in that country on the same basis as for local people. You can download this form from europa.eu – search for 'Useful forms for social security rights'. As with all the rules described in this section, they may change if and when Brexit goes ahead.

Even within the EEA, you may need to top up the state healthcare with private insurance. Retiring to a non-EU country, you will normally be expected to have private health insurance. This can become costly as you age because of the increasing risk of having to claim.

Information and advice about tax

The main source of information about UK taxes is gov.uk. It has general guides to most aspects of the taxes discussed in this chapter, and also forms and helpsheets that accompany the Self-Assessment tax return: gov.uk/self-assessment-forms-and-helpsheets. If you need to check the detailed tax rules, HMRC publishes the manuals which its own tax inspectors use; you can find these at gov.uk/government/collections/hmrc-manuals, and the letter of tax legislation is available from legislation.gov.uk. HMRC has a variety of helplines to help with all aspects of tax listed at gov.uk/contact-hmrc and a dedicated IHT and probate helpline on 0300 123 1072.

There are also some well-informed non-government guides to tax, such as the Low Incomes Tax Reform Group's site: litrg.org.uk. If you are looking for an offline source, try *The Daily Telegraph Tax Guide 2020* by David Genders, published by Kogan Page (new edition due May 2020).

Many people have straightforward tax affairs and can manage them for themselves. However, in some situations, you may want the help of a professional (contact information for the following and other professionals/organizations is available in the online directory that accompanies this book at www.koganpage.com/GRG2020):

- if you run a business, you might employ an accountant to help you draw up your accounts and complete your tax returns;

- if you have complex tax affairs, want advice on saving tax or are in a dispute with HMRC about the amount of tax you owe, you might want to consult a tax adviser, such as a member of the Chartered Institute of Taxation (CIOT);

- if you want advice about IHT, estate planning or setting up a trust, consider a member of the Society of Trust and Estate Practitioners (STEP);

- if you need tax advice but cannot afford the fees that professionals normally charge, you may be eligible for free help from Tax Aid (for tax problems you've been unable to resolve with HMRC, only if your income is below about £20,000 a year), or Tax Help for Older People (if you are aged 60 and have income of less than £20,000 a year).

There are also firms that offer to fill in your tax return for you. They do not all have formal qualifications, so you might want to consider a member of the Association of Tax Technicians (ATT).

If you intend to retire abroad, you may want to consult a financial adviser – there is information about this in Chapter 1. However, be aware that many financial advisers are not authorized to advise clients outside the UK so, once you move, you may need to seek out a suitably qualified and registered local adviser.

There are various online calculators that can help you estimate how much tax and National Insurance you may have to pay on your salary. These include:

- gov.uk/estimate-income-tax;

- listentotaxman.com;

- moneysavingexpert.com/tax-calculator.

Check which.co.uk/money/tax/tax-calculators to calculate the tax implications when drawing a lump sum from your pension savings, as well as dividends and IHT.

05
Investment

Whether you have a lot to invest or only a little, deciding on the right investment strategy for you depends on your goals and other factors.

General investment strategy

Investments differ in their aims, their tax treatment and the amount of risk involved. One or two types are best suited to the wealthy who can afford to take significant risks. But, if you are taking the idea of investing seriously, the aim for most people is to acquire a balanced portfolio, which typically means diversifying your saving and wealth across a mix of investments from the four main 'asset classes':

1 *Cash investments* are savings accounts with banks, building societies and National Savings & Investments (NS&I), and similar investments. These are generally short-term and many offer easy access to your money. They are lower risk and so the potential returns are much less than other types of investment. Your money is generally secure, but there is a real risk it will lose value due to tax and inflation.

2 *Bonds* are, effectively, an IOU from the government or big companies. When you buy one, you are lending money that earns an agreed fixed rate of interest. Government bonds (gilts) are backed by the state and are as good as guaranteed, whereas corporate bonds carry greater risk but offer the possibility of improved returns. Another way of investing in loans to companies is peer-to-peer lending.

3 *Investing in property* either directly as a buy-to-let investor or indirectly through investment funds that hold mainly commercial property and/or shares in property companies. These carry more risk than the previous two asset classes, but can be a relatively stable source of income. Property prices go down as well as up, and it can take longer to sell property, so you need to be prepared for delays in getting your money back.

4 *Equities (shares)* basically means backing the companies that drive economic growth. You can do this by buying shares in individual companies or by investing through a professionally managed investment fund. There are a variety of funds available, each with different objectives and each carrying different levels of risk and reward.

The precise mix of asset classes that is right for you depends on your life stage, circumstances and personal views about investing. In general, when you are young, experts generally recommend that you have all or the vast majority of your long-term investments in equities. In the past, the standard advice was to gradually shift towards lower risk investments, such as bonds and shares, during the last 10 years before your intended retirement. (An often-quoted rule of thumb was subtract your age from 100 and that's the proportion of your portfolio to have in equities – for example, at age 60, have 40 per cent in equities.) However, the policy of pension freedom and choice introduced from April 2015 (see Chapter 3) means that it will be appropriate for many people to have substantial sums invested in equities even after retirement.

Source of investable funds

If you are looking at your investment options, you will need first to work out where your investable funds are likely to be found. Possible sources include:

- *Your pension savings.* As explained in Chapter 3, many people these days have defined-contribution pension schemes (where you build up your own personal pot of savings) and, during your working years, you may want to get involved in how these savings are invested. Since the new pension freedoms introduced in April 2015, on reaching retirement, many people are looking at drawdown as a way to provide retirement income. This means leaving your pension savings invested and so requires you to make choices about how to invest them. You can also draw cash lump sums out of your pension scheme before, at or during retirement. That's fine if you are planning to spend the money or give it away. However, with the exception of your tax-free lump sum at retirement, it's generally a bad idea to withdraw money from a pension scheme simply to save or invest it elsewhere – see *Make the most of tax* later in this chapter.

- *Individual Savings Accounts (ISAs)* are a way of investing tax-efficiently. There are different types and, although cash ISAs are the most popular, others let you invest in a range of investments of your choice.

- *Insurance policies* designed to mature on or near your date of retirement. These are normally free of tax in your hands (though tax will have been paid by the insurer). You may also have ongoing policies that let you choose how you want to invest your money, from a range of investment funds.

- *Profits on your home*, if you sell it and move to smaller, less expensive accommodation. Provided this is your main home, there is no capital gains tax (CGT) to pay.

- *Redundancy money*, golden handshake or other farewell gift from your employer. You are allowed £30,000 redundancy money free of tax and you may receive other taxable sums too, such as pay in lieu of notice and a lump sum for holiday you are owed.

- *Sale of SAYE* and other employee shares. The tax rules vary according to the type of scheme, the date the options were acquired and how long the shares were held before disposal. You can check the rules at gov.uk/tax-employee-share-schemes.

- *Saving out of your income* may mean drip-feeding quite small amounts into your savings accounts or investments, but small sums quickly build up and there are some advantages to saving on a regular basis. If you reinvest the return from your savings, you benefit from compounding (earning a return on the reinvested sums as well as your original investment), which accelerates the growth of your savings.

Your goal

Some saving and investment goals are fairly universal. For example, everyone's first saving priority must be to build up and maintain a 'rainy day' fund (also called an emergency fund). If you are still working, ideally you should aim for at least three months' outgoings. This ensures that if your earnings stop, for example because of illness or redundancy, you can still cope financially until your situation improves or you can adapt to your new circumstances. If you're already retired, provided you have a secure income, you might be able to manage with a smaller emergency fund. Whatever your age or stage of life, this fund should be enough to cover unexpected expenses, for example, home and car repairs, replacing essential home appliances, and so on. An emergency fund should be held in accounts you can access immediately.

Another universal goal is having a secure income in retirement, but how you tackle this goal depends on your life stage. If you're of working age, your goal is to build up (accumulate) the funds you need. If you have reached retirement, your aim is to draw on (decumulate) your savings in a sustainable way that ensures you can maintain your living standards throughout retirement. While you are in the accumulation stage, you are likely to have a high proportion of your investments in equities, possibly gradually switching to the cash and bond asset classes as retirement approaches, depending on your intended choices at retirement. But, if you plan to use drawdown, you are likely to maintain a high proportion of shares in your portfolio at least through the earlier years of retirement.

Other goals vary substantially from one individual to another, for example, saving to buy a home, for a holiday, to leave an inheritance. For a goal to be workable, you need to think about:

- Scale. How much will you need? This determines how much you must save or how much you need to draw from existing savings.

- Timescale. When will you need to draw on your savings, or how long must they last?

- Degree of flexibility. Does it matter if you miss your goal? By how much?

The choice of savings and investments for achieving your goal depends crucially on the amount of risk you are willing and able to take, the degree to which the tax system may help you build up or maintain the sums you need, and how much of your return is lost in charges.

Understand risk

In an ideal world you would be able to invest your money securely and achieve amazing returns. In the real world, those opportunities do not exist. If a deal sounds too good to be true, it really is. It will be a scam or have hidden charges or both. Don't be fooled. If you want a safe home for your money, the return will be low. If you want a higher return, you will have to take on some risk. And, if you want very high returns, you'll be taking on a lot of risk.

The asset classes in broad order of increasing risk are: cash, gilts, corporate bonds and peer-to-peer lending, property, and shares. Putting all your eggs in one basket, for example by investing in the shares of a single company, will be more risky than spreading your money across a range of different companies. Similarly, you can reduce risk by investing across a spread of industries (sectors) and countries. Investment funds are a useful way of achieving a spread of risks, because you buy into a ready-made portfolio rather than having to choose each investment for yourself. You can manage risk further by spreading your money across the different asset classes. Some investment funds do that for you, or you can pick several different investment funds to achieve the asset class mix that you want.

There are three dimensions to consider when thinking about risk: comfort, need and capacity. The first is the level of risk you feel comfortable taking. In general, there is no point taking on so much risk that you have sleepless nights. However, you must balance that against the level and type of risk that you need to take in order to achieve your goal. Thirdly, you should consider your capacity for loss. This means not taking risks with money that you really cannot afford to lose. For example, if you need a given minimum level of income to get by in retirement, it makes sense to secure that using low-risk investments like annuities rather than a higher-risk strategy such as drawdown. (However, drawdown would be fine to provide any income over and above your minimum needs.)

Look out for tax and charges

Your money has to work harder for you if part of your return is lost in taxes and charges. Chapter 4 explains the tax treatment of savings and investments, but you should always choose your savings and investments primarily on the basis of your goals and circumstances, not simply to get a tax break.

Charges also eat into the returns you make. In the case of savings, there are usually no explicit charges – they are simply reflected in the interest rate on offer. Use price comparison websites to find the best returns, or check the tables published in the personal finance sections of newspapers. In general expect to get a higher return if you have to lock up your money for a while (notice accounts and term bonds). Take note if the return includes a 'teaser rate' (payable for the first few months only), and be prepared to switch to a different account once the teaser rate ends.

If you invest direct in bonds and shares, you will have dealing charges to pay. For many people, it's more convenient and economical to invest through investment funds. However, these come with a range of fees and charges. Look for the 'ongoing charges' figure which bundles together the main charges into a single figure. Charges are typically expressed as a percentage per year of the amount you have invested. There are two points to note: the level of annual charges may sound low, but because they are taken year after year they have a substantial impact on the final value of your investment. For example, charges of 1 per cent a year, would reduce the value of your investments by a sixth after 20 years, and a quarter after 30 years. Secondly, charges are deducted regardless of whether your investment has grown or not, so the fund managers get paid even if your investments earn you nothing or have fallen in value. So always check what charges you will pay and, if they are high, make sure you are satisfied that the extra charges are justified by the superior or extra service you expect to receive. If not, choose a cheaper alternative.

More information

The sections which follow give details of the different types of savings and investment available. Except for annuities and National Savings & Investments, which have sections to themselves, the different types of investment are listed by groups, as follows: bank and building society accounts, fixed-interest securities, peer-to-peer lending, equities and investment-type life insurance. Here, in addition, are some websites that are well worth checking out and have information on savings and investments:

- Chartered Institute for Securities and Investment (financial planning principles) cisi.org/cisiweb2/fpweekmicrosite/what-is-financial-planning;
- FE Trustnet (fund information): trustnet.com and morningstar.co.uk;
- Money Advice Service: moneyadviceservice.org.uk;
- Moneyfacts: moneyfacts.co.uk;
- Money Supermarket: moneysupermarket.com;
- This is Money: thisismoney.co.uk;
- Which?: which.co.uk;
- Eiris (ethical and sustainable investing): yourethicalmoney.org/.

Annuities

Annuities are financial products from insurance companies that give you an income in exchange for a lump sum. The income may be for a fixed period (a temporary annuity) or for life (lifetime annuity). The lump sum you buy it with may be your pension savings (in which case, you buy a pension annuity) or from any other source (in which case you buy a 'purchased life annuity') – the distinction matters because the two types of annuity are taxed in different ways.

Pension annuities

In the past, the most popular way to convert the money saved up in a pension pot into income was to buy a lifetime annuity. It promises to pay a guaranteed income for life, no matter how long you live, in return for you handing over your pension savings. This type of annuity is best thought of as a type of insurance, because it protects you against living longer than your savings would otherwise last. The money is paid to you by the annuity provider (insurer) and can be paid monthly, quarterly or annually, in advance or in arrears. Pension annuity income is taxed just like any other form of income (see Chapter 4).

You choose at the outset what type of annuity you want to buy and from which provider. Once you've made the purchase, you cannot change your mind and you are locked into whatever deal you have struck. There are several factors that determine the amount of income you'll get from a lifetime annuity:

1 **Interest rates.** To guarantee it can pay the income, the insurance company offering the annuity will invest the money you've paid in low-risk income-producing investments, such as government stocks (gilts) and high-quality corporate bonds. The return on these is linked to the general level of interest rates in the economy. When interest rates are low (as they have been for the last 10 years), annuity incomes will also be low.

2 **Life expectancy.** When you buy an annuity, you are basically put in a pool with lots of other people of the same age as you. The average life expectancy of people in the pool determines the level of annuity income you are all offered. If life expectancy generally is rising, the amount of annual income you're offered will fall because it is expected to be paid out for longer. Recently, it looks as though life expectancy has stopped rising, which may help to stabilize the income offered.

3 **Your personal life expectancy.** The older you are when you buy an annuity, the higher the income you will be offered, because your remaining life is expected to be shorter than when you were younger. You can also get a higher-than-average annuity income if your health is poor, you

smoke, or you are affected by other factors that tend to reduce your life expectancy. Women tend to live longer than men and so, in theory, should be offered a lower annuity income, but since 2012 it has been illegal for insurance companies to offer different terms to men and women.

4 **The type of annuity you choose.** A standard annuity offers a level income that is the same year after year. Disadvantages are that the income stops when you die, even if you die soon after purchase, and that inflation reduces the buying power of the income. There are all sorts of different types of annuity that aim to overcome these disadvantages and offer other options too. The more special features you add to an annuity, the lower the starting income tends to be.

Be aware that some pension schemes promise to pay annuities at a rate that was set some time ago – these are called 'guaranteed annuity rates' (GARs). Often, these rates were set many years ago when the general level of interest rates was much higher, and so the GARs offer a more generous income than you can normally get today. Your pension scheme provider may offer to buy out your GAR for a cash sum (to be transferred to another pension scheme or possibly, if you are aged 55 or over, to be paid out). Think carefully before accepting such a deal as you will be giving up a valuable secure retirement income. If your GAR is worth £30,000 or more, you will be obliged to get professional financial advice before making a decision.

You don't have to use your whole pension pot to buy an annuity. For example, you might use part to buy an annuity to top up your retirement income to the minimum secure income you want and then put the rest into drawdown. You could use part of your savings to buy an annuity now and another tranche to buy another annuity later on. You don't have to buy a lifetime annuity: you could buy a temporary annuity that provides an income for a set number of years, and then shop around later on to buy a further annuity if you want to.

Purchased annuities

Purchased lifetime annuities (PLAs) are similar to the type of lifetime annuity you buy with your pension pot, except they tend to offer slightly worse value and are taxed in a different way.

You buy a PLA with any non-pension lump sum. The insurance company invests that money in order to be sure of paying you the promised income. Part of every income payment you get is treated for tax as if it were a return of a bit of your original lump sum and is tax-free; only the remaining part of each payment you receive is treated as income and is taxable in the same way as interest (see Chapter 4). The size of the tax-free part depends on how long you are expected to live (the longer your life expectancy, the lower the tax-free part). The insurance company will tell you how much taxable interest you are getting and will normally deduct the tax due from your payments before you receive them.

Types of annuities

Whether you are considering a pension annuity or a purchased life annuity, there is a whole range of annuities you can buy. A useful guide to shopping around for the right type of annuity for you and the income on offer from different providers is available at moneyadviceservice.org.uk/en/tools/annuities.

Conventional/level annuities

You will receive a fixed income for life. This is the simplest and most straightforward annuity available. Approximately 85 per cent of people who buy an annuity choose this type because they know what their income will be for the rest of their life, no matter how long they live. However, to some extent, this certainty is an illusion, because inflation will over the years reduce the amount that this level income can buy.

Enhanced/impaired-life annuities

This type of annuity means more cash for smokers or those with poor health. They offer extra cash if your life is likely to be shorter than average. Poor health can mean a richer annuity because the insurance company calculates the length of time you are likely to live. Some 40 per cent of people should consider buying an enhanced annuity as it could make a huge difference to their income. You can qualify on grounds such as blood pressure, high cholesterol or being overweight.

Annuity with guarantee

A reason why people are reluctant to buy an annuity is the fear of dying soon after and so receiving too few payments to recoup the outlay. Annuities with guarantee address this problem by paying out for a set number of years (often five or 10), even if you die. Such guarantees reduce the level of income you get, but not dramatically unless you are fairly elderly. If you die within the guarantee period, your nominee will receive the balance of the guarantee as income. Bear in mind that an annuity with guarantee is not a good way of providing for someone who is financially dependent on you (or co-dependent because you share bills), because they may survive much longer than the remaining guarantee period – consider a joint-life annuity instead.

Capital-protected annuity

This type of annuity is similar to an annuity with guarantee, except that it pays out a lump sum to your nominee if you die during the early years. A capital-protected annuity guarantees to pay out as much as you originally paid for the annuity. If you die before your payments equal the full amount, the balance is paid to your nominee. If you were under 75 at the time of death, the payment is normally tax-free. If you were older, your nominee pays income tax on the lump sum at their normal rate.

Joint-life annuities

These annuities continue to pay out after one partner dies. They are particularly suitable if you are married or in a civil partnership, and more especially if one partner has no pension. But they come at a cost: you will receive a lower income level. Joint-life annuities pay out as long as one of a couple is living, and you have a choice of percentages for the survivor's pension, such as 100 per cent, 50 per cent or two-thirds, which are commonly offered.

Escalating annuities

This is where income grows each year either by a set amount or in line with inflation. Inflation can have a detrimental effect on your income after you retire, so if you want your annuity to partially or fully increase with the cost of living, this is the type to choose.

While planning for the impact of inflation is extremely sensible, don't automatically opt for an inflation-linked annuity. The starting income will be a lot lower, so it will be many years before the total income you get from the inflation-linked annuity matches what you would have had from a conventional annuity. An alternative strategy would be to choose a conventional annuity but make sure you save part of it for use later on in maintaining your standard of living. Moreover, there are not many providers of inflation-linked annuities, so the market is relatively uncompetitive, often making inflation-linked annuities poor value for money.

Investment-linked annuities

The amount you get from this type of annuity is dependent on the performance of stock market investments. These annuities expose your pension funds to the ups and downs of the stock market. There is the possibility of rising retirement income: you are taking the risk that you may get less in the hope you will get more. This type of annuity should be considered only after taking financial advice, and by those who have other assets on which they can live should the income level drop.

Flexible annuities

These are annuities where the income you receive changes in a pre-defined way or alters if specified events occur. They are sometimes described by the shape that the income would make if plotted against time on a graph. For example, a U-shaped annuity starts with a relatively high income to support active early retirement, declines in the years when perhaps you stay home more and kicks up again in the later years when you might need care. Other variable annuities might pay an income that is normally level, but increases if you develop care needs. Although flexible annuities became a possibility in the UK from 2015 onwards, to date they have not really taken off.

Alternatives to annuities

The main alternative to buying an annuity is to put your pension pot into a drawdown fund where it remains invested and you can flexibly draw out income and lump sums as and when you want to.

Because insurance companies make sure they can keep on paying the income an annuity promises by investing in relatively low-risk investments, there is little point investing your drawdown fund in those same types of investment, or, worse still, cash – you'll simply get the similar low-risk, low-return income that an annuity would provide, but without the guarantee that your income will continue for life. For drawdown to produce a superior income, the fund needs to be invested in higher-returning, but higher-risk, investments such as equities. This gives the best chance of generating a higher income over the long term that can keep pace with inflation even after paying the charges associated with drawdown funds. However, the value of equities can go down as well as up, so you need to be prepared for an income that, while hopefully on a rising trend, may nevertheless need to go down in some years.

From time to time, so called 'third-way' products come onto the market. These work in a variety of ways but basically aim to offer the best of both worlds: a secure income (like an annuity) but higher (by linking to the stock market like drawdown). The charges for these products are often high, and you should question whether you really need them since you can usually create your own DIY third way by using part of your pension pot to buy an annuity and putting the rest into drawdown.

How to obtain an annuity or drawdown

In general, you should shop around to see which providers offer the best annuity rates. The Money Advice Service comparison tool is a good place to start: moneyadviceservice.org.uk/en/tools/annuities. However, you are strongly recommended to get advice from a financial adviser specializing in annuities and drawdown. They can help you decide on a suitable strategy for you and, if annuities are part of that strategy, which type to choose and whether you may be eligible for the higher income that comes with an enhanced or impaired-life annuity. Bear in mind that your pension pot is a juicy target for scammers, so never take advice from strangers who contact you out of the blue or anyone who offers you a deal that sounds too good to be true. Seek out an adviser for yourself and check they are legally authorized before you do business with them by checking their entry on the Financial Services Register: fca.org.uk/firms/financial-services-register. Here are some organizations that can help you find a suitable adviser:

- The Chartered Institute for Securities and Investment: financialplanning. org.uk/wayfinder;
- The Money Advice Service: moneyadviceservice.org.uk/en;
- The Personal Finance Society: thepfs.org/yourmoney/find-an-adviser;
- The Society of Later Life Advisers: societyoflaterlifeadvisers.co.uk;
- Unbiased.co.uk: unbiased.co.uk.

National Savings & Investments (NS&I)

NS&I is one of the biggest savings institutions in the country, tasked with raising money for the government. It deliberately does not try to out-compete banks and building societies and its products are ultra-safe because they are backed by the government, so you will not get the highest return on your savings. Nevertheless, for many people, NS&I is attractive because the government guarantee is unlimited (compared with the maximum £85,000 per person per institution with other savings), and it offers some unique products such as Premium Bonds and (when available) tax-free Savings Certificates. The default way to invest is online at nsandi.com, though some NS&I products can be managed by post.

Most types of investment offered by NS&I are broadly similar to those provided by banks and other financial bodies. Full details of all their products are listed on their website.

Bank and building society accounts

Banks, building societies and credit unions offer a range of accounts and savings products. As with NS&I (mentioned above), what distinguishes all these products is that the amount you originally invest is generally secure (no capital risk) and the return you get is in the form of interest, which can either be rolled up in the account or, depending on the product, paid out. Unlike NS&I products, if your bank, building society or credit union went bust, your savings would be protected only up to a maximum of £85,000 (see *Investor protection*, later in this chapter, for more about this), so you might want to spread your money across several institutions if you have a large amount of savings.

Broadly speaking, there are two types of products on offer: transaction accounts and savings accounts.

Transaction accounts

Transaction accounts are the ones you use for managing your money day to day, typically a current account, and usually pay no interest. With interest rates on savings being very low over the last decade, understandably some people now just leave savings to build up in their current account. However, it's still better to use savings accounts even with low rates of return – every little helps! Some accounts have a 'sweeping' facility that lets you automatically transfer any left-over balance in your current account into a savings account. Online banking and some smartphone apps let you set up sweeping for yourself.

There is a huge difference between being in credit and dipping into the red. Charges on current account overdrafts can be high (especially if you do not agree the overdraft with your bank in advance), confusing and hard to compare. Some accounts come with a small free overdraft facility which can be a useful buffer. If you are worried about going accidentally overdrawn, you could consider a basic bank account, which has most of the features of a current account except you cannot go overdrawn. All the big banks offer basic bank accounts, though they tend not to publicize this, so ask if you are interested in banking this way. If you have a smartphone, there are also apps either from your own bank or separate app providers that you can set up to send you alerts if the balance in your account dips below a pre-set level. There are even apps these days that let you automatically transfer a short-term loan from a separate provider into your bank account if you're about to go overdrawn, which can be cheaper than a traditional overdraft.

Savings accounts

Banks and building societies also offer a wide range of savings accounts. These differ in a variety of ways: whether you operate the account online, by phone or post, or can visit physical branches; whether your money is readily accessible or locked in for a while (in which case you should expect a higher return); whether the interest you get is variable or fixed; whether the interest is taxable or tax-free; the minimum you have to save, whether as a lump sum or regular amount; and how the return is paid to you, as income or a lump sum.

Interest rates vary considerably and change over time, so you should regularly check whether you are still getting a good deal and be prepared to switch if necessary. This is especially important with accounts that pay a 'teaser rate', meaning a higher interest rate for the first few months which makes the return look tempting but then fall back to a less competitive standard rate. Although keeping track and switching may be fairly time-consuming, at least comparing the rates offered by different savings institutions has become very much easier, as there are a host of price comparison websites that let you compare the deals on offer and the personal finance sections of newspapers publish a selection of deals from these services. It's best to use at least a couple of sites rather than rely on just one, for example:

- moneyfacts.co.uk;
- moneysavingexpert.com;

- moneysupermarket.com;
- which.co.uk.

When comparing interest rates, you'll see that comparison sites and advertisements for savings products quote a figure called the 'annual equivalent rate' (AER). This provides a true comparison when comparing one return with another because it takes into account teaser rates coming to an end, the frequency of interest payments and how often interest is compounded (added to your balance so that it too can earn interest in future).

A word of caution: although less common these days, some accounts are marketed especially as being suitable for older savers. But these do not necessarily offer the highest returns. Don't ignore the rest of the market that may well serve you better.

Here are some of the different types of savings accounts available.

Instant-access savings account

This attracts a relatively low rate of interest, but it is both easy to set up and very flexible, as you can add small or large savings when you like and can usually withdraw your money without any notice. It is an excellent temporary home for your cash if you are saving short-term for, say, a holiday. However, it is not recommended as a long-term savings plan.

High-interest savings account

Your money earns a higher rate of interest than it would in an ordinary savings account. However, to open a high-interest account you will need to deposit a minimum sum, which could be £500 to £1,000. Although you can always add to this amount, if your balance drops below the required minimum your money will immediately stop earning the higher interest rate. Terms vary between providers.

Fixed-term savings account

You deposit your money for an agreed period of time, which can vary from a few months to over a year. In return for this commitment, you will normally be paid a superior rate of interest. As with high-interest accounts, there is a minimum investment: roughly £1,500 to £10,000. If you need to withdraw your money before the end of the agreed term, there are usually hefty penalties. (Sometimes these accounts are called 'bonds', which can be a bit confusing because the name 'bond' is used for a variety of other types of saving and investment too.)

Equity-linked savings account

This offers a potentially better rate of return, as the interest is calculated in line with the growth in the stock market. Should the market fall, you may lose the interest, but your capital should normally remain protected. The minimum investment varies from about £500 to £5,000 and, depending on the institution, the money may need to remain deposited for perhaps as much as five years. Do ensure you fully understand all the terms and conditions, as rules vary.

ISA savings

The advantage of a cash ISA is that your interest will be tax-free and, as far as anyone can tell, that will continue to be the case for as long as your account continues to be an ISA. (This contrasts with relying on your Personal Savings Allowance to make your interest tax-free, since the allowance could be reduced in future years.) You can use up to the full amount of your annual ISA allowance (£20,000 in 2019/20) to invest in a cash ISA. While ISAs generally can be thought of as a tax wrapper that you fill up with investments of your choice, cash ISAs are invariably a single account that comes ready wrapped as an ISA. So, if you are interested in taking out a cash ISA, you must search for accounts with the word 'ISA' in their name.

You can take out a cash ISA with only one provider each year, but you can choose a different provider every year. Once you have an ISA, you can transfer it to another provider if you want to. A word of warning though: do not cash in the ISA with a view to reinvesting with the new provider – that way you lose the tax-free ISA status. Instead, tell the new provider you want to make a transfer, and they will deal directly with your old provider to make the transfer and retain the tax-free status.

More information

To find out about a particular transactions or savings account, click on the link provided on a comparison website, go direct to the provider's website or, if they have a high street presence, enquire at your nearest branch. There is such a wide range of providers and accounts that it is advisable to look at a number of them, as the terms and conditions may vary quite widely.

Fixed-interest securities

'Fixed-interest securities' (also called fixed-income securities) is a generic name for bonds that are traded on the stock exchange. Yes, there's that confusing term 'bond' again! In this case, 'bond' means a loan that an investor makes to a government, local authority, company or other organization. The loans are used by government to fund its spending programmes, by companies to finance investment, and so on. However, instead of the investor waiting until that organization eventually pays the loan back, you can sell the loan on the stock market, and similarly buy existing loans there too. For as long as you are the owner of the bond, you usually receive regular interest payments. Each bond has a similar structure as follows:

- **Term.** The original period for which the loan is made. It's usually a fixed number of years.

- **Redemption date.** The date at the end of a fixed term when the loan is paid back.

- **Redemption value.** The amount the investor gets back on the redemption date.

- **Nominal value** (also called par value or face value). A handy unit used to talk about bonds – just as you might talk of bottles if investing in wine or bars if investing in gold. For a UK bond, the nominal value is typically £100. With most bonds, the redemption value is set to be the same as the nominal value.

- **Coupon.** The amount of interest the bond pays each year. It is usually a fixed number of pounds and expressed as a percentage of the nominal value. For example, if the bond pays £3 a year for each nominal £100 of bonds you hold, the coupon is 3 per cent. As the coupon is a fixed rate of interest, that's why these bonds are called 'fixed-interest securities'.

The return from investing in fixed-interest securities comes in two parts: the interest you get, and any gain or loss you make on selling the bond or at redemption. The return you personally get depends on the price you paid for the bond. For example, buying a bond with a 3 per cent coupon for £80 and selling it a year later for £81 would mean getting an income (the coupon) of £3 and a gain of £1, so £4 altogether which would be a return of 5 per cent (£4 as a percentage of £80). If you sold it for only £79, you'd get £3 coupon offset by a loss of £1, giving a return of £2 or just 2.5 per cent (£2 as a percentage of £80). So although bonds are called 'fixed-interest securities', the overall return you get goes up or down depending on the stock market price of the bonds. But, in pounds, the coupon payments are almost always all for the same amount and paid at regular intervals, regardless of what happens to the stock market, so bonds can be a good choice if you are seeking a regular income (and it's why insurance companies that offer annuities invest in bonds).

There are two risks with fixed-interest securities: credit risk and interest rate risk.

Credit risk is the risk that the issuer of the bond will not make all the promised payments of interest and pay the redemption value. This depends on both the financial soundness of the issuer and, if it does become insolvent, where in the pecking order a particular bond stands as regards to investors being paid back. Credit risk is one of the main determinants of the price of a bond: the higher the risk of the issuer defaulting, the bigger the return the investor needs in order to be persuaded to take on the risk. This means a high-risk bond must either have a high coupon (in other words, the issuer has to pay a high rate of interest to borrow the money it wants) and/or investors must be able to buy it at a low price. In general, government bonds are considered very low risk (because governments can as a last resort use tax or monetary policies in order to keep up the loan repayments or buy back the bonds). Therefore, the return on gilts is lower than the return from the corporate bonds of a well-established company which itself is lower than the return from bonds of a new-venture company. Specialist credit-rating agencies assess the risk of default and give bonds a rating, the highest of which is AAA (triple-A).

Interest rate risk is simply the risk of future interest rates changing in a way that makes your bond investments less profitable. You've seen that the return on a bond depends on the stock market price at which it can be bought or sold. If interest rates in the economy as a whole rise, the stock market price of bonds will fall (so that the return – the fixed interest as a percentage of the market price – rises in line with other interest rates). That's good news if you are a new investor. But, if you already hold the bonds, the value (market price) of your asset falls. That's not a problem if you were intending to hold the bond until redemption (because the redemption value is fixed and unaffected by changes in the stock market), but does mean crystallizing a loss if you have to sell on the stock market before then. Conversely, if interest rates in the economy as a whole fall, the stock market price of bonds will tend to rise, making them more expensive for new investors but generating a capital gain (or at least a smaller capital loss) for existing bond holders.

Interest from bonds is taxable as savings income, but any gains from gilts and most corporate bonds are free of CGT (see Chapter 4). However, even the interest is tax-free if you invest through a pension scheme or a stocks and shares ISA. Whatever you invest uses part (or even all) of your annual ISA allowance (£20,000 in 2019/20).

While all bonds work in a similar way, the next sections take a closer look at two types of bond that are sometimes bought direct by private investors. For a wider range of bond investments, you are more likely to use an investment fund – see *Investment funds* later in this chapter.

Gilt-edged securities

Gilts, or gilt-edged securities, are bonds issued by the UK government that usually offer the investor a fixed interest rate for a predetermined, set time, rather than one that goes up or down with inflation. While their value, like shares, is prone to fluctuation, gilts are well known for their security and are viewed as one of the safest of investments, hence their original name, 'gilt-edged securities'. While stock has a redemption date, typically between five and 25 years, it can be sold at any time for the present market price. By the time the redemption date is reached, the government will pay the investor the fixed face value of the stock, which could be more or less than the original price paid, providing a capital gain or loss.

Gilts are suitable for a variety of investment aims. Firstly, gilts can be actively bought and sold hopefully to generate capital gains as well as income. Gilt value (stock market price) is influenced by many factors, including inflation, other competing forms of investment and the time left till maturity. Buying gilts is best done when interest rates are high and look likely to fall (in other words market price is low and likely to rise). Gilts with a lower coupon and/or a longer remaining term tend to have more volatile prices. It is even possible to buy 'gilt strips' where you buy the right not to the whole stream of payments from a bond, but just the right to a separate coupon payment or just the redemption value, and the market price of these is particularly sensitive to changes in general interest rates. Alternatively, if the intention is to hold a gilt until redemption, the return (coupon payments plus redemption value) is known, fixed and guaranteed from the time of purchase. This strategy can therefore be used to provide a secure income. In a refinement to this strategy, the investor could even buy a series of gilt strips in order to build a stream of income payments exactly tailored to their needs. Due to their low credit risk, investors tend also to invest in gilts as a safe haven, and in recent years this has (along with low interest rates) pushed up their prices. The result has been that the available return on gilts has fallen.

Index-linked gilts

Index-linked gilts work in very much the same way as conventional gilts. However, both the coupon and redemption value increase over time in line with inflation. The measure of inflation used is the Retail Prices Index (RPI). The RPI has largely been discredited as a flawed measure of price increases, and has been replaced as the UK's official measure of inflation by the Consumer Price Index (CPI). However RPI is still used for index-linked gilts and, since RPI tends to overstate inflation by around 1 per cent a year, this is to the advantage of investors.

Index-linked gilts are one of the few opportunities available to investors to secure a guaranteed inflation-proofed return on their investments. (The usual strategy for hedging against inflation is to invest in equities but, although their value tends to keep pace with inflation over the long term, this is not guaranteed.)

Permanent interest-bearing shares (PIBS)

These are a form of fixed-interest investment previously offered by some building societies as a means of raising share capital and still available to purchase on the stock market. They have several features in common with gilts, as follows. They pay a fixed rate of interest (coupon) that is set at the date of issue; and the actual return on offer is determined by the movement of their stock market price. The interest is usually paid twice yearly and – again, similarly to gilts – there is no CGT on profits. Unlike most gilts, as the name suggests, PIBS are 'permanent', in other words, they have no redemption date. This means that the only way to get your money back is to sell them on the stock market or to accept whatever offer is made if the issuer decides to buy back the PIBS. Moreover, the market in PIBS is not particularly active, so you might struggle to sell at a good price.

Despite the fact that PIBS are issued by building societies, they are very different from normal building society investments and have generally been rated as being in the medium-to-high risk category. Anyone thinking of investing their money should seek professional advice.

More information

For comprehensive information about gilts, visit the government's Debt Management Office (DMO) website at dmo.gov.uk. To get started, search on 'Publications' for its useful guide for private investors. The Building

Societies Association has a handy guide to PIBS: bsa.org.uk/information/consumer-factsheets/general/what-are-pibs. A useful source of information about all fixed-interest prices and returns is fixedincomeinvestor.co.uk.

Corporate bonds are often bought and sold in quantities that exceed private investors' means, but 'retail bonds' are corporate bonds tailored specifically for the private investor market. Information on what's available and current prices can be found at londonstockexchange.com/exchange/prices-and-markets/retail-bonds/retail-bonds-search.html.

You can buy and sell bonds either when first issued or on the stock market. You can do this through a stockbroker, and the London Stock Exchange has a searchable register you can use to find a broker: londonstockexchange.com/exchange/prices-and-markets/stocks/tools-and-services/find-a-broker/locate-a-broker-search.html. If you want to invest through an ISA, choose a broker that offers this option. You will only be able to hold bonds directly through a pension scheme, if you have a Self-Invested Pension Plan (SIPP), and many brokers offer this arrangement. Alternatively, for gilts, the DMO provides a dealing service for private investors: dmo.gov.uk/responsibilities/gilt-market/buying-selling/purchase-sale-service. A stockbroker can offer advice if you want it, while the DMO provides just an 'execution-only' service (carrying out your dealing instructions but no advice). With both, you pay dealing charges, and the DMO service may be cheaper.

Peer-to-peer lending

Traditionally, savers have deposited their money with banks, which then lend the money to individuals and firms who want to borrow. By charging borrowers more than the interest paid to savers, banks turn a profit on this role as the intermediary bringing savers and borrowers together. The internet has disrupted this traditional relationship. Now savers can lend direct to borrowers without the bank as a middleman by going through platforms (websites with the appropriate information and tools). This is called peer-to-peer lending.

Peer-to-peer platforms do not have the branch networks and infrastructure of banks and building societies, so can operate at low cost and typically charge fees to borrowers. While the details of each platform vary, as an investor, you normally spread your money across loans to a wide range of borrowers for a set term and, in return, receive interest. You can often choose the level of risk you want to take and receive a higher return for making riskier loans.

Marketing for peer-to-peer lending often targets savers who would traditionally have used bank and building society accounts, questioning why you would leave your money languishing at low interest rates when you can get much higher returns from peer-to-peer lending. But make no mistake: peer-to-peer lending is not the same as putting your money in a savings account. You are lending to individuals and businesses that may default on their loans, so this is more like investing in corporate bonds. However, unlike corporate bonds, there is no stock market for peer-to-peer lending, and you might struggle to find an investor willing to take over your loans if you want your money back early and/or have to pay a fee to the platform. Be aware too that peer-to-peer loans do not count as deposits for regulatory purposes and so the deposit-protection scheme that protects up to £85,000 of bank and building society savings does not apply to peer-to-peer lending. Some peer-to-peer platforms have set up their own compensation schemes, but these have yet to be fully tested.

The interest you earn from peer-to-peer loans is taxable and taxed in the same way as savings income (see Chapter 4). If you make a loss because a borrower defaults, you can deduct the loss from other peer-to-peer loan interest you get before working out the tax due. (You cannot set losses off against any other type of income.) However, where the platform offers this route, you can invest in peer-to-peer lending through an Innovative Finance ISA in which case your interest will be tax-free. Whatever you invest this way uses part of your annual ISA allowance (£20,000 in 2019/20).

More information

The Peer2Peer Finance Association is a trade body for peer-to-peer platforms and aims to promote high standards. Its website p2pfa.org.uk/ contains information and data about this form of investment, as well as a list of its members.

To invest, go to the platform you are interested in. The largest UK platforms are:

- **Funding Circle,** which lets you invest in businesses: fundingcircle.com;
- **Ratesetter,** which offers investment in loans to individuals, property developers and car dealers: ratesetter.com;
- **Zopa,** which offers investment in loans to individuals: zopa.com.

For details about the taxation of peer-to-peer loans, visit gov.uk/guidance/peer-to-peer-lending.

Equities

Companies need money when they first start up, and often later on to fund new investment. You have already seen that one way they do this is to issue corporate bonds. Another way is to issue equities (shares). Unlike corporate bonds, shares do not (usually) offer you a fixed return. Instead, shareholders can expect to receive a share of the profits the company makes, through the payment of dividends. However, companies do not always make profits and, even when they do, they usually keep back some or all of them to reinvest in the business. So it may be many years before a new company starts to pay dividends and, once it does, the dividends are not guaranteed and could be reduced or stop altogether. However, shareholders may still make a return from their shares if they can sell them at a higher price than they originally paid for them.

In a private company, the shares are all normally owned by the people who set up and are running the business. But, at some stage, the owners may want to cash in their shares and they can do this by 'going public' – in other words, offering the shares to the general public, and later on they might issue further new shares in order to raise extra money. Existing shares in public companies can be bought and sold by investors through a stock market. The main stock markets in the UK are the London Stock Exchange where well-established companies trade and the Alternative Investment Market (AIM) for newer and smaller companies. So when you buy shares, you in effect become an owner of a small part of the business, and shareholders can usually have a say in how the company is run by voting at its annual general meetings.

The money you invest is unsecured. This means that, quite apart from any dividends, your capital could be reduced in value – or if the company goes bankrupt you could lose the lot. Against this, if the company performs well you could substantially increase your wealth. The value of a company's shares is decided by the stock market. Thousands of large and small investors are taking a view on each company's prospects, and this creates the market price. The price of a share can fluctuate daily, and this will affect both how much you have to pay if you want to buy and how much you will make (or lose) if you want to sell. However, shares tend to give higher returns over the long run (10 years or more) than either cash or bonds. It's easy to see why: when experts talk about economic growth, they are really talking about the collective output of all the firms in the country. So investing in shares means you are investing in the growth of the economy. Providing you will not need your money back soon or at short notice and so can sit out any short-term dips in the stock market, shares are likely to be the backbone of your investment portfolio.

Chapter 4 explains how dividend income from shares is taxed and how you may need to pay CGT if you make substantial gains from shares. However, most private investors do not pay tax because dividends fall within their Dividend Allowance (£2,000 in 2019/20) and their gains are less than their annual CGT exemption (£12,000 in 2019/20). Moreover, income and gains from equities will be tax-free if you hold them through a pension scheme or stocks and shares ISA.

Holding shares in just one company would be risky, and it is more usual to have a spread of shares in different companies, across different industries and across different countries too. If you have the time and inclination, researching and choosing your own share portfolio can be a lot of fun. However, for most people, the best way to invest in shares is through an investment fund – see the next section.

More information

Information about share prices is published daily in some newspapers, including The Financial Times, and is available online, for example, on stockbrokers' websites and the London Stock Exchange site at londonstockexchange.com/prices-and-markets/markets/prices.htm. Another useful source is Yahoo Finance: uk.finance.yahoo.com.

You can buy and sell shares either when first issued or on the stock market. You can do this through a stockbroker, and the London Stock Exchange has a searchable register you can use to find a broker: londonstockexchange.com/exchange/prices-and-markets/stocks/tools-and-services/find-a-broker/locate-a-broker-search.html. Brokers offer three levels of service:

- execution-only, where they just carry out your buying and selling instructions;
- advisory, where they provide reports and recommendations as well as carrying out your dealing instructions;
- discretionary management, where the broker makes the buying and selling decisions and runs a portfolio for you that is suitable given your goals and circumstances.

The more input you have from the broker, the more expensive the service. Thus, execution-only is the cheapest option. These days, dealing is normally done through an online platform, though there are still some high-street brokers and banks that offer stockbroking through their branches or by phone. You may be charged commission on each trade, and you can expect to pay about £10 to £12 per trade if that's the only charge. But usually there is a regular platform fee, say £25 a quarter. Sometimes this regular fee is called an 'inactivity fee' and is reduced if you make some trades, or alternatively you pay the full platform fee and your first few trades are free or lower cost. Stamp duty is charged on purchases (but not sales) of existing shares (but not new shares), normally at a rate of 0.5 per cent of the size of the transaction. If the value of your purchase or sale is more than £10,000, you will have to pay a 'PTM levy'. This funds the work of the Panel on Takeover and Mergers (PTM) which supervises and regulates deals between companies that affect shareholders.

If you want to invest through an ISA, make sure the broker you choose offers this option. You will only be able to hold shares directly through a pension scheme if you have a SIPP, and many brokers offer this arrangement. Charges for SIPPs vary, so do shop around and make sure not to pay over the odds for SIPP services that you don't need – for example, if all you really want to do is invest in investment funds, you do not need to pay for a SIPP that allows you to invest in shares, bonds and commercial property as well.

To learn more about investing in shares and other stock market investments, a good read is *How the Stock Market Works* by Michael Becket of the Daily Telegraph, published by Kogan Page.

Investment funds

Investment funds are ready-made portfolios of shares, bonds and/or other investments. There are literally thousands of funds to choose from with a huge diversity of investment aims and risk-return profiles. While this can be confusing, once you find your way around, mixing and matching different funds offers an abundance of ways to tailor your asset allocation to your particular needs and circumstances. There are many different categories of investment fund but, broadly, you can invest in:

- **The money market.** This corresponds to the cash asset class, but you are investing at wholesale money market rates that tend to be higher than the returns you can get from bank and building society accounts.

- **Government and corporate bonds.** Some funds specialize in gilts, others UK corporate bonds, and yet others the bonds of overseas government and companies. These funds are often useful for investors seeking income.

- **Equities.** This includes funds investing in UK equities, global equities or the shares of companies in particular countries or regions, such as Europe, Asia or the US. Regardless of region, some funds focus on well-established companies, others on smaller ones. Some funds specifically aim to produce a steady income, while others focus mainly on capital growth.

- **Property.** These funds either invest directly in property – usually commercial premises, such as office blocks, shopping centres, care homes and student accommodation – or they invest in the shares of developers and other property firms. Because property generates rental incomes, these funds can be particularly useful for income investors.

- **Mixed investment.** The best portfolio for you will often require a mix of asset classes. Some funds offer this mix ready-made, with a choice of the proportion of the fund invested in equities up to, say, 35, 60 or 85 per cent. Some funds achieve the mix by directly holding assets from the different classes. However, others are 'funds of funds', in other words a single fund that invests in a selection of other funds. A point to watch out for with funds of funds is that you have two layers of charges, which can make them expensive.

- **Absolute return funds.** These aim to achieve a positive return after charges in all market conditions. However, there is no guarantee, and these funds do not have a particularly good track record.

- **Specialist.** There are also a whole host of funds investing in assets, such as gold, the oil sector, fintech, healthcare, and so on.

Investment funds can be structured in a variety of different ways: unit trusts and open-ended investment companies, investment trusts, exchange traded funds, life insurance funds and pension funds. What they have in common is that your money is pooled with that of lots of other investors, and professional managers select the investments in the fund.

The main advantages of investing through an investment fund are:

- **Affordability and risk management:** unless you have a lot to invest, it would be hard for you to spread your money across as many different shares, bonds or other investments as a fund can. With an investment fund, investing as little as £500 as a lump sum or £50 a month can give you a more diversified portfolio that better targets the right level of risk for you.

- **Convenience:** if you invest through a fund, you are not involved in the administration of making trades, gathering dividends and looking after each investment in your portfolio. This is an especially welcome advantage if you want to invest in assets in another country where the systems involved may be very different from those in the UK. In addition, someone else makes decisions about which investments to buy and sell and when, saving you the time and effort of acquiring skills and researching this for yourself.

The downside of using an investment fund is that there are a variety of middlemen involved who all have to be paid, including for example the fund managers, the custodians responsible for the safe-keeping of assets and the dealers who carry out the fund's buying and selling instructions. The higher the charges, the less of the return on the underlying assets is left for you. The precise range and nature of charges vary depending on how the fund is structured, but a key figure to look for is 'ongoing charges' which bundles together the main charges into a single figure that you can use to compare the costs of one fund with another. Significantly, though, the ongoing charges figure does not include the dealing costs incurred when the fund buys and sells assets.

A large part of the ongoing charges figure is the annual management charge (AMC) which pays the professionals who run the fund. The AMC will be higher for a fund that uses 'active management', meaning that the fund managers are trying to 'beat the market' by picking stocks and the timing of deals that they think will do well. This contrasts with passive investment, which simply aims to replicate the market return. (Passive funds tend to have 'tracker' or 'index' in their name, or refer directly to the index they track, such as the FTSE 100.) Research by the UK's financial regulator, the Financial Conduct Authority (FCA), in 2016 found that the average AMC for active funds is 0.9 per cent a year, compared with just 0.15 per cent a year for passive funds. Paying higher charges could be worthwhile if active funds consistently deliver superior returns. But there have been numerous studies over the decades that suggest this is not the case, and the FCA's research reinforced these findings. Taking into account the fact that active funds not only have higher ongoing costs but also trade more frequently and so have higher dealing costs, the FCA estimated that over a 20-year investment term a passive investor would be £14,439 better off than a typical active-fund investor.

More information

Before you invest, you should be given or directed to a Key Investor Information Document (KIID) or Key Facts Document, which sets out the aims, charges and risks of the investment fund, and broadly where your money will be invested. The KIID is set out in a standardized way that will help you compare one fund with another. Funds also usually publish their own factsheet with further information. You can obtain these documents either direct from the fund manager or from the broker or other intermediary through which you invest.

You can find a lot of information and data about investment funds on the websites of the two main trade bodies for the sector:

- the **Investment Association**: the trade body representing unit trusts, open-ended-investment-companies (OEICs), insurance funds and, since 2019, eligible exchange traded funds (ETFs). These are all types of investment fund (called 'open-ended') where the price you pay closely reflects the value of the underlying assets in the fund: theia.org;

- the **Association of Investment Companies**: the trade body representing investment trusts, venture capital trusts and similar funds. These are all types of investment fund (called 'closed-ended') that you buy and sell on a stock market and the price you pay may be at a discount or premium to the value of the assets in the fund: theaic.co.uk.

Other useful websites for general information, news and data about investment funds include:

- yourethicalmoney.org/;
- trustnet.com;
- morningstar.co.uk;
- moneyweek.com;
- thisismoney.co.uk/money/investing/index.html.

There are a variety of ways to invest. Some are available only if you are using a financial adviser. With others, you can contact the fund managers direct. If you have a pension plan or investment-type life insurance, the provider gives you access to the available funds. However, a common way to buy investment funds these days is through online investment platforms, often called 'fund supermarkets'. These typically offer unit trusts and OEICs, and some now offer investment trusts too. In general, though, you need to use a stockbroker if buying investment trusts and ETFs. That said, there is a blurring between brokers and fund supermarkets, with many brokers offering online investment platforms, complete with the option to set up an ISA or SIPP if you want to. Traditionally, you would access an investment platform through a computer, but increasingly you can use smartphone apps. Some apps offer a limited range of portfolios to suit different risk appetites, removing the need to select your own funds. Some well-known investment platforms and apps are:

- A J Bell: youinvest.co.uk/dealing-account;
- Fidelity: fidelity.co.uk/services/investment-account;
- Hargreaves Lansdown: hl.co.uk/Investment/Platform;
- Interactive Investor: ii.co.uk;
- iWeb: www.iweb-sharedealing.co.uk/share-dealing-home.asp;
- Nutmeg: nutmeg.com;
- True Potential: tpinvestor.com;
- Wealthify: wealthify.com.

To find a stockbroker, use the London Stock Exchange searchable register: londonstockexchange.com/exchange/prices-and-markets/stocks/tools-and-services/find-a-broker/locate-a-broker-search.html.

Investment-type life insurance

Life assurance can provide you with one of two main benefits: it can provide your successors with money when you die, and/or it can be used as a savings plan to provide you with a lump sum (or income) on a fixed date or when you decide to cash in the policy. There are three basic types of life assurance: term policies, endowment policies and whole-life policies.

Term policies involve a definite commitment. You elect to make regular payments for an agreed period, for example until such time as your children have completed their education, say eight years. If you die during this period, your family will be paid the agreed sum in full. If you die after the end of the term (when you have stopped making payments), your family will normally receive nothing. So term insurance is not used for investment.

Endowment policies also promise to pay out on death within a fixed period of time, but unlike term policies, endowment policies also pay out a cash sum if you survive to the end of the term. This makes endowment policies expensive if all you need is life cover, but a possible basis for a savings plan or lump-sum investment bond. As a savings plan, you sign a contract to pay regular premiums over a number of years and in exchange receive a lump sum on a specific date. Most endowment policies are written for periods varying from 10 to 25 years. Once you have committed yourself, you have to go on paying every year. There are heavy penalties if, having paid for a number of years, you decide that you no longer wish to continue. As an investment bond, you pay in a lump sum which can either be left to grow or can be used to provide a regular income.

Whole-life policies are designed to pay out on your death. In its most straightforward form, the scheme works as follows: you pay a premium every year and, when you die, your beneficiaries receive the money. An important point to note is that the insurance holds good only if you continue the payments. If one year you did not pay and were to die, the policy could be void and your successors would receive nothing. Because, assuming you keep the policy going, it will definitely pay out one day, it builds up a cash-in value. That cash-in value makes whole-life policies suitable as a basis for investment.

Both whole-life policies and endowment policies offer three basic options: with profits, without profits or unit-linked:

- *Without profits.* This is sometimes known as 'guaranteed sum assured'. What it means is that the insurance company guarantees you a specific fixed sum (provided of course you meet the various terms and conditions). You know the amount in advance and this is the sum you – or your successors – will be paid. This type of policy is expensive because of the guarantee.

- *With profits.* You are assured a relatively low guaranteed fixed sum plus an addition, based on the profits that the insurance company has made by investing your annual or monthly payments. By definition, the profits element is not known in advance, but often the aim is that it will reach a target sum. This is the type of policy that in the past was popularly combined with an interest-only mortgage to form an 'endowment mortgage'. However, in recent times the widespread failure of the endowment policies to produce enough to pay off the mortgage in full means that endowment mortgages are less common these days.

- *Unit linked.* The premiums you pay are invested in one or more investment funds. These may be the insurance company's own funds or a selection of unit trusts and OEICs. The value of your policy depends on the performance of the investments in the funds.

Insurance policies come with a range of charges, and you should in particular be aware that there are often hefty penalties if you want your money back sooner than originally anticipated. Before you invest, you should receive a Key Information Document or Key Features Document. This will include a summary figure for the costs which you can use to compare the costs of one policy with another.

Tax

The taxation of life insurance policies is quite complex and has pros and cons depending on your personal tax situation.

Policies can be divided into 'qualifying' and 'non-qualifying'. Broadly speaking, most regular premium endowment and whole-life policies with an original term of at least 10 years are qualifying policies. When your policy matures, the proceeds are entirely tax-free in your hands. However, that's not to say that these are necessarily a tax-efficient way to save or invest, because a UK-based insurance company will, in most cases, have already paid tax on the income and gains from the investments underpinning the policy. That inevitably reduces the pay-out you get, and you cannot reclaim the tax the company has paid. The tax paid by the company will typically be more than you personally would have paid if you pay income tax at the basic rate or less and/or do not use your full CGT allowance each year. In those cases, if you are investing on a unit-linked basis, you might instead get a better return from investing in unit trusts and OEICs. If you are a higher-rate taxpayer, additional-rate taxpayer or do regularly use up your CGT allowance, the life insurance route can be tax-efficient. Also be aware that in some situations the insurance company will not have paid tax. This applies in the case of tax-exempt friendly society plans and life companies that are based offshore.

Insurance policies that don't meet the qualifying conditions are non-qualifying policies. This applies, for example, to all single-premium policies. Confusingly, the profit you make from a life insurance policy is called a 'gain' even though it is treated as income for tax purposes. If you make a gain, there is no basic-rate income tax to pay on it; this is in recognition of the fact that the insurance company has already paid tax on the income and capital gains from the underlying investments. However, if your income is high enough, you will have to pay higher-rate and additional-rate tax on the gain. But you may be able to reduce the tax payable by claiming 'top-slicing relief'. Using this relief, you divide the gain on the policy by the number of years it has run and add the resulting average gain (the slice) to the rest of your income for the year. Then work out tax on the slice, and multiply it by the number of years the policy has run. This may reduce your tax bill if the slicing prevents your gain spilling into a higher tax bracket.

Another feature of non-qualifying policies is that you can draw out a sum each year equal to 5 per cent of the amount you originally invested without triggering an immediate tax bill. For example, if you invested a lump sum of £10,000, you can draw off £500 each year without paying tax. The withdrawals are added to any gain when the policy matures and may be taxable, but only at whatever rates of tax then apply to you. So, if by then you are a basic-rate taxpayer, you could have no personal tax bill to pay at all on the gain. As with qualifying policies, people who pay income tax at the basic rate or less and do not use their full CGT allowance may get better returns from unit trusts and OEICs rather than investing in funds through life insurance.

More information

For more information about the tax treatment of life insurance, download the HMRC Helpsheet HS320 *Gains on UK life insurance policies* from gov.uk.

To invest through a life insurance policy, either contact insurance companies direct or arrange through a financial adviser.

Investor protection

There are stringent rules on businesses offering investment services, and a powerful regulatory body, the FCA. This is charged by Parliament with responsibility for ensuring that firms are 'fit and proper' to operate in the investment field and for monitoring their activities on an ongoing basis. Investment businesses (including firms giving financial advice) are not at liberty to operate without authorization or exemption from the FCA. Operating without such authorization or exemption is a criminal offence. You can check whether a firm is authorized and for which types of business by looking them up in the Financial Services Register:

fca.org.uk/firms/financial-services-register. If the firm is not authorized or you have any doubts, do not do business with it.

Authorized firms must comply with the FCA's high level principles and detailed conduct of business rules. The principles include treating customers fairly, and the conduct rules include matters such as marketing and promotions being fair and you being given timely information before and after you invest about the services the firm offers and any products that it sells you. Unsolicited visits and telephone calls to sell investments are for the most part banned. Where you do take up a product, you typically have a cooling-off period (typically seven or 14 days) within which to change your mind. The cooling-off period gives you time to explore other options before deciding whether to cancel the contract or not. Firms must also have a proper complaints procedure, with provision for customers to receive fair redress, where appropriate.

Complaints and compensation

If you have a complaint against an authorized firm, in the first instance you should take it up with the firm concerned. You may be able to resolve the matter at this level, since all authorized firms are obliged to have a proper complaints-handling procedure.

The Financial Ombudsman Service (FOS) advises that the best approach is to start by contacting the person you originally dealt with and, if you phone, to keep a written note of all telephone calls. If complaining by letter, it helps to set out the facts in logical order, to stick to what is relevant and to include important details such as your policy or account numbers. You should also keep a copy of all letters, both for your own record purposes and as useful evidence should you need to take the matter further. If you have gone through the firm's complaints procedure, or if after eight weeks you are still dissatisfied, you can approach the FOS, which will investigate the matter on your behalf and, if it finds your complaint is justified, may require the firm to pay compensation; depending on your losses, this could be up to £350,000. If you disagree with the Ombudsman's decision, this does not affect your right to go to court should you wish to do so. See financial-ombudsman.org.uk.

The Financial Services Compensation Scheme (FSCS) is the compensation fund of last resort for customers of authorized financial services firms. If a firm becomes insolvent or ceases trading, the FSCS may be able to pay compensation to its customers. See fscs.org.uk. The amount of compensation varies depending on the type of product involved: up to £85,000 per person per institution in the case of bank, building society and credit union accounts; up to £85,000 in the case of investments; and up to 100 per cent without limit in the case of life insurance products (including annuities).

However, be aware that these complaints and compensation arrangements protect you if you have been unfairly or dishonestly treated by a firm. They do not provide protection against investment risk. Unless you were misled or badly advised to take on a risky investment, the ups and downs of bonds, shares, investment funds and similar investments are just an inherent part of those assets. There is no protection against those risks if the decision to invest was yours and the outcome turns out not to be the one you were hoping for. This is a strong reason for being wary of making your own investment decisions unless you are comfortable and confident doing so. If you have any reservations, get professional advice.

Scams

In 2018, at least £197 million was lost in investment scams, with an average loss of £29,000 per person. According to the FCA, the most common scams involve shares, bonds, foreign exchange and cryptocurrencies. In the past many scams started with a cold call, but these days e-mail, websites or social media are even more common ways for scammers to try to get your money.

It's easy to be over-confident and think you can spot a scam, but fraudsters are becoming increasingly sophisticated. When approached with a deal, the most common check that over-55s say they carry out is to go to a company's website, but fraudulent websites can look very professional these days. Here is the FCA's list of warning signs that should make you alert to a scam:

1 unexpected contact: traditionally scammers cold-call, but contact can also come from online sources such as e-mail or social media, post, word of mouth or even in person at a seminar or exhibition;

2 time pressure: they might offer you a bonus or discount if you invest before a set date or say the opportunity is only available for a short period;

3 social proof: they may share fake reviews and claim other clients have invested or want in on the deal;

4 unrealistic returns: fraudsters often promise tempting returns that sound too good to be true, such as much better interest rates than elsewhere;

5 false authority: using convincing literature and websites, claiming to be regulated, speaking with authority on investment products;

6 flattery: building a friendship with you to lull you into a false sense of security.

To stay safe, as a minimum, the FCA recommends that you do not respond to any contact out of the blue, check the firm against the Financial Services Register at fca.org.uk/firms/financial-services-register; and against the FCA warning list of known scams, fca.org.uk/scamsmart/warning-list, and get professional advice before handing over any money. If you are a victim of investment fraud, report the scam to Action Fraud: 0300 123 2040, actionfraud.police.uk. Unfortunately, the chances of getting your money back may be slim, especially if the fraudsters are based overseas, but at least you will help others avoid being scammed in the same way.

There is a lot more advice and information about known scams on the FCA's ScamSmart website: fca.org.uk/scamsmart and the Action Fraud website.

06
Your home

Nearly a third of people see property as the safest way to save for retirement, according to the Equity Release Council. The home is seen as a valuable asset that provides a kind of super-emergency fund. However, this begs the question of how the home will be converted into cash if the need arises – for example to provide extra income or pay for care. Moreover, your home is not just an investment, it is a place to live. So other considerations as you age are how well your home still meets your needs. For some people, the right option may be to move to a smaller property that releases cash or is easier to manage. For others the answer may be to stay put and adapt their present home.

Before you come to any definite decision, ask yourself a few down-to-earth questions: What are your main priorities? Do you want to be close to your family? Would a smaller, more manageable home be easier for you to run? Would a reduction in running costs be helpful? What about realizing some capital to provide you with extra money for your retirement? Have you thought about living in a particular town or village that you know and like and where you have plenty of friends? Or does the security of being in accommodation that offers some of the facilities you may want as you become older sound attractive? Would, say, a resident caretaker and the option of having some of your meals catered for, appeal to you?

Whatever you decide is bound to have advantages and drawbacks; life is full of compromises. But it is important that you weigh up the pros and cons carefully, so that you don't end up making a choice that – while attractive in the short term – you regret later on.

Staying put

Since moving house is said to be one of the most stressful things in life, if you're a homeowner who needs more space, it makes sound common sense to extend rather than sell up. If this idea appeals to you, spend a bit of time working out whether there are ways of adapting your home to provide what you want.

Extending and improving your home

There are all kinds of ways to improve your property and maximize its potential: from relatively simple cosmetic updates (such as redecorating) to more complicated work including adding a new kitchen or bathroom. Before embarking on any improvements, it is sensible to work out which ones will be most suitable and add value to your property. Large-scale projects such as loft conversions and extensions inevitably involve some financial investment. But the total cost of improving your home may be lower than the cost of moving, once fees and stamp duty are taken into account. A loft conversion is popular as it can add an extra bedroom and possibly even a bathroom. Building an extra room as an extension is the next favourite, followed by adding a conservatory, a new kitchen, central heating, bathrooms and new windows. But there are some exciting options available to those ready for a challenge. Whatever you decide, stick to the rules. Any new work must comply with building regulations (gov.uk/building-regulations-approval). Most important, under the Party Wall Act (gov.uk/guidance/party-wall-etc-act-1996-guidance), where appropriate you must also notify your neighbours.

Adding an extension to the back of your property is one of the most popular ways to add space – because this is where most people have their garden. It is also the most practical option. Costs vary depending on the quality of the fixtures and fittings, as well as local labour rates. Smaller extensions to the rear or side of a property can often be built without having to make a planning application, provided that the design complies with the rules for permitted development (see gov.uk/planning-permission-england-wales – and follow the links from there if you live in Scotland or Northern Ireland). It is wise to always check with your local authority first before committing to any work.

The most ambitious scheme, of course, would be to become your own neighbour, by purchasing the next-door property and knocking through. This solution to requiring more space (whatever the reason might be – such as moving relatives close to you while retaining some independence) works for some people. Knocking through allows more space than an extension without incurring moving costs or leaving the neighbourhood. This option is neither cheap nor simple. However, it is possible to knock through almost any age or style of property so long as it is adjoining. Professional advice from an architect is essential so that the required planning permissions can be sought. Also it is sensible to take a holistic approach so that the finished conjoined house looks right. This makes selling the property much easier in the future, and it is vital to bear this point in mind however you plan to extend your property.

Alternatively, if you live in an apartment you might be able to buy the adjoining unit or the one above or below then knock through or install a staircase to achieve double living space. Any construction work being undertaken must, of course, adhere strictly to planning and building regulations, and you must ensure the project is completed properly. Although it may be tempting to cut corners, it is never advisable. Things can come back to haunt you at a later date should you want to sell. With regard to any home extension or 'knock-through' option, provided you can remain living in the property while the building work is being carried out, the disruption is less dramatic. Owners living onsite often make for a smoother and swifter conclusion to the project.

Despite being pricier than a conventional extension, if there is no scope to go outwards or upwards, extending below ground level is proving increasingly popular (creating a so-called 'iceberg home'). This is particularly so in higher-value areas such as central London. Planning permission is normally required, but is not usually an obstacle, even within a conservation area, because the new space has no visual impact on the street-scape. Some local authorities don't even require a planning application. On the other hand, there have been some high-profile neighbour disputes, so you need to proceed with care. Converting an existing cellar is less expensive and does not usually require planning permission (however, do check first with your local authority). For further information see www.basements.org.uk.

Another popular way to increase space in your home is to build above a garage. A conversion of this kind is reasonably simple and increases the size of your home easily and quickly. Remember to do your sums before you start. You will want to compare building costs with how much value the extra rooms are likely to add to your home – and remember that any scheme would be subject to appropriate planning permission being granted, because of the extra height and alteration to the roof line. Whether your garage is single size or double, attached or detached, this type of extension is one of the quickest 'wins' because you are working with what you've got and you are spared the necessity of digging new foundations (however, existing foundations will need to be checked to prove they can sustain the extra load). Also, there are few implications for disruption to the rest of the house, particularly if the garage is detached. You could of course extend into the garage itself as well as building above, if it's not being used to house the car. Rooms above a detached garage make an ideal guest suite, office, study, granny or nanny flat (or somewhere to carry on a noisy hobby). Should this idea appeal, there are some specialist companies dealing solely with garage conversions.

A few judicious home improvements carried out now could make the world of difference in terms of comfort and practicality. Many of us carry on for years with inefficient heating systems that could be improved relatively easily and cheaply. Stairs need not necessarily be a problem, even when you are very much older, thanks to the many types of stair lifts now available. Even so, a few basic facilities installed on the ground floor could save your legs in years to come. Similarly, gardens can be redesigned to suit changing requirements. Areas that now take hours to weed could be turned into extra lawn or a patio. Decking is also a popular option, but can be slippery and high maintenance.

Options if you have a leasehold property

There are two ways of owning your home: freehold or leasehold. With freehold, you own your home indefinitely and it's up to you what improvements or other changes you want to make to it and even the extent to which you keep your property in good repair. With leasehold, you own the property for a set period of time – when first created, leases are typically anything from 99 years to 999 years, though you may have bought from a previous leaseholder and so have a shorter period left. When the lease ends, the property reverts to the freeholder and, in the meantime, you pay an annual sum in ground rent to the freeholder, though traditionally just a nominal (peppercorn) amount. Another aspect of leasehold is that you and the freeholder have joint responsibility for the property. The freeholder may organize regular maintenance, but require you to pay an annual service charge to cover the costs. If major work is required, the freeholder may ask you for a lump sum towards the cost. You may also have to pay a permission fee if you want to make changes to the property, such as building an extension or adding a conservatory.

Long leases are rare in Scotland, but in England and Wales, most flats are leasehold. Historically, most houses have tended to be freehold, although there are more exceptions in recent years. Under the law, as it stands, the leasehold owner of a house usually has the right to buy the freehold or claim a lease extension. Similarly, owners of flats can individually buy a lease extension and have the right collectively to buy the freehold of their building. Even if flat-owners do not want to buy the freehold, they have the right to take over the management of their block and so better control spending on the common areas. Another option (which has not really caught on) is for the leaseholders to buy out the freeholder and create a commonhold, which means individual flats are owned on a freehold basis, but with obligations to maintain the common areas of the building.

Many people do not necessarily want to buy the freehold or extend the lease but do want protection from a landlord. Among other rights, where leaseholders believe that their service charges are unreasonable they can get free, independent advice from the government-funded Leasehold Advisory Service (lease-advice.org) and, if necessary, ask a tribunal, rather than a court, to determine what charge is reasonable. This includes work that has been proposed but not yet started. Also, where there are serious problems with the management of a building, tenants can ask the tribunal to appoint a new manager. Importantly, a tribunal is less formal than a court and avoids the risk of potentially unknown costs being awarded. Further information is available at gov.uk/housing-tribunals. For information about leasehold rights in Northern Ireland, see housingadviceni.org/leaseholders-freeholders-and-ground-rent.

Another useful source of information and help for leaseholders is the Federation of Private Residents' Associations Ltd (FPRA), which is the national not-for-profit organization for private residents and residents' associations: fpra.org.uk.

Moving to a new home

If you do decide to move, it makes sense that the sooner you start looking for your new home the better. There is no point in delaying the search until you retire unless you have to. With time to spare, you will have a far greater choice of properties and are less likely to indulge in any panic buying. Beware of taking on commitments such as a huge garden. While this might be a great source of enjoyment when you are in your 60s, it could prove a burden as you become older. If you are thinking of moving out of the neighbourhood, there are other factors to be taken into account such as access to shops and social activities, proximity to friends and relatives, availability of public transport and even health and social support services. While these may not seem particularly important now, they could become so in the future. Couples who retire to a seemingly 'idyllic' spot often return quite quickly. New friends are not always easy to make.

The question of downsizing is something that affects many over-60s. While a smaller house will almost certainly be easier and cheaper to run, make sure that it is not so small that you are going to feel cramped. Remember that, when you and your partner are both at home, you may need more room to avoid getting on top of each other. Also, if your family lives in another part of the country, you may wish to have them and your grandchildren to stay. For more information on how to downsize without pain, contact APDO UK (the Association of Professional Declutterers and Organisers): apdo.co.uk.

You should also consider the area you are moving to. Even if you think you know an area well, check it out properly before coming to a final decision. If possible, take a self-catering let for a couple of months, preferably out of season when rents are low and the weather is bad. A good idea is to limit your daily spending to your likely retirement income rather than splurge as most of us do on holiday. Do your research and visit propertydetective.com or findahood.com. To check out local crime rates, visit www.police.uk.

This is even more pertinent if you are thinking of moving abroad: for more information, see *Retiring abroad* later in this chapter. For the financial implications of living overseas, see Chapter 4.

Counting the cost

Moving house can be an expensive exercise but, if you can afford to move, some good bargains can be had. It is estimated that the cost is between 5 and 10 per cent of the value of a new home, once you have totted up extras such as stamp duty, valuation fees, legal fees, estate agent's commission and removal charges. If you are moving to release some of your housing wealth, you are probably a cash buyer and so will not need a mortgage. While this saves on some upfront and ongoing costs (such as the 'booking fee' typically charged for many mortgage deals and regular mortgage repayments), do not be tempted to skimp on other areas that a mortgage lender would have insisted on, such as a valuation and buildings insurance.

SDLT and its equivalents

Stamp Duty Land Tax (SDLT) is a tax on the purchase (but not sale) of a property in England and Northern Ireland. There are equivalent taxes in Scotland (Land and Buildings Transaction Tax, LBTT) and Wales (Land Transaction Tax, LTT). What you pay for the property is divided into slices, and a different SDLT rate applies to each slice. Assuming this is your only home, the first slice up to £125,000 is tax-free; the next £125,000 is taxed at 2 per cent; the next £675,000 at 5 per cent, the next £575,000 at 10 per cent and anything over that at 12 per cent. (There are special rates for first-time buyers buying a property up to £500,000: the first £300,000 is tax-free and the next £200,000 is taxed at 5 per cent.)

If you already own another residential property, an extra 3 per cent SDLT is added to the above rates. So the first slice of £125,000 is taxed at 3 per cent, the next £125,000 at 5 per cent, and so on. This would apply, for example, if you bought your new home before selling your old one. However, you can claim a refund of the extra 3 per cent SDLT, provided you sell the additional home within 36 months.

You don't have to do the sums yourself. There is a stamp duty calculator at www.tax.service.gov.uk/calculate-stamp-duty-land-tax/#/intro.

CASE STUDY

Marloes decided to sell her four-bedroom house and buy a bungalow closer to where her son lives. There was no immediate buyer for her house, but she went ahead and bought the bungalow on 6 June 2019 for £320,000, using money from her pension fund and other savings. This meant she had to pay an extra 3 per cent SDLT. The tax bill worked out as (3% x £125,000) + (5% x £125,000) + (8% x £70,000), or £15,600 in total. As long as she sells her old house by 5 June 2022, she will be able to claim back £9,600 of the SDLT (3% x £320,000).

Survey or valuation fee

When buying a new home, especially an older property, it is essential to have a full building (structural) survey done before committing yourself. This will cost in the region of £600 for a small home, more for a larger property, but is worth every penny. In particular, it will provide you with a comeback in law should things go wrong. A home valuation report, while cheaper (say, around £250), is more superficial and may fail to detect flaws that could give you trouble and expense in the future. To find a surveyor, visit the Royal Institution of Chartered Surveyors (RICS) website at rics.org.

If you are buying a newly-built house, there are a number of safeguards against defects. Look for a National House Building Council (NHBC) warranty or its equivalent. The NHBC operates a 10-year 'Buildmark' residential warranty and insurance scheme under which the builder is responsible for putting right defects during the first two years. It is designed to protect owners of newly-built or newly-converted residential housing if a problem does occur in a new home registered with NHBC. If the homeowner and builder do not agree on what needs to be done, NHBC can carry out a free independent resolution investigation and, if judged necessary, will instruct the builder to carry out repair works. If a problem becomes apparent after more than two years, the homeowner should contact NHBC, as the Buildmark covers a range of structural aspects as well as double glazing, plastering and staircases. See nhbc.co.uk/Homeowners/.

Legal costs

As both a seller and a buyer, you will in effect have two sets of legal fees though you will normally appoint the same solicitor or conveyancer to handle both transactions. Expect to pay £1,250 upwards (including VAT at 20 per cent). In addition to the legal expert's own fees, there will also be the cost of local searches they carry out, for example, to check whether the property you are buying will be affected by any planning applications or unusual obligations, such as contributing to the maintenance of a local church (in which case, your solicitor will probably advise you to take out chancel repair liability insurance). There is a handy calculator on the Rightmove website that can give you a ball-park figure for legal costs: rightmove.co.uk.

Most properties in England and Wales are these days recorded on the HM Land Registry, with just 14 per cent of land now unregistered. Similar registers apply in Scotland and Northern Ireland. Your solicitor or conveyancer will search the register to check that you and the other seller are the rightful owners and to check out anything unusual in the deeds of the home you are buying, such as covenants that restrict how you use the property, who is responsible for boundaries, and so on. However, you can also carry out searches of the relevant register yourself if you want to:

- England and Wales: gov.uk/government/organisations/land-registry;
- Scotland: ros.gov.uk/our-registers/land-register-of-scotland;
- Northern Ireland: nidirect.gov.uk/articles/searching-the-land-registry.

Estate agents

Using an estate agent is free if you are a buyer, but you pay if you are a seller. The agent is acting on behalf of the seller (not prospective buyers) and should be aiming to get the best price consistent with achieving a sale. However, estate agents also have the normal obligations of any business to treat its customers honestly and fairly whether you are a buyer or a seller. What's more, the 1993 Property Misdescriptions Act prohibits estate agents and property developers from making misleading or inflated claims about a property, site or related matter.

Anyone can set up as an estate agent, so you might want to choose one that is a member of the National Association of Estate Agents (NAEA) Propertymark scheme. Propertymark requires its members to observe professional standards, such as having relevant qualifications, insurance, and a complaints procedure if things go wrong. You can find a Propertymark member by looking out for the logo or visiting propertymark.co.uk/how-we-protect-you/vendors-buyers/#find-an-expert.

All estate agents by law must belong to one of the two approved complaints bodies: The Property Ombudsman Service (TPOS) or the Property Redress Scheme (PRS). You must have complained first to the estate agent involved and allowed up to eight weeks for a response. If the estate agent does not reply or you are unhappy with the response, then you can take your complaint to TPOS or PRS, according to which one the agent belongs to. You have 12 months to do this. Both schemes can order the estate agent to put matters right which could include compensation if appropriate. For more information about TPOS, go to tpos.co.uk. For information about the PRS, visit theprs.co.uk.

Beyond professional standing, what should you look for in an estate agent? As a seller, you want an agent who is well-informed about the maximum price your home can realistically fetch, so with a good knowledge of what similar homes in your area have sold for. You want to be sure that your home will be marketed well, for example locally in the estate agent's window and relevant newspapers and also nationally through web platforms, such as Rightmove, Zoopla and OnTheMarket. Cost is also a factor and there is a wide variation from around 1 to 3 per cent of the sale price plus VAT at 20 per cent. However, a few estate agents charge a flat fee of, say, £900 to £1,400 including VAT. As a buyer, finding your dream house may prove harder than you think. It can take months of exhaustive searching, yet some people catch sight of their perfect future home by casually searching on the internet or scanning the property pages of a local paper or windows of local estate agents. Websites are often a good place to start, so try rightmove.co.uk, zoopla.co.uk and onthemarket.com.

Energy Performance Certificate (EPC)

As a seller in any part of the UK, you will need to have an Energy Performance Certificate (EPC) that rates your property's energy use and suggests ways to make energy-saving improvements. As a buyer, you will want to inspect the EPC for the new home you are considering as it will give you a clue to potential running costs and any potential outlay required to make the property more energy efficient.

The EPC rating is on an A–G scale (like the EU energy label used on fridges and other white goods); the higher the rating, the more energy efficient the home is. The average UK home has a 'D' rating, and the Energy Saving Trust suggests you think carefully before choosing any home with an 'F' or 'G' rating. For its size it will be expensive to heat, and your carbon footprint will also be larger. Newer homes generally use less energy, so buyers or renters looking at a recently built home would expect to see an EPC rating of 'B' or above. EPCs are valid for 10 years. You do not need an EPC for a listed property.

EPCs are produced by accredited Domestic Energy Assessors and cost from £45 to £100, depending on the size of the property. Your estate agent can arrange an EPC for you, but you will usually pay less if you arrange it yourself. To find an assessor in Scotland, use the online directory at https://www.scottishepcregister.org.uk/. For the rest of the UK, visit epcregister.com.

Bridging loans

With a home to sell, many older buyers do not need a mortgage. However, it's not always possible to align the timing of your sale and purchase. Tempting as it may be to buy before you sell, unless you have the money available to finance the cost of two homes – including the extra stamp duty involved as explained above – you need to do your sums very carefully indeed. Bridging loans are a way of getting over the problem, but can be a very expensive option. As an alternative to bridging loans, some of the major institutional estate agents operate chain-breaking schemes and may offer to buy your property at a discount (some 10 or 12 per cent less than the market price). Some companies that could help include:

- BridgingLoans.co.uk: bridgingloans.co.uk;
- Best Bridging Loans: bestbridgingloans.co.uk;
- BridgingLoansUK.co.uk: bridgingloansuk.co.uk.

Removals

Professional help is essential for anyone contemplating a house move. Whether you are moving to the next street, or halfway across the world, using a reputable firm of removers and shippers will remove many of the headaches. A full packing service is something that should be considered, and saves much anxiety and a lot of your time. Costs vary depending on the type and size of furniture, the distance over which it is being moved and other factors, including insurance and seasonal troughs and peaks. Obviously, valuable antiques will cost more to pack and transport than standard modern furniture. It pays to shop around and get at least three quotes from different removal firms. Remember, however, that the cheapest quote is not necessarily the best. Find out exactly what you are paying for and whether the price includes packing and insurance.

The British Association of Removers (BAR) promotes excellence in the removals industry; for approved firms all of whom work to a rigorous code of practice, see bar.co.uk.

Retiring abroad

Do you dream of retiring to the sun? It could be a real option, but think carefully before making the leap. You will need to consider the cost and legal aspects of buying property in the country you are looking at. Local taxes, inheritance laws and many other aspects can be very different. A number of people contemplating an adventurous retirement raise funds on their family home in the UK and purchase a small property abroad, becoming what is known as 'residential tourists'. This means they travel to and from their other house without much luggage and spend several months at a time in their overseas home. Such a property abroad tends to fall into the category of 'lock up and leave' so that travelling to and from it is fairly easy. This bridges the gap between selling up and moving completely from the country you've lived in for years. It allows a certain amount of thinking time before you make a decision on whether or not the foreign property will at some point become your 'forever' home.

Should you be considering retiring abroad, this needs a lot of careful planning. If the country is English-speaking, no new language skills will be needed. While a pleasure for some people, the thought of having to learn a new language could for others be quite a challenge. Also, there are a number of additional costs, besides purchasing the property, which can sometimes get overlooked: legal expenses, notary fees, transaction tax (equivalent to stamp duty), registration fees and local taxes, costs of a solicitor and surveyor, to name a few. The purchase of another car, insuring the vehicle, new furniture, washing machine, dishwasher, fridge and freezer have to be taken into account, and there will be the costs of making a new will. Removal costs from the UK to the new country can be quite heavy too. You should also look at the information in Chapter 3 about UK state and private pensions paid to you if you live abroad, and Chapter 4 which considers the circumstances in which you may still be liable for UK tax.

So if you decide to retire overseas, be careful. Some ways of protecting yourself when buying property abroad include:

- Get all documents translated.
- If you are given something to sign, make sure you have a 14-day cooling-off period.
- Take the documents home to the UK and speak initially to a lawyer and financial adviser over here rather than in the country overseas (though be aware that a UK-based financial adviser may not be authorized to give you advice once you live abroad, so at some stage you may want to hire a local financial adviser).
- Make sure the lawyer you use is independent and not involved in the sale in any way.
- Do not use a lawyer recommended by the seller.
- If you are buying a repossessed property, find out what happened.
- If you are borrowing money, go to a reputable bank. The bank manager will want to be sure the deal is sound – this adds another layer of checks and protection.

There are many websites offering advice and information on retiring abroad:

- buyassociation.co.uk/category/overseas-property/;
- expatfocus.com – provides essential information and advice for a successful move abroad;
- expatria.com – a wealth of information, including reports for some of the most popular retirement destinations;
- gov.uk/moving-or-retiring-abroad;
- propertyinretirement.co.uk/RetiringAbroadCategory.html;
- retirementexpert.co.uk/RetiringOverseasCategory.html.

Homes that are different

Not everyone wants to live in a conventional home, and some people get to a stage where they welcome some extra support. However, be aware that the alternatives to a conventional freehold home often involve extra costs and/or less security, so make sure you understand what you are getting into before you make the leap.

Retirement housing and sheltered accommodation

The terms 'retirement housing' and 'sheltered accommodation' cover a wide variety of housing, and while you may not wish to move into this type of accommodation just now, if the idea interests you in the long term it is worth planning ahead, as there are often very long waiting lists. See Chapter 13 for more detail.

Caravan or park home

Many retired people consider living in a caravan or park home. These can be kept either in a relative's garden or on an established site, possibly at the seaside or in the country. If you want to live in a caravan on land you own or other private land, you should contact your local authority for information about any planning permission or site licensing requirements that may apply. If, on the other hand, you want to keep it on an established site, there is a varied choice.

As anyone who has holidayed in a caravan will know, these are not always the small affairs that you hitch to the tow bar of your car. Many caravans are spacious and, while capable of being moved, are largely static, being permanently sited on a dedicated holiday or residential park. Park homes are similar in that they are technically classified as mobile homes, but are larger, more substantial prefabricated bungalows. Whether you are looking at a caravan or a park home, if this is to be your only or main home, you need to be aware of your rights and the range of issues that you need to check out. The information given here applies to England in particular, but the rules are very similar in the rest of the UK.

When you choose to live in a park home (or caravan), you typically buy the home but rent the land (called the pitch) on which it stands from the owner of the site where the park home is situated. If you want this to be your permanent home, it is essential that you check a number of facts about the site. First, does the site owner have planning permission and a licence to use the land as a caravan or park home site? Does the licence allow residential use rather than just holiday use and, if both, is the home you are interested in located in the residential part of the site? Is the permission indefinite or time-limited? If time-limited, your right to remain on the land will also expire, so it's essential that you choose a site with indefinite permission.

Provided the site is licensed for residential use and can have mobile homes on it all year round, you are likely to have a 'protected agreement' which means that the law gives you certain rights. This includes security of tenure, the right to give your home to another family member or to leave it in your will, and the right to sell your home. The site owner has obligations to maintain the pitch and provide the infrastructure of the park (pathways, lighting, pipework and so on), but also has rights which include a commission equal to 10 per cent of the sale price if you sell your home to someone else. However, the governments of both England and Wales are looking at possibly changing or phasing out the 10 per cent commission.

You will be entering into a contract with the site owner, so you need to check the terms and conditions carefully. There may be restrictions on who can live on the site – for example, over-50s only, no children and only some types of pets. Importantly, you need to check the rent for the pitch – called the pitch fee – and how it can be reviewed, plus any other charges and the arrangements for services, such as gas, electricity, water and sewerage. Commonly, pitch fees are increased annually in line with inflation and often the site owner contracts with the providers of services and resells to you the energy, water and so on, but may not charge more than they paid (plus VAT). Some site owners levy an annual service charge, which can be variable (depending on what the owner has spent on maintaining the site). However, this smacks of double-charging since the pitch fee is meant to cover these sorts of costs, and the government has proposed that variable service charges should be banned from some future date yet to be decided.

Park homes are becoming an increasingly mainstream form of housing, and you can search for them on exactly the same sites as you would when looking to buy any other home, such as rightmove.co.uk, zoopla.co.uk and onthemarket.com. You buy either from the site owner or from an existing park homeowner. Park homes, while usually cheaper than a conventional home of similar size, are nevertheless often surprisingly expensive given that you are not acquiring the land on which they stand. Technically, you don't need a solicitor, but you will be spending a substantial sum and are strongly recommended to get legal advice and also to have a survey of the home done before you buy.

For more information about your rights when buying and living in a park home, visit the following sites:

- England: gov.uk/park-mobile-homes;
- Wales: gov.wales/park-mobile-homes;
- Scotland: gov.scot/policies/homeowners/mobile-homes;
- Northern Ireland: nidirect.gov.uk/information-and-services/buying-selling-and-renting-home/living-mobile-home-or-caravan.

For advice about buying and owning a park home, contact the Leasehold Advisory Service (LEASE): parkhomes.lease-advice.org.

Self-build

Up to one in 10 new homes (around 12,000) completed each year in the UK are self-build homes. This is much lower than some other countries – for example 80 per cent of new homes in Austria. With typical cost savings estimated at between 25 and 40 per cent, the number of people wanting to self-build has been high and growing – a YouGov survey in 2011 suggested that over half of people in the UK would consider self-build if they had the opportunity. What holds them back is thought to be a shortage of suitable land, along with barriers to gaining finance and planning permissions and just general bureaucratic 'red tape'. As a result, the government introduced a statutory 'right-to-build' in England from October 2016. (There is no equivalent legislation in the rest of the UK.) Under this new right, people can register their interest in self-building with the local authority where they want to build, and the local authority has a duty to consider granting planning permissions for suitably serviced self-build plots to meet local demand. You can find your local register on your local council's website or through the National Custom & Self Build Association (NaCSBA) website: nacsba.org.uk/campaigns/right-to-build-portal.

New building methods have been developed that defy the assumption that you need to be fit or young to undertake such a project, and many older people have successfully become self-builders or custom builders (a sort of halfway house where you work with specialist developers who tailor the build to your requirements). No prior building experience is necessary, although this of course helps. Most self-builders work in groups and/or employ subcontractors for some of the more specialized work, but individuals who wish to build on their own can make arrangements with an architect or company that sells standard plans and building kits.

Some lenders offer self-build mortgages to enable borrowers to finance the purchase of land plus construction costs. However, as with any mortgage, it is essential to make sure that you are not in danger of over-committing yourself. The Building Societies Association publishes a useful guide, *Lending information for self build in the UK*, available from bsa.org.uk.

Here are some useful websites:

- buildstore.co.uk: advice on self-build, renovation, plots of land for sale, buying building materials and seeing how others build their own home, including a UK map of land for sale, plot search and calculator for working out your self-build costs.

- cat.org.uk: the Centre for Alternative Technology provides a free information and advice service on sustainable living and environmentally responsible building.

- gov.uk/guidance/self-build-and-custom-housebuilding: guidance on legislation and the local authority registers where you can declare your interest in obtaining a serviced plot.

- homebuilding.co.uk: self-build and renovation website, featuring house plans, building costs, house design, land for sale, exhibitions and all the information you will need, including a self-build cost calculator.

- selfbuildportal.org.uk: website from NaCSBA with comprehensive information and guidance on all aspects, including an interactive guide to help you decide whether your project is feasible, links to local authority registers and a diary of shows, workshops and other events for people interested in custom or self-build.

How green is your house?

In June 2019, outgoing prime minister, Theresa May, announced an ambitious target for the UK: zero net carbon emissions by 2050. With so much publicity about global warming, recycling, going green and reducing carbon footprints, becoming eco-friendly is something everyone should consider. You could set about such home improvements straight away with the specific aim of making your home as energy saving, economical and convenient as possible. Improvements are often easier to afford when you are still earning a regular salary. So if you are still working, you may find it easier to put up with the mess when you are not living among it 24 hours a day. The sooner you start, the earlier you will reap the benefit.

Solar panels

For eight years, the government actively encouraged homes to fit solar panels through a system of feed-in tariffs that paid households for selling their excess electricity to the national grid. Although government-backed incentives have gone, the price of solar panels has dropped dramatically and it is likely that commercial energy companies will become increasingly willing to strike deals with households for their excess energy as they seek themselves to become largely green suppliers.

Even if your solar panels do not generate an income, they will save on your energy bills. The Energy Saving Trust suggests the savings could currently be between £90 and £240 a year. That would mean a payback period of between 67 and 25 years on the average cost of around £6,000 to install a system. The expected life of solar panels is about 25 years and there may be period maintenance requirements. On the face of it, that doesn't make solar panels an attractive financial proposition. However, if the UK is to meet its 2050 target, the cost of energy may well rise in future increasing the savings on bills, and there is that possibility of an income from selling your excess supply. Moreover, this is not just about people's personal finances, but the social gain of reducing emissions, so you may feel solar panels are worthwhile as a way of doing your bit to tackle climate change.

One of the drawbacks of solar energy has been that storage technology has lagged behind the ability to capture the sun's energy when the sun is shining. However, there is a growing convergence between home generation of electricity and electric cars, with the possibility that car batteries could act as a store of energy, drawing the power they need from the domestic supply and also feeding electricity back to the household when required.

The best place to find out more is the Energy Saving Trust at energysavingtrust.org.uk.

Insulation

When you retire, you may be at home more during the day so are likely to be using your heating more intensively. One of the best ways of reducing those now alarmingly increasing utility bills is to get your house properly insulated. Heat escapes from a building in four main ways according to the Energy Saving Trust: through the roof, walls, floor and loose-fitting doors and windows. Insulation not only can cut the heat loss dramatically, but will usually more than pay for itself within four or five years.

Loft insulation

As much as 25 per cent of heat in a house escapes through the loft. The answer is to put a layer of insulating material, ideally 220 to 270 millimetres thick according to the material used, between and across the roof joists. You may be able to lay this yourself. The materials are readily available from builders' merchants. If you prefer to employ a specialist contractor, you can find one through the National Insulation Association (NIA) website: nia-uk.org.

Doors and windows

A further 20 per cent of heat escapes through windows and doors, half of which could be saved with double glazing. There are two main types: sealed units and secondary sashes (which can be removed in the summer). Compared with other forms of insulation, double glazing is expensive; however, it does have the additional advantage of reducing noise levels. Since April 2002, any replacement doors and windows installed have to comply with strict thermal performance standards. The work will need to be done by an installer who is registered under the FENSA scheme; see the Glass and Glazing Federation website at ggf.org.uk.

Effective draughtproofing saves heat loss as well as keeping out cold blasts of air. It is also relatively cheap and easy to install. Compression seals are the simplest and most cost-effective way to fill the gap between the fixed and moving edges of doors and windows. They are mounted by a variety of methods and supplied in strip form. For draughtproofing older sliding-sash windows and doors, wiper seals, fixed with rustproof pins and screws, need to be used. For very loose-fitting frames, gap fillers that can be squeezed from a tube provide a more efficient seal between frame and surround, but this is normally work for a specialist. If you do fit draught seals, make sure you leave a space for a small amount of air to get through, or you may get problems with condensation. If the house is not well ventilated, you should put in a vapour check to slow down the leakage of moisture into the walls and ceiling. For advice on durable products and contractors, see the Draught Proofing Advisory Association website at dpaa-association.org.uk.

Heat loss can also be considerably reduced through hanging heavy curtains (both lined and interlined) over windows and doors. If you make sure your curtains cover the windowsill or rest on the floor you will keep warmer. It is better to have curtains too long than too short.

Wall insulation

More heat is lost through the walls than perhaps anywhere else in the house: it can be as much as 45 per cent. If your house has cavity walls – and most houses built after 1930 do – then cavity wall insulation should be considered. This involves injecting mineral wool (rock wool or glass wool), polystyrene beads or foam into the cavity through holes drilled in the outside wall. It is work for a specialist and, depending on what grants are applicable, may be free or could cost upwards of £350 depending on the size and type of home you live in. Against this, you could expect a typical saving of around £90 to £315 off your heating bill each year. In most cases the initial outlay should be recovered in less than four years. Make sure that the firm you use is registered with a reputable organization, such as the British Standards Institution, or can show a current Agrément Certificate for the system and is approved by the British Board of Agrément (BBA). If a foam fill is used, the application should comply with British Standard BS 5617 and the material with BS 5618.

Solid wall insulation can be considerably more expensive, but usually worthwhile, providing similar savings of around 25 per cent off your annual heating bill. Again, this is work for a specialist and involves applying an insulating material to the outside of the wall, plus rendering or cladding. Alternatively, an insulated thermal lining can be applied to the inside. For further information and addresses of registered contractors, see:

- British Board of Agrément: www.bbacerts.co.uk;
- British Standards Institution: bsigroup.co.uk;
- Cavity Insulation Guarantee Agency (CIGA): ciga.co.uk;
- Insulated Render & Cladding Association Ltd: inca-ltd.org.uk;
- National Insulation Association: nia-uk.org.

Floor insulation

Up to 15 per cent of heat loss can be saved through filling the cracks or gaps in the floorboards and skirting. If you can take up your floorboards, rock wool or glass wool rolls can be extremely effective when fixed underneath the joists. Filling spaces with papier mâché or plastic wool will also help, especially if a good felt or rubber underlay is then laid under the carpet. Be careful, however, that you do not block up the underfloor ventilation, which is necessary to protect floor timbers from dampness and rot. Solid concrete floors can be covered with cork tiles or carpet and felt or rubber underlay. See energysavingtrust.org.uk.

Hot water cylinder insulation

If your hot water cylinder has no insulation, it could be costing you several pounds a week in wasted heat. A British Standard insulating jacket fitted around your hot water cylinder will cut wastage by three-quarters. Most hot water tanks now come ready supplied with insulation. If not, the jacket should be at least 75 millimetres thick. See energysavingtrust.org.uk.

Benefits and grants

If you are over State Pension age, you will usually automatically qualify for the Winter Fuel Payment, which is a lump sum each winter of between £100 and £300 to help with your heating bills (though in fact you can spend the money in any way you choose). If you've deferred your State Pension (see Chapter 3), you are still eligible, but may need to make a claim by calling 0800 731 0160. For more details see gov.uk/winter-fuel-payment. Regardless of age, if you are getting means-tested benefits (because your income is low), you will automatically get an extra amount (£25 for each seven-day period), called the Cold Weather Payment, if the average temperature between November and March is below zero for seven days in a row. For more information, see gov.uk/cold-weather-payment.

The largest energy providers have an Energy Company Obligation (ECO) to provide help with energy-saving home improvements if you are claiming means-tested or disability benefits, or if you live in social housing with an EPC rating of E or above. While the range of possible improvements is wide, the focus is mainly on cavity wall and loft insulation. The improvements might be free or you might be required to contribute towards the cost. To find out if you are eligible, contact your energy supplier.

If you're getting the Guarantee Credit part of Pension Credit (see Chapter 3) and your energy provider is part of the Warm Home Discount Scheme, you may qualify automatically for a one-off discount off your electricity bill for the winter months. For winter 2019, the discount was £140. If you qualify for winter 2020, you will have received a letter between October and December 2019. If you don't qualify automatically, but your income is low, contact your supplier to see if you can be included in the scheme. If you live in a park home, there is a form you can complete in order to be sent details: parkhomeswhd.com.

The availability of other help with your energy bills and energy-saving home improvements varies across the nations and council regions of the UK. To find out what is available in your area, if you live in England or Wales, use the grant finder on the Simple Energy Advice site at www.simpleenergyadvice. org.uk/grants. If you are in Scotland, visit the Home Energy Scotland website at energysavingtrust.org.uk/scotland/home-energy-scotland. For Northern Ireland, see nidirect.gov.uk/information-and-services/energy-wise/energy-saving-grants.

Here are some other websites that give advice and information on this subject:

- energysavingtrust.org.uk;
- freeinsulation.co.uk;
- getinsulation.co.uk;
- government-grants.co.uk;
- homeheatingguide.co.uk;
- insulationgrants.info.

Heating

It may be possible to save money by using different fuels or by heating parts of your house by means of different systems. This could apply especially if some rooms are only used occasionally. Organizations that provide guidance on different forms of heating include:

- **Energy Saving Trust**: go to the section on Heating and hot water: energysavingtrust.org.uk;
- **Solid Fuel Association**: for advice and information on all aspects of solid fuel heating, including appliances and installation: solidfuel.co.uk;
- **Which?**: go to the section called Home heating systems: which.co.uk.

When buying equipment, check that it has been approved by the appropriate standards approvals board. For electrical equipment, the letters to look for are BEAB (British Electro-technical Approvals Board) or CCA (CENELEC Certification Agreement), which is the European Union equivalent. For gas appliances, look for the CE mark, which denotes that appliances meet the requirements of the Gas Appliance (Safety) Regulations Act 1995. Domestic solid fuel appliances should be approved by the Solid Fuel Appliances Approval Scheme; check the sales literature.

Gas appliances should only be installed by a Gas Safe Register registered installer. Registration is compulsory by law, and as a further safeguard, all registered gas installers must carry a Gas Safe Register ID card with their photo, types of gas work they are competent to do, their employer's trading title and the Gas Safe Register logo. After a gas appliance has been installed, you should receive a safety certificate from the Gas Safe Register, proving that it has been installed by a professional. You should keep this safe, as you may need it should you want to sell your home in the future. See gassaferegister. co.uk. Additionally, members of the Building & Engineering Services Association (BESA) can advise on all types of central heating. All domestic installation work done by member companies must meet rigorous standards. See thebesa.com.

Electricians should be approved by the NICEIC. All approved contractors are covered for technical work by the NICEIC Complaints Procedure and Guarantee of Standards Scheme and undertake to work to British Standard 7671. Any substandard work must be put right at no extra cost to the consumer. For local approved contractors see niceic.org.uk.

An alternative source for finding a reputable electrician is the Electrical Contractors' Association. Its members, all of whom have to be qualified, work to national wiring regulations and a published ECA Code of Fair Trading. There is also a work bond, which guarantees that, in the event of a contractor becoming insolvent, the work will be completed by another approved electrician. See eca.co.uk.

Tips for reducing your energy bills

Energy can be saved in lots of small ways. Taken together, they could amount to quite a large cut in your bills. Here are some quick win suggestions from energysavingtrust.co.uk and the amount they could save you each year:

- turn your heating thermostat down one degree: saves £80;
- use smart heating controls: saves £75;
- fit a water-efficient shower head: saves £70;
- replace all your light bulbs with LED lights: saves £35;
- don't leave appliances on standby: on average saves £30;
- use a bowl for washing up rather than a running tap: saves £25;
- draught-proof doors and windows: saves £20;
- if you have chimneys, install a draught excluder: saves £15;
- turn off lights when no-one's in the room: saves £14;
- cut your time in the shower by one minute a day: saves £7;
- don't overfill your kettle: saves £6;
- do one less wash a week: saves £5.

If you do all those things, the saving per person could add up to a massive £382 a year! You can also save by shopping around regularly for the cheapest energy supplier and being prepared to switch. The energy regulator,

Ofgem, has a list of approved price comparison websites that can help you do this: ofgem.gov.uk, go to the section called *Compare gas and electricity tariffs: Ofgem-accredited price comparison sites*. In some areas, communities have turned tables on the energy providers and formed buyers' clubs which invite suppliers to compete for a bulk deal to supply all the households in the club. Your local council may be able to advise if there is a buyers' club operating in your area, or try an internet search.

Improvement and repair

If your house needs structural repairs, a wise first step would be to contact RICS to help you find a reputable chartered surveyor. See rics.org.

Local authority assistance

The Regulatory Reform Order gives local authorities greater discretionary powers to provide assistance – such as low-cost loans and grants – to help with renovations, repairs and adaptations to the home, or to help someone move to more suitable accommodation if that is a better solution. Any assistance given, however, must be in accordance with the authority's published policy. For further information contact the environmental health or housing department of your local authority.

Disabled facilities grant (DFG)

Available in England, Wales and Northern Ireland, this helps towards the costs of adapting your home to enable you to live there, should you become disabled. A grant can be obtained from your local council. It can cover a wide range of improvements to enable someone with a disability to manage more independently, including, for example, adaptations to make the accommodation safe for a disabled occupant, work to facilitate access either to the property itself or to the main rooms, the provision of suitable bathroom or kitchen facilities, the adaptation of heating or lighting controls, or improvement of the heating system. Provided the applicant is eligible, a mandatory grant of up to £30,000 may be available in England for all the above (local authorities may use their discretionary powers to provide additional assistance), £25,000 in Northern Ireland and up to £36,000 in Wales.

As with most other grants, there is a means test. The local authority will want to check that the proposed work is reasonable and practicable according to the age and condition of the property, and the local social services department will need to be satisfied that the work is necessary and appropriate to meet the individual's needs. The grant can be applied for either by the disabled person or by a joint owner or joint tenant or landlord on his or her behalf. For further information, contact the environmental health or housing department of your local authority. See gov.uk/disabled-facilities-grants/. If you live in Scotland, visit the Scottish Government website for guidance on equipment that you either buy yourself or might be able to get from the NHS or your local authority: gov.scot (see the section on *Support and social care*).

Do not start work until approval has been given to your grant application, as you will not be eligible for a grant once work has started.

Other help for disabled people

Your local authority may be able to help with the provision of certain special facilities such as a stair lift, telephone installations or a ramp to replace steps. Apply to your local social services department and, if you encounter any difficulties, ask for further help from your local disability group or Age UK group.

Many local Age UK branches operate a handyperson service, providing someone who can undertake small jobs around the home, such as putting up shelves, fitting a smoke alarm or grab rails, installing window locks or energy-efficient lightbulbs and so on. Call the Age UK advice line on 0800 678 1602 or visit the website to see if this is available in your area: ageuk.org.uk/services/in-your-area/handyperson-services. To find other tradespeople, here are some useful contacts:

- **APHC Ltd** (Association of Plumbing and Heating Contractors Ltd) maintains a national register of licensed members and can put you in touch with a reputable local engineer. See aphc.co.uk/competent_persons_scheme.asp.
- The **Association of Master Upholsterers & Soft Furnishers Ltd** has a list of over 500 approved members; see upholsterers.co.uk/member-directory/.
- The **Chartered Association of Building Engineers** can supply names of qualified building engineers/surveyors. See cbuilde.com/find-a-member/.
- The **Chartered Institute of Plumbing and Heating Engineering** can provide a list of professional plumbers. See ciphe.org.uk.

- The **Federation of Master Builders**: lists of members are available from regional offices. See fmb.org.uk/find-a-builder/.

- The **Guild of Master Craftsmen** can supply names of all types of specialist craftspeople including, for example, carpenters, joiners, ceramic workers and restorers. See guildmc.com and findacraftsman.com.

- The **Royal Institute of British Architects** has a free Clients Service which, however small your building project, will recommend up to three suitable architects. See architecture.com.

- **RICS** will nominate qualified surveyors in your area, who can be recognized by the initials MRICS or FRICS after their name. See rics.org.

- The **Scottish and Northern Ireland Plumbing Employers' Federation** is the national trade association for all types of firms involved in plumbing and domestic heating in Scotland and Northern Ireland. See snipef.org.

Home improvement agencies

Home improvement agencies (sometimes known as 'staying put' or 'care and repair' agencies) work with older or disabled people to help them remain in their own homes by providing advice and assistance on repairs, improvements and adaptations. They also advise on the availability of funding and welfare benefits, obtain prices, recommend reliable builders and inspect the completed job.

- **Foundations** is the national body for home improvement agencies in England: foundations.uk.com.

- **Care & Repair Cymru** is the organization to contact if you are in Wales: careandrepair.org.uk.

- **Care & Repair Scotland**: careandrepairscotland.co.uk.

- **Housing Advice NI** is the contact for Northern Ireland: housingadviceni.org/grants-financial-assistance.

- Information on home improvement agencies and care and repair in the UK can also be found by contacting **EAC** (Elderly Accommodation Counsel) which helps older and elderly people with their housing, support and care needs. See housingcare.org.

- If you are a veteran, the **British Legion** runs a service that can help with home improvements: www.britishlegion.org.uk/get-support/care-and-independent-living/independent-living.

Safety in the home

The vast majority of accidents are caused by carelessness or by obvious danger spots in the home that for the most part could very easily be made safer. Tragically, it is all too often the little things that we keep meaning to attend to, but never quite get round to, that prove fatal. Here are a few suggestions for you to make your home safer.

Steps and stairs should be well lit, with light switches at both the top and the bottom. Frayed carpet is notoriously easy to trip on. On staircases especially, defective carpet should be repaired or replaced as soon as possible. All stairs should have a handrail to provide extra support – on both sides if the stairs are very steep. It is also a good idea to have a white line painted on the edge of steps that are difficult to see – for instance in the garden or leading up to the front door. It may be stating the obvious to say that climbing on chairs and tables is dangerous – and yet we all do it. You should keep proper steps, preferably with a handrail, to do high jobs in the house such as hanging curtains or reaching cupboards.

Floors can be another danger zone. Rugs and mats can slip on polished floors and should always be laid on some form of non-slip backing material. Stockinged feet are slippery on all but carpeted floors, and new shoes should always have the soles scratched before you wear them. Remember also that spilt water or talcum powder on tiled or linoleum floors is a major cause of accidents.

The *bathroom* is particularly hazardous for falls. Sensible precautionary measures include using a suction-type bathmat and putting handrails on the bath or alongside the shower. For older people who have difficulty getting in and out of the bath, a bath seat can be helpful. Soap on a rope is safer in a shower, as it is less likely to slither out of your hands and make the floor slippery. Regardless of age, you should make sure that all medicines are clearly labelled. Safely dispose of any prescribed drugs left over from a previous illness.

The *kitchen* is another place where it is important to be careful. Spills should be wiped up immediately to avoid slips. Any items you use regularly should be kept easily within reach. If you are having trouble preparing meals or doing the cleaning, your local social services can assist you with advice on helpful equipment. The Disabled Living Foundation can provide equipment such as handrails, automatic lights and kettle tippers: dlf.org.uk.

Falls are a great risk for older people. For every two people who fracture a hip in later life, one never regains the same level of mobility. So it pays to try to prevent such accidents. If you have a fall, stay calm. If you're unhurt, look for something firm to hold on to and get slowly to your feet again – then sit down and rest. If you are injured, try to get comfortable, stay warm, and shift position every half hour or so until help arrives.

Fires can all too easily start in the home. If you have an open fire, you should always use a fireguard and sparkguard at night. The chimney should be regularly swept at least once a year, maybe more if you have a wood-burning stove. Never place a clothes horse near an open fire or heater, and be careful of flammable objects that could fall from the mantelpiece. Upholstered furniture is a particular fire hazard, especially when polyure-thane foam has been used in its manufacture. If buying new furniture, make sure that it carries a red triangle label, indicating that it is resistant to smoul-dering cigarettes. Furniture that also passes the match ignition test carries a green label. 'Combustion modified foam' that has passed the BS 5852 test now has to be used.

Portable heaters should be kept away from furniture and curtains and positioned where you cannot trip over them. Paraffin heaters should be han-dled particularly carefully and should never be filled while alight. Avoid leaving paraffin where it will be exposed to heat, including sunlight. If pos-sible, it should be kept in a metal container outside the house. Never dry clothes near a portable heater or open fire.

Gas appliances should be serviced regularly by British Gas or other Gas Safe Register registered installers. You should also ensure that there is ade-quate ventilation when using heaters. Never block up air vents: carbon monoxide fumes can kill. *If you smell gas or notice anything you suspect could be dangerous, stop using the appliance immediately, open the doors and windows and call the National Grid 24-hour emergency line free: 0800 111 999.*

More than one in three fires in the home are caused by accidents with *cookers*. Chip pans are a particular hazard: only fill the pan one-third full with oil and always dry the chips before putting them in the fat or, better still, use oven-ready chips that you just pop into the oven to cook. Pan han-dles should be turned away from the heat and positioned so you cannot knock them off the stove. If you are called to the door or telephone, always take the pan off the ring and turn off the heat before you leave the kitchen.

Cigarettes left smouldering in an ashtray could be dangerous if the ash-tray is full. Smoking in bed is a potential killer.

Faulty electric wiring is another frequent cause of fires, as are overloaded power points. The wiring in your home should be checked every five years and you should avoid using too many appliances off a single plug. Ask an electrician's advice on the maximum safe number, and use only plugs that conform to the appropriate British Standard (usually 1363). It is a good idea to get into the habit of taking the plug out of the wall socket when you have finished using an appliance, whether TV or toaster.

All electrical equipment should be regularly checked for wear and tear, and frayed or damaged flexes immediately replaced. Wherever possible, have electric sockets moved to waist height to avoid unnecessary bending whenever you want to turn on the switch. In particular, *electric blankets* should be routinely overhauled and checked in accordance with the manufacturer's instructions. It is dangerous to use both a hot water bottle and electric blanket – and never use an under blanket as an over blanket.

Electrical appliances are an increasing feature of labour-saving *gardening* but can be dangerous unless treated with respect. They should never be used when it is raining. Moreover, gardeners should always wear rubber-soled shoes or boots, and avoid floppy clothing that could get caught in the equipment.

As a general precaution, keep *fire extinguishers* readily accessible. Make sure they are regularly maintained and in good working order. Make sure you install a smoke alarm on each floor of your home and test them monthly. Here are some useful websites:

- ageuk.org.uk/information-advice/care/housing-options/home-safety/;
- dlf.org.uk;
- firekills.campaign.gov.uk;
- independentliving.co.uk;
- saferhouses.co.uk/FireSafetyCategory.html.

Home security

According to the Home Office, the elderly are no more at risk from crime than any other section of society. Should you feel nervous or vulnerable, the crime prevention officer at your local police station will advise you on how to improve your security arrangements. He or she will also tell you whether there is a Neighbourhood Watch scheme and how you join it, or how to set one up. This is a free service that the police are happy to provide.

Most burglaries are opportunist crimes – so don't be an easy target. The most vulnerable access points are doors and windows. Simple precautions such as fitting adequate locks and bolts can do much to deter the average burglar. Prices for a good door lock are about £60 to £80 plus VAT, and prices for window locks are about £15 to £20 plus VAT per window. Doors should have secure bolts or a five-lever mortise lock strengthened by metal plates on both sides, a door chain and a spy hole in the front door. Additionally, you might consider outside lights (ideally with an infrared sensor) to illuminate night-time visitors and an entry-phone system requiring callers to identify themselves before you open the door.

Windows should also be properly secured with key-operated locks. The best advice is to fit locks that secure them when partially open. Install rack bolts or surface-mounted security press bolts on French windows, and draw your curtains at night so potential intruders cannot see in. Louvre windows are especially vulnerable because the slats can easily be removed. A solution is to glue them in place with an epoxy resin and to fit a special louvre lock. An agile thief can get through any space larger than a human head, so even small windows such as skylights need properly fitted locks. Both double glazing and Venetian blinds act as a further deterrent. If you are particularly worried, you could also have bars fitted to the windows or install old-fashioned internal shutters that can be closed at night. Alternatively, many DIY shops sell decorative wrought-iron security grilles.

Increasingly these days you can fit smart devices, including video cameras both inside and outside the home that are wirelessly connected to a home hub and link to your smartphone. These alert you when someone approaches or enters your home, show you video or photos of who is there and even let you hold a remote conversation with them. You can also use smart devices to control lighting and other aspects of your home (such as automated blinds), making it appear that your home is occupied. These devices have been taking off very fast and are seen as a challenge to traditional burglar alarms (see below), particularly because smart devices can be self-installed and the cost starts from as little as £200 (though £500 to £600 is probably a more reasonable estimate for an average home).

Another obvious security safeguard is to ensure that your home is securely locked, both front and back doors, whenever you go out, even for five minutes. If you lose your keys, you should change the locks without delay. Insist that official callers such as meter readers show their identity cards before you allow them inside. If in doubt about unexpected callers, keep them out. Gas, electric and water companies can give meter readers and engineers a password so you know they are genuine. You could fit a locking chain and spy hole on your front door for peace of mind. If you install a smart meter, this will automatically relay readings to your supplier, reducing the number of uninvited callers visiting your home.

If you are going away, even for only a couple of days, remember to cancel the milk and the newspapers. You might also like to take advantage of the Royal Mail's Keepsafe service, which will store your mail while you are away and so avoid it piling up and alerting potential burglars to your absence. There is a charge for the service, which starts at £15 for up to 10 days. See royalmail.com/personal/receiving-mail/keepsafe. However, bear in mind that these days mail is delivered by a wide range of companies, and Royal Mail will only hold onto mail sent by their own service.

If your home will be unoccupied for any length of time, it is sensible to ask the local police to put it on their unattended premises register. Finally, if you are not using smart devices to control your lights and other home appliances, consider a time switch (cost around £15) that will turn the lights on and off when you are away and can be used to switch on the heating before your return.

If you want to know of a reputable locksmith, you should contact the Master Locksmiths Association: locksmiths.co.uk.

Further useful information is supplied by:

- **Victim Support,** a support and witness service for those affected by crime: victimsupport.org.uk.

- **Trustmark Scheme,** which finds reliable, trustworthy tradesmen: trustmark.org.uk.

- **Age UK Advice,** provide a booklet *Staying Safe: Personal security at home and out and about*. See ageuk.org.uk.

- **Trading Standards** can be contacted if you have problems or disagreements with suppliers of goods or services; from overcharging to faulty goods, from dodgy workmanship to reporting unscrupulous traders ('cowboys') or scams. To find your local trading standards office, see gov.uk/find-local-trading-standards-office.

Burglar alarms and safes

More elaborate precautions such as a burglar alarm are among the best ways of protecting your home. Although alarms are expensive – installation costs from about £450 to well in excess of £1,000 for sophisticated systems and, if you are linked to a monitoring service, there are ongoing charges – they could be worth every penny. In the event of a break-in, you can summon help or ask the police to do what they can if you are away.

Many insurance companies will recommend suitable contractors to install burglar alarm equipment and some arrange discounts for their policyholders with manufacturers of security devices. The National Security Inspectorate website lists approved contractors in your locality that install burglar alarm systems to, among others, British and European standards. The National Security Inspectorate will also investigate technical complaints: nsi.org.uk.

If you keep valuables or money in the house, think about buying a concealed wall or floor safe. If you are going away, it is a good idea to inform your neighbours so that if your alarm goes off they will know something is wrong. Burglar alarms have an unfortunate habit of ringing for no good reason (a mouse or cat can trigger the mechanism), and many people ignore them as a result. It is advisable to give your neighbours a key so that they can turn off and reset the alarm should the need arise.

Personal safety

Older people who live on their own can feel particularly at risk, especially when out and about. However, crime statistics show that older people are far less likely to be attacked than younger people. A number of personal alarms are now available that are highly effective and can generally give you peace of mind. A sensible precaution is to carry a 'screamer alarm', sometimes known as a 'personal attack button'. These are readily available in department stores, electrical shops and alarm companies. While the dangers are often exaggerated, it must be sensible to take all normal precautions. The police are of the view that many muggings could be avoided if you are alert, think ahead and try to radiate confidence.

A smartphone or traditional landline can also increase your sense of security. Some families come to an arrangement whereby they ring their older relatives at regular times to check that all is well. With a smartphone, you can set a family locator app so that family members or friends can remotely check where you are. You can also set up your smartphone with emergency information, including a contact person and details of any health condition you have or drugs you need, to help the emergency services if you are involved in an incident.

Many councils run community alarm schemes. For a small fee you get a panic button, usually on a pendant or wristband, so you can contact an emergency operator if you have a fall or are taken ill at home, or suspect a break-in. The operator phones a friend, relative or the emergency services. Age UK has been running its alarm scheme for 30 years, but try your council first.

Home insurance

There are two types of home insurance that you need to consider: buildings insurance, which covers the structure of your home, and contents insurance, which covers your possessions inside it. You can take out separate policies for each or combine them in a single policy which may be cheaper and can be simpler if you need to make a claim that affects both (for example, due to a break-in, fire or flood). Another important extra feature of home insurance is 'public liability cover'. This is designed to meet claims against you as a homeowner, tenant or landlord – for example if a visitor tripped and was injured in your home (contents insurance) or if a tile fell from your roof and damaged a neighbour's car (buildings insurance) – and you are found liable for the damage or injury.

If you rent your home, your landlord is responsible for insuring the building. If you own your home and still have a mortgage, your lender will insist that you have buildings insurance, though normally you choose the insurer and arrange the policy. Once your mortgage is paid off, it's up to you whether you have buildings cover, but you'd be very unwise to skimp on this cover. Your home is (perhaps along with your pension savings) probably the most valuable asset you have. If it were destroyed by a fire, say, you would need to rebuild it or have the wherewithal to buy a replacement home, so insurance is essential. Similarly, it makes sense to cover your possessions even though it's not compulsory to have contents insurance.

A brief word about flooding: with climate change and past policies that allowed developers to build on flood plains, around one in six English properties are deemed to be at risk of flooding, according to government data – that's over 5 million homes, and more once the other nations of the UK are included. The number of homes affected has been rising and households who had already been flooded or were at the highest risk were finding their insurance premiums soaring to unaffordable levels or even being refused cover altogether. To tackle this problem, in 2016, a joint initiative between government and insurers was set up, called Flood Re. Broadly, the scheme allows for average home insurance premiums to be a bit higher so that insurance can be offered to homes at highest risk at a more affordable price (albeit still high). The scheme is set to last for 25 years, after which insurers are expected to revert to pricing each household's insurance on their own particular risk. The 25 years was perceived as a breathing space during which flooding can be tackled in other ways, such as dredging rivers and sea defences. However, some experts suggest that it is simply not economic to protect all homes from the effects of climate change, for example, from coastal flooding and erosion. If you already live in a home that is at serious risk of flooding, in addition to paying high insurance premiums, you may find it hard to sell your home making it impossible to move elsewhere. Your only option may be to make your home as flood resilient as you can and there is useful information on the Know Your Flood Risk website: knowyourfloodrisk.co.uk. For people who are looking to move house, you may want to be wary of buying a home that could flood. You can find out about the flood risk of different areas of England on the Environment Agency website: gov.uk/check-flood-risk. For similar information for the other regions of the UK, visit:

- sepa.org.uk/environment/water/flooding (Scotland);
- naturalresources.wales/flooding/?lang=en (Wales);
- infrastructure-ni.gov.uk/topics/rivers-and-flooding (Northern Ireland).

The Association of British Insurers has information on various aspects of household insurance and loss prevention: www.abi.org.uk.

Buildings insurance

The amount you need to insure for is the full rebuilding cost of your home in the thankfully unlikely but extreme event of it being totally destroyed, for example by fire. This is not the same as the market value of your home (what someone is willing to pay to buy it). While the rebuilding value is often less than the market value, it can be higher. This can seem perplexing since, even if the home were destroyed, you would usually still have the land on which it stands. However, full rebuilding costs include the cost of clearing the site and rebuilding in similar materials and to similar standards which may be more expensive than current building norms, with the aid of architects and surveyors who all charge fees. If you don't insure for the full value, any claim you make (even small claims for, say, a window or broken bathroom fitting) will be scaled back proportionately.

For guidance on the rebuilding cost of your home, you can use the RICS Building Cost Information Service, which includes a calculator for residential rebuilding costs: calculator.bcis.co.uk. Once you have an insurance policy, the rebuilding cost you have declared is normally automatically increased each year in line with inflation, but it's a good idea to use the RICS calculator to recheck from time to time that the insured value is still in line with the rebuilding cost.

Contents insurance

Make sure you have the right level of cover. If you insure for more than your belongings are worth, you are wasting money. However, if you insure for less (underinsure) you risk having any claim scaled back proportionately. Once you stop work, you may need to review the value of your home contents. You may have new items you have bought with a retirement lump sum.

With older possessions, you should assess the replacement cost and make sure you have a 'new for old' or 'replacement as new' policy. Most insurance companies offer an automatic inflation-proofing option for both building and contents policies. You should not forget to cancel items on your contents policy that you no longer possess. You must also add new valuables that have been bought or received as presents. In particular, do check that you are adequately covered for any home improvements you may have added, such as a new kitchen or garage, conservatory, extra bathroom, swimming pool or other luxury.

Where antiques and jewellery are concerned, simple inflation-proofing may not be enough. Values can rise and fall disproportionately to inflation, and depend on current market trends. For a professional valuation, contact the British Antique Dealers' Association (bada.org) or LAPADA (Association of Art & Antiques Dealers): lapada.org. Either of these organizations can advise on the name of a specialist. Photographs of particularly valuable items can help in the assessment of premiums and settlement of claims, as well as give the police a greater chance of recovering them in the case of theft – do include something like a coin or ruler in the photo to show the scale of the item. Property marking, for example with an ultraviolet marker, is another useful ploy, as it will help the police trace your possessions should any be stolen.

Finding and buying insurance

Insurers have long had a practice of offering attractive premiums for new customers while hiking up the renewal cost for loyal customers who stay put. This means to get a fair deal it has been important to shop around each year and be prepared to switch to a new provider. Price comparison websites and brokers can help you do this.

Price comparison websites include:

- **Comparethemarket**: comparethemarket.com;
- **Confused.com**: confused.com;

- **GoCompare:** gocompare.com;

- **MoneySuperMarket:** moneysupermarket.com.

To find an insurance broker in your area, use the Find a member directory of the British Insurance Brokers Association: biba.org.uk; or try My Local Adviser: mylocaladviser.co.uk.

Comparison websites do not necessarily cover the whole market, and may feature companies that pay them commission more highly than others, so the golden rule is always to check deals on at least two sites. Bear in mind, too, that some companies like DirectLine do not market themselves on comparison sites at all. Similarly, insurance brokers do not necessarily cover the whole market and may be selecting your policy from a panel of insurers, and the broker will receive commission from the provider of the policy you take out. An advantage of using a broker is that they will also help you if you need to make a claim. Using a broker is also a good route if you are a non-standard customer – for example, you live in a thatched property or you will spend significant periods of time away from home.

While reviewing your provider each year still makes sense, the UK's financial regulator, the Financial Conduct Authority (FCA) has been investigating insurance companies' pricing practices and, although its enquiry is ongoing, there have been some changes already. Insurance trade bodies have published guidelines urging insurers to reduce unfairly penalizing loyal customers with excessively higher prices and some insurers are now actively advertising their compliance with this new approach.

Some insurance companies offer home and contents policies for older people (age 50 and over) at substantially reduced rates. The rationale behind such schemes is that older people are less likely to leave their homes empty on a regular basis (ie 9 to 5), and are therefore less liable to be burgled. In some cases, policies are geared to the fact that many retired people have either sold or given away many of their more valuable possessions and therefore need to insure their homes only up to a relatively low sum. These policies are not necessarily cheaper than the deals you can get elsewhere, so do get some mainstream quotes too, but the following websites will give you more information on some of the policies aimed at older people:

- ageco.co.uk/insurance (Age UK's insurance arm);

- esure.com/home-insurance/over-50s;

- lv.com/home-insurance/over-50s-home-insurance;

- postoffice.co.uk/home-insurance/over-50s;

- rias.co.uk;

- saga.co.uk/insurance.

Apart from shopping around, there are some other ways to keep down the cost of insurance. One is to agree to a voluntary excess, which means the first part of a claim that you will bear the cost of yourself. The higher the excess, the lower your premium. It is standard these days that you build up a no-claims discount with every year that you have home insurance and do not make a claim. The flip side of this discount is that, if you do claim, your premium at renewal is likely to rise sharply. This may mean that it's simply not worth making modest claims at all. Alternatively, you could pay extra to protect your no-claims discount, which means that you can make one or two claims without your premium increasing as a result.

Raising money on your home – equity release

Many homeowners find that when they reach later life they have wealth tied up in their home, but fewer savings or less income than they would like – a classic case of asset-rich but income-poor. If you are in this situation, you could consider using your home as a source of extra cash. The most obvious way to raise money from your home would be to sell it and buy somewhere cheaper (often referred to as 'downsizing'). If you don't want to move, or can't move, another option is equity release – releasing wealth from your home while continuing to live there. It is important to check before taking such a step that it is the right choice for you, both now and in the future.

There are two types of equity release scheme: a lifetime mortgage and a home reversion plan. Both are designed to run until you die or move out, for example if you move permanently into a care home. You can have a scheme just for yourself, or for you and your partner. In the latter case, the plan runs until you both no longer need the home. To use equity release, you need either to own your home outright or, if you do still have a mortgage, part of the equity you release will be used to pay this off.

If equity release does look suitable for you, consider the type of scheme and features that will suit you best. Make sure you understand how the scheme works, what your options will be if your circumstances change, for example, you want to move home and your obligations, for example, to keep your home in a good state of repair and to have buildings insurance.

In addition to financial advice, you will also need the advice of a valuer – this is especially important in the case of a home reversion scheme – and a solicitor. It is important that these experts are acting for you and not the equity release provider.

For more information about equity release generally and members who subscribe to the Equity Release Council code of practice, visit equityreleasecouncil.com.

Using your home to earn money

Rather than move, many people whose home has become too large are tempted by the idea of taking in tenants. At best, it could provide you with extra income and the possibility of pleasant company. At worst, you could be involved in a lengthy legal battle to regain possession of your property.

There are three broad choices: taking in paying guests or lodgers; letting part or all of your home as self-contained accommodation; and other schemes, such as renting your drive as a parking space. In all cases, for your own protection it is essential to have a written agreement and to take up bank references, unless the let is a strictly temporary one where the money is paid in advance. Otherwise, rent should be collected monthly or quarterly, and you should arrange a hefty deposit to cover any damage. An important point to be aware of is that there is now a set of strict rules concerning the treatment of deposits, with the risk of large fines for landlords and agents who fail to abide by them. You are also required to check that your tenants (but not B&B guests) have the right to be in the UK, by copying their passport or other immigration documents, and you can be fined if you fail to do this. If you are renting your home or buying with a mortgage, you should get permission from your landlord or mortgage lender before going ahead.

Paying guests or lodgers

This is the most informal arrangement, and will normally be either a casual holiday-type bed-and-breakfast let or a lodger who might be with you for a couple of years. In either case, the visitor will be sharing part of your home, the accommodation will be fully furnished, and you may be providing at least one full meal a day and possibly also basic cleaning services. To encourage people to let out rooms in these ways, the government allows you to earn up to £7,500 (£3,750 if letting jointly) a year free of tax under the

Rent-a-Room-Relief scheme. If your rental income comes to more, you can either just pay tax on the income above the tax-free amount or you can work out tax on the profit (rather than income) you make by deducting allowable expenses from the rental income. For further information see gov.uk/rent-room-in-your-home/the-rent-a-room-scheme. If you have a mortgage or are a tenant yourself (even with a very long lease), check with your building society or landlord that you are entitled to sublet.

You do not have to commit to having a lodger around the house fulltime; you can start with a short-term arrangement to see how you find it. Some employees and lecturers need a room only between Monday and Friday, keeping your weekends clear. Foreign students are around all term time but not in the holidays. Foreign language students might need a room only for one six-week term. You can stipulate whether to take younger or older people.

There are few legal formalities involved in these types of lettings, and rent is entirely a matter for friendly agreement. As a resident owner you are also in a very strong position if you want your lodger to leave. Lodging arrangements can easily be ended, as your lodger has no legal rights to stay after the agreed period. A wise precaution is to check with your insurance company that your home contents policy will not be affected, since some insurers restrict cover for households with lodgers. On the other hand, sometimes your premium falls on the basis that the home is likely to be occupied for more of the time, reducing the risk of burglary. Unless you make arrangements to the contrary, you should inform your lodger that his or her possessions are not covered by your policy.

In the case of a lodger or B&B accommodation for no more than six people at a time, your home continues to be subject to council tax. However, if you offer B&B on a larger scale, you will have to pay business rates. There is a useful guide at gov.uk/government/publications/rating-of-guest-houses-and-bed-and-breakfasts.

Having more than one lodger or using your home as a B&B means that part of any gain you make if you sell your home could be liable to capital gains tax – see Chapter 4 for more information.

Letting part or all of your home

You could convert a basement or part of your house into a self-contained flat and let this either furnished or unfurnished. Alternatively, you might let out the whole of your home if you will be living elsewhere for a time. In England and Wales, this is usually done by creating an assured shorthold tenancy, typically for a fixed term of six or 12 months, but alternatively as a rolling monthly contract. The rent you charged is set for the fixed term, but can be increased at renewal. Your tenant agrees to pay the rent for the full fixed term unless you have a break clause written into the agreement. The let will automatically cease at the end of that fixed period, though you and the tenant may agree to renew for a further term or move onto a rolling contract. If the arrangement is on a more ad hoc basis with no specified leaving date, it may be legally necessary to give at least four weeks' notice in writing – the position over notices to quit will vary according to circumstances. Should you encounter any difficulties, it is possible that you may need to apply to the courts for an eviction order.

In Scotland, there is an equivalent type of tenancy contract called a short-assured tenancy. However, for new lettings from 1 December 2017 onwards, this has been replaced by a new arrangement called the private residential tenancy, which gives tenants more security of tenure and more predictable rents. For information, see gov.scot/policies/private-renting/private-tenancy-reform.

As a landlord, you are responsible for ensuring the property is safe. This includes, for example, making sure that electrical and gas appliances are checked regularly, and that there are smoke alarms on each level of the property and escape routes in the event of fire. Before you can advertise the property, you must get an Energy Performance Certificate (see earlier in this chapter) so that your tenants have an idea of what their energy bills might be like. Both you and the tenants will want to inspect the property and have an inventory before they move in, and you will typically ask for a deposit. When the tenants move out, you can take money from the deposit to cover the cost if there is any damage caused by the tenants. In the meantime, you must keep your tenant's money safe by lodging it in a government-backed deposit protection scheme. For more information, see:

- gov.uk/renting-out-a-property (England and Wales);
- mygov.scot/renting-your-property-out/your-responsibilities (Scotland);
- housingadviceni.org/advice-landlords/thinking-becoming-landlord (Northern Ireland).

When you come to sell your property, if you have made a profit, there may be capital gains tax to pay on the share of the profit that represents the part of the property that was let out and/or the proportion of time for which it was let. Providing the property has been your own home at some stage, you may be able to reduce the tax bill by claiming lettings relief.

Other schemes

If you think a little extra cash might be useful, depending on where you live (such as near a festival site or theme park), you could turn your garden into a 'micro campsite' and earn, say, £40 per night. campspace.com aims to create a community of like-minded garden hosts and campers who will offer and use the temporary micro campsites in preference to overcrowded and under-plumbed festival ones. The only proviso is that fresh water should be available. Whether you want a queue of muddy festival goers outside your bathroom in the morning is a matter for you to decide. Similarly, if you live near a station, airport or business area and have a large or unused driveway, you can rent it out as a parking space to commuters and travellers, through sites like parkonmydrive.com, yourparkingspace.co.uk and parklet.co.uk.

Should you have extra space in your house and don't mind renting out a room, or you want to rent out your home for a week or two while you are away, by signing up to certain websites you can reach potential guests from all round the world. Try gumtree.com, airbnb.co.uk, wimdu.co.uk, spareroom. co.uk or roomgo.co.uk. If you'd rather not have people, you can make extra money out of the empty space in your house by renting out your cellar, loft or garage as storage space: see storemates.co.uk and parklet.co.uk.

You can offer your home for film and advertisement locations if you can cope with a lot of disruption. But it pays good money, and film producers need other types of homes besides stately ones. Look at locationshub.com and locationworks.com.

The great news is that, since April 2017, you can earn up to £1,000 of income from using your property completely tax-free. It could cover all the ideas in this section and also rental income from a lodger – though you cannot claim this £1,000 allowance as well as Rent-a-Room Relief, so you are probably better off claiming the latter. If your property income comes to more than £1,000, you can either pay tax on the excess or pay tax instead on your profit (income less allowable expenses). There's more information at gov.uk/guidance/tax-free-allowances-on-property-and-trading-income.

Holiday lets

Buying a future retirement home in the country and renting it out as a holiday home in the summer months is another option worth considering. As well as providing you with a weekend cottage at other times of the year and the chance to establish yourself and make friends in the area, it can prove a useful and profitable investment.

As long as certain conditions are met, income from furnished holiday lettings enjoys most – but not all – of the benefits that there would be if it were taxed as trading income rather than as investment income. In practical terms, this means that you can claim capital allowances on such items as carpets, curtains and furniture as well as fixtures and fittings, thereby reducing the initial cost of equipping the house. The running expenses of a holiday home, including maintenance, advertising, insurance cover and council tax (or business rates – see later in this chapter), are all largely allowable for tax, excluding that element that relates to your own occupation of the property. Married couples should consider whether the property is to be held in one spouse's name, or owned jointly. A solicitor or accountant will be able to advise you.

To qualify as furnished holiday accommodation, the property must be situated in the UK, be let on a commercial basis, be available for holiday letting for at least 210 days during the tax year, and be actually let for at least 105 days. But do not include long-term lets to the same tenant for more than 31 consecutive days. This still leaves you with plenty of time to enjoy the property yourself.

There is always the danger that you might create an assured tenancy, so do take professional advice on drawing up the letting agreement. Similarly, if you decide to use one of the holiday rental agents to market your property, get a solicitor to check any contract you enter into with the company. For more information see rics.org.

A further point to note is that tax inspectors will take a tough line as to what is 'commercial', and loss-making ventures could lose their tax advantages. To safeguard yourself, it is important to draw up a broad business plan before you start and to make a real effort to satisfy the minimum letting requirements. Also make sure you keep good records and report your profits correctly through the Self-Assessment system (see Chapter 4). Recent research estimated that £8 billion of Self-Assessment tax goes unreported each year, and the biggest culprits are property owners, with a quarter failing to report and pay all the tax they owe. This could make property owners more liable to HMRC enquiries into their tax affairs.

Help with housing costs

If your income and savings are low, you may be entitled to state help with your mortgage or rent. The rules are often complex and you can find more information at gov.uk. In some cases, you claim different benefits depending on whether you are under or over State Pension age, but note that there was an important change to the rules on 15 May 2019. Before that date, only one member of a couple had to be over State Pension age for the household to be eligible for pension-age benefits. For new claims from that date onwards, both members of the couple have to be over State Pension age. This means, for example, that if one of you is aged, say, 68 and the other 65, you would have to claim Universal Credit rather than Pension Credit until the younger person also reached State Pension age. Since Universal Credit is typically a less generous benefit, this can have a serious impact on your income – though help with housing costs is broadly the same.

There are several online calculators that you can use to check whether you qualify and how much you might get:

- **Entitledto:** entitledto.co.uk;
- **Policy in Practice:** betteroffcalculator.co.uk;
- **Turn2Us:** benefits-calculator.turn2us.org.uk.

You might also qualify for help with your council tax bill, but this is no longer a national scheme. Your local authority decides on the level of help and who qualifies.

Useful sources of information and advice about help with housing costs include:

- **Citizens Advice Bureau:** citizensadvice.org.uk;
- **Shelter,** the housing and homelessness charity: shelter.org.uk.

Paying a mortgage

The main means-tested benefit for people who have reached State Pension age is Pension Credit (see Chapter 3) or, if you (or your partner) are still of working age, Universal Credit. In either case, if you still have a mortgage you may qualify for help with paying the interest on that loan – through Support for Mortgage Interest (SMI). Take a look at the section on equity release earlier in this chapter for some things to think about when comparing this state help with taking out a commercial equity release scheme.

If you are getting Pension Credit, SMI starts at the same time as your Pension Credit claim. In other cases, there is a nine-month waiting period. SMI covers interest only (not any capital repayments), and is limited to interest on a maximum of £100,000 of your loan if you are on Pension Credit, or £200,000 otherwise. When you claim Pension Credit or Universal Credit, you will normally be asked questions to work out if you are eligible for SMI as well and, if so, you will be offered an SMI loan. It's up to you whether or not you decide to take it up. You can find more information at gov.uk/support-for-mortgage-interest.

Paying rent

If you (and your partner too if you have one) are over State Pension age and renting, you might qualify for Housing Benefit to cover at least part of your rent. You might be able to get Housing Benefit even if your income is too high for you to get Pension Credit. If you (or your partner) are younger, Housing Benefit is one of several benefits that have been replaced by Universal Credit, and so the total you get each month may include help with your housing costs.

In addition to your income being low, eligibility for Housing Benefit also depends on your savings. If you are getting the Guarantee Credit portion of Pension Credit (see Chapter 3), each £500 of savings above £10,000 that you have will be deemed to produce £1 a year of income, and this deemed income will be included in the means test. In other cases, each £250 of savings above £6,000 will be deemed to produce £1 a year of income and, in addition, you will be completely ineligible if your savings exceed £16,000.

If you rent from your local council or a housing association, Housing Benefit is based on the rent you pay plus service charges, for example, for maintenance of communal parts of the building. However, what you get is reduced if you are deemed to be living in a home that is larger than your needs, based on the number of bedrooms (sometimes called the 'bedroom tax'). If you have one spare room, your Housing Benefit is reduced by 14 per cent; if you have two or more spare rooms, your Housing Benefit is reduced by a quarter. In making this judgement, it's assumed, for example, that couples will share a room, unless that's impossible because of disability.

If you rent privately, Housing Benefit is based on either what you actually pay or a Local Housing Allowance (LHA), whichever is the lower. The LHA that applies to you depends on the number of bedrooms you can claim for and the area in which you live. LHA is based on the 30 per cent of cheapest rents in an area for homes of each size (one-bedroom up to four), and is also capped at a maximum amount. As a result, it is unlikely that Housing Benefit will cover the full amount of the rent you are paying. You can find the LHA for your area using the government's online tool at lha-direct.voa.gov.uk/search.aspx.

If you live in a mobile home or houseboat, you may be able to claim benefit for site fees or mooring charges. If you live in a private nursing or residential care home you will not normally be able to get Housing Benefit to help with the cost. However, you might be eligible for help with care-home fees if your income and savings are low – see Chapter 13 for more information.

If you claim Pension Credit, the Pension Service will ask you questions at that time to assess whether you are eligible for Housing Benefit too. Housing Benefit is administered by your local council, and the Pension Service will automatically forward your claim to your council. If you are just claiming Housing Benefit on its own, contact your local council – you can find contact details at gov.uk/apply-housing-benefit-from-council.

If you're renting from your council or a housing association, Housing Benefit will be paid direct to your landlord. If you are renting privately, you receive the money and are responsible for ensuring your rent is paid. This means you may need to budget carefully – see Chapter 2 for guidance on this. For more information about Housing Benefit, see gov.uk/housing-benefit.

Paying council tax

Council tax is based on the value of the dwelling in which you live (the property element) and also consists of a personal element – with discounts and exemptions applying to certain groups of people.

The property element

Most domestic properties are liable for council tax, including rented property, mobile homes and houseboats. The value of the property is assessed according to a banding system, with eight different bands (A to H). The banding of each property is determined by the government's Valuation Office Agency. Small extensions or other improvements made after this date do not affect the valuation until the property changes hands.

Notification of the band is shown on the bill when it is sent out in April. If you think there has been a misunderstanding about the valuation (or your liability to pay the full amount), you may have the right of appeal.

Liability

Not everyone pays council tax. The bill is normally sent to the resident owner or joint owners of the property or, in the case of rented accommodation, to the tenant or joint tenants. Married couples and people with a shared legal interest in the property are jointly liable for the bill, unless they are students or severely mentally impaired.

The personal element

The valuation of each dwelling assumes that two adults will be resident. The charge does not increase if there are more adults. However if, as in many homes, there is a single adult, you can claim to have your council tax bill reduced by 25 per cent. Certain people are disregarded when determining the number of residents in a household. There are also a number of other special discounts or exemptions, as follows:

- People who are severely mentally impaired are disregarded or, if they are the sole occupant of the dwelling, qualify for an exemption.

- Disabled people whose homes require adaptation may have their bill reduced to a lower band.

- People on a low income may qualify for a reduction in their council tax through their local authority's Council Tax Reduction or Council Tax Support scheme. In Northern Ireland, help with domestic rates may be available through Housing Benefit.

- Disabled people on higher-rate Attendance Allowance need not count a full-time carer as an additional resident and therefore may continue to qualify for the 25 per cent single (adult) householder discount. Exceptions are spouses or partners and parents of a disabled child under 18 who would normally be living with the disabled person, and whose presence therefore would not be adding to the council tax.

- Young people over 18 but still at school are not counted when assessing the number of adults in a house.

- Students living in halls of residence, student hostels or similar are exempt; those living with a parent or other non-student adult are eligible for the 25 per cent personal discount.

- Service personnel living in barracks or married quarters will not receive any bill for council tax.

Discounts and exemptions applying to property

Certain property is exempt from council tax, including:

- Property that has been unoccupied and unfurnished for less than six months.

- The home of a deceased person; the exemption lasts until six months after the grant of probate.

- A home that is empty because the occupier is absent in order to care for someone else.
- The home of a person who is or would be exempt from council tax because of moving to a residential home, hospital care or similar.
- Empty properties in need of major repairs or undergoing structural alteration can be exempt from council tax for an initial period of six months, but this can be extended for a further six months. After 12 months, the standard 50 (or possibly full 100) per cent charge for empty properties will apply.
- Granny flats that are part of another private domestic dwelling may be exempt, but this depends on access and other conditions. To check, contact your local Valuation Office.

Business-cum-domestic property

Business-cum-domestic property is rated according to usage, with the business section assessed for business rates and the domestic section for council tax. For example, where there is a flat over a shop, the value of the shop will not be included in the valuation for council tax. Likewise, a room in a house used for business purposes will be subject to business rates and not to council tax. However, if you are an employee who works from home, or you run a small business from home, using, say, a bedroom as a home office or selling goods from your home by post is unlikely to incur business rates. For more information, see gov.uk/introduction-to-business-rates/working-at-home.

Appeals

If you become the new person responsible for paying the council tax (eg because you have recently moved or because someone else paid the tax before) on a property that you feel has been wrongly banded, you have six months to appeal and can request that the valuation be reconsidered. Otherwise, there are only three other circumstances in which you can appeal:

- if there has been a material increase or reduction in the property's value;
- if you start, or stop, using part of the property for business or the balance between domestic and business use changes;
- if either of the latter two apply and the listing officer has altered the council tax list without giving you a chance to put your side across.

If you have grounds for appeal, you should take up the matter with the Valuation Office. If the matter is not resolved, you can then appeal to an independent valuation tribunal. For advice and further information, contact your local Citizens Advice Bureau.

Council Tax Reduction or Support

Before April 2013, there was a national scheme to provide help with your council tax bill if your income and savings were low. However, since then, responsibility for this type of help passed to local councils who set their own rules about who is eligible and how much help you might get. The help is called either Council Tax Reduction or Council Tax Support. In either case, it takes the form of a reduction in your council tax bill (rather than you being paid cash).

To apply for help, contact your local council – you can find contact details at gov.uk/apply-council-tax-reduction.

07
Leisure activities

Whatever amount of leisure time you have available in retirement, there is almost certainly something you will be looking forward to doing. Whether you tend towards studying, sports or crafts there are loads of suitable activities for everyone's tastes on offer locally or nationally. You may need to do a bit of research, but that is easy on the internet. Most clubs and societies have websites, giving information for potential members. Many organizations have concessionary rates for people of retirement age – or indeed from age 60, which to many of us does not feel old enough for retirement at all – as do a number of theatres and other places of entertainment. Given the immense variety of tantalizing options available, it's not surprising that many retired people find they have never been so busy.

But did you know that according to Ofcom, a third of people aged 65 to 74 and nearly half of those aged 75 and over are still 'digitally excluded' – missing out on all the many benefits of being online? While a whole series of initiatives has made some inroads, this still remains stubbornly high. It cuts people off from opportunities not just to participate in study and leisure activities taking place over the internet, but also to easily track down what is on offer in the physical world around them. For everything listed here, the latest information is always available on the relevant website, so it is recommended that you check there for further details.

Adult education

Opportunities for education abound, and there are scores of subjects easily available to everyone, regardless of age or previous qualifications. You might be a leisure learner or among the many older people studying with a view to taking on a new career in later life.

Formal learning

Not all educational courses are free, and this can deter a number of people from taking the opportunity to learn. However, there is no age limit for applying for a student loan to cover university tuition fees and, because of the way the rules work, you probably will not have to pay back all or even any of the loan. Student loan rules work differently in the different nations of the UK:

- **England and Wales:** loans for undergraduate study start to be repaid the April after you leave the course, or four years after you started. You repay only when your income exceeds £494 a week or £2,143 a month (2019/20), and the balance is written off after 30 years. Postgraduate loans start to be repaid the April after you leave, and only when your income exceeds £404 a week or £1,750 a month (2019/20), with the balance written off after 30 years.

- **Scotland and Northern Ireland:** loans for undergraduate or postgraduate study start to be repaid the April after you leave the course or (undergraduate) four years after you started. You repay only when your income exceeds £364 a week or £1,577 a month (2019/20). In Scotland, the balance of undergraduate loans is written off after 30 years and, in Northern Ireland, after 25 years. Postgraduate loans are written off after 30 years.

To be eligible for a student loan, you must not be studying at the same level as a degree you already have, unless your new qualification is in a STEM (science, technology, engineering or maths) subject or healthcare. While most universities require you to have some minimum qualifications (such as A-levels), the UK's largest distance-learning higher education institution, the Open University, is specifically open to learners regardless of whether or not they have prior qualifications.

The UK has two specialist distance learning universities: the Open University (open.ac.uk), and Arden (arden.ac.uk). However, increasingly, traditional brick universities are also offering online distance learning, which you might find more convenient than attending a campus. Many universities offer a choice of part-time or full-time study. A specialist in part-time study is Birkbeck, University of London, a world-class research and teaching institution, and London's only specialist provider of evening higher education. See bbk.ac.uk.

You may be interested in courses that offer pre-university or professional qualifications. See *Training opportunities* in Chapter 9 for some suggestions.

Informal learning

There are also increasing opportunities for informal learning, both at university and other levels, online and in the physical world. Agencies such as Age UK (ageuk.org.uk) and LaterLife (laterlife.com) will supply information on free and subsidized educational courses. Local libraries and your council are two of the best places to obtain information on local opportunities, such as adult education and life skills courses in, for example, literacy, numeracy, digital skills and financial capability. If you are interested in learning online, here are some of the leading websites where you can study informally for free:

- **BBC Bitesize:** learn with the BBC through online courses and study. See bbc.com/bitesize/subjects.
- **Coursera:** this online platform offers low-cost massive online open courses (MOOCs) from universities around the world. See coursera.org.
- **edX:** another MOOC platform offering courses from universities around the world. See edx.org.
- **FutureLearn:** an online MOOC platform, founded by the Open University with courses from that and many other universities. See futurelearn.com.
- The **Open University** (OU): free courses are available on its OpenLearn platform, some of which tie in with TV programmes that the BBC and OU co-produce. See open.edu/openlearn.

Many universities offer non-degree courses for adults and public lectures, sometimes in the evening or during vacation periods. In addition, there are non-university organizations that offer a wide range of lectures, talks and courses. Here are just a few possibilities:

- **Guardian Masterclasses:** life skill, career and hobby-related courses with a leaning towards writing, media and the arts from the Guardian newspaper group, held in London. See theguardian.com/guardian-masterclasses.
- **U3A** (the University of the Third Age) is the national representative body for the Universities of the Third Age in the UK. U3As are self-help,

self-managed, lifelong learning cooperatives for older people. The U3A website has a diverse list of courses available online, which have been specifically designed for those in later life who are looking to learn some new skills. See u3a.org.uk.

- The **Women's Institute** (WI) Denman College offers half-day, day and residential courses for men as well as women, both WI members and non-members, at the WI's college in Oxfordshire. Over 650 courses covering a wide range of subjects from cookery and Tai Chi to history and photography. Some bursaries are available to cover the fees. See denman. org.uk.

- The **Workers' Educational Association** is the UK's largest voluntary sector provider of adult learning with part-time adult education courses for everyone, delivered locally through partner organizations. See wea.org.uk.

Arts

Wherever you live you can enjoy the arts. Whether you are interested in active participation or just appreciating the performance of others, there is an exhilarating choice of events, including theatre, music, exhibitions, film making and so on. Many entertainments offer concessionary prices to retired people.

Regional Arts Council offices

The Arts Council England works to get great art to everyone by championing, developing and investing in artistic experiences that enrich everyone's lives. For information and details of its investment in your region and contact details for your regional office, see artscouncil.org.uk/what-we-do/your-area.

For those who wish to join in with amateur arts activities, public libraries keep lists of choirs, drama clubs, painting clubs and similar in their locality.

Films

Cinema is a hugely popular art form. Should you enjoy film, you might think of joining a film society or visiting the National Film Theatre. Here are some other ideas:

- **Cinema for All** (formerly the British Federation of Film Societies) is the national organization for the development and support of the film society and community cinema movement in the UK. It offers a wide range of services and resources dedicated to the needs of community cinemas. See cinemaforall.org.uk.

- The **British Film Institute** has a world-renowned archive, cinemas, festival, films, publications and learning resources to inspire you. See bfi.org.uk.

Music and ballet

From becoming a friend and supporting one of the famous 'houses' such as Covent Garden to music making in your own right, here are some suggestions:

- Becoming a Friend of **Covent Garden** is the best way to keep up with events at the Royal Opera House, attend talks, recitals, study days, master classes and some 'open' rehearsals of ballet and opera. See roh.org.uk/memberships/friend.

- As a Friend of the **English National Opera**, you support the work of the Company and enjoy privileges such as priority booking, dress rehearsals and many other events. See eno.org/support-us/how-to-support/become-a-member.

- Members of **Sadler's Wells** receive priority booking and up to 20 per cent off tickets. See sadlerswells.com/support-us.

Music making

Whatever style of music you enjoy, there are associations to suit your taste. Here are some contacts:

- **Handbell Ringers of Great Britain** promotes the art of handbell tune ringing in all its forms. See hrgb.org.uk.

- **Making Music** supports and champions over 3,000 voluntary and amateur music groups throughout the UK. See makingmusic.org.uk.

- The **National Association of Choirs** represents and supports over 500 choirs and 26,000 voices, all of them amateur and voluntary, throughout the UK. See nationalassociationofchoirs.org.uk.

- The **Society of Recorder Players** brings together recorder players of all ages from all over the UK. See srp.org.uk.

Poetry

There is an increasing enthusiasm for poetry and poetry readings in clubs, pubs and other places of entertainment. Special local events may be advertised in your neighbourhood.

The **Poetry Society** is a charitable organization providing support and information, and aims to create a central position for poetry in the arts. See poetrysociety.org.uk.

Television and radio audiences

People of all ages, backgrounds and abilities enjoy participating as members of studio audiences and contributors to programmes. For those wishing to take part, there are a couple of websites that can help:

- The **Applause Store** is the one-stop shop for literally thousands of free television and radio audience tickets to the very best entertainment, music, comedy, chat, sitcom, reality and award shows, produced at locations around the world. See applausestore.com.
- **BBC Shows:** be in the audience – free tickets for shows. See bbc.co.uk/showsandtours/tickets.

Theatre

Details of current and forthcoming productions for national and regional theatres, as well as theatre reviews, are well advertised in the press and on the internet. Preview performances are usually cheaper, and there are often concessionary tickets for matinees:

- **Ambassador Theatre Group** sells tickets from the UK's largest theatre group and offers annual membership discounts. See atgtickets.com.
- The **Barbican** is the largest multi-arts and conference centre in Europe, presenting a diverse range of art, film, music, theatre, dance and education events. See barbican.org.uk.
- The **National Theatre** stages over 20 theatre productions each year in three auditoriums – the Lyttleton, Dorfman and Olivier theatres. See nationaltheatre.org.uk. Many cinemas now show livestreams or encores (repeats) of National Theatre performances; for details, see ntlive. nationaltheatre.org.uk.

- **Official London Theatre** is the capital's only official theatre website. It has the latest news on listings, what's on, how to buy tickets, and events. See officiallondontheatre.com.

- The **Scottish Community Drama Association** is a community-based organization operating through 24 district committees throughout Scotland. See scda.org.uk.

- **UK Theatre Network** is a social network and online magazine for the performing arts industry with news and features, as well as national and regional theatre listings and review guides. See Twitter feed: @realuktheatre.

Visual arts

If you enjoy attending exhibitions and lectures, membership of some of the arts societies offers a good choice:

- The **Art Fund** exists to secure great art for museums and galleries all over the UK for everyone to enjoy. All funding is privately raised, and the Art Fund has over 80,000 members. There are art tours at home and abroad led by experts. See artfund.org.

- The **Contemporary Art Society** exists to support and develop public collections of contemporary art in the UK. Members' events include visits to artists' studios and private collections, previews and parties at special exhibitions, and trips outside London and overseas. See contemporaryartsociety.org.

- **The Arts Society** (formerly National Association of Decorative & Fine Arts Societies) is an arts-based charity with over 340 local decorative and fine arts societies in the UK and mainland Europe. It promotes the advancement of arts education and appreciation and the preservation of our artistic heritage with day events and tours organized both in the UK and abroad. See theartssociety.org.

- Friends of the **Royal Academy of Arts** receive many benefits, including unlimited access to the world-renowned exhibition programme with guests, and the award-winning *RM* quarterly magazine. See royalacademy.org.uk.

- The **Tate** is a public institution, owned by and existing for the public. Its mission is to increase public knowledge, understanding and enjoyment of British modern and contemporary art through its collections at four locations: Tate Modern and Tate Britain, both in London, Tate Liverpool and Tate St Ives. Members have unlimited free entry to exhibitions, special events and member-only rooms with refreshments. See tate.org.uk.

Painting as a hobby

If you are interested in improving your own painting technique, art courses are available at your local adult education institute. Your library may have details of painting groups and societies in your area.

The **Society for All Artists**, which exists to inform, encourage and inspire all who want to paint, whatever their ability, provides all that you need to enjoy this hobby. See saa.co.uk.

Computing and IT

As mentioned at the beginning of the chapter, there are still a large number of over-65s who are 'digitally excluded' – not using computers or the internet. Computing is one of the most popular adult education classes among retired people – and in most cases, learning these skills is completely free.

Local libraries have set times throughout the week for retired people to either learn computing skills or update skills they already have. Library staff will teach retired people on a one-to-one basis, and this service is entirely free of charge. Some banks also provide free digital training and, while their hope is that this will encourage you to take up online banking, the training is more general and wide-ranging than that. Ask at your local branch or get your local library or a digitally-enabled friend to search online for sessions near you.

For further ideas for developing and honing your digital expertise, see the section *IT skills* in Chapter 9.

Creative writing

It is said that there is a book in everyone, and many retired people have a yen to write. As this is a solitary occupation, you may find that joining a writing group is a worthwhile and pleasurable thing to do. The National Association of Writing Groups – nawg.co.uk – is one place to find a local group; another is Writers Online, writers-online.co.uk.

If the range of writing-related options interest you, something else to check is *Writing Magazine*. This is a monthly journal designed to help aspiring and actual writers.

Dance/keep fit

Clubs, classes and groups exist in all parts of the country offering ballroom, old-time, Scottish, folk, ballet, disco dancing and others. Additionally, there are music and relaxation classes, aerobics and more gentle keep-fit sessions. Many of the relaxation and keep-fit classes are particularly appropriate for older people. Find out what is available in your area from your library, or see the list below (there are further suggestions in Chapter 11, *Health*):

- The **British Dance Council** is the governing body of all competition dancing in the UK. It can put you in touch with recognized dance schools in your area. See british-dance-council.org.

- The **English Folk Dance and Song Society** is one of the leading folk development organizations in the UK. It aims to place the indigenous folk arts of England at the heart of our cultural life. See efdss.org.

- The **Imperial Society of Teachers of Dancing** is a registered educational charity providing education and training for dance teachers, from ballet to ballroom. See istd.org.

- The **Keep Fit Association** offers 'fitness through movement, exercise and dance' classes. There are hundreds of classes throughout the UK for all ages and abilities. See keepfit.org.uk.

- The **Royal Scottish Country Dance Society** aims to preserve and further the practice of traditional Scottish country dancing. It has 170 branches worldwide offering instruction at all levels. See rscds.org.

- The **Sport and Recreation Alliance** is the umbrella organization for the governing and representative bodies for all sport in the UK. See sportandrecreation.org.uk.

Games

Many local areas have their own backgammon, bridge, chess, whist, dominos, Scrabble and other groups that meet together regularly in a club, hall, pub or other social venue to enjoy friendly board games. Information on local clubs should be available from your library. Here are some national organizations which will put you in touch with local groups:

- The **Association of British Scrabble Players** promotes interest in the game and coordinates all Scrabble tournaments in the UK. See absp.org.uk.

- The **English Bridge Union** is a membership organization committed to promoting the game of duplicate bridge. Members receive a wide range of services, including details of tournaments and bridge holidays at home and abroad. See www.ebu.co.uk.

- The **English Chess Federation** aims to promote the game of chess as an attractive means of cultural and personal advancement, providing information about chess clubs and tournaments throughout England. See englishchess.org.uk.

Gardens and gardening

Courses, gardens to visit, special help for people with disabilities, and how to run a gardening association; these and other interests are all catered for by the following organizations:

- The **English Gardening School** teaches all aspects of gardening. Courses range from one day to an academic year, at Chelsea Wharf. See englishgardeningschool.co.uk.

- **Garden Organic** is the national charity for organic gardening and has been at the forefront of organic gardening for over half a century. Based at Ryton in Warwickshire. See gardenorganic.org.uk.

- The **Gardening for Disabled Trust** provides practical and financial help to disabled people who want to continue to garden actively despite advancing age or disability. See gardeningfordisabledtrust.org.uk.

- The **National Gardens Scheme** has over 3,700 gardens to choose from in England and Wales, mostly privately owned. Over half a million visitors enjoy visiting gardens that open to the public just a few days each year. See ngs.org.uk.

- The **National Society of Allotment & Leisure Gardeners Ltd** aims to protect, promote and preserve allotments for future generations. It acts as a national voice for allotment and leisure gardeners. See nsalg.org.uk.

- The **Royal Horticultural Society** is the UK's leading gardening charity, dedicated to advancing horticulture, promoting gardening and inspiring all those with an interest in gardening. See rhs.org.uk.

- **Scotland's Gardens Scheme** facilitates the opening of large and small gardens throughout Scotland that are of interest to the public. See scotlandsgardens.org.

- **Thrive** is a small national charity that uses gardening to change the lives of disabled people. See thrive.org.uk.

History

People with an interest in the past have so many activities to choose from – visit historic monuments, including ancient castles and stately homes, in all parts of the country; explore the City of London; study genealogy or research the history of your local area. Here are some organizations to consider:

- **Age Exchange** is the UK's leading charity working in the field of reminiscence, and works to improve the quality of life for older people through reminiscence-based creative workshops. See age-exchange.org.uk.

- **Ancestry** is a global network of family history websites that together form the world's largest collection of family trees. It has collections of census and many other historical data records. See ancestry.co.uk.

- The **Architectural Heritage Society of Scotland** is concerned with the protection, preservation, study and appreciation of Scotland's buildings. Six regional groups organize local activities and carry out casework. See ahss.org.uk.

- **Bekonscot Model Village** is the world's oldest model village, with 1.5 acres of model railways, towns and landscapes. See bekonscot.co.uk.

- The **British Association for Local History** aims to encourage and promote the study of local history as an academic discipline as well as a rewarding leisure pursuit. See balh.co.uk.

- The **City of London Corporation** website has a section called 'Visit the City' with a wealth of information about London's museums and historic sites, which include, for example, St Paul's Cathedral, the Guildhall, Dr Johnson's House, the Monument, Barbican and the Central Criminal Court. See cityoflondon.gov.uk.

- **English Heritage** champions our historic places and advises the government and others to help today's generation get the best out of our heritage and ensure it is protected for future generations. See www.english-heritage.org.uk.

- The **Federation of Family History Societies** is an educational charity that exists to represent the interests of family historians generally and especially the preservation and availability of archival documents. See ffhs.org.uk.

- The **Gardens Trust** is dedicated to the conservation and study of historic designed gardens and landscapes. It has helped save or conserve scores of important gardens. See thegardenstrust.org.

- The **Georgian Group** exists to preserve Georgian buildings and to stimulate public knowledge and appreciation of Georgian architecture and town planning. Members enjoy day visits and long weekends to buildings and gardens, private views of exhibitions and a programme of evening lectures in London. See georgiangroup.org.uk.

- **Historic Houses** represents 1,500 privately owned historic houses, castles and gardens throughout the UK. Around 300 houses are open to the public for day visitors. See historichouses.org.

- The **Historical Association** supports the study and promotes the enjoyment of history. It believes that historical awareness is essential for the 21st-century citizen. See history.org.uk.

- The **Monumental Brass Society** is for all those interested in any aspect of monumental brasses and incised slabs of all dates and in all countries. See mbs-brasses.co.uk.

- The **National Trust** exists to protect historic buildings and areas of great natural beauty in England, Wales and Northern Ireland. Membership gives you free entry to the Trust's many properties and to those of the National Trust for Scotland. See nationaltrust.org.uk.

- The **National Trust for Scotland** cares for over 100 properties and 183,000 acres of countryside. Members also enjoy free admission to any of the National Trust properties in England, Wales and Northern Ireland. See nts.org.uk.

- The **Northern Ireland Tourist Board** has a free information bulletin, *Visitor Attractions*, listing historic sites and other places of interest. See discovernorthernireland.com.

- The **Oral History Society** promotes the collection, preservation and use of recorded memories of the past for projects in community history, schools, reminiscence groups and historical research. See ohs.org.uk.

- The **Society of Genealogists** promotes the study of family history and the lives of earlier generations. Its library houses a huge collection of family histories, civil registration and census material. See sog.org.uk.

- The **Victorian Society** campaigns to preserve fine Victorian and Edwardian buildings in England and Wales for future generations. See victoriansociety. org.uk.

Museums

Most museums organize free lectures, guided tours and sometimes slide-shows on aspects of their collections or special exhibitions. If you join as a friend, you can enjoy certain advantages, such as access to private views, visits to places of interest, receptions and other social activities. Here are some suggestions:

- The **British Association of Friends of Museums** is an umbrella organization that acts as a national forum for friends and volunteers who support museums around the UK. See bafm.co.uk.

- The **Ashmolean Museum of Art and Archaeology** is a university museum and a department of the University of Oxford. Its mission is to make its collections available to the widest possible audience, both now and in the future. See ashmolean.org.

- **British Museum** members enjoy free entry to exhibitions and evening openings as well as information about lectures, study days, tours and members' room. See britishmuseum.org.

- Friends of the **Fitzwilliam Museum** receive regular mailings with information about museum events, including exhibitions, concerts, lectures and parties in the Cambridge area and throughout the UK. See fitzmuseum.cam.ac.uk.

- Friends of the **National Maritime Museum** enjoy the museum complex, housed in Greenwich Park, which comprises the largest maritime museum in the world, Wren's Royal Observatory and Inigo Jones's Queen's House. See rmg.co.uk/national-maritime-museum.

- Friends of the **Victoria and Albert Museum** (V&A) have free admission to exhibitions, members' previews, a programme of events, a free subscription to *V&A Magazine* and members' room. See vam.ac.uk.

- Membership of the **National Museums of Scotland** gives regular mailings and the *Explorer* magazine, invitations to lectures and other events, and free admission to exhibitions and some sites. See nms.ac.uk.

Nature and conservation

Many conservation organizations are very keen to recruit volunteers; the majority are therefore listed in Chapter 10, *Voluntary work*. Also, many of those concerned with field studies arrange courses and other special activity interests where there is usually a residential content, so more are listed in Chapter 12, *Holidays*. Here are a few that don't appear elsewhere in this book:

- The **Field Studies Council** is an environmental educational charity committed to helping people understand and be inspired by the natural world. Fieldwork and cross-curricular courses inspire thousands of students each year through its countrywide network of centres across the UK. See field-studies-council.org.

- The **Forestry Commission**'s mission is to protect and expand Britain's forests and woodlands, and increase their value to society and the environment. See forestryengland.uk.

- The **Inland Waterways Association** is a national charity run by over 17,500 volunteers, which campaigns for the use, maintenance and restoration of Britain's inland waterways. See waterways.org.uk.

- **Wildlife Trusts** is the largest UK voluntary organization dedicated to conserving the full range of the UK's habitats and species. There are 47 local Wildlife Trusts caring for 2,500 nature reserves and campaigning for the future of our threatened wildlife. See wildlifetrusts.org.

Public library service

The public library in the UK is an endangered species and needs your support. Britain's public library service has been under tremendous threat recently due to local authority spending cuts. Although a number have been closed, many local support groups have sprung into action to save their local libraries, with – in some cases – volunteers taking over the running of the entire premises.

The UK library service is a huge resource, which not only lends millions of books free each year, but also CDs, DVDs, large-print and braille books, audio books and ebooks. Most are equipped with the internet, so visitors can browse websites and do research. One of its traditional main attractions is as a source of masses of information about both local and national activities. Additionally, there are often reference sections containing newspapers and periodicals as well as local historical archives and a wide selection of reference books covering any subject, although these physical collections are in many cases being replaced by online resources. If the information you require is not available in the library itself, the trained staff will normally do their best to tell you where you might find it. Local libraries are also often a venue for a wide range of community groups and activities.

The UK's public library service is excellent – please help to keep it going by using your local facilities and volunteering your time to keep it open.

Sciences and other related subjects

If astronomy, meteorology or geology fascinate you, there are several societies and associations that may be of interest:

- The **British Astronomical Association** is open to all people interested in astronomy. See britastro.org.
- The **Geologists' Association** organizes lectures, field excursions and monthly meetings at Burlington House. See geologistsassociation.org.uk.
- The **Royal Meteorological Society,** which includes among its membership both amateurs and professionals, exists to advance meteorological science. See rmets.org.

Special interests

Whether your special enthusiasm is stamp collecting or model flying, most of the associations listed organize events, answer queries and can put you in contact with kindred spirits:

- **Birdlife International,** the site full of information for those interested in bird life across the globe. See birdlife.org.
- The **British Association of Numismatic Societies** helps to coordinate the activities of the many local societies, whose members are interested in the study or collection of coins and medals. See www.coinclubs.org.uk/.
- The **British Beekeepers Association** aims to promote the craft of beekeeping and educate the public on the importance of bees in the environment. See bbka.org.uk.
- The **British Model Flying Association** is responsible nationally for all types of model flying, organizing competitions and fun-fly meetings and advice and guidelines on model flying. See bmfa.org.
- The **Miniature Armoured Fighting Vehicle Association** is an international society providing advice and information on tanks and other military vehicles and equipment. See mafva.net.

- The **National Association of Flower Arrangement Societies** (NAFAS) has over 50,000 members who attend NAFAS events, the National Show, and take part in courses in floral art and design. See nafas.org.uk.

- The **National Philatelic Society** is for those interested in stamp collecting, buying and selling stamps through the society's auctions or postal packet scheme. See ukphilately.org.uk.

- The **Railway Correspondence and Travel Society** is Britain's leading railway enthusiast group for those interested in railways past, present and future. See rcts.org.uk.

- The **RSPCA** is the UK's leading animal welfare charity. Its website is all about animals: pets, horses, wildlife and farm animals. See rspca.org.uk.

- The **Wildfowl & Wetlands Trust** is a leading conservation organization saving wetlands for wildlife and people across the world. See wwt.org.uk.

Sport

Retirement is an ideal time to get fit and take up a sporting hobby. To find out about opportunities in your area, contact your local authority recreational department or your local sports or leisure centre.

Angling

The **Angling Trades Association** promotes the interests of anglers and angling, including educational and environmental concerns, where to find qualified tuition, local tackle dealers and similar information. See anglingtradesassociation.com.

Badminton

Badminton England is the sport's governing body in England. Many categories of membership are available. Most sports and leisure centres have badminton courts and give instruction. See badmintonengland.co.uk.

Bowling

The **Bowls Development Alliance** is the united body of Bowls England, the English Indoor Bowling Association, the English Short Mat Bowling Association and the British Crown Green Bowling Association. It is a game

that is available to everyone from 8 to 80. See esmba.co.uk, www.
bowlsengland.com, eiba.co.uk and bcgba.org.uk.

Clay pigeon shooting

The **Clay Pigeon Shooting Association** is an association of individual shoot-
ers and a federation of clubs. As a member you have public liability insurance, your scores are recorded in the national averages and you can compete
in national events. See cpsa.co.uk.

Cricket

To play, watch or help at cricket matches, contact your local club, or contact
the **England and Wales Cricket Board** to get in touch with your county
cricket board. See ecb.co.uk.

The **Kia Oval** is home to the Surrey County Cricket Club and one of the
main venues for international and county cricket. Club membership entitles
you to free or reduced price tickets for the Members' Pavilion to watch
international matches as well as county events. See kiaoval.com.

Lord's Cricket Ground offers a conducted tour of Lord's that includes the
Long Room, the futuristic Media Centre and the MCC Museum, where the
Ashes urn is on display. Senior citizens can attend County Championship
matches and the National League matches for half price. See lords.org.

Croquet

A number of local authorities as well as clubs now offer facilities for croquet
enthusiasts. The **Croquet Association** runs coaching courses and can advise
about clubs, events, purchase of equipment and other information. See
croquet.org.uk.

Cycling

Cycling UK protects and promotes the rights of cyclists. There is also a
veterans' section. See cyclinguk.org.

Darts

The **British Darts Organisation** organizes over hundreds of darts events
throughout the country each year. See bdodarts.com.

Golf

England Golf is one of the largest sports governing bodies in England, looking after the interests of over 1,900 golf clubs and 651,000 members. See englandgolf.org, or elsewhere in the United Kingdom:

- **Golfnet** (bringing together the Golfing Union of Ireland and the Irish Ladies Golf Union): golfnet.ie;
- **Scottish Golf**: scottishgolf.org;
- **Wales Golf**: walesgolf.org.

Rowing

British Rowing is the governing body for the sport of rowing both indoors and in water. See britishrowing.org.

Running

The **Association of Running Clubs** (ARC) is the governing body for running clubs. Their website gives information on road-running clubs and their activities throughout the UK. See runningclubs.org.uk.

Swimming

Swim England is the national governing body for swimming in England. See swimming.org, or contact:

- **Swim Ireland**: swimireland.ie;
- **Swim Scotland**: swimscotland.co.uk;
- **Swim Wales**: swimwales.org.

Table tennis

Table Tennis England is the association for this sport, enjoyed by people of all ages and all levels of competence. See tabletennisengland.co.uk.

The **Veterans English Table Tennis Society** (VETTS) holds regional and national championships including singles and doubles events for various ages over 40. See vetts.org.uk.

Tennis

The **Lawn Tennis Association** provides information about anything to do with tennis, from advice on choosing a racquet to obtaining tickets for major tournaments. See lta.org.uk.

Seniors Tennis GB promotes competitions for older players in various age groups from 35 years up, with information on club, county and international events. See lta.org.uk.

Walking

The **Ramblers' Association** provides comprehensive information on all aspects of walking, and can advise on where to walk, clothing and equipment and organized walking holidays, as well as details of the hundreds of local groups throughout the country. See ramblers.org.uk.

Windsurfing

Seavets, affiliated to the Royal Yachting Association, aims to encourage the not-so-young of all abilities to enjoy the challenge of windsurfing. See seavets.co.uk.

Yachting

The **Royal Yachting Association** has thousands of affiliated clubs and recognized training centres throughout the UK. It provides comprehensive information for boat owners, with advice on everything from moorings to foreign cruising procedure. See rya.org.uk.

Women's organizations

Women today participate in almost any activity on equal terms with men. But there are women's clubs and organizations that continue to enjoy enormous popularity:

- **Association of Inner Wheel Clubs UK** (the Inner Wheel was originally for the wives of Rotarians) – see associationofinnerwheelclubs.co.uk.

- The **Mothers' Union** promotes Christian care for families internationally in 84 countries, with over 4 million members. See mothersunion.org.

- The **National Association of Women's Clubs** has around 130 clubs with nearly 5,000 members nationally, open to women of all ages, faiths and interests. See nawc.org.uk.

- The **National Women's Register** has groups across the UK of 'lively minded women' who meet informally in members' homes to enjoy challenging discussions. The groups choose their own topics and many also arrange a varied programme of social activities. See www.nwr.org.uk.

- The **Scottish Women's Institute** is one of the largest women's organizations in Scotland and has thousands of members of all ages who enjoy social, recreational and educational activities. See theswi.org.uk.

- **Townswomen's Guilds** is one of the UK's leading women's organizations, providing fun, friendship and a forum for social change since 1929. Over 20,000 women nationwide have joined. See the-tg.com.

- The **Women's Institute** (WI) is the largest national organization for women, with nearly 220,000 members in local WIs across Britain. It plays a unique role in providing women with educational opportunities and the chance to take part in a wide variety of activities and campaigns. See thewi.org.uk. If you live in Northern Ireland, there is the Federation of Women's Institutes of Northern Ireland – see wini.org.uk.

For people with disabilities

In large part due to legislation, facilities for people with disabilities have improved dramatically in recent decades, so there are fewer activities from which disabled people are now excluded. Fencing is one which is fun and exciting, and a good way to keep in shape. It involves panache, style and grace, and can be done in a wheelchair. While wheelchair fencing is very different from the sport of ambulant fencers, the weapons and their usage remain the same. To find out more about wheelchair fencing, a good starting point is British Disability Fencing. Its website offers a huge amount of information, including how and where you can find a local fencing club. See britishdisabilityfencing.co.uk.

For blind or partially-sighted people, the following websites may be of interest, as they feature talking books:

- **Calibre Audio Library** has audio books that bring the pleasure of reading to people who have sight problems, dyslexia or other disabilities that prevent them from reading a print book; this service is entirely free. See calibre.org.uk.

- **Listening Books** is a UK charity providing a large collection of audio books to over 50,000 people nationwide who find it difficult or impossible to read due to illness or disability. Audio books are sent through the post on CD, or can be downloaded or streamed from listening-books.org.uk.

- **RNIB**'s Talking Book Service offers over 26,000 audio books, paid for by annual subscription, and delivered direct to your door. The RNIB's library has books available in audio, digital, braille and giant print. See rnib.org.uk.

Public transport

One of the big benefits of reaching retirement age is the availability of cheap travel. Local authorities are now required to offer people over State Pension age concessionary bus fares. Coaches very often have special rates for older people, usually from age 60. Senior Railcards, available to men and women over 60, offer wonderful savings on rail travel. Details of all these are given in Chapter 12, *Holidays*.

08
Starting your own business

Retirement as a time of endless leisure is not necessarily an appealing prospect, but it can be the opportunity to try something different that happens to involve self-employment or to fulfil a long-held ambition to start your own business. Of course, working in retirement may be a necessity if income is short or you are bridging a gap until your pension starts, and in that case you should seriously weigh up the option of taking a paid job working for someone else versus working for yourself. Running your own business can seem to offer an attractive flexibility over how, when and where you work, but it is no soft option. If your business is to be a success, it may require a great deal of mental, physical, emotional and time input, though this will vary with the type of business you choose.

If you do opt for self-employment, you will be part of a growing trend. Government data shows that one in six of the UK labour force (4.8 million people) is now self-employed, compared with one in eight back in 2001. Much of this growth represents people working on their own or with a partner but without employees, and this micro-business group totals 4 million. While the growth has affected all age groups, it has been particularly marked among people aged 65 and over, who now number just under half a million. When it comes to earnings, in common with all ages, older self-employed people earn less if they work full-time than full-time employees. However, bucking the trend, part-time older businesspeople earn slightly more than their peers who are employees.

Government research has found that, for most people of all ages, the key motivation to becoming self-employed was not financial, but the lure of independence, flexibility and job satisfaction, with flexibility top of the list (mentioned by 46 per cent of the people surveyed). Most planned to remain self-employed until they retired. For the minority who intended to quit self-employment to become an employee, by far and away the most common reason was greater security. Three out of five self-employed had additional sources of income, such as a partner's income, rental income or a pension, and the majority of this group said being self-employed was not essential. This reveals one of the big advantages of starting a business in later life. While the most common problems that younger business owners face tend to be financial – dealing with periods when earnings drop due to illness, having enough surplus to save for a pension and applying for a mortgage when earnings are variable and insecure – as an older entrepreneur, you are more likely to be past these issues and more free to take real pleasure in your business.

Taking stock

The range of business opportunities is limitless. Some of the areas you might be thinking of are:

- Consultancy work, selling specialist knowledge and skills built up over your career to a range of clients, who might include your former employer.
- Turning an existing hobby into a business, for example, carpentry, metalwork, sewing, jewellery-making or baking. This might entail selling things you make, holding workshops where you train others in these skills, or both.
- Selling skills you already have, such as gardening, catering, a handyperson service, teaching languages, tutoring or coaching, musical and performance arts, driving, housekeeping, care or companionship services.
- Acquiring new skills that you can sell, such as plumbing, web design or book-keeping.
- Running a location-based business, such as a café or shop.
- Starting a social enterprise, where the aim is not to make profit for yourself but to benefit your community – for example, giving debt advice, running an animal rescue centre or providing support for the homeless.

Different types of business require different levels of commitment from you and have different financial requirements. The sections that follow aim to get you thinking about how well you and your business idea marry up.

Time and flexibility

A major attraction of being your own boss is choosing when you work, and some types of business lend themselves well to this, for example arranging your own workshops and classes to teach a skill, building up a small clientele for regular gardening services, or taking on contracts that simply specify delivery deadlines. However, being able to flex your hours does not necessarily mean you can work short hours, and some businesses will struggle if you are too flexible. For example, if you run a shop or café where you rely on customers dropping in without an appointment or booking, you will rapidly lose custom if your business is only open at random and unpredictable times. Nobody will want to make the effort of travelling to your premises only to find you closed.

There are similar issues if you work as a consultant. Firms often use consultants and freelancers to deal with lumpy or unexpected workloads. As such, you will often be contracted to deliver your work to tight and possibly very short deadlines. This may mean burning the midnight oil to meet a deadline, even though once it's done you can take time out. A further issue with consultancy is that much of your work may come from repeat contracts from happy clients or referrals because of the great job you did. Thus, while you're building your reputation, turning down a job because you'd prefer some free time could mean that you lose not just that one contract but also repeat work from that client and others. Once you are established, this may be less of a problem. Similar issues may apply if you are building up a business such as catering for, or performing at, special events – if you say no, the customer is likely to move on and find an alternative, and you may also lose referrals as a result.

If you are selling things you make, you may need to schedule your workload around peaks and troughs in your market. Will your sales be bunched in the Christmas period or during the summer? If so, you will need to build up your stock ahead of these periods. How you sell can also create the rhythm for your work – if, say, you sell at a monthly craft fair, you will want your stock to be highest just before each sale. If, on the other hand, you sell mostly online, your sales might be more evenly spread and you might even be in the happy position of being able to make items to order.

Be aware too that there is a fair amount of admin that goes with running a business: keeping records of sales and everything you buy; drawing up accounts; dealing with tax; complying with regulations, such as waste disposal; and so on. You may be able to hire others to take on some of these tasks, though that has to be arranged and monitored too. In many areas, from catering to finance, there are additional regulations, and, if you provide professional services, you may have continuing professional development (CPD) requirements to comply with. These will all require time on top of what it takes to run your core business.

Personal resilience

Resilience is the ability to carry on in stressful situations and to recover quickly if something goes wrong. It's a capacity that's important in all aspects of life, but especially when running your own business, when you can sometimes feel very alone with your responsibilities, concerns and challenges.

We have all had days when we are brimming with optimism and feel we can achieve anything. On days like that, the tasks we set ourselves are done in quick time and the amount of work we get through is amazing. Other days are sluggish and full of stop-starts and doubts, making it hard to complete any task. Often, the difference between these days is a matter of focus. If there are too many commitments and worries crowding your mind, it can be hard to prioritize and focus on any one task. Running your own business inevitably means that you must to some extent keep a watching brief on many different aspects, but it is important when necessary to prioritize, focus on a single task and blot out distractions.

There are various techniques you can use to help you develop the art of focusing. Psychologists suggest using mindfulness techniques (focusing on breathing in order to still the mind and bring your thoughts into the present) can help. Exercise can have a similar effect – for example, going for a short, brisk walk can help your thoughts to untangle. Then there are more practical things you can do. Turning off your phone and logging out of your e-mail account for a while will reduce distractions. Writing a 'to-do list' shifts your mental load onto paper and can help you to see which tasks to prioritize. Dividing an overwhelming job into small chunks makes it manageable. With both to-do lists and chunking, ticking off each task as you complete it is a way of giving yourself positive feedback and a sense of achievement.

Experts, like Dr Geetu Bharwaney, talk about the importance of emotional resilience and the way self-worth, self-control and mood are essential components. For example, a positive mood promotes expansive thinking, while negative moods can leave you working below your full potential. The techniques she advocates include a 'feelings check in' where you acknowledge your mood, analyse the reasons for it and take active steps to change it. She also suggests self-soothing – choosing a coping strategy that engages your senses, which might be a few moments of stretching, sipping tea, smelling flowers, watching clouds or whatever works for you. You can find out more about Bharwaney's ideas at https://www.eiworld.org/resilience.

The degree of personal resilience you need will vary with the types of business you have in mind and the type of person you are. For example, if you are a shy person, a business that requires you to spend a lot of time negotiating with or presenting to customers could be very stressful and require high degrees of resilience, while a more extrovert person might thrive. A business that lets you quietly work from home could suit a reserved person, but create stressful levels of loneliness in others. So choosing the business that suits your personality is important and will reduce the incidence of situations that call on your resilience. Nevertheless, any business is likely to have some stressful moments, so it's good to develop some of the techniques mentioned to help you build and manage your resilience.

Your skill set

Knowledge and skills you already have or plan to develop may be at the heart of your core business idea. However, there is a wide range of peripheral tasks involved in starting and running a business – compliance with laws and regulations, web design, marketing, ordering supplies, reviewing contracts, creating and keeping records, calculating and paying tax, choosing payment and delivery systems and troubleshooting when things go wrong, to name just a few. Some tasks can be outsourced to experts, such as an accountant, whose fees will be a cost to the business. Maybe you have a partner or other family member who is willing to take on some aspects. Generally, though, there will be a range of non-core business tasks that you will have to undertake yourself.

It's worth thinking through all the elements involved in running your chosen business and conducting a skills audit on yourself to see which tasks you can readily take on and which might be a challenge. You could use a traffic-light system in your skills audit – green for tasks where you already have the necessary skills, amber for areas where you could get by but would benefit from updating or further developing your skills, and red for any skills gaps. Decide how you will tackle the gaps – for example, tool yourself up through training, or outsource to someone else who does have the skills. If you decide on training, decide what sort of training you need, where you can access it and by when you need to have done it. See Chapter 9 for some ideas on adult learning.

Financial resources

Some businesses require very little money (capital) to set up. For example, if you are selling your skills as a gardener locally, you could operate from home and simply advertise on neighbourhood websites or local public noticeboards to find customers, with very little outlay beyond some gardening tools (which you might already have). Launching other businesses may not be possible at all without substantial upfront finance, for example, to buy premises, fittings and machinery, meet regulatory requirements, pay for marketing, or buy an existing business from the outgoing owner. You will find information about possible sources of finance later in this chapter under *Financial matters*.

Whatever your business, you are likely to need some working capital. This finances the delay between your spending on raw materials, equipment and other inputs and receiving the proceeds from selling your services or products. The length of the delay will vary with the type of business, the conditions it faces and the terms you have with your customers. For example, if you provide consultancy work, it is typical to require payment within 30 days of presenting your invoice. In practice, clients are often much slower to pay. (The law allows you to charge business customers interest if they are late paying, but in practice you might be reluctant to do this if you want to foster an ongoing relationship with that customer.) If you are selling things that you make, you normally get revenue as soon as you make a sale, unless you offer customers credit. However, if sales are slow, you may instead see your stocks pile up and have a long wait to recoup the cost of making the items. You may be in a position to fund the working capital you need from your own savings or non-business income. If not, you may need to agree an overdraft or loan from your bank.

Your access to capital can be a defining factor in whether you can afford to start your chosen business.

Buying a franchise

An alternative to setting up your own business from scratch is to buy a franchise, where you buy the right to run an outlet based on a tried-and-tested business format for a specified term of years (often 10), after which you may be able to renew for further periods. The franchise is your own business, but you do not have total freedom because you are constrained to run it in the way set out by the franchise agreement. Moreover, you do not keep all the money you make because some of it will go back to the franchisor (the seller of the franchise). On the other hand, you should be investing in a proven business format, which should increase the chance of your business succeeding. Statistics from a regular survey run by the British Franchise Association (BFA) and NatWest Bank show that, in 2018, 93 per cent of franchises were profitable and fewer than 1 per cent a year close down due to commercial failure. By contrast, government data suggests that around one in eight of all small businesses failed in 2017.

You pay a fee upfront for a new franchise or a resale price for an existing franchise. There may also be other upfront costs, such as for training you are required to do, buying in stock, and so on. Total start-up costs vary greatly depending on the type of business. The BFA/NatWest survey gives examples of £5,000 to start a dancing-for-toddlers franchise up to £450,000 to start up a franchised gym, but with half of franchisors saying the start-up costs would be less than £40,000. Banks are normally willing to lend money to help you buy a franchise, though you will be expected to put up a substantial proportion of the money yourself. Usually, you also pay an ongoing annual fee to the franchisor which may be a percentage of sales rather than profit; and you may be required to buy stock from the franchisor which gives you little control over this key cost.

What you should get from the franchisor is an established brand and on-going marketing. It is essential that you go over the terms and conditions of the franchise with a fine tooth comb and, to do this, you should engage an accountant and solicitor experienced in franchising, for example from thebfa. org/affiliate-members/. Your advisers should always be independent from those advising the franchisor. With such potentially significant upfront costs, you will need to carry out substantial research and investigation to ensure that the franchise you are considering looks to be a sound investment over the term of the franchise and that it is the type of business that will suit you.

There is a wealth of information and guidance about franchising and the franchising opportunities available on the BFA and other websites. See, for example:

- British Franchise Association: thebfa.org;
- Franchise Direct: franchisedirect.co.uk;
- whichfranchise.com.

Getting organized

Occasionally businesses spring spontaneously to life – you leave an employer who asks if you'll continue a project on a freelance basis, or a friend asks if you'll make them one of the seats you built for your own garden, and it snowballs from there. However, in most cases, you will need to do some serious planning to convert your business idea into reality. Creating a business plan will help you – and others – see if your idea is financially viable, and you need to make other key decisions, such as the structure of your business, your business name, where you will work and what insurance you need.

Your business plan

If you will need to raise finance, you will need to show your bank or backers a business plan so they can gauge how sound their lending or investment will be. Even if you will not be seeking finance, you are still well advised to draw up a business plan because the process of doing so will help you to make a realistic appraisal of your business viability and where you might face challenges. It will also establish a baseline to compare against later when you are reviewing the progress of your business. Your business plan should contain the following elements:

- The name of your business, what you will sell and its unique selling proposition (USP). The USP is essentially what will make you succeed against the competition. For example, you may have a novel product, cheaper costs, better quality or a special location.
- The experience and skills you and anyone else involved will bring to the business.
- The market you will operate in, who the customers are and who your competitors are.
- How you will get your customers and your pricing strategy.
- How your business operates – for example, where it's located, your suppliers, equipment you need, how you get your goods or services to market, significant risks and how you will manage compliance requirements (such as data protection).
- Financial projections, including expected revenue, profit and cash flow.
- Financing requirements.
- Business targets for the short-, medium- and long-term.

If you will be presenting your plan to your bank or potential backers, you should include an executive summary at the start of the plan that concisely draws together the key points from the whole plan. This summary should ideally be no more than a couple of pages, and its function is to excite and interest the potential financier enough to want to know more. This is important because, if the summary does not grab their attention, they might never read the rest of your plan.

You can draw up your plan from scratch yourself, or there are many business plan templates that you can buy online – just search using the words 'business plan'. Even better, some templates and guidance are available free, for example from The Prince's Trust. Although this organization exists to support young people, its resources are available to all – see princes-trust. org.uk/help-for-young-people/tools-resources/business-tools/business-plans.

Your business structure

There are three main ways to structure your own business: sole trader, partnership or company. Small-scale or casual self-employment might not need to be formally structured at all.

Small-scale and casual self-employment

Since April 2017, you can have up to £1,000 of trading income each year tax-free and without having to declare it on a tax return. The £1,000 limit applies to revenue, not profit, and you cannot claim tax relief for any expenses. Trading allowance might be enough to cover your business if it is very small-scale. Similarly you can have £1,000 of property income tax-free without the need to declare it. This could cover, for example, money you make from letting out your driveway as a parking space, or from occasionally renting out your home through an internet platform.

In either case, if the revenue you get is more than £1,000, you can choose to deduct either the £1,000 allowance or your actual expenses. You then pay tax on what remains. The allowance cannot be used to create a loss, but deducting expenses can. Trading income of more than £1,000 must be declared each year on a tax return. There is a section of the return for 'Other income', and this includes casual earnings from, say, occasional freelance work that falls short of running a business.

A note of caution: HM Revenue & Customs (HMRC) will only accept that you are running a bona fide business if you are doing so with a view to making a profit (even if in some years you actually make a loss). It will not accept that a hobby you do for fun, not profit, is a business.

Sole trader

This is the simplest business format. Legally, there is no separation between you and your business; you are one and the same (though you may choose a business name that you trade as). This has the disadvantage that, if something goes wrong in your business, all your personal wealth could be in the firing line and, in the extreme, lost. But the advantage is simplicity in accessing the money you make and a minimum of bureaucracy and admin.

To start up, you simply start trading. You must register with HMRC as soon as possible, which will ensure that you are on the system for the various taxes you need to pay – the main tax is income tax on your business profits. While there is no fine for a delay in registering your business, there will be interest and penalties if you fail to deal with tax correctly. You must keep records and draw up your accounts each year. These will form the basis of your tax bills. There is more information about tax later in this chapter in the section *Dealing with tax*.

Sole trader status can be particularly suitable for trades (such as plumbing or carpentry) and vocations (for example, writing or music) when they are small-scale.

Partnership

For tax purposes, partnerships are essentially a group of two or more sole traders working together, and each partner is treated as if their share of the partnership is their own business.

There is no absolute requirement to draw up a partnership agreement, but you would be wise to do so. However well you and your partner(s) feel you get on, business and money disagreements can quickly turn any relationship sour. Therefore, it's best to be very clear right from the start how the partnership will work, such as how you will share its management, workload, income and expenses. A solicitor or accountant can help you draw up an agreement.

Partners are jointly and severally liable for the expenses and debts of the business and, like sole traders, partners' personal wealth can be called on to pay off any debts of the business. 'Jointly and severally' means that, even if the partnership agreement says you intend to share everything equally, if one partner cannot pay his or her way, then the remaining partner(s) must normally pick up the liability. The exception is where you set up a limited liability partnership (LLP). An LLP is a sort of halfway house between an ordinary partnership (sole-trader-type status) and limited company. Some key differences are:

- **Identity:** Like a limited company (see the following section), an LLP has a separate legal identity from its participants. This means the LLP can enter into contracts in its own right.

- **Limited liability:** More like a limited company, some or all partners in an LLP have limited liability, meaning that their personal wealth is not at risk. The maximum loss is the money they put into the partnership, and they are not responsible for the losses of other partners.

- **Public accountability:** The flip side of limited liability is that the LLP has to be more transparent than an ordinary partnership, so it is required to register and file annual accounts with Companies House (gov.uk/government/organisations/companies-house), and these are open to public inspection.

- **Tax:** Like an ordinary partnership, partners in an LLP pay income tax on their share of the profits, while a company pays corporation tax.

- **Management:** The partners jointly manage a partnership or LLP, while a company is ultimately answerable to its shareholders.

- **Joiners and leavers:** It is straightforward for new partners to join an LLP (or ordinary partnership), and when someone leaves their share of the business normally just devolves to the remaining partners. It is more complicated for shareholding employees to join and leave a company.

While you can just start trading as a partnership, it may make sense to enlist the help of a solicitor in drawing up a partnership agreement. If you opt for an LLP, you could set this up yourself, and forms and guidance on doing this are available at gov.uk/guidance/set-up-and-run-a-limited-liability-partnership-llp. A more normal route, however, is to get the help of an accountant, solicitor or specialist company formation agent (see *Sources of help and advice* at the end of this chapter). They can also advise on whether an LLP is the best structure for your business.

Limited company

A company has a separate legal identity from the people running it. This means, for example, that it is the company, not you directly, that enters into contracts with customers and suppliers and receives the money earned. The company issues shares and the shareholders are the ultimate owners of the company. This is the basic structure of companies quoted on a stock exchange (public companies), as well as a small business that you set up for yourself where all the shares are privately owned (private company).

Day-to-day running of a company is the responsibility of the company's directors (who may also hold some or all of the shares). In a public company, there is also a company secretary who keeps a register of shareholders, calls meetings and generally deals with the administrative side of things. In a private company, there is no requirement to have a company secretary and, in that case, a director takes on these responsibilities. There must be at least one director. A company must hold an annual general meeting (AGM), and additional meetings if extraordinary events arise. Shareholders usually get to vote at these meetings, typically with one vote per share – this means that, provided you own the majority of the voting shares in your company, you have control over your business.

As a director, you are an employee of your company. The company must pay corporation tax on its profits and, as an employee, the main tax you pay is income tax on any earnings you draw. Some or all of the company's profits can be paid out as dividends on the shares and these, too are subject to income tax (see *Dealing with tax* later in this chapter for more information). You may also be able to borrow money from the company through a director's loan account, in which case you owe your company the money and must repay it at some stage.

If you set up your business as a limited company, you have the advantage of limited liability. This means that, provided you do not trade while knowingly insolvent, the maximum loss you can incur is the cost of the shares you hold, so your personal wealth is not at risk. That said, if the company needs to borrow money from a bank, the bank may insist that the loan is secured against your personal assets, often your home, and in that case, if the loan could not be repaid, the assets used as security could be seized. In return for limited liability, companies must be registered with Companies House (gov. uk/government/organisations/companies-house) and must file various documents, including, for example, details of the director(s) and annual accounts, which can be inspected by the public.

You can deal with the form-filling required to set up a company yourself, but most people get help from an accountant or company formation agent (see *Sources of help and advice* at the end of this chapter).

A company structure will often be most suitable for larger businesses and those offering trades rather than services. An accountant or company formation agent can advise on the structure that might best suit you. However, if your business involves offering personal services, such as IT, consultancy or supply teaching, you may find that your clients expect you to operate as a company. This is because the tax rules about employment status are sometimes unclear (see *Dealing with tax* later in the chapter) and clients want to protect themselves from disputes with HMRC that could result in them having to pay tax as if you were their employee. You could set up your own company or another option is to join an 'umbrella company' (a 'managed service company'). This is operated by an agency and you, along with many other service providers, are employees of the umbrella company. The company collects your receipts from clients and passes them on to you as earnings after deducting relevant taxes and the agency's fee.

Your business name

There are relatively few restrictions on what you call your business if you set up as a sole trader or an ordinary partnership. You can trade under your own name or choose something different, in which case, you will need to include your own name as well as your business name on your invoices and correspondence. There are a few restrictions, for example, you cannot include words that would suggest you are a company or have limited liability, such as 'Limited', 'Ltd', 'LLP' and so on.

If you set up your business as an LLP or company, there are similar rules about the name you can give to your business. You must register your business with Companies House and it cannot have a name that is the same or close to the name of any other business already on the register. Companies House has an online tool where you can check if the name you are thinking of has already been taken: beta.companieshouse.gov.uk/company-name-availability. The name of a private company with limited liability must end in 'limited' or 'Ltd' (though you may instead choose the Welsh equivalent, 'cyfyngedgig' or 'cyf', if your company is registered in Wales). An LLP's name must end with 'Limited Liability Partnership' or 'LLP' (or Welsh equivalent if registered in Wales).

Whatever your business structure, your business name must not be offensive, or suggest a connection with government or a public authority. Moreover, unless you have official permission, the name must not include any words or expressions that have been designated in legislation as being sensitive. These include, for example, 'association', 'bank', 'Britain', 'dental', 'mutual', 'queen' and 'trust'. For more information, see gov.uk/government/publications/incorporation-and-names/incorporation-and-names.

You cannot normally stop any other business using your own name, company name or trading name unless you register it as a trademark, for which there is a fee of £170 (online application) or £200 (paper application), see gov.uk/how-to-register-a-trade-mark. By the same token, if somebody has already registered as a trademark the name you want to trade under, you will be infringing their trademark if you trade using the same name. This applies even if the name is available for registration with Companies House (which has a different function unconnected with trademarking), so you should separately also check the trademark register: gov.uk/search-for-trademark. This is important because the consequences of being involved in a trademark dispute can be severe.

Another issue to think about if you intend to have a website is whether a domain name is available that matches your business name or the trading name you intend to use. You can check this using the UK official domain name registry firm: theukdomain.uk.

Where you will work

For many small businesses, there is a choice: work from home or from dedicated business premises. With some service businesses, such as hairdressing, there is a third option of operating out of your home, but delivering the service in your customers' own homes.

Working from home has a number of advantages: it keeps your costs low, you don't lose time travelling to a workplace, it may be easier to combine work with family commitments, you may have more control over making your working environment a pleasant place to be, and home may be ideal if you have a disability that restricts your capacity to travel or operate from another space. However, there are drawbacks too: your home might lack the space you need, home services such as broadband may be less efficient and reliable than you need, working from home can be lonely, it can be hard to close the door on work leading to excessive hours, or, on the other hand, family distractions may make it hard to get enough time and focus for work.

In addition, there may be legal constraints on your ability to work from home. If you have a mortgage or you rent, you should get permission from your lender or landlord before setting up a business at home. As a home-owner, with or without a mortgage, you should check your deeds for any covenants that restrict working from home or the types of business that can be located there. You might decide to go ahead even if there are covenants restricting home working, since covenants are effective only if someone – typically a neighbour – decides to take legal action to try to enforce them. This may be likely if your business intrudes in some way on your neighbours' enjoyment of their own properties, for example, because your business is noisy, creates a lot of waste, or means that there is a string of delivery vans parking outside. If you are just quietly beavering away at a computer or sewing machine, it's unlikely your neighbours will notice or want to complain.

Local tax is another consideration. Where a property is residential, you pay council tax (domestic rates in Northern Ireland). On a business property you pay business rates. Where part of a residential property is used wholly for business, business rates will be due on that part, for example, where you have converted the garage into a workshop, built an office in the garden or your home is above your shop. If you use one or more rooms in the house for business, but those rooms are still used domestically as well, then business rates will not normally be payable. This might apply where you use a room as your office weekdays, but at the weekend you use it to pay domestic bills, create a newsletter for the friends of the local park, and so on. The position is not always clear cut, so you may want to get advice from a tax adviser (see *Sources of help and advice* at the end of this chapter) or talk to your local council. Be aware too that, while mixed business-private use may save you business rates, it will limit the home-related expenses you can claim for income tax – see *Dealing with tax* later in the chapter.

If you decide to work in dedicated business premises, you will need to buy, lease or rent space suitable for your particular business. If your work will be desk-based, you might consider renting in a shared-office-space complex. There are a variety of options: your own office, your own desk or hot desking. Some of these complexes also have meeting rooms you can book and shared refreshment areas. There are often small locally-based complexes, but also large multi-location providers. Some sources and providers that can help you find business property include:

- local estate agents;
- property websites, such as **Rightmove**, rightmove.co.uk and **Zoopla**, zoopla.co.uk;
- local craft centres – they may have workshops for rent;
- **Official Space** – a shared-office-space provider: officialspace.co.uk;
- **Regus** – a shared-office-space provider: regus.co.uk;
- **Workspace** – shared-office-space complexes in London only: workspace.co.uk;
- **Expert Market** – a search engine to help you find business services, including office space: expertmarket.co.uk (select Operations).

Be aware that some spaces that have previously been free may no longer be so if you are using them for commercial purposes. This includes many local parks. If you are thinking of setting up as a fitness coach holding sessions in the park, first check out with your local council or park operator whether there is a charge.

Insurance

There are not many types of insurance that are compulsory. However, there are several that you would be wise to consider if you run a business – and some clients may insist you have certain types of cover before they will do business with you. The types of insurance you may need include:

- **Motor insurance**: this is compulsory if you are going to drive or park a vehicle on public roads. The minimum cover required by law is third-party cover to compensate other people if you injure them or damage their property.

- **Employer's liability insurance**: you must by law have this if your business has employees. It is designed to pay out if employees are injured or become ill because of the work they do for you.

- **Business premises insurance**: the equivalent of home buildings insurance but for your office, shop, café or other business premises. It covers damage to, or destruction of, the fabric of the building and its fittings against a wide range of perils, such as fire, flood, storm damage, subsidence, break-in damage, and so on. This insurance is not required by law but, if you have taken out a mortgage or other loan secured against the premises, the lender will normally insist that you have insurance cover.

- **Business contents/equipment insurance**: this covers your office furniture, computers, copiers and other equipment, books, journals, raw materials, stock of finished goods, and so on against perils, such as fire, flood and theft. If you work from home, your normal home contents policy is unlikely to automatically cover business possessions, so you may want to seek an extension to your home policy.

- **Public/product liability insurance**: cover for legal costs and compensation should a customer, client or any member of the public suffer injury or loss because of using your products or services or due to accidents on your premises, or damage you cause while carrying out your services at customers' premises. Not compulsory, but essential if you are selling products, have premises that clients or the public visit, or you work at other people's premises.

- **Professional indemnity insurance**: this covers legal costs and compensation if a client claims they have suffered loss because of a problem with your work, for example, regarding accuracy, late delivery, incompleteness or infringing someone else's copyright. Especially useful for consultants, advisers and tutors.

- **Professional treatment liability insurance:** optional cover for legal costs and compensation should a client claim that your services or advice has led to the client suffering an injury. Useful for, for example, personal trainers and hairdressers.

- **Key man insurance:** this pays out if a partner or employee who is vital to the success of the business has to leave because of illness or dies.

- **Cyber insurance:** this covers the financial consequences of data breaches, malicious hacks and similar IT-related threats.

A business insurer or broker can typically put together a package of the different types of insurance relevant to your business, so that you just have one policy rather than several different ones to worry about. Some useful contacts include:

- **British Insurance Brokers Association.** The trade body for insurance brokers. It has a searchable database of members and you can specify the type of insurance you are seeking, for example 'commercial': biba.org.uk.

- **Direct Line for Business.** Part of the Direct Line insurance group, specializing in insurance for small businesses and professionals. Like the rest of the group, it deals with customers direct so is not usually included on price comparison sites: directlineforbusiness.co.uk.

- **Hiscox.** An international broker and leading provider of business insurance to UK professionals, consultants and small- and medium-sized firms in all sectors: hiscox.co.uk.

- **Price comparison websites.** Some have sections where you can compare quotes for business insurance, such as: comparethemarket.com and moneysupermarket.com.

- **Simply Business** (XBridge Limited). A UK-based broker specializing in business insurance across 1,000 different trades: simplybusiness.co.uk.

Finding customers

Without customers you have no business, so it is essential to have a sound plan for how to reach them. The strategies you adopt depend very much on the type of business that you have.

If yours is a very local business, for example, providing gardening, plumbing or other services or trades provided in people's homes, your focus will be on how to make your local community aware of your existence and building a good reputation which will help you to get further business through word of mouth. Some possibilities include putting printed flyers through people's doors, placing ads in community magazines and on community noticeboards, and joining and posting on online community sites, such as eBay Local (ebay.co.uk/local), Gumtree (gumtree.com) and Nextdoor (nextdoor. co.uk). There are also a number of websites that you could join, where would-be customers either search for traders in their area or post their job requirements which the site then matches to traders. Typically, these sites are free for customers to use, but you pay a fee to be listed, agree to abide by a code of conduct or ethics, and agree to provide information that enables the website operators to check you comply with their standards. Customers can leave feedback which can help you to build your reputation. It's important that you check the terms and conditions before joining a site to ensure that it caters for your type of business, you are happy with how the site works and the fees it charges, and you can meet its requirements. Examples of such sites include:

- **Checkatrade** (Vetted Limited): checkatrade.com;
- **FindaTrade Ltd**: findatrade.com;
- **Rated People Ltd**: ratedpeople.com;
- **TrustaTrader**: trustatrader.com;
- **Trusted Traders** (part of the consumer advocacy group, Which?): trustedtraders.which.co.uk.

If you will be selling things you make from a stall or food van, your main outlet may be local craft fairs and events, such as festivals and agricultural shows. You typically pay a fee for your stall or pitch, and gain access to all the visitors as potential customers. You can find information about local craft fairs and events from your local council, community Facebook pages, local churches and schools. You can search for events by location on event websites, such as eventbrite.co.uk, list.co.uk, stallandcraftcollective.co.uk, stallfinder.com, and ukcraftfairs.com.

If you plan to sell beyond your local community, the easiest route for many small businesses is through online sites, such as eBay and Amazon Marketplace. You may previously have sold items privately on eBay, in which case your listing would have been free and you paid eBay a percentage of the price you received. The fees are different if you are selling as a business, and there are a variety of options, including creating your own virtual shop. You can find details at ebay.co.uk/help/fees-invoices. For details of how to advertise and sell on Amazon, visit services.amazon.co.uk/services.html.

Where you are selling your expertise as a consultant, your approach to finding clients is likely to be very different. Contracts with the government or other public bodies normally have to go through a tendering process. You typically pitch for the business by responding to an invitation to tender (ITT), which will usually be posted on a tendering website. Therefore, your first step is to register with relevant websites and check them regularly for contracts that may be of interest to you. You can find guidance on how to sell your goods and services to the public sector at gov.uk/tendering-for-public-sector-contracts. There is also a searchable database of contracts over £10,000 with the public sector at gov.uk/contracts-finder. The devolved governments have their own procurement systems – for guidance on using these, see:

- Scotland: publiccontractsscotland.gov.uk;
- Wales: businesswales.gov.wales/sell2wales-selling-public-sector-0;
- Northern Ireland: finance-ni.gov.uk/topics/procurement.

Outside the public sector, you could contact potential clients direct to find out what opportunities might be available and how to bid for them. There are also many intermediary websites that you can join for a fee that offer tender-finding services and provide automatic alerts when relevant contracts come up, such as b2bquotetenders.co.uk, bespokebids.com, creativetenders. co.uk and supply2govtenders.co.uk.

However, in the consultancy world, invitations to bid for, or take on, pieces of work often come through people you know or have worked with before or through referrals. Therefore, it is important to develop and maintain a good business network. This can be challenging in later life as people who were good business contacts retire, so you should be continually working on developing new links, for example by joining relevant professional bodies and attending events and conferences. Invitations to bid for work can also come through social media. For example, joining LinkedIn (linkedin. com), and keeping your profile up to date can attract contact from businesses looking for people with your areas of expertise. Some organizations will tweet about opportunities, so it's worth having a Twitter account and following the firms you would be interested in working with: twitter.com.

Financial matters

However passionate you are about your business and however much you enjoy what you do, your business will not thrive if the finances do not stack up. It's common to make a loss at the start because you may need to invest heavily and building a customer base takes time, but you should be able to forecast the point at which you will start to make a profit and anticipate the points at which you may experience cash flow pressures. If you have ever watched the BBC TV programme, *Dragon's Den*, you will know that having a sound grasp of your business finances is also essential if you are to attract outside backing – and this includes banks.

While forecasts are essential, the future does not always go as planned and, despite your best efforts, your business could nevertheless fail, so it's important to be able to distinguish a temporary financial blip from the signs of more systemic problems.

Financial forecasts

Forecasting the finances of your business needs to begin well before you start up. The initial task is to check that you have a viable business at all. Forecasts are at the heart of the business plan that you draw up (see earlier in this chapter) and then rolling forecasts become the compass for your ongoing business. You cannot effectively plan ahead and avoid crises if you have no idea of where your business is meant to be going.

Forecasting, by its nature, can never be 100 per cent accurate, but the assumptions and guesstimates you build in should be based on the best information you can gather. After you have been trading for a while, forecasting should become easier because you will have some past track record to guide you, though changing external factors mean that the future will seldom simply replicate the past. At the start of your business, forecasting will be more challenging, and you may need to research widely to make your figures as realistic as you can.

There are two types of forecast that you will need to make: cash flow and profit. They are not the same. Cash flow is all about the timing of receipts and expenses and will help you understand what working capital you need and when. The profit forecast will show whether you are making money. You may have seen reports of firms, like Uber, that have yet to make any profit, but nonetheless keep trading because they are able to manage their cash flow. Conversely, a profitable business can be brought to its knees if it does not have enough cash to meet its immediate expenses.

Cash flow forecast

A cash flow statement is a record of all the money flowing into the business and all the money flowing out during a particular time period. A cash flow forecast is the same, but estimating forward rather than looking back. You can think of this as being like a tank of water with income as a tap that when it is opened starts to fill the tank and expenses like a plug at the bottom which when pulled drains water from the tank. What's in the tank is a reservoir of cash and that, typically, will be your business bank account. (Note that a company, being a separate legal identity, must have its own company bank account quite separate from any accounts you personally may have. If you operate as a sole trader, you do not have to open a separate bank account for your business, though in most cases it will make managing your business finances easier if you do.) It follows then that the first item in your cash flow forecast is the starting bank balance and the final item in any period is your closing bank balance. Looking ahead to the first year or two of your forecast, you should normally draw up your forecast on a month-by-month basis. Table 8.1 gives an example of the format you might use. This example is for a very small business working from home with no employees. A bigger business might have VAT (see *Dealing with tax* later in this chapter) to pay, rent and business rates and a wage bill, and so require many more items. However, this is not a set of accounts and you do not need to list every minute detail. The aim here is to block in the main revenue and expense areas, and it's fine to gather similar items together under a single broad heading.

Table 8.1   Cash flow forecast

Items	January	...	December
Opening bank balance (A)	....		....
Receipts	....		....
Revenue from sales	....		....
Receipts from debtors	....		....
New capital	....		....
Other receipts	....		....
Total receipts (B)	....		....
Expenses	....		....
Payments to suppliers	....		....
Stationery, office supplies and marketing			
Heating and lighting	....		....

(*continued*)

Table 8.1   (Continued)

Items	January	...	December
Phone and broadband	....		....
Postage and packaging	....		....
Accountant's fees	....		....
Bank charges and interest	....		....
Tax	....		....
Capital expenditure	....		....
Personal drawings	....		....
Other expenses	....		....
Total expenses (C)	....		....
Closing bank balance (A + B – C)	....		....

In Table 8.1, *Revenue from sales* is the cash you expect to receive when you sell something. If your customers or clients will not pay you straight away, do not include that amount here. Instead, they will become debtors of the company and, only when they do pay you what they owe does it enter the cash flow under *Receipts from debtors*.

Revenue from sales is probably the most difficult figure to forecast. You will need to estimate the volume of your sales, including any seasonal pattern, and also the price at which you will sell your goods or services. If you are making something that is already on the market, you can look at the price charged by competitors while taking relative quality into account. When selling consultancy services, it can be much more difficult – for example, you may want to charge different rates to different clients.

New capital is any money that will come into the business from outside. This could be a loan from a bank, receipts from selling new shares to an investor, money you transfer to your business from your savings or other income, and even expenses that you will pay for personally.

Payments to suppliers are the amounts you pay for your raw materials (if any). You should investigate who you would use as your suppliers, and what they will charge to help you estimate these costs. Put these items under the month in which you will actually make the payment (not the month you will be billed if that's earlier). The same goes for *stationery, office supplies and marketing*. If you are working from home, you will need to decide what proportion of the bills for heating, lighting, broadband and phone corresponds to business use, and record these items in the months that you will pay these household bills. *Postage and packaging* may be a significant item if you will be mailing your products to customers.

In a very small business, you might decide to keep your own accounts, but more often businesses hire an accountant. Also, although it is common for personal bank accounts to be free if you are in credit, with business bank accounts there will normally be charges, for example a monthly fee and a charge for each transaction. If you run an overdraft, you will be charged interest. Thus, *fees, charges and interest* are a 'leakage' from your bank account that needs to be taken into account. Your cash flow forecast will also need to include any taxes, recorded in the months when they will fall due for payment.

Capital expenditure is the place to enter what you will pay for any equipment needed for the business, such as tools, machinery, computers, and so on. *Personal drawings* is money that you want to plan now that you will take out of the business – this may be essential if you will be relying on money from the business to meet some or all of your day-to-day living expenses. Other expenses may include, for example, interest payments if your business is financed partly by borrowing.

When all the receipts are added to the opening bank balance and all the expenses deducted, the result is the closing bank balance. This becomes the opening bank balance for the next month. If the closing bank balance in any month is a positive amount, then the business will be paying its way. If the closing balance is negative, you'll need to decide how to deal with the shortfall – for example, borrow from the bank, put in extra cash yourself or look for a way to reduce expenses.

Profit forecast

This forecast does not need to be broken down month-by-month, but you might want to look at it on a quarterly or half-yearly basis rather than annual. The figures in the profit forecast are related to the cash flow forecast, but organized in a different way to answer a different question: whether your business is likely to make money, and when. A simplified version of a profit forecast is shown in Table 8.2.

In Table 8.2, *sales revenue* is the volume that you will sell during the period multiplied by the price (regardless of whether payment is received immediately or later). *Cost of sales* is all the expenses that vary directly with the volume of sales, called the variable costs. The most obvious variable cost is raw materials that go into making a product, plus the cost of labour,

Table 8.2 Simplified profit forecast

Items	Year 1, Quarter 1	...	Year x Quarter 4
Sales revenue	....		....
Less cost of sales	....		....
Gross profit (A)	....		....
Expenses	....		....
Depreciation	....		....
Interest	....		....
Taxes	....		....
Total deductions (B)	....		....
Net profit (A – B)	....		....

electricity used, and so on. Subtracting these costs from sales gives the *gross profit*. This figure is telling you whether production of the product or service itself generates revenue. If it doesn't, that's a clear signal that the business is not viable.

However, gross profit does not tell you whether the business as a whole is profitable. To work that out, you need to subtract the *expenses* that do not vary with your level of production – your overheads or fixed costs. They include, for example, the cost of your premises and running an office. If you have employees, some may be involved in admin, say, that has to be done whatever the level of production and so are fixed rather than variable costs.

Rather than deducting the cost of capital equipment in the periods when you buy it, in the profit forecast, it is more usual to include *depreciation* – the value lost each year because of wear and tear and simply becoming out of date. Depreciation is often calculated simply by dividing the original cost by the predicted useful lifetime of the asset. By subtracting this amount each year, you are taking account of the annual cost of using up the asset.

The profit remaining is not the end of the story, because if the business has borrowed money, there will be *interest* to pay and, finally *taxes*. What's left is called *net profit* – the amount ultimately available to the business owners. Provided net profit is positive, the business is financially viable. For many businesses, net profit will be negative in the early start-up phase. What you are looking for in your profit forecast is the break-even point where your sales have built up sufficiently that you cross from losses into net profit.

Balance sheet forecast

Unlike companies, sole traders are not required to produce a balance sheet. However, it is good practice to have one, and to include forecasts of it in your business plan, since a balance sheet forecast will help you cross-check that your profit forecasts make sense and that your business will be solvent (meaning that its assets – what it owns – exceed its liabilities – what it owes). Table 8.3 shows the basic structure of a balance sheet.

The balance sheet is a snapshot of everything a business owns and owes on a particular date, typically the business financial year end. Current assets and current liabilities cover items that normally turn over during a year and tend to be very liquid (easily turned into cash or called in for payment). By contrast, other assets and other liabilities tend to be held for many years and are typically less liquid.

Current assets include, for example, *cash in bank accounts*, money owed by customers or clients (*debtors*), items not yet received that the business has already paid for, and finished goods yet to be sold (*inventory*) and raw

Table 8.3   Balance sheet forecast

Assets	Balance sheet date	Liabilities	Balance sheet date
Current assets		**Current liabilities**	
Cash at bank	....	Overdraft	....
Debtors	....	Creditors	....
Payments in advance	....	Accounts payable	....
Inventory and supplies	....	Taxes payable	....
Other	....	Other	....
Total current assets (A)	....	*Total current liabilities (D)*	....
Other assets		**Other liabilities**	
Property, plant and equipment	....	Long-term loans	....
Investments	....	Bonds	....
Intangible assets	....	Owner's/shareholders' equity	....
Total other assets (B)	....	*Total other liabilities (E)*	....
Total assets (A + B) = C	....	**Total liabilities (D + E) = C**	....

materials (*supplies*). Other assets include things like buildings, machinery, office equipment, vehicles (*property, plant and equipment*), any *investments* the business has (for example, holding shares in another company), and *intangible assets*, such as customer goodwill and the value of brand names (due to customer recognition and loyalty).

Current liabilities include any *overdraft* at the bank, money the business owes for example for supplies already received (*creditors* and *accounts payable*) and for *taxes* due but not yet paid. Other liabilities includes *long-term loans* from banks and other organizations, and money the business has borrowed by issuing *bonds* (securities usually tradeable on a stock exchange). The difference between these two groups of liabilities and total assets is what belongs to the owner of a sole-trader business or the shareholders of a company (*owner's/shareholders' equity*), and by convention this is shown in the liability section of the balance sheet.

The general principle behind the balance sheet is double-entry book-keeping, which means that for every entry in one area of a business's accounts there is an equal and opposite entry in a corresponding area. The result is that, in the balance sheet, by definition total assets and total liabilities (shown in the final line in Table 8.3) must be equal. For example, if the business has made a net profit that increases owner's/shareholders' equity on the liability side, there will usually be an equal increase in cash at bank on the asset side.

Comparing the balance sheet forecast from one year to the next can help you track the likely ongoing health of your business. For example, a healthy sign would be owner's/shareholders' equity increasing from one balance sheet to the next. If current assets are less than current liabilities, this indicates a situation in which a business may struggle to meet immediate debts and so may face liquidity problems.

Raising finance

As mentioned at the start of this chapter, many older entrepreneurs have other sources of income apart from their business. That income, existing savings or a lump sum drawn from pension savings (see Chapter 3) may be enough to start a business without needing to raise finance elsewhere.

As noted earlier, there are two reasons for needing finance: as working capital, or as a longer-term investment to finance start-up or expansion. Working capital is – or should be – short-term by its nature, since the aim is to cover the lag between spending on production and receiving the receipts from sale. Typically, you might use a bank overdraft, which is a short-term form of borrowing, to cover your working capital needs. You have seen how a cash flow forecast can help you to spot when you will need an injection of working capital. A bank is likely to be more impressed by your overdraft request if you make it well in advance in anticipation of your forecast needs with a clear indication of when the overdraft will be paid off than if you have to borrow in a crisis.

Friends or family may also be a source of short-term financial help, but you should bear in mind that if you are unable to repay the money when agreed your relationship with them could be at risk. Similarly, you might want to be wary of inviting friends and family to make a longer-term investment in your business and consider how the situation might develop if you lost their money.

For a small business, banks have traditionally been a source of longer-term business loans. You can approach any bank that offers small business loans; it doesn't have to be your normal bank. However, an alternative is to borrow through a peer-to-peer platform, such as Funding Circle (fundingcircle. com), Assetz Capital (assetzcapital.co.uk) and Thin Cats (thincats.com). Peer-to-peer platforms bring would-be investors directly together with borrowers, without any bank or other intermediary in the middle. This generally means that savers can get a better return and borrowers may pay less than a bank would have charged. Many peer-to-peer lenders belong to the trade body, Peer-2-Peer Finance Association – you can find a list of its members at p2pfa.org.uk/platforms.

If you are thinking of business on an altogether larger scale, you may want to seek funding from 'business angels' – individuals and organizations that back entrepreneurs or venture capital funds. This will usually involve selling shares in your company in exchange for an injection of capital. For more information, see the UK Business Angels Association (ukbaa.org.uk) and the British Private Equity and Venture Capital Association (bvca.co.uk).

Recognizing problems

Few businesses operate completely smoothly without a few downs as well as ups, so it can be hard to distinguish a temporary problem from signals that the business is failing. The most important thing is to keep an eye on your financial records. Cash flow forecasts and balance sheets may seem like a dry set of numbers but, like a painting-by-numbers set, once you colour them in, they become rich pictures of the state of your business, so this is a good place to start. You should regularly – say, monthly or quarterly, depending on the scale of your business – check how your business is performing against the previous forecast and then roll your forecast forward, revising it as necessary in the light of performance so far and any other new information. Based on these forecasts, you can set out a budget that reflects your plans for dealing with any problems the forecasts throw up.

In the cash flow forecast, an occasional end-period negative bank balance is likely simply to indicate the 'lumpiness' of the timing of receipts and expenses. If you and your bank are happy with an occasional temporary overdraft to cover this, it need not be a problem. However, you might want to investigate the cause of the lumpiness and whether there are steps you can take to smooth out the flows, for example, finding new sales outlets for low-season periods, getting customers to pay more quickly or spreading your purchases more evenly. Over time, you could aim to retain more profit within the business bank account to build up the business's working capital.

However, if the cash flow forecast shows a consistent and growing negative bank balance, then you have a liquidity problem that needs action now to stop it getting worse. Broadly, there are five possible underlying problems: your sales are too low, your prices are too low, customers are failing to pay you on time (or at all), your costs are too high, or you are expanding out of line with the working capital you have available. You need to identify and resolve the underlying problem.

While you do so, you may be able to increase your working capital by injecting more cash yourself, borrowing more, finding new investors or reorganizing your balance sheet. If you are already borrowing heavily, lenders may be unwilling to lend you more and you may struggle to keep up the repayments. New investment may look unattractive unless you have a convincing way to tackle the underlying problem. There may be assets on the balance sheet that could be sold to raise cash, but it may take time to sell them and they may have to be sold at a knock-down price. Selling could be a false move if the assets are essential to the business, though you might investigate whether leasing equipment or vehicles you need could be more cost-effective than owning them. You might be able to replace short-term debt (such as an overdraft) with cheaper, longer-term debt. However, you should be wary of restructuring your debts if it means securing new ones against your home because, if the loan repayments are not met, you could lose your home. While on this unhappy journey, you might also adopt some other strategies, such as failing to pay your suppliers on time – but this could cause more problems, as it puts stress on their businesses, and they may stop supplying you or insist on money upfront.

If you get to the point where the liabilities (excluding owner's/shareholders' capital) on your balance sheet exceed your assets, the business is insolvent. A company is also deemed insolvent under the Insolvency Act 1986 if it can no longer meet its day-to-day obligations. At the point of insolvency, your business is bust. If your business is a limited company, as a director you lose the protection of limited liability and can be made personally liable for the company's debts if you trade while knowingly insolvent. The same applies to partners in an LLP. Sole traders and partners in an ordinary partnership do not in any case have limited liability and so are always putting their personal assets at risk.

When you are in the thick of running your business, it can be very hard to be objective and admit that the business has no future. Ideally, you need to spot the signs and stop before you reach the point of insolvency. Alarm bells should ring if any of the following apply:

- Your cash flow forecasts show a persistent deficit, especially if it is growing.
- You are no longer paying some or all of your suppliers on time.
- One or more major customers or clients are failing to pay you on time.
- You are up to your overdraft limit with the bank.
- Your gearing ratio (liabilities as a percentage of assets) is high.
- You have been refused further credit or loans for your business.
- Your current asset ratio (current assets divided by current liabilities) is close to or below one.
- You are having to sell business assets.

Dealing with tax

The taxes you pay as a result of running a business depend mainly on your business format, but can also be affected by the size of your business, and your age. You may have to collect tax on your sales and pay tax related to your business premises, profits and any gain you make on the sale of your business.

Tax on sales

Whatever the format of your business, you must by law register for Value Added Tax (VAT) if your turnover (revenue from sales) will be more than £85,000. VAT is a tax on sales that is ultimately paid by the final consumer, but it is collected by each business in the supply chain. If you are registered for VAT, you must normally charge VAT on your sales (called your outputs in the language of VAT) by adding 20 per cent (2019/20 rate) to the price you charge your customers, but you can claim back VAT you paid on your purchases (inputs). Regularly (usually once a quarter), you complete a VAT return in which you report the VAT you've collected and the amount you are claiming, and hand over the difference to HMRC.

There are some exceptions because some goods and services are exempt from VAT, including for example Royal Mail postal charges (but not postal services provided by others), many financial and insurance services (but not advice or bookkeeping). Some organizations are exempt, in particular charities. Some goods and services are subject to VAT, but the rate is set at 0 per cent – this includes, for example, most food and drink (but not hot food, confectionary, snacks, ice cream, soft drinks or mineral water), children's clothes, books and water supplies. Domestic energy supplies are taxed at a low rate of 5 per cent (but supplies to business premises are usually taxed at the standard rate of 20 per cent). The distinction between exempt and zero-rated might seem a bit academic. However, an exempt supplier cannot claim back VAT on inputs, while a zero-rated supplier can.

Being VAT-registered normally poses no problem if your customers are other businesses, since they can normally claim back the VAT you charge them (since your output is their input). However, if your customers are individuals and households, adding VAT inevitably makes your prices higher. This could be a problem if many of your competitors are too small to have to pay VAT. In that situation, either you add VAT to your ideal price and see your competitors undercut you or you have to reduce your base price (and so your profit margin) in order to align your end-price (including VAT) with the rest of the market.

If your turnover does not exceed £85,000, you can if you choose voluntarily register for VAT. This might be worth doing if, for example, your customers are other businesses and you pay VAT on most of your supplies which you could reclaim if registered. Being registered for VAT might also lend extra credibility to your business in the eyes of clients or customers. However, since April 2019, being VAT-registered has become more onerous because of a new system for reporting VAT called Making Tax Digital (MTD).

MTD is a government initiative to make the reporting of more taxes electronic, starting with VAT (though with plans eventually to extend it to corporation tax and income tax). It applies to VAT-registered businesses with a turnover above £85,000. If you are registered but your turnover is less, you don't have to join, but can voluntarily opt into MTD. Under MTD, you have to keep your VAT records digitally and submit returns using software that is compatible with HMRC systems; Excel spreadsheets will not suffice. Compatible software is provided by many commercial accounting software providers, and HMRC has an online search tool of suppliers at gov.uk/guidance/find-software-thats-compatible-with-making-tax-digital-for-vat. For a small business that does not already use a commercial accounting package, the software might cost from around £9 a month, though you will not need your own software if your accountant (if you use one) manages MTD for you. In limited cases you can ask to be exempted from MTD, for example, because you cannot use computers or the internet due to age, disability or where you live. To claim exemption, call HMRC VAT general enquiries on 0300 200 3700.

For more information about VAT, see gov.uk/vat-businesses. For guidance on how to register, see gov.uk/vat-registration.

Business rates

Business rates are a tax due on most non-domestic properties, such as shops, offices, workshops, holiday rental homes, guest houses and stables. They may also apply to any part of your home that you use exclusively for business (see *Where you will work* earlier in this chapter). Business rates are administered by your local council.

Business rates are calculated by multiplying the rateable value of the property by a multiplier. However, the detail of business rates differs depending on which nation of the UK you live in. In England, rateable value is the commercial rental value of the property on 1 April 2015. There are two multipliers: a standard multiplier and a lower small business multiplier which applies to properties with a rateable value below £51,000. In 2019/20, the small business multiplier is 49.1p. For example, if the rateable value of your business premises is £10,000 a year, your business rates would be £4,910 a year (£10,000 x 49.1p). However, you may qualify for one of several business rate reliefs which reduce or eliminate the bill. In particular, you might be able to get small business rate relief, in which case, there are no business rates on a property with a rateable value of £12,000 or less (100 per cent relief) and, for values between £12,001 and £15,000, the relief gradually tapers from 100 to 0 per cent. You might be able to get hardship relief if you are facing financial difficulties. For a full list of the various reliefs available, see gov.uk/apply-for-business-rate-relief.

The system in Wales is broadly the same as for England, but small business rate relief is 100 per cent for premises with a rateable value up to £6,000 and tapered between £6,001 and £12,000. For further details about the various reliefs, visit businesswales.gov.wales/business-rates-relief-in-wales. In Scotland, rateable values were last reviewed in 2017. The multiplier is called 'poundage' and is slightly lower for small businesses at 49p in 2019/20. Scotland has a more extensive range of reliefs, which are outlined at mygov.scot/business-rates-relief/. Rateable values were last assessed in 2013 in Northern Ireland. There are two parts to the multiplier: a regional rate set by the Northern Ireland Executive (34.01p in 2019/20) and a district rate set by the local council and different in each part of the nation. For more information, see nibusinessinfo.co.uk/content/business-rates-basics.

If you think business rates will apply to you, contact your local council when you first start up in order to be included in the rating system and to apply for rate relief: gov.uk/find-local-council.

Tax for sole traders and partners

As explained earlier in this chapter, there is no separate legal identity for a business run by a sole trader or partner. The profits from the business are part of their personal income and subject to income tax along with all their other income. You might also have to pay National Insurance contributions, but not if you have reached State Pension age – see Chapter 3 for information. The income tax rules for sole traders and partners are more generous than for employees (allowing the self-employed, for example, to claim tax relief for a wider variety of expenses and also for losses), so you may need to satisfy HMRC that you are genuinely self-employed.

Are you self-employed?

Whether or not you count as genuinely self-employed for tax purposes depends on the facts of your relationship with each client or customer. Confusingly, the tax legislation on employment status is separate from the employment legislation, so HMRC could deem that you are really an employee for tax purposes, even if the organization hiring you does not and so does not give you the rights that an employee would have (such as a minimum wage, sick pay and paid holiday leave). The sort of facts that will tend to indicate you are genuinely self-employed rather than an employee, include:

- you have the right to turn down work;
- you choose where you work;
- you choose the hours you work;
- you are paid a fixed sum for the work;
- your own money is at risk;
- you have to put right mistakes at your own cost;
- you provide the main equipment needed to do your work;
- you have the right to provide a substitute to do the work;
- you can employ others to help you carry out the work;
- you have more than one customer or client.

HMRC is also concerned to distinguish self-employment from activities that do not amount to running a business, such as hobbies or one-off transactions. HMRC uses 'badges of trade' to help it make these judgements, and you are more likely to be deemed to be genuinely in business if your intention is to make a profit, the activity is systematic and repeated, the things you are selling have value mainly through being sold, the way you sell them is typical for a trading organization, and the things you are selling are normally in your possession for only a short time.

GOV.UK has an employment status indicator tool that can help you work out if you are likely to be accepted as self-employed: gov.uk/guidance/check-employment-status-for-tax.

Registering your business

To ensure that you pay the right taxes on time and so avoid any penalties, you should register your business as soon as possible after starting up. You are, in any case, required to let HMRC know of any untaxed source of income within six months of the end of the tax year in which you received the income, so the very latest you should register is 5 October in the tax year after the one when you started up. You can register your business either through HMRC's online services system or by completing form CWF1. For details, see gov.uk/log-in-file-self-assessment-tax-return/register-if-youre-self-employed or phone the Self-Assessment helpline on 0300 200 3310.

National Insurance

Business people who are sole traders or partners, who are under State Pension age, must usually pay Class 2 and Class 4 National Insurance.

Class 2 contributions are set at a flat weekly rate (£3 a week in 2019/20). However, they are voluntary if your profits (or share of profits in the case of a partner) are less than a small profits threshold (£6,365 in 2019/20). Class 2 contributions help you build up state retirement pension. The maximum number of years of contributions that you need for the maximum State Pension is 35. Therefore, if you have fewer than 35 years of National Insurance contributions on your record, it is likely to be worth paying Class 2 contributions even if your profits are below the small profits threshold. Each year's worth of contributions would cost you £156 and qualify you for over £250 a year of index-linked State Pension. (Bear in mind though that you need at least 10 years of contributions to qualify for any State Pension at all.) The requirement to pay Class 2 contributions stops from the start of the week in which you reach State Pension age.

Class 4 National Insurance contributions are a percentage (9 per cent in 2019/20) of your annual profits between a lower and upper limit (£8,632 and £50,000, respectively in 2019/20) and 2 per cent of profits above that limit. Class 4 contributions do not carry any entitlement to build up State Pension. Class 4 contributions stop from 6 April following the year in which you reach State Pension age.

Both Class 2 and Class 4 contributions are collected through the Self-Assessment tax system that applies to income tax (see the following section).

Income tax

Your business profits are added to your other income for the tax year, and income tax is then calculated as described in Chapter 4. However, there are many adjustments you can make when calculating your business profits, and there can be a substantial delay between making the profits and paying tax on them.

Your profit is basically your sales revenue less expenses, so your profit and loss account is the starting point for calculating your profit for tax purposes. For tax, you are allowed to deduct all expenses that you incur 'wholly and exclusively' for business purposes. In practice, where mixed expenses can be transparently split between private and business, you can also deduct the business part. For example, if you work from home, you can deduct a proportion of the cost of energy bills, basing the proportion on the number of rooms in the home and the percentage of time that one or more rooms are used for business. You will not need to apportion by time if you use part of your home exclusively for business. However, exclusive business use could mean that you have to pay capital gains tax (CGT) on part of any profit you make when you sell your home (see Chapter 4) and might mean you are liable for business rates on that part.

Some expenses are disallowed, including the cost of capital items and depreciation. Instead, you claim capital allowances which are, broadly speaking, depreciation calculated according to standardized tax rules. If you make a loss, you usually have several options, including, for example, carrying the loss forward to set against future profits or carrying the loss 'sideways' to set against other non-business income for the same tax year. If you use an accountant, he or she can advise you on what you can claim. If you want to check the rules yourself, there is a wealth of information at gov.uk/hmrc-internal-manuals/business-income-manual.

Once your business has been running for a while, you will normally be taxed on the profits you made during your accounting year which ends in the current tax year. (A tax year runs from 6 April to the following 5 April.) It's up to you to choose your accounting year end – for example, you might choose the calendar year to 31 December, or the year to 30 April. In the first example, your taxable income for 2019/20 would include the profits you made in the year to 31 December 2019 (since that date falls in the 2019/20 tax year). In the second example, taxable income for 2019/20 would include profits made in the year to 30 April 2019. This means that the earlier in the tax year your accounting date falls, the longer the delay before your profits are taxed. Slightly different rules apply in the first few years of your business and the closing years, and you can find details in the HMRC Helpsheet HS222 *How to calculate your taxable profit* available from gov.uk. If you choose an accounting year of 31 March, your accounting year will be treated as if it is the same as the tax year (called 'fiscal accounting'), in which case there are no special opening and closing year rules. This simplifies your tax affairs, but does minimize the period between making the profits and paying tax on them.

You must fill in a tax return each year in which you declare all your income, including your business profits. Once you have registered your business, HMRC will automatically contact you to remind you to do this. There is a separate section of the return for self-employment and the questions guide you through the amounts you need to enter. There is a short version of the section that you can use if your turnover is less than £85,000 (2019/20). You can complete a paper version of the tax return, though most people these days complete the online version using HMRC's free software. Paper tax returns must be sent in (filed) by 31 October following the end of the tax year, and online returns by 31 January. For example, the 2019/20 tax return will have to be filed by 31 October 2020 (paper) or 31 January 2021 (online). If you miss the 31 January filing deadline, there is an automatic £100 fine.

If you owe less than £3,000 in tax and want it collected through Pay-As-You-Earn (PAYE) (for example, by deduction from a private pension that you get), you will need to submit your return by 31 December (so, 31 December 2020 in the case of the 2019/20 tax return). For information about PAYE, see Chapter 4. If the PAYE option does not apply, you pay tax in two payments on account: the first on 31 January during the tax year; the second on 31 July following the end of the tax year, unless your last Self-Assessment bill was less than £1,000. For example, the tax you owe for 2019/20 is paid on 31 January 2020 and 31 July 2020. These are estimates which are set at half the income tax for the previous year less any part paid through PAYE and half the National Insurance bill for the previous year. Once your tax return is filed (by January 2021 for the 2019/20 tax year), the exact bill can be calculated and you will either have a balancing charge to pay by 31 January (for the 2019/20 tax return if there is extra tax to pay, on 31 January 2021) or receive a refund if you have overpaid.

Note that three important events happen on 31 January: it's the latest date for filing your tax return; it is also the latest date for paying any balancing charge due on last year's income; and it is the date on which the first payment on account for this year's income is due. If your profits are rising, this can mean you have a hefty sum to pay on 31 January, as the case study shows.

CASE STUDY

Margaret runs a business from home making chutneys and preserves. These have become popular and she has had several large orders, leading to an expansion in her production and rising profits. In 2018/19, her income tax and National Insurance bill was £10,000. For 2019/20, her payments on account were each set at half this, so she paid £5,000 on 31 January 2020 and £5,000 on 31 July 2020. When she files her tax return on 31 January 2021, it turns out that her total tax bill for the year is £14,000. She has already paid £10,000 through the payments on account, but that leaves a £4,000 balancing charge to be paid by 31 January 2021. On that date, she must also pay her first payment on account for the 2020/21 tax year, which is set at half her 2019/20 bill, in other words £7,000 (half of £14,000). Therefore, the total Margaret must pay on 31 January 2021 is £11,000 (£4,000 + £7,000).

You need to keep the records on which the business section of your tax return is based for five years after the filing date. You can be fined £3,000 if you cannot produce your records. In practice you may want to keep your records for longer, because HMRC can go back up to 20 years if they suspect tax fraud. HMRC can and do get things wrong, but it would be hard to defend your position if you no longer had the records on which your tax declarations were based.

Tax if you operate as a company

If you set up your business as a company, it has a separate legal identity from you. Your company and you have different taxes to pay.

Corporation tax

As explained earlier in this chapter, you must register your company with Companies House. Normally, this automatically triggers its registration for tax and, within 14 days, you should receive the company's tax number from HMRC. In some cases – for example, if you registered with Companies House by post or through an agent – you will need to make a separate registration for corporation tax, and you should do this within three months of starting to do business to avoid any penalty. Further information is at gov. uk/limited-company-formation/set-up-your-company-for-corporation-tax.

For tax purposes, the profits a small company makes are calculated in broadly the same way as described for a sole trader above. The company must pay corporation tax on these profits at a rate of 19 per cent (2019/20), due to fall to 18 per cent in 2020/21. The after-tax profits may be retained within the company or all or part may be paid out to shareholders.

Corporation tax has to be paid no later than nine months and one day after the end of the company's accounting year. For example, if the accounting year end is 31 December, the tax must be paid by the following 1 October. Most small companies hire an accountant who will deal with corporation tax reporting and payment details, along with the company's other annual filing commitments.

National Insurance

As a director of your company, you are an employee. You may decide to draw a salary from the company, in which case both you and the company normally have to pay Class 1 National Insurance.

Assuming you are under State Pension age, employee contributions are paid at a rate of 12 per cent on earnings between a primary threshold (£166 a week in 2019/20) and an upper earnings limit (£962 a week in 2019/20) and 2 per cent on earnings above that. Earnings of at least a lower earnings limit (£118 a week in 2019/20) count towards building up state retirement pension. Therefore, if you have not already reached the 35 years of contributions needed to qualify for the maximum State Pension, you might want to make sure your company pays you at least the amount of the lower earnings limit. Once an employee reaches State Pension age, they stop paying National Insurance.

Your company has a number of obligations as your employer. It must pay employer's National Insurance contributions at a rate of 13.8 per cent on any of your pay above a secondary threshold of £166 a week (2019/20). This applies even where the employee is over State Pension age. Unless all employees (including you) earn less than the lower earnings limit, the company must also set up a PAYE system to collect any income tax and National Insurance you (the employee) owe, and pass all the National Insurance and income tax to HMRC. There is information at gov.uk/paye-for-employers. However, many small companies contract this task out to their accountant or a specialist payroll company. To find a payroll company, search online for 'payroll services'.

Any earnings your company pays you count as expenses of the business and so reduce the amount of corporation tax the company pays.

Income tax

As an employee, if you draw earnings from your company, these are taxable in exactly the same way as earnings from any other job would be (see Chapter 4).

As a shareholder, you may receive dividends paid out by your company. Dividend income is also subject to income tax, but at different rates from those applicable to earnings. Chapter 4 explains how the income tax personal allowance and tax bands are applied to different types of income in a strict sequence. The tax you pay on dividends depends on the tax band into which they fall:

- no tax on dividends covered by your personal allowance;
- the first £2,000 (2019/20) of dividends that fall into the basic-, higher- or additional-rate bands are tax-free because they are covered by your Dividend Allowance;

- remaining dividends that fall into the basic-rate band are taxed at a rate of 7.5 per cent;

- remaining dividends that fall into the higher-rate band are taxed at a rate of 32.5 per cent;

- remaining dividends that fall into the additional-rate band are taxed at a rate of 38.1 per cent.

The tax rates on dividends are lower than the rates on, say, earnings, pensions and savings income, reflecting the fact that they have already had some tax (corporation tax) deducted while in the hands of the company.

For younger taxpayers, a big attraction of being paid with dividends rather than earnings is that there is no National Insurance to pay on dividend income. You might think this advantage does not apply if you are already over State Pension age, since you no longer pay National Insurance in any case, but bear in mind that your company does still have to pay employer's National Insurance on earnings, so dividends would reduce the total tax payable by your company and you.

CASE STUDY

George is a plumber and operates through a limited company. He is aged 60 and a basic-rate taxpayer. The company has made £10,000 profit before tax this year, and George is considering a couple of different ways of drawing this money out:

- Take maximum earnings. This would be an expense for the company, deductible when working out profits. The profits would therefore be zero, wiping out any corporation tax bill. However, the £10,000 would need to cover both the earnings paid to George and the employer National Insurance contributions on those earnings. The company can afford to pay George £8,807 with an employer's National insurance bill of £1,193. On earnings of £8,807, George would pay employee's National Insurance of £1,037 and income tax of £1,761. Out of the £10,000, George would receive £6,009 and HMRC £3,991.

- Take maximum dividends. The company would pay corporation tax at 19 per cent (2019/20) on the profits, leaving £8,100 to be paid out as dividends. In George's hands, the first £2,000 of dividends would be tax-free (covered by his Dividend Allowance) and the remainder taxed at 7.5 per cent. Out of the £10,000, George would end up with £7,642 and HMRC £2,358.

Personal service companies beware

As you can see from the case study above, director/shareholders of a company have the potential to save tax by paying themselves fully or partly in the form of dividends – a happy state of affairs! Clients have also been happy with this arrangement because it has meant they have not been involved in the administration of tax on the amounts they pay you – that was all dealt with by your own company. However, in the case of personal service companies, this state of affairs has been under a sustained attack from HMRC, starting with some rules introduced in 2000 and generally referred to as 'IR35', which have been tightened further in recent years and are now also known as the 'off-payroll working' rules.

A personal service company is not defined in law but is basically where, through your own company, you are providing consultancy, IT skills or similar to your clients. Often, providing these types of services involves working at your client's premises, possibly for set hours, using their office equipment and maybe being paid by the hour rather than a set fee. If you look back to the section of this chapter called *Are you self-employed?*, you can see that these kind of work arrangements might be considered closer to being an employee of the client rather than genuinely running your own business. HMRC has described the purpose of the rules as follows:

> 'A worker is involved in off-payroll working when they work for a client through their own intermediary, often a personal service company (PSC), but would be an employee if they were providing their services directly. As off-payroll workers are paid through their own intermediary, they pay Income Tax and National Insurance contributions (NICs) in a different way to an employee. The off-payroll working rules are in place to make sure that where an individual would've been an employee if they were providing their services directly, they pay broadly the same tax and NICs as an employee.'

Currently, the rules work in different ways depending on whether a client is a public sector organization or a private sector firm. If public sector, that organization is responsible for deciding if you would in effect be an employee apart from the existence of your company and, if so, must deduct tax and National Insurance from the fees it pays you as if you were its employee. If your client is in the private sector, then, until 2020, you are responsible for deciding if the rules apply, and your company will need to pay income tax and National Insurance as if your fee income is paid as earnings from your company (even if in fact you draw part or all of the money out as dividends).

There are penalties and interest charges if HMRC deems you have got the decision wrong. The rules apply on a contract-by-contract basis, so you could find that you are deemed genuinely in business for yourself regarding one contract but a de facto employee with another. For more information about how the rules work, see gov.uk/guidance/ir35-what-to-do-if-it-applies. From April 2020, your private sector clients will take over responsibility for deciding your employment status and operating the rules (in the same way as public sector clients already do).

The rules are controversial and the application of them is seldom clear-cut. However, you should be prepared for clients to take a cautious approach, which means they are likely to tax you as if you are an employee just to be on the safe side and protect themselves from potential HMRC investigation and penalties.

Tax when you sell your business

If your business involves simply selling your skills – whether as, say, a consultant or a gardener – there might not be any business as such to sell when you decide to stop working. However, other types of business may have substantial value, in their premises, brands, patents for unique products, stock of raw materials and finished goods and other assets. This means that you may be able to sell your business as an ongoing concern or sell off assets if the business is to close down. If you make a profit from the sale, you may have to pay CGT. However, you can usually claim entrepreneur's relief.

CGT is a tax on any gain made when you dispose of an asset (although some assets and disposals are exempt – see Chapter 4). 'Disposal' extends beyond just selling an asset, so would also cover giving your business away (for example, to your adult children). Gains are added to any taxable income made in the same year to determine the rates at which CGT is charged. The normal rates of CGT on gains (other than from residential property) are 10 per cent for gains falling into the basic-rate band of tax and 20 per cent for anything more. Entrepreneur's relief reduces the rate to 10 per cent on the whole gain.

The relief is available whatever the format of your business (sole trader, partnership, company). For sole traders and partners, to be eligible you must have owned the business for at least two years before you sell it. In the case of a company, you must have been an employee or office-holder (meaning an unpaid director or company secretary) for at least two years, and the company's main activities must be trading (as opposed to simply holding investments, say).

There is further information at gov.uk/entrepreneurs-relief.

Other rules and regulations

Depending on the type of business you have and the activities it involves, there may be a whole range of other rules and regulations that you will need to be aware of and abide by. It is not possible to cover every possibility here, but this section highlights a few of the most common areas.

Data protection

There have long been laws to protect people's personal data, but they became tougher with the introduction of the General Data Protection Regulation (GDPR) from May 2018. Personal data means any data by which an individual can be recognized, such as their name, address, e-mail address and, depending on how data is used and combined with other information, could include many other aspects too. See ico.org.uk for more information. You are likely to be handling and processing personal data in relation to your customers and any employees that you have.

You must have a lawful purpose for needing personal data. This might be, for example, that the data is essential for you to carry out the contract you have with the individual, or you are legally required to have the information. Before gathering personal data, you must make clear to the person involved why you need their data, how it will be used, how long you will keep it and whether you will be sharing the data with others – details such as these should be set out in a 'privacy notice'. You must obtain the person's explicit consent to collecting and using their data and, in most cases, they can withdraw their consent at any time, in which case you should normally erase their data. You must use the data only for the purposes you stated and store it no longer than necessary. The data must be stored securely and destroyed safely when no longer required and, if a data breach does occur, you must report it promptly to the Information Commissioner's Office (ICO). Individuals have a right to request a copy of the personal data you hold about them. Anyone in your business who handles personal data needs to understand their responsibilities and obligations under GDPR.

The ICO has produced guidance and an interactive checklist for small businesses to understand what personal data they use and their obligations under the law: ico.org.uk/for-organisations/in-your-sector/business.

Hiring employees

Of the 4.8 million people recorded in government statistics as being self-employed, 4 million work on their own or with a partner but have no employees at all. Moving from working alone to employing someone is a big leap both in costs and administration. Some aspects to consider are touched on below. A good source of further information is Acas (Advisory, Conciliation and Arbitration Service): acas.org.uk.

Avoiding discrimination

Under the Equality Act 2010, it is illegal to discriminate in the workplace because of a 'protected characteristic': age, disability, gender reassignment, marriage and civil partnership, pregnancy and maternity, race, religion or belief, sex, or sexual orientation. This applies to all aspects of work, including recruitment. Unless there is some objective reason that is crucial to the work, your job advertisements cannot discriminate either in favour of or against anyone with a protected characteristic. Be alert to indirect as well as direct discrimination – for example, you would be indirectly discriminating on the grounds of age if you asked for new graduates or people with a minimum number of years' experience. Be aware too that data protection legislation gives applicants the right to see any personal data you hold about them, including notes you make about why you turned them down for a job.

Right to work in the UK

The government requires you to check that anyone you take on has the right to work in the UK. You can be fined up to £20,000 per worker if you fail to make this check. If you do employ someone illegally, you could be sent to jail for up to five years and face an unlimited fine.

The check normally involves inspecting the person's passport and, if applicable, their biometric residence permit. You are required to satisfy yourself that the document is genuine, dates for the right to work have not expired, photos look like the applicant and information across multiple documents is consistent. If the right-to-work is time-limited, you will need to do a further check later on to see if it has been extended. You must keep a copy of the documents. If the person cannot produce appropriate documents, you are required to ask the Home Office to check their immigration employment status. There is further information at gov.uk/government/collections/right-to-work-checks-employer-guidance.

Insurance

If you have employees, you must by law take out employer liability insurance. This provides you with cover against legal costs and compensation if an employee claims they have been injured or made ill by the work they do for you. Typically, the minimum level of cover will be £5 million. See the section on *Insurance* earlier in this chapter for how to buy this cover.

Contract of employment

A contract of employment is the agreement you make with your employee about their work, pay and conditions. The contract is not what is written down anywhere, but what you agreed which might have been purely orally. However, within a month of starting, your employee has the right to a written statement, outlining the main terms of the employment, and this should be based on the contract you agreed.

Minimum Wage

You must by law pay your employees at least the National Minimum Wage (under 25-year olds) or National Living Wage (25 and over). In 2019/20, the minimum hourly rates are:

- 25 and over: £8.21;
- 21 to 24: £7.70;
- 18 to 20: £6.15;
- under 18: £4.35;
- apprentice (any age): £3.90.

If you pay exactly the minimum, you will need to increase your employees' pay each April when the minimum rates change. Rates are published at gov. uk/national-minimum-wage-rates.

Working hours and paid holiday

Under current laws (stemming from European legislation), you cannot normally require employees to work more than 48 hours a week. However, an employee can choose to opt out of this restriction. They must do this in writing. More restricted hours apply to employees aged under 18.

Full-time employees are entitled by law to at least 5.6 weeks (28 days) paid holiday a year, which can include bank holidays. Part-time workers are entitled to a pro rata amount – for example, someone working three days a week would be entitled to 16.8 days of paid holiday (3 x 5.6). For more information, see acas.org.uk.

Registering as an employer and PAYE

If any of your employees (including you if you are an employee of your own company) earns at least the lower earnings limit (£118 a week in 2019/20), you will have to operate a PAYE system to report their earnings to HMRC and to collect and hand over the correct tax deductions. See gov.uk/paye-for-employers.

The first step is to register with HMRC as an employer up to two months before you start paying your employee(s), and before the first payday. HMRC will issue you with a PAYE reference number (takes about five days). You may already have registered if you operate as a company and pay yourself at least the lower earnings limit. To register, visit gov.uk/register-employer.

Automatic enrolment into a pension

All employers, regardless of size, must enrol their eligible employees into a pension scheme, pay at least a minimum contribution to the scheme and collect and pay in any contribution required from the employee. (This does not apply if the only employee is you as sole director of your own company.)

Eligible employees are those aged between 22 and State Pension age, earning more than a trigger amount (£10,000 a year in 2019/20). You must automatically enrol them in a pension scheme, although they have the right to opt out if they want to. You will need to re-enrol anyone who opts out every three years. Some other employees, while they do not have to be automatically enrolled, can ask to be included in the scheme (opt in). They are: employees aged 16 to 21 earning more than £10,000, employees who have reached State Pension age and earn more than £10,000, and employees aged 22 to 74 earning between £6,136 and £10,000 (2019/20 rates). Other employees can ask to be put into a pension scheme (not necessarily the automatic enrolment scheme), but you do not have to pay any contributions for them.

In 2019/20, the minimum contribution is 8 per cent of your employee's gross pay between a lower and upper limit (£6,136 and £50,000 in 2019/20), of which you must pay at least 3 per cent. The remaining contribution can come from the employee, in which case they would pay 4 per cent and a further 1 per cent will come from tax relief paid direct to the pension scheme by HMRC.

A financial adviser can help you choose and set up a suitable workplace pension scheme, though the simplest solution might be to enrol them in the government-backed scheme, NEST (the National Employment Savings Trust): nestpensions.org.uk. For full details about automatic enrolment, see thepensionsregulator.gov.uk.

Sick pay

If your employee on average earns at least the lower earnings limit (£118 per week in 2019/20), you must pay them Statutory Sick Pay (SSP) if they are unable to work due to illness for four or more days in a row. You must pay this from the fourth day of illness. The first three days may be paid at their normal rate or unpaid, depending on the terms in their contract of employment. Your employee must tell you they are off sick within seven days, or a shorter period if the contract of employment sets an earlier deadline. If your employee is off for more than seven days, they must provide a 'fit note' from their doctor. This will set out whether they can do no work or might be fit enough for some duties. In the latter case, you can discuss with your employee what work they could manage – for example, shorter hours, working from home or different tasks. If, when your employee returns, they have a disability, bear in mind that this is a protected characteristic, so you must not discriminate against them. Moreover, you have a duty to make reasonable changes in the workplace to enable them to do their job. Note that conditions such as cancer count as a disability.

SSP must be paid at a rate of £94.25 a week (in 2019/20) for a maximum of 28 weeks. You can pay more than this and/or for longer, if you choose. You make the payments through the payroll in the normal way, deducting income tax and National Insurance if applicable. There is no government help for employers with paying SSP. For more information, see the employer's guide to SSP at gov.uk/employers-sick-pay.

Parental rights

Employees who are parents usually have the right to a range of benefits that you must provide. They include:

- **Maternity leave** of up to 52 weeks for a new mother, part of which can be transferred to the father (called Shared Parental Leave).

- **Statutory Maternity Pay** (SMP) for new mothers up to 39 weeks which must be at least 90 per cent of average pay for the first six weeks and, after that, at least £148.68 a week (2019/20) or 90 per cent of average pay, whichever is lower. Part of this can be transferred to the father under the Shared Parental Leave scheme.

- **Paid paternity leave** of up to two weeks (in addition to any Shared Parental Leave). Statutory Paternity Pay (SPP) is payable during the two weeks at the same rate as SMP.

- **Adoption leave** for up to 52 weeks, and Statutory Adoption Pay (SAP) for up to 39 weeks at the same rates as SMP.

- **Unpaid parental leave,** after the employee has been with you for a year, of up to 18 weeks in total per child up to their 18th birthday. This is limited to a maximum of four weeks a year, unless you agree to a longer period.

- **Time off for family and dependents** to deal with an unexpected emergency, such as a child suddenly falling ill, childcare arrangements falling through at the last moment or an elderly parent having a fall. There is no minimum or maximum time off, but it should be 'reasonable'.

Find useful employer guides to all of these entitlements at gov.uk/browse/employing-people/time-off. You may be able to claim back from the government most or all of the amounts you pay out in SMP, SPP, SAP and Shared Parental Leave Pay. If you cannot afford to make the payments, you can apply for an advance. For details, see gov.uk/recover-statutory-payments.

Bear in mind that sex and pregnancy are both protected characteristics, so you may not discriminate either in recruitment or after appointment against an employee who takes time off for children.

Dismissal

Especially in a very small business, it can be tough if it turns out that you and your employee do not get on or they do not perform their job well. However, employees have rights and, if you dismiss an employee unfairly, they could take their case to an Employment Tribunal and you could end up being ordered to pay compensation.

While some employee rights – such as protection from discrimination and the right to sick pay – start from day one of their employment, full rights against unfair dismissal come into effect only once your employee has been with you for two years. Before that, you must still follow correct procedures, but it is easier to say goodbye to an underperforming employee. Moreover, it makes sense to have a probationary period (say, six months) during which you and your employee both know you are testing the water to see how the appointment works out. Dismissal should be the last resort, and you should talk through any problems with your employee, offering mentoring and training as required to bring them up to speed. Acas publishes a *Code of practice on disciplinary and grievance procedures* which sets out guidance on dealing with problems between employer and employee and the procedures to follow. While following the code is not a legal requirement, being able to show that you have followed it would support your side of the case if it did come to an Employment Tribunal. You can find the code at acas.org.uk.

In case you do decide to part company with an employee, it's important that the contract of employment sets out how much notice you will give them. Commonly, this might be one week during the probationary period and one month after that. If the contract does not include this information, statutory notice periods will apply which are: one week during the first two years (except the first month, when there is no minimum), two weeks when they have been with you two years, and at least one extra week for every year beyond two years.

Licence to practice

In some areas of work, it is illegal to offer your services to the public unless you have particular qualifications, abide by code of conduct rules, undertake regular continuous professional development and/or are recorded on a register of practitioners. For example, this applies throughout much of the financial services industry and the health industry if you will be in a public-facing role.

In other areas, while having a licence may not be a legal requirement, your standing may be enhanced if you are qualified or belong to a recognized professional body.

Waste disposal

If you spent most of your life as an employee, where discarded paper, old computers and other business waste magically disappears, it may come as a shock to find how difficult it can be to organize waste disposal as a small business.

Over the years, increasingly tough regulations have been introduced to ensure that waste is disposed of responsibly and recycled where possible. A domestic household taps into this system through local council kerbside collections and household recycling centres. However, you can be fined heavily for putting business waste into the household system. Businesses need alternative arrangements, and must usually pay to use these.

Some councils run schemes whereby local businesses can buy trade refuse sacks which are suitable for certain types of waste, such as paper. Other councils expect businesses to take out contracts with commercial waste handling firms. Council-run recycling centres will also usually accept business waste for a fee but, if you take waste there yourself, you will need a waste carrier's licence. Alternatively, you will need to hire a firm that does have a licence to take your waste there. You can find out about getting your own licence at gov.uk/waste-carrier-or-broker-registration. The licence is usually free if you are just transporting your own waste.

It is worth considering waste disposal at the time you buy supplies and you may wish, for example, to buy printer supplies from makers that run recycling schemes. Also check with your local council to see what arrangements it has for business waste: gov.uk/find-local-council. Use a search engine to find commercial waste contractors serving your area – try searching for 'business waste'.

Working with children or vulnerable adults

If your self-employment involves working with children or vulnerable adults – for example, because you tutor children, run children's dance classes or provide care services – your clients may want to be sure you have no unspent criminal convictions that would make you unsuitable for this work, by asking you to have a Disclosure and Barring Service (DBS) check. Even if not a requirement, you may feel that being able to provide the results of such a check will enhance your customers' or clients' confidence in you.

The DBS system is not really designed for the self-employed. Its main purpose is for employers to check whether employees and job applicants are suitable for roles that involve children or vulnerable adults. However, it is possible to request a basic check on yourself, which will result in a certificate that you can show to customers or clients. To do this, see gov.uk/request-copy-criminal-record. A basic check costs £25 (in 2019). There are more detailed DBS checks which you could obtain by going through an intermediary called a 'responsible organization' – for a list of these, see gov.uk/guidance/responsible-organisations.

Sources of help and advice

For help setting up and running a business, including the tax implications, consider using an accountant. The following professional bodies can provide a list of members:

- **Association of Chartered Certified Accountants**: accaglobal.com;
- **Institute of Chartered Accountants in England and Wales**: icaew.com;
- **Chartered Accountants Ireland**: charteredaccountants.ie;
- **Institute of Chartered Accountants of Scotland**: icas.com.

If you will be entering into a partnership, you are strongly advised to get legal advice from a solicitor. You can search the member lists of the following bodies:

- The **Law Society** – use its Find a Solicitor service to find legal advice in England, Wales and Scotland: solicitors.lawsociety.org.uk;
- The **Law Society of Northern Ireland**: lawsoc-ni.org/solicitors.aspx.

Information on tax and the laws applicable to small business is available at gov.uk.

There are several membership bodies that represent small businesses, for example lobbying government to promote small business interests, and often provide members with access to a range of benefits, such as guidance, membership events, legal advice, insurance deals, and so on. They are typically funded through annual membership fees. Organizations include:

- the **Association of Independent Professionals and the Self Employed**, which specializes in representing independent contractors, freelancers and consultants: ipse.co.uk;
- the **Federation of Small Businesses**: www.fsb.org.uk;
- the **Forum of Private Business**: fpb.org;
- your **local chamber of commerce** – find it through the website of the national body, British Chamber of Commerce, which includes a searchable directory of local chambers: britishchambers.org.uk;
- the **Professional Contractors Group**, which represents independent contractors and consultants in knowledge-based industries: pcgroup.prg.uk;
- the **Small Business Association**: sbauk.org.

09
Looking for paid work

Money is not the only benefit that flows from work. Studies show that work can also be a source of identity, self-esteem, social contact and even better health. In the UK, legislation against age discrimination in recruitment and workplace opportunities is well established, and it is gradually becoming the norm that retirement is no longer the cliff edge it once was. Many people enjoy moving into a phase of life where work continues but on a part-time or otherwise less frenetic basis, either with their existing employer or a new one.

Points to consider when choosing retirement employment should include:

- previous employers who might consider you for part-time jobs if you have enjoyed working for them;
- researching temporary job recruitment websites to find jobs that will be enjoyable;
- learning new skills that can lead to wider job options, if a fresh start is needed;
- when retirement is about to happen, asking present employers for part-time hours to help the transition;
- if money is not a factor, considering volunteer work or teaching and lecturing to pass on previous skills;
- not jumping at the first job offered – take time to weigh up your options and don't be scared to hold off for the right job.

Note that this chapter looks at work in retirement where you take on a job with an employer. Another option is to do freelance work or start your own business, and you'll find ideas on that in Chapter 8.

Financial considerations

Continuing to work can be a way of increasing your income, but there are some other financial aspects to consider.

Decisions about your State Pension

Your entitlement to State Pension depends purely on reaching State Pension age, and is not affected by whether you continue to work or how much other income you have. However, if you're still working, you might not need your State Pension yet and it may be pushing you into a higher tax bracket, so it may be worth deferring your State Pension – in which case it will be higher once it does start. For further details, see Chapter 3.

Decisions about your private pensions

Normally, employers cannot these days impose any particular retirement age. However, pension schemes can still set a normal pension age at which your full pension starts. If you start your pension earlier than the normal pension age, your pension will usually be lower and, if you start it later, it may be increased. (Chapter 3 has more details.)

Private pensions are of two types: you might belong to a company pension scheme run by your existing employer and/or a previous employer; and you might have one or more personal pension schemes that are either workplace schemes you took out through your job or schemes you arranged for yourself.

Company scheme with your existing employer

In many cases, you can start drawing your retirement pension even while continuing to work for the same employer. However, in some cases your pension payments stop or are reduced if you go back to work, particularly in public sector jobs. Check the rules of your scheme carefully and note any particular steps you need to take if you want to have both your pension and earnings from that job. If you retired early on health grounds with an ill-health pension, this is likely to stop if you recover enough to return to work, but could be replaced with your normal pension if you have reached the normal pension age for your scheme. If you received an enhanced early pension on taking voluntary redundancy, there may be restrictions on your coming back to work for the same employer.

You may be able to decide to put off starting your pension, in which case the pension might be higher when it does start – but check what rules apply in your scheme. If you start your pension, it's unlikely that any earnings you then get will count as pensionable, so you will not build up any further pension (and no pension contributions will be deducted from your pay). However, you could still save for a pension if you wanted to, using a personal scheme.

Company scheme with a previous employer

There is nothing to stop you drawing a pension from a previous employer's scheme and taking on work with a different employer. Check the scheme rules to see whether putting off starting the pension will mean it's higher when it does start.

Personal pension schemes

Whether workplace schemes or ones you arranged for yourself, with personal pensions you can decide when you want to start drawing your money out. You can draw a pension whether you are still working or not. There are more details about pensions in Chapter 3 and more about investments in Chapter 5.

National Insurance contributions (NICs)

Under current rules, once you reach State Pension age, you no longer pay National Insurance contributions (NICs) even if you carry on working.

When you reach your State Pension birthday, you need to show your employer proof of your age – usually your birth certificate or passport, if you have one. However, if you do not want your employer to see your documents, you can ask HMRC to provide you with a letter confirming that you've reached State Pension age. You might have a 'certificate of age exemption' issued some time ago. HMRC no longer issues these, but, if you have one, you can show that to your employer as proof.

Redundancy

If you have just been made redundant, or fear this is a possibility, see the information in Chapter 2, *Money and budgeting*.

Special measures to assist disabled people to work

Disability, like age, is a 'protected characteristic'. This means that, under the Equality Act 2010, it is illegal to discriminate in the workplace either directly or indirectly against someone with the characteristic. Direct discrimination can happen where you are deliberately excluded, for example from recruitment, training or promotion, because the employer decides you could not manage. Indirect discrimination can occur when your employer fails to make reasonable adjustments, such as making all general areas accessible for wheelchair users. You have these rights whether your disability is a physical or mental condition. It has been established that someone living with cancer has the same rights as anyone else with a disability.

The mental health charity, Scope, suggests that reasonable adjustments at work might include, for example, adapted equipment such as special chairs and voice-recognition software, lowered desks, modified entrances, changing your responsibilities, transferring tasks to a colleague, flexible working, working from home, reduced hours, or training colleagues to support you (for example, through deafness awareness training). If you are caring for someone with a disability, there is no requirement for your employer to make reasonable adjustments, but they must still not treat you less favourably than other employees because of the disability – if they do, it is called direct discrimination by association.

If you feel you are disadvantaged at work because of a disability, contact your human resources department to discuss measures that would help you. You might like to take a colleague, union representative, family member or friend with you to the meeting. If you're unhappy with your employer's response, seek advice, for example from your union if you belong to one or the Acas (Advisory, Conciliation and Arbitration Service) helpline: 0300 123 1100 or via online chat on the website: acas.org.uk. If Acas cannot help you reach agreement with your employer, you have the right to take your complaint to an employment tribunal.

Age discrimination and equality

Anti-age-discrimination legislation came into force in October 2006, and was enshrined in the Equality Act 2010. Under the Act, age is a 'protected characteristic' and it is illegal, except in a few situations, for employers to discriminate directly or indirectly against candidates or employees on account of age. Such discrimination might affect, for example, decisions about recruitment, training, pay, promotion or redundancy. The exception is where there is an objective reason for taking age into account, for example, the requirement for a young person to act the part of a youth in a theatrical production. While ageism is mainly thought of as affecting older workers, it is equally illegal to discriminate against younger people on the grounds of age.

Provided individuals are capable of doing their job, an employer cannot normally require them to retire at a specific retirement age. However, upper age limits are permitted in some jobs, such as the police, firefighting and the Armed Forces, because of the physical demands of the job. There is also an exception for pension schemes so that they are still allowed to set a normal pension age at which a person's full pension usually starts. But, in general, capacity to do the job should be based on the same objective factors, whatever the age of the employee and, if an older worker is underperforming, they should be given the same opportunities for improvement as any other employee.

Employees also have a right to request flexible working and, if (say) that option is available to younger workers with children, it might be discrimination if similar working arrangements were denied to older workers. However, while an employer must consider any request for flexible working, they can refuse if there are business grounds for doing so.

If you feel you have been discriminated against at work, you could raise the matter with your line manager, your trade union or the human resources department. If the issue cannot be resolved informally, you could pursue it further through your employer's formal grievance procedure. If that does not produce a satisfactory outcome, the next step is to use the Acas conciliation service and finally you could take your case to an employment tribunal. Acas publishes a useful guide called *Discrimination. What to do if it happens* which is available from the Publications section of the Acas website: acas.org.uk.

You have the same rights to complain and, if necessary, take your case to a tribunal, if you believe you have been unfairly treated during a recruitment process because of your age. However, it can be difficult to obtain evidence that age was a factor. Under data protection legislation, you have the right to request and see any notes made about you during the recruitment process if they are held on computer or in a structured filing system.

Assessing your abilities

Some people know exactly what job they want. They have planned their action campaign for months beforehand, done their research, prepared a CV and followed up selective openings. But, if you are not one of those few, knowing what you have to offer is an essential first step. Make a list of everything you have done, in both your formal career and ordinary life, including your outside interests. In particular, consider adding any practical or other skills, knowledge or contacts that you have acquired over the years. These could now prove especially useful. If, for example, you have done a lot of public speaking, fundraising, committee work or conference organization, these would be excellent transferable skills that would make you attractive to a prospective employer. As a result of writing everything down, many people find that they have far more to offer than they originally realized.

In addition to work skills, you should include your personal attributes and any special assets that would attract an employer. The list might include organizational abilities, a good telephone manner, communication skills, the ability to work well with other people, access to a car or willingness to do flexible hours. Maturity can also be a positive asset. Many employers prefer older people: they can be more reliable and less likely to be preoccupied with family and social demands. Also, in many newly established companies, run by young directors, a senior person's accumulated experience is often rated as especially valuable.

If you spend some time working on your personal branding, how to market yourself and to whom, you will become much more focused. It will help you form a clearer idea of the sorts of jobs that would suit you. Although it's sensible to keep an open mind and not limit your applications too narrowly, the worst mistake you can make is to answer scores of advertisements indiscriminately – and end up with a sackload of rejections, or, worse, no response at all. As a general rule when job hunting, the more accurate and targeted you can be in the application process, the more likely you are to succeed.

Many people find this extraordinarily difficult. After years of working in one occupation, it takes quite a leap in imagination to picture yourself in another role, even if it is in the same or a related area. If you intend to do something completely different it will be harder still, as your knowledge of what the job entails will probably be second-hand. Also, quite apart from the question of what you would enjoy, in many parts of the country the issue may be more a matter of what is available.

Talking to other people helps. Friends, family, work colleagues or business acquaintances may have useful information and moreover will quite likely be able to appraise your abilities more objectively than you can yourself. It could also be sensible to consult outside experts who specialize in adult career counselling, and whose advice may be more realistic than that of friends in the context of the current job market. If you are claiming Jobseeker's Allowance or means-tested out-of-work state benefits, you will have a 'work coach' whose role is, in theory, to identify your skills and help you find suitable work. But in practice, like so many public services, this area tends to be under-resourced; your work coach may have little more than 10 minutes to advise you and may be more concerned to ensure that your claim for benefits is valid rather than advise you on finding a job. Whatever you decide to do, remember that with age and experience comes wisdom. You have the power to negotiate and you have the power to decide what you want to do next. Make sure you take a job that is right for you.

Training opportunities

Knowing what you want to do is one thing, but before starting a new job you may want to brush up existing skills or possibly acquire new ones. Most professional bodies have a full programme of training events, ranging from one-day seminars to courses lasting a week or longer. Additionally, adult education institutes run a vast range of courses or, if you are still in your present job, a more practical solution might be to investigate open and flexible learning, which you can do from home.

Open and flexible learning

Open and flexible learning is successfully helping to provide a greater range and flexibility of vocational education and training opportunities for individuals of all ages. In particular, it is designed to increase the scope for participants to learn at a time, place and pace best suited to their own particular circumstances.

The following organizations offer advice and an excellent range of courses:

- **Arden University:** offers online learning leading to degree-level qualifications particularly in more vocational subjects, such as accounting and finance, computing and healthcare management. See arden.ac.uk.

- **Avado** offers online courses leading to professional qualifications aimed at career developers and changers, in subjects such as accounting and HR. See avadolearning.com.

- **Coursera**: this online platform offers low-cost massive online open courses (MOOCs) from universities around the world. Study can be informal or to gain certificates or credit towards qualifications. See coursera.org.

- **edX**: an online platform, founded by Harvard and MiT, offering MOOCs from universities around the world. Either study for free or pay to access assessment and certificates of learning or qualifications. See edx.org.

- **FutureLearn**: an online platform, founded by the Open University, offering MOOCs from universities around the world. Either study for free or pay to access assessment and certificates of learning. See futurelearn.com.

- The **National Extension College** offers a vast range of home study courses, leading to GCSEs, A-levels and professional qualifications, and has been providing distance learning courses for over 50 years. See nec.ac.uk.

- The **Open and Distance Learning Quality Council** is the UK guardian of quality in open and distance learning and includes a list of accredited providers on its website. Set up originally by the government in 1968, it is now an independent organization. See odlqc.org.uk.

- The **Open University** (OU) is a world leader in modern distance learning, the pioneer of teaching and learning methods that enable people to achieve their career and life goals studying at times and in places to suit them. In addition to its paid-for degrees, the OU offers a huge range of free courses on its OpenLearn platform, some of which are specifically aimed at developing employability skills. See open.ac.uk and open.edu/openlearn.

IT skills

If you are considering a change in direction, some new qualifications may be advantageous. IT skills are essential, so if you are not confident about your computer literacy and don't have much IT experience or specialist knowledge, here are some useful websites to look at:

- **Alison.com**: a MOOC platform that includes digital literacy from the basics onwards. See alison.com/courses/core-it-skills.

- **Digital Skills Scotland:** free online courses for individuals and business. See digitalskillsscotland.co.uk.

- **FutureLearn:** courses available on this MOOC platform include a suite from Accenture on digital skills mainly for business and career development. See futurelearn.com/career-advice/grow-your-digital-skills.

- **Google Digital Garage:** mainly aimed at businesses and career developers. See learndigital.withgoogle.com/digitalgarage.

- **Home and Learn** offers a free computer courses and tutorials site. Courses are aimed at beginners: all you do is click on a computer course that interests you and start. See homeandlearn.co.uk.

- **Microsoft:** the basics, including safety online, netiquette and accessing digital content. See microsoft.com/en-gb/digitalliteracy/home.

- **OpenLearn:** includes courses such as Digital Literacy: succeeding in a digital world that introduce skills such as staying safe online and finding information online. See open.edu/openlearn.

Help with finding a job

If you plan to work in retirement, the best way is to start looking while you still have a job. Prospective employers may prefer applicants who are busy and actively working rather than those who have had a period of non-employment for whatever reason. However, whether you are hoping to go straight from one job to another, or have had an enforced period of not working, this should not affect the way you approach your job search. If you have been retired for some time and want to return to work, you might consider doing some voluntary work in the meantime. This would provide a ready answer to the inevitable interview question 'What have you been doing?'.

When starting to look for work, make sure you tell your friends and acquaintances that you are in the market for work, and include your present or recent employer. Some firms encourage consultancy links with former executives, or at least are prepared to respond to a good idea. A greater number are more than happy to take on previous employees over a rush period or during the holiday season. Social media is also an increasingly important part of job searching. Use your LinkedIn (linkedin.com) account to search for job opportunities and let contacts know you are in the market – if you don't have a LinkedIn account, consider setting one up. Similarly, if you don't yet tweet, now is a good time to open a Twitter account and follow the organizations you would like to work for – it is common these days for companies to tweet about their key vacancies.

If you are a member of a professional institute, talk to them and tell them of your availability. Many institutes keep a register of members wanting work and, encouragingly, receive a fair number of enquiries from firms seeking qualified people for projects, part-time or temporary work, interim management or sometimes even permanent employment. Any clubs to which you belong could provide useful leads, as well as any committees you sit on, or any other group with which you are involved. Often someone you know will be the perfect link between you and your next employer.

If you intend to follow up advertisements, selectivity is the name of the game. Limit your applications to those that sound genuinely promising – you will save yourself a lot of time this way. With so many vacancies being advertised online, it pays to have a CV and covering letter ready for submission straight away. Sign up to a select number of sites that will keep you posted about work opportunities. Check out where there are skills shortages, and see if any of your transferable skills would help plug that gap.

A direct approach to likely employers is another possible option. Do your research carefully both on the internet and among your personal network. Ask your colleagues, contacts and friends for their advice on which organizations might be interested in employing someone with your abilities. If possible, find out the name of the appropriate person to contact and the best method to reach them. If someone you know can prepare the ground in advance by way of introduction, and act as a referrer, this is far more likely to get you noticed. Some other tips:

- Making the most of previous employment skills is another important point when hunting for retirement jobs.

- Widen the job search: the more employment sources searched, the greater the amount of opportunities and contacts.

- Contact previous employers to enquire about part-time work.

- Search online job boards on sites such as Craigslist (geo.craigslist.org/iso/gb) and Gumtree (gumtree.com) for local jobs.

- Local job centres should provide good results, and jobs can be sourced on online job centre websites.

- Contact local colleges and universities who are always looking for teachers with a wide variety of employment skills.

- The internet has become one of the most useful job search tools and should not be underestimated when searching for that perfect retirement job.

There are many online recruitment websites, but the following websites may be particularly useful for more mature workers:

- **Laterlife.** Its job search section through partner skilledpeople.com focuses on jobs for the over-50s and will assist you with all the information and services you need. See laterlife.com.

- **Prime Candidate** is the employability arm of the Age Diversity Forum, which campaigns against age bias, and includes a job search section for older workers. See primecandidate.org.

- **Redundancy Expert** was formed to provide comprehensive information and advice on redundancy and a section of its website is dedicated to finding work and getting a job. See redundancyexpert.co.uk.

- **Vercida** is a job search site specializing in helping employers to have diverse workforces, including employees over 50. See vercida.com/uk.

CV writing

Regardless of whether you use contacts, advertisements or agencies – or preferably all three – a prime requirement will be to have a well-presented CV. This is your personal sales document and it will be helpful if it can be e-mailed to prospective employers. It should contain:

- your name and contact number(s);
- e-mail and website addresses;
- key achievements to date;
- qualifications and work experience, past employers, positions held and responsibilities;
- referees.

Your CV should be no longer than two pages of A4, which after a long career means being selective about the information you include. While some CVs are highly professional, one that is too long is often counterproductive – it should be targeted to the job on offer, emphasizing those elements of your experience and skills that are relevant. It is customary these days to include a brief summary either as part of your CV or in your covering letter showing how you meet the specific job and person specification that was advertised. This is the place where you need to really grab the attention of whoever is trawling through possibly hundreds of applications. There are companies that will professionally produce CVs, and although this can be worthwhile, there will be a fee attached. There are plenty of websites where CV templates can be downloaded for free, such as myperfectcv.co.uk. A well-set-out CV can make all the difference when it comes to catching an employer's interest. Older workers should concentrate on their main employment skills and employers when updating a CV.

Interview technique

If you have worked for the same employer for a number of years, your interview skills may be a little rusty. It is a good idea to list all the questions you expect to be asked (including those you hope won't be brought up) and then get a friend to rehearse you in your answers. In addition to questions about your previous job, have answers prepared for the following: what you have done since leaving employment, whether your health is good, why you are interested in working for this particular employer, and, given the job requirements, what you think you have of special value to offer. You may also be asked what you know about the organization, so do your research. Obvious mistakes to avoid are claiming skills or knowledge that you do not possess, giving the impression that you have a series of stock answers to problems, and criticizing your former employer.

Be prepared to have an answer to the question: how much money would you expect? You may have to strike a balance between what you would like and what is realistic in the current market.

Part-time openings

Part-time work may for some people be the ideal solution; others may regard it as second-best. With the job market so competitive, many part-time or temporary assignments offer the perfect way into employment that may develop into full-time work in future. This is especially true of small firms, which may be cautious about recruitment while the business is relatively young.

With the average job now lasting between 1.8 and three years, temporary or project-based professional and executive assignments that last a specific time are becoming increasingly common. People with specialist expertise are actively sought, so it is important to be aware of the growth areas in employment. Over a fifth of all new jobs are now on a contract basis, the average being for six months or a year. Mature candidates have everything to gain here because of the greater turnover of jobs. Serial part-time work, perhaps supplemented by freelance work, can easily develop into a full-time occupation. Many retired businesspeople take on two or three part-time jobs and then find themselves working as hard as they have ever done in their life.

Employment ideas

Interim management

Interim managers represent a huge growth area in recruitment over the past few years. An interim manager gives a company instant access to a 'heavy-weight yet hands-on executive' with a proven track record. Typically hired for three to nine months, interim managers help organizations undergoing major change, implement critical strategies or plug a crucial management gap. Many of the best jobs go to those who have recently taken early retirement or been made redundant. Assignments could be full-time or involve just one or two days' work a week.

The following organizations could also assist:

- EO: executivesonline.co.uk;
- Interim Partners: interimpartners.com.

Secondment to another organization

Secondment from your current employer to another organization, often charitable, is something worth considering. This can be part-time for a few hours a week or full-time for anything from a few weeks to two years. It can also often lead to a new career. Normally only larger employers are willing to consider the idea since, as a rule, the company will continue to pay your salary and other benefits during the period of secondment. If you work for a smaller firm it could still be worth discussing the suggestion, as employers benefit from the favourable publicity the company attracts by being seen to support the local community.

Business in the Community is a business-led charity which works with businesses to build a sustainable future for people and the planet. It has secondment opportunities for both employers and individuals. See bitc.org.uk.

Public appointments

Opportunities regularly arise for individuals to be appointed to a wide range of public bodies, such as tribunals, commissions and consumer consultative councils. Many appointments are to local and regional bodies throughout the country. Some are paid, but many offer an opportunity to contribute to the community and gain valuable experience of working in the public sector on a part-time, expenses-only basis. Public appointments vacancies in the UK at local, regional and national levels are found on publicappointments. cabinetoffice.gov.uk and you can be alerted to new opportunities by following the government Twitter account @publicappts.

Non-executive directorships

Many retiring executives see this as the ideal solution; however, these appointments carry heavy responsibilities. If you are able and committed and have the necessary experience, see these websites:

- **First Flight Placements:** ffplacements.co.uk;
- **NED Exchange:** nedexchange.co.uk.

Paid work for charities

Although charities rely to a very large extent on voluntary workers, most charitable organizations of any size have a number of paid appointments. Other than particular specialists that some charities may require for their work, the majority of openings are for general managers or administrators, fundraisers and those with financial skills. Salaries have been improving, but in general are still considerably below the commercial market rate. Anyone thinking of applying for a job in a charity must be sympathetic to its aims and style.

Agencies specializing in charity recruitment advise that it is a good idea to work as a volunteer before seeking a paid appointment, as this will provide useful experience. The following organizations may help:

- **Charity JOB:** charityjob.co.uk;
- **Charity People:** charitypeople.co.uk;
- **Harris Hill:** harrishill.co.uk;
- **NCVO KnowHow:** knowhow.ncvo.org.uk/studyzone/working-for-a-charity;
- **ProspectUs:** prospect-us.co.uk;
- **TPP Not for Profit:** tpp.co.uk.

Market research

Surveys are going on all the time – to inform business, politics, academic research and more. There are several ways in which you could get involved. The first is to be a panel member. The big market research firms all conduct regular 'omnibus surveys' – large-scale surveys that bring together questions from many clients on a diverse range of topics. The results are then often statistically treated to predict how the country as a whole would respond to those questions. The raw data for those predictions comes from a large standing panel of respondents. Typically, omnibus surveys are online, so you will need a computer and internet connection. It's up to you which surveys you opt into, and you receive a small payment for each one you complete. Market research companies also recruit people to gather data as mystery shoppers and to conduct phone surveys and face-to-face surveys on the street or in people's homes. If this all sounds interesting, try these companies:

- **Ipsos MORI:** ipsos.com/ipsos-mori/en-uk/careers-at-ipsos#become;
- **NatCen:** natcen.ac.uk/careers;
- **Populus:** populuslive.com;
- **YouGov:** yougov.co.uk/join-community.

Sales

Almost every commercial firm in the country needs good sales staff. Many people who have never thought of sales could be excellent in the job because of their specialist knowledge in a particular field combined with their enthusiasm for the subject. There is always a demand for people to sell advertising space. Also, many firms employ demonstrators in shops or at exhibitions for special promotions. The work is usually temporary or freelance, and while pay is normally good, the big drawback is that you could be on your feet for long periods of the day. If the idea of selling fires you with enthusiasm, there are many opportunities to tempt you.

Tourist guide

Tourist guide work is something that will appeal to extroverts and the super-fit with oodles of stamina and a liking for people. It requires an academic mind as well, since you will need to put in some fairly concentrated study. While there are numerous possible qualifications, some are easier than others – training for the coveted Blue Badge takes up to two years. The Blue Badge itself is no guarantee of steady work, since openings are largely seasonal. In fact, most tourist guides are self-employed and the field is highly competitive, but opportunities are greatest in London, especially for those with fluency in one or more foreign languages. See the national membership association for Blue Badge Tourist Guides: britainsbestguides.org.

You could sign on as a lecturer with one of the growing number of travel companies offering special interest holidays. To be eligible you need real expertise in a subject, the ability to make it interesting and an easy manner with people. Pay is fairly minimal, although you may receive tips – plus of course the bonus of a free holiday. See Chapter 12, *Holidays*, for the names of tour operators that may be worth contacting.

Other tourist work

If you live in a popular tourist or heritage area, there is a whole variety of seasonal work, including jobs in hotels, restaurants, shops and local places of interest. Depending on the locality, the list might also include jobs as deckchair attendants, play leaders for children, caravan site staff, extra coach drivers and many others.

Teaching and training skills

If you have been a teacher at any stage of your career, there are a number of part-time possibilities.

Coaching

With examinations becoming more competitive, demand has been increasing for ex-teachers with knowledge of the public examination system to coach youngsters in preparation for A and AS levels, GCSEs and common entrance exams. Contact local schools, search the internet or contact a specialist educational consultancy.

Gabbitas Educational Consultants is one of the UK's leading educational consultancies offering advice and support in all aspects of independent education. It also maintains an extensive register of appointments for teachers and tutors. See gabbitas.com.

Specialist subjects

Teachers are in demand for mathematics, physics, chemistry, technology and modern languages. People with relevant work experience and qualifications may be able to teach or give tuition in these subjects. A formal teaching qualification is required to teach in state-maintained schools. See the Teaching Regulation Agency website at https://teacherservices.education.gov.uk.

Before engaging with children, you will need a Disclosure and Barring Service (DBS) check (formerly called a Criminal Records Bureau or CRB check) – see *Caring for other people* later in this chapter. Retired teachers, linguists and others with specialist knowledge can earn good money from tutoring – see hometutors.org.uk. Alternatively, you could oversee exams as an invigilator. The British Council may have work – check out britishcouncil. org and fejobs.com.

University tutors

Many universities employ tutors, often called associate lecturers, to work directly with students, delivering tutorials either online or face-to-face and marking their work. There is no general requirement to have a formal teaching qualification to tutor at university level, but you will usually have an advantage if you have a teaching certificate and/or fellowship of Advance HE: heacademy.ac.uk. With more vocational subjects, your experience and professional qualifications will be valued. Jobs in this area may be part-time or full-time. Contact universities direct to find out about their tutoring vacancies and try specialist recruitment sites such as timeshighereducation. com/unijobs/listings/tutors.

English as a foreign language

There is an ongoing demand for people to teach English to foreign students. Opportunities are concentrated in London and the major academic cities such as Oxford, Cambridge, Bath and York. Good English-language schools require teachers to have an initial qualification in teaching English to those who have a different first language. For more information see tefl.org and tefltraining.co.uk.

Caring for other people

With an ageing population, there are growing opportunities for paid work in this field. If you are considering working with vulnerable people (young or old), you will be required to have a full DBS check with enhanced disclosure, designed to protect those who need to rely on other people and to ensure that no one unsuitable is appointed to a position of trust who is likely to abuse it. These checks are extremely thorough and can take several weeks or even months to process. Please be patient and as accurate as possible when asked to provide information by prospective employers, charities or not-for-profit organizations. For further information about DBS checks and why they are required, see gov.uk/dbs-check-applicant-criminal-record.

Your employment status will depend on the facts that apply in your case. You may be employed by a council, other organization or an agency. Alternatively, if you work direct for the person or family who needs help, you may be their employee (and they will be responsible for operating PAYE to deduct tax from your pay, and so on). If you work direct but have multiple clients, you might count as self-employed.

Domestic work

A number of private domestic agencies specialize in finding temporary or permanent companions, housekeepers and extra-care help for elderly and disabled people or for those who are convalescent. Pay rates vary depending on which part of the country you live in and the number of hours involved. The following agencies may be of interest:

- **Anchor Care:** anchor.org.uk;
- **Consultus Care & Nursing Agency Ltd:** consultuscare.com;
- **Country Cousins:** www.country-cousins.co.uk;
- **Universal Aunts Ltd:** universalaunts.co.uk.

The Lady magazine, published every Wednesday and online at lady.co.uk, has classified advertisements for domestic help.

Home helps

Local authorities sometimes have vacancies for home helps, to assist disabled or elderly people in their own home by giving a hand with the cleaning, light cooking and other chores. Ask your local social services department.

Childcare

If you work as a childminder, you will normally be self-employed. However, if you work as a nanny on either a daily or live-in basis, you will be an employee of the family for whom you work. Some useful sites for finding nanny positions include:

- care.com;
- childcare.co.uk;
- lady.co.uk;
- nannyjob.co.uk.

Busy parents may need someone reliable to meet children at airports, stations or even travel with them. See universalaunts.co.uk or enter 'children's escort' in job agency websites.

Nursing

Qualified nurses are in great demand in most parts of the country and stand a good chance of finding work at their local hospital or through one of the many nursing agencies. Those with suitable experience, although not necessarily a formal nursing qualification, could apply to become a care support worker for the newly merged charity Carers Trust. Crossroads Care and The Princess Royal Trust for Carers have merged to form the leading carers' charity. See carers.org.

Home sitting

Taking care of someone else's home while they are away on holiday or business trips is something mature, responsible people, usually non-smokers with no children or pets, can do. It is a bit like a paid holiday, and you get paid every week (extra if care of pets is involved), depending on the responsibilities and on the size of the house or flat. Food and travelling expenses are normally also paid. It is useful to have your own car. Firms specializing in this type of work include:

- **Homesitters Ltd:** homesitters.co.uk;
- **Housesitters Ltd:** housesitters.co.uk;
- **Rest Assured House Sitters:** restassuredhousesitters.co.uk;
- **Universal Aunts Ltd:** universalaunts.co.uk.

10
Voluntary work

Volunteering is not just about giving back; it can enhance your own life too. A quarter of people say they volunteer so they can meet new people and make friends, almost the same proportion see it as a way of using their existing skills and one in six welcome it as a chance to learn new skills, according to a government survey. So if this appeals to you, why not give it some thought? Here are some suggestions as to what you might do.

Types of work

Clerical

Any active group is likely to need basic administrative help, from typing and stuffing envelopes to answering the telephone and organizing committees. This may involve a day or so a week or occasional assistance at peak times. Many smaller charities in particular would also greatly welcome hearing from individuals with IT expertise to assist with setting up databases, a website, etc.

Fundraising

Every voluntary organization needs money, and when donations are static or falling, more creativity and ingenuity are required to help bring in funds. Events are many and varied, but anyone with energy and experience of organizing fundraising events would be welcomed with open arms as a volunteer.

Committee work

This can cover anything from very occasional help to a virtually full-time commitment as branch treasurer or secretary. People with business skills or financial or legal backgrounds are likely to be especially valuable, and those whose skills include minute-taking are always in demand.

Direct work

Driving, delivering 'meals on wheels', counselling, visiting the housebound, working in a charity shop, helping with a playgroup, respite care for carers: the list is endless and the value of the work incalculable. While certain qualifications and experience – financial, legal, nursing and social work – have particular value in some circumstances, there is also a multitude of interesting and useful jobs for those without special training or with abilities like driving or computer skills. Similarly, the time commitment can vary to suit both helper and organization. It is far better to give just one morning a month and be reliable than to promise more time than you can spare and end up cancelling or letting people down. Equally, as with a paid job, before you start you should be absolutely clear about all the terms and conditions:

- What sort of work is involved?
- Who will be working with you?
- What is expected?
- When will you be needed?
- Are expenses paid? What for? How much?

If you have all this mapped out in the beginning there will be less chance of any misunderstandings. You will find that voluntary work is not only very rewarding in its own right, but also allows you to make a real contribution to the community.

You will be required to have a full Disclosure and Barring Service (DBS) check (formerly called a Criminal Records Bureau or CRB check) with enhanced disclosure if you are considering working with vulnerable people (young or old). For further information about DBS checks and why they are required, see gov.uk/dbs-check-applicant-criminal-record.

Choosing the right voluntary work

Once you've decided that you might take on some volunteering, the next question is what to do. You will need to find out where the opportunities are in your local area and what particular outlet would suit your talents. You may have friends or neighbours who are already involved in volunteering locally. Asking their advice would be a start, as they may well have some good suggestions or know which organizations are in need of extra pairs of hands. However, if you don't know where to start, the organizations listed here are arranged in broad categories of interest. As there are literally thousands of voluntary groups, national and local, that need help in some way or other, it is impossible to include them all or describe all their activities and volunteering opportunities. The following act as signposts to help you learn more about them and how you can get involved:

- The **Do-It Trust** is a digital charity that operates an online hub bringing together volunteers and organizations that need them. See do-it.org.

- The **National Council for Voluntary Organisations** (which has taken over the previous role of Volunteering England) is a member organization for charities and similar organizations. Its website includes a directory for finding your local volunteering centre. See ncvo.org.uk.

- **REACH** is the skilled volunteering charity, encouraging people to take on new challenges and make a difference to their community. See reachskills. org.uk.

- The **Royal Voluntary Service** (RVS) is an 80-year old organization that mobilizes volunteers to work particularly in hospitals and the community. See royalvoluntaryservice.org.uk.

- Volunteer centres. Most towns have a body of this kind that seeks to match up volunteers with local organizations seeking help. Ask your local council for contact details.

- **Volunteering Matters** (formerly Community Service Volunteers) lets you search for local volunteering opportunities, with separate sections for the different British nations. See volunteeringmatters.org.uk.

- **Volunteer Scotland** is the national centre for volunteering in Scotland. See www.volunteerscotland.net.

- **Volunteering Wales** is the website of Third Sector Support Wales, bringing together volunteering support across the Welsh local councils and third-sector organizations. See volunteering-wales.net.

- The **Wales Council for Voluntary Action** is an umbrella body for voluntary activity in Wales. See wcva.org.uk.

If you do have an idea of a cause to which you would like to donate your time and expertise, here are some more specific places to start.

General:

- The **British Red Cross**: redcross.org.uk;
- **Citizens Advice Bureau**: citizensadvice.org.uk;
- **Lions Clubs British Isles**: lionsclubs.co;
- The **Royal Voluntary Service**: royalvoluntaryservice.org.uk;
- **Toc H**: toch-uk.org.uk.

Animals:

- The **Cinnamon Trust**: cinnamon.org.uk;
- **Guide Dogs for the Blind Association**: guidedogs.org.uk;
- **PDSA**: pdsa.org.uk;
- **Pet Fostering Service Scotland**: pfss.org.uk;
- **Pets As Therapy**: petsastherapy.org;
- The **Royal Society for the Prevention of Cruelty to Animals** (RSPCA): rspca.org.uk;
- The **Wildfowl & Wetlands Trust**: wwt.org.uk.

Bereavement:

- **Cruse Bereavement Care**: cruse.org.uk.

Children and young people:

- **Action for Sick Children**: actionforsickchildren.org;
- **Barnardo's**: barnardos.org.uk;
- The **Children's Society**: childrenssociety.org.uk;
- The **Children's Trust Tadworth**: thechildrenstrust.org.uk;
- **Save the Children UK**: savethechildren.org.uk;
- The **Scout Association**: scouts.org.uk;
- **Sea Cadet Corps**: ms-sc.org.

Conservation outdoors:

- The **Architectural Heritage Society of Scotland**: ahss.org.uk;
- The **British Trust for Conservation Volunteers**: tcv.org.uk;
- The **Campaign to Protect Rural England**: cpre.org.uk;
- **Friends of the Earth**: friendsoftheearth.uk;

- Greenpeace: greenpeace.org.uk;
- The **Ramblers' Association**: ramblers.org.uk;
- The **Royal Society for the Protection of Birds**: rspb.org.uk.

The elderly:

- **Abbeyfield**: abbeyfield.com;
- **Age UK**: ageuk.org.uk;
- **Carers Trust**: carers.org;
- **Carers UK**: carersuk.org;
- **Contact the Elderly**: contact-the-elderly.org.uk.

The family:

- **Marriage Care**: marriagecare.org.uk;
- **Relate**: relate.org.uk.

Health:

- **Attend**: attend.org.uk;
- **BackCare**: backcare.org.uk;
- **Blind Veterans UK**: blindveterans.org.uk;
- **British Heart Foundation**: bhf.org.uk;
- **Calibre Audio Library**: calibre.org.uk;
- **Cancer Research UK**: cancerresearchuk.org;
- **Disability Snowsport UK**: disabilitysnowsport.org.uk;
- **Leonard Cheshire Disability**: leonardcheshire.org;
- **Mind**: mind.org.uk;
- The **Riding for the Disabled Association**: rda.org.uk;
- The **Royal National Institute of Blind People**: rnib.org.uk;
- **St John Ambulance**: sja.org.uk;
- **Scope**: scope.org.uk;
- **Thrive**: thrive.org.uk.

Heritage and the arts:

- **Council for British Archaeology**: archaeologyuk.org;
- **English Heritage**: www.english-heritage.org.uk;

- The **National Trust**: nationaltrust.org.uk;
- **Society for the Protection of Ancient Buildings**: spab.org.uk.

Those in need:

- **Citizens Advice**: citizensadvice.org.uk;
- **Oxfam**: oxfam.org.uk;
- The **Samaritans**: samaritans.org.

Offenders and the victims of crime:

- **Change Grow Live**: changegrowlive.org;
- **Nacro**: nacro.org.uk;
- **New Bridge Foundation**: newbridgefoundation.org.uk;
- **Victim Support**: victimsupport.org.uk.

Politics:

- The **Conservative Party**: conservatives.com;
- The **Green Party**: campaigns.greenparty.org.uk;
- The **Labour Party**: labour.org.uk;
- The **Liberal Democrats**: libdems.org.uk;
- **Plaid Cymru**: plaidcymru.org;
- The **Scottish National Party**: snp.org;
- The **Social Democratic and Labour Party** (SDLP): sdlp.ie;
- **UKIP**: ukip.org.uk;
- The **Ulster Unionist Party**: uup.org.

Service personnel and veterans:

- **ABF The Soldiers' Charity**: soldierscharity.org;
- **Combat Stress**: combatstress.org.uk;
- **Help for Heroes**: helpforheroes.org.uk;
- **SSAFA**: ssafa.org.uk;
- The **Royal Air Force Benevolent Fund**: rafbf.org;
- The **Royal Alfred Seafarers' Society**: royalalfredseafarers.co.uk;
- The **Royal British Legion**: britishlegion.org.uk.

Long-term volunteering

If you are thinking of a long-term, probably residential commitment there are a number of organizations in need of voluntary help for a wide variety of projects abroad. Many require specialist skills, such as engineering or medicine; others essentially need people with practical qualities, common sense and enthusiasm. Each organization has a minimum period of service. Couples without dependent children are welcome, as long as both have the necessary skills.

There are various opportunities for suitably qualified people to work in the developing countries of Africa, Asia, the Caribbean and the Pacific on a semi-voluntary basis. General conditions are similar for all of them; training is provided; travel is paid, plus a living allowance or salary that is based on local levels rather than on expatriate rates; and medical insurance is paid for. Support with resettlement and re-employment is provided on completion of the tour.

Skills most in demand include civil engineering, mechanical engineering, water engineering, architecture, urban, rural and regional planning, agriculture, forestry, medicine, teaching English as a foreign language, maths and physics training, and economics. As a general rule, there is an upper age limit of 65 (VSO accepts volunteers up to 75), and you must be willing to work for a minimum of two years.

The following are the major agencies involved in this kind of work:

- **International Service**: internationalservice.org.uk;
- **Skillshare International**: skillshare.org;
- **Voluntary Service Overseas** (VSO): vsointernational.org.

Volunteering abroad for the over-50s is often referred to as 'golden gapping'. It is gaining popularity among many 50–75-year-olds. Thousands of mature people have enjoyed gap years recently, and the number is growing. If a life-changing experience and doing some voluntary work abroad before or just after you retire appeal to you, gapwork.com and goabroad.com should be able to help.

11
Health

People retiring today are often younger in looks and behaviour than previous generations, and should be able to enjoy many healthy years of life. But, remember, bodies do require care and attention if they are to function at their best. There is no need to get out of shape: making time for the changes that help you to feel good should mean you are likely to have a far longer and more enjoyable retirement.

Keep fit

Emphasis on and availability of every type of keep fit activity are on the increase. It is a welcome innovation, as there are a growing number of opportunities for older people, including those with disabilities. Information should be available online, or in your local newspaper or library. The following organizations may be able to help you:

- **emduk** (Exercise, Move, Dance) is the national governing body for group exercise with a mission to improve the nation's health through dance and exercise. Find classes near you: emduk.org.
- **Extend** provides gentle exercise classes for older people, and anyone of any age who has a disability, throughout the UK. See extend.org.uk.
- **Fl-exercise** is a nationwide exercise network for people of all ages, with an emphasis on friendship as well as fitness. See fl-exercise.com.
- **Medau Movement** encourages the body to move with energy, strength, stamina, suppleness and coordination. Classes are held throughout the country. See medau.org.uk.

Pilates

Pilates is an invigorating form of exercise for your mind and body that can improve your strength, flexibility and overall mobility. See The Pilates Foundation website at pilatesfoundation.com.

Yoga

Yoga is popular with all ages and is a means of improving fitness and helping relaxation:

- **British Wheel of Yoga** is a registered charity and the largest yoga organization in the UK. With thousands of qualified teachers, it promotes yoga classes, workshops and events for its members and the public. See bwy.org.uk.

- **Yoga for Health and Education Trust** is a not-for-profit company and charity dedicated to bringing yoga to all, whether fit and well or disabled. See yoga-health-education.org.uk.

Sensible eating

While regular exercise is important, so is sensible eating. Advice on healthy eating seems to change so fast, it's hard to keep up. But with more than one in four adults in Britain being obese according to the National Health Service (NHS), it is a worrying trend that so many people are seriously overweight. The more excess weight you carry, the greater the risks to your health. In particular, there is an increased risk of type-2 diabetes, heart attack and stroke, as well as surgery being made more difficult. As age increases, there is greater likelihood of restricted mobility, which is only exacerbated if you are overweight.

The *Eat Well* section of the NHS website has lots of advice on food and eating a balanced diet, including recipes and, should you need it, a weight-loss plan: nhs.uk/live-well/eat-well.

As every health magazine advises, crash diets are no solution for long-term fitness. Many people need a boost to get started, and whatever method you choose is fine as long as it works. Two excellent websites are:

- **Livestrong.com**, which believes that everyone has the power to change their lives, is a daily health, fitness and lifestyle destination. See livestrong.com.

- **WW** (formerly known as Weight Watchers), whose aim is to help members establish a healthy, balanced approach to weight loss, with emphasis on making small, lifetime changes that can be maintained for the long term. See weightwatchers.com/uk.

Keeping healthy in the heat

The older we get the more conscious we need to be of the sun and how it affects us. The NHS warns that anyone over the age of 65 is in the 'high-risk' category for heat-related illness. Too much sun or getting overheated can induce sunstroke and dehydration, while also causing other issues – such as exacerbating existing health problems such as heart disease and high blood pressure. These guidelines should help you keep your cool:

- *Stay hydrated*. One of the most common effects of prolonged periods in the heat is dehydration. The hotter months are definitely the time you should get at least six to eight glasses of fluids a day. Keep a bottle of water with you, especially when on the road, and remember that caffeine and alcohol dehydrate you.

- *Wear sunscreen*. The older we get, the more susceptible to certain types of skin cancer we are. Find the right sunscreen for you, and top up regularly.

- *Protect your eyes*. Protecting eyes from the brightness and UV rays of the sun will promote better eyesight and prevent cataracts. Wear wrap-around sunglasses that offer UV protection and a wide-brimmed hat that will shade your eyes while also protecting your ears, nose and head from sunburn.

- *Lower your temperature*. Even when out of direct sunlight your temperature can be too high. If you're feeling too hot, taking a cool shower is an effective way of maintaining a safe temperature. If you often feel discomfort from the heat, aim to spend the warmest parts of the day in air-conditioned areas.

- *Be prepared*. Keep a sunhat in the car, spare water bottles in your fridge and stock up on sunscreen. Our weather is unpredictable, and whether you are a sun worshipper or prefer the shade, it's best not to get caught out.

Food safety

As most readers will know, basic rules on food safety are important. Elderly people who are afflicted by food poisoning will typically suffer much more severe symptoms than younger people. Dehydration can become a serious factor and can lead to decreased blood pressure. This in turn affects the blood supply to vital organs such as the kidneys. It is very important that fluids are replaced as soon as possible should dehydration occur.

There are a few ways that food poisoning can occur; one of the most common is by consuming food that is past its use-by date. Older people on a budget often buy food that is close to its use-by date in order to save money. There are a number of precautions that should be taken to reduce the risk of food poisoning. These include:

- not eating food products that are past their sell-by or use-by dates;
- always making sure food is stored in refrigerators set at the right temperature;
- following cooking instructions carefully;
- not eating raw or undercooked meat products or eggs;
- always washing hands and work surfaces that have been used to prepare meat, seafood and eggs;
- always washing raw vegetables thoroughly, especially vegetables that are not going to be cooked;
- ensuring that frozen foods are completely thawed before cooking and never refreeze thawed foods;
- never eating undercooked foods in restaurants. Always send undercooked food back to be cooked completely;
- having two chopping boards: one for meat and one for everything else;
- covering the food in your fridge with shrink-wrap or beeswax wraps; this includes leftovers;
- never keeping cooked and uncooked food together, as they can contaminate each other;
- keeping all parts of your kitchen clean;
- not reheating food more than once and not keeping cooked food longer than two days.

Drink

Retirement is no reason for giving up pleasures, and in moderate quantities alcohol can be a very effective nightcap and can also help to stimulate a sluggish appetite. However, bear in mind that alcohol-related deaths have been increasing in the UK and are highest among women aged 50 to 59 and men aged 60 to 64, according to the Office for National Statistics. Alcohol dependency is far more likely among those who are bored or depressed, who drift into the habit of having a drink to cheer themselves up or to pass the time. Because the early symptoms appear fairly innocuous, the danger signs can often go unnoticed.

Whereas most people are sensible enough to be able to control the habit themselves, others may need help. The family doctor will be the first person to check with for medical advice. But additionally, for those who need moral support, the following self-help groups may be the answer:

- **Al-Anon Family Groups UK & Eire** provides support to anyone whose life is, or has been, affected by someone else's drinking. There are over 800 support groups in the UK and Republic of Ireland. See al-anonuk.org.uk.

- **Alcohol Change UK** (formed by the merger of Alcohol Research UK and Alcohol Concern) is the national agency on alcohol misuse, campaigning for a society free from alcohol harm through an effective alcohol policy and improved services for people whose lives are affected by alcohol-related problems. See alcoholchange.org.uk.

- **Alcoholics Anonymous** is a fellowship of men and women who share their experience, strength and hope with each other so that they may solve their common problem and help others recover from alcoholism. See alcoholics-anonymous.org.uk.

Smoking

Any age is a good one to cut back on smoking, or preferably to give up altogether. Smokers are 20 times more likely to contract lung cancer; they are at more serious risk of suffering from heart disease and stroke, and they are more liable to chronic bronchitis and other ailments. Dozens of organizations concerned with health publish leaflets about giving up smoking. Here are three of them:

- **NHS Scotland** offers free advice, counselling and encouragement to those wishing to give up smoking. See nhsinform.scot/healthy-living/stopping-smoking.

- **Quit** aims to reduce unnecessary suffering and death from smoking-related diseases, and aims towards a smoke-free UK future. See quit.org.uk.

- **Smokefree** offers help and advice to smokers who want to quit and gives information about local services, including nicotine replacement therapy and group support. See nhs.uk/smokefree.

Accident prevention

One of the most common causes of mishap is an accident in the home. The vast majority of these could be avoided by taking normal common-sense precautions, such as repairing or replacing worn carpets and installing better lighting near staircases. For a list of practical suggestions, see Chapter 6, *Your home*.

If you are unlucky enough to be injured in an accident, whether in the street or elsewhere, the Law Society offers a free service called the Accident Line (accidentlinedirect.co.uk) to help you decide whether you can make a claim. You will be entitled to a free consultation with a local solicitor specializing in personal injury claims. Alternatively, you could consult the National Accident Helpline at national-accident-helpline.co.uk.

Aches, pains and other abnormalities

There is nothing about becoming 50, 60 or even 70 that makes aches and pains inevitable. Age itself has nothing to do with the vast majority of ailments. Many people ignore the warning signs when something is wrong, yet treatment when a condition is still in its infancy can often cure it altogether, or at least help to delay its advance. The following should always be investigated by a doctor:

- any pain that lasts more than a few days;
- lumps, however small;
- dizziness or fainting;
- chest pains, shortness of breath or palpitations;
- persistent cough or hoarseness;
- unusual bleeding from anywhere;
- unnatural tiredness or headaches;
- frequent indigestion;
- unexplained weight loss.

Health insurance

Private medical insurance

This type of insurance covers the cost of private treatment if you need hospital care. People with private medical insurance often get a nasty shock when they reach retirement age, particularly if they were previously covered under a company scheme. Their premiums start to rocket – just at the point when their income has been reduced to a pension. However, switching to a cheaper scheme often gets more difficult as we get older. Some policies have maximum age limits, but a more frequent problem is that if you have already developed a health condition, you will lose cover for it if you switch insurers, since pre-existing medical conditions, including associated complaints, will normally be excluded when you take out a new policy.

Nevertheless, if your current policy has become unaffordable, you may feel that you have no alternative but to look for something cheaper. Some leading insurers offer lower-cost policies for 'older' people, but these policies aren't necessarily cheaper than those of other companies. Things to watch out for with lower-cost policies are that they provide less cover, such as limited outpatient cover. Other providers, in order to make the premiums affordable, require policyholders to accept far higher excesses (the amount they have to contribute themselves) in order to obtain cover. More positively, some insurers offer discounts if you exercise regularly and encourage this by providing gym-membership discounts and free fitness trackers. Premiums are also sometimes cheaper if you agree to a restricted list of hospitals or consultants. Another variant is a six-week waiting policy, where you claim for private treatment only if the NHS waiting period for the treatment you need is longer than six weeks.

Be aware too that private medical insurance only covers 'acute' conditions, meaning health problems that can be cured or alleviated. It does not cover chronic conditions – the sort of health problems that can often be managed to some extent, but are not curable. With ageing, unfortunately, chronic conditions are more likely to develop, so not all of the health issues you experience will be covered by your health insurance.

Older people sometimes opt out of private medical insurance cover and, despite concerns about adequate funding and the demands of an ageing population, the NHS means that in the UK medical insurance is not usually a necessity. The NHS has, generally, an excellent record in dealing with urgent conditions and accidents. However, it sometimes has a lengthy waiting list for the less urgent and more routine operations, and NHS-funded treatment may simply not be routinely available for treatments that are considered low priority. By using health insurance to pay for private medical care, you will probably get faster treatment, as well as greater comfort and privacy in hospital. Here are just a few of the organizations that provide cover:

- **AXA PPP Healthcare:** axappphealthcare.co.uk;
- **BUPA:** bupa.co.uk;
- **Exeter Family Friendly Society:** the-exeter.com;
- **Saga Services Ltd:** saga.co.uk;
- **Vitality:** vitality.co.uk/health-insurance.

With so many plans on the market, selecting the one that best suits your needs can be quite a problem. An independent financial adviser or specialist insurance broker could advise you, such as a member of the Association of Medical Insurance Intermediaries. See amii.org.uk.

Private patients – without insurance cover

If you do not have private medical insurance but want to go into hospital in the UK as a private patient, there is nothing to stop you, provided your doctor is willing and you are able to pay the bills. The choice if you opt for self-pay lies between the private wings of NHS hospitals or hospitals run by charitable or non-profit-making organizations, such as:

- **BMI Healthcare:** bmihealthcare.co.uk;
- **Nuffield Health:** nuffieldhealth.com.

Some private hospitals run their own credit schemes, so you can pay for treatment plus interest by instalment. Do check that you can afford the repayments before you go ahead. Self-pay is also an option if the procedure you need is outside the scope of NHS-funded treatments.

Hospital cash plans

These are inexpensive alternatives to medical insurance policies. They are not intended to cover the cost of private treatment. Instead, they pay out a cash sum in the event that a wide range of health-related events happen to you.

These include, for example, having to go into hospital (NHS or private) and receiving routine care, such as visiting the dentist, optician, physiotherapist, and so on. You use the cash in any way you like – for example, if you go into hospital, the cash could help a family member visit you. There is an annual limit on each pay-out. The higher the monthly premium you pay, the higher the cash limits. In effect, cash plans are not so much insurance but a way of spreading the cost of healthcare through the monthly payments. To make them worthwhile, make sure you claim each time you can.

Different cash plans cover different ranges of treatment, so choose whichever best matches the healthcare that you use. Some providers to check out include:

- **BHSF** (originally the Birmingham Hospital Saturday Fund): www.bhsf. co.uk;
- **Orchard Healthcare**: orchardhealthcare.co.uk;
- **SimplyHealth**: simplyhealth.co.uk;
- **Sovereign Healthcare**: sovereignhealthcare.co.uk;
- **WHA Direct**: whahealthcare.co.uk.

Medical tourism

Medical tourism, or 'global healthcare' as it is now known, involves travelling to a foreign country for a medical procedure, and has been growing rapidly over recent years. While the medical procedures needed can be urgent, the majority are elective treatments such as cosmetic surgery or dental care. One way to find out about this growing market and to meet some of the providers of such services is to search the following websites:

- **Medical Tourism**: medicaltourism.com;
- **Treatment Abroad**: treatmentabroad.com.

Make sure you are confident about the standards of treatment and care you will receive before going down this route.

Long-term care plans

An emergency operation is one thing; long-term care because an individual can no longer cope unaided is quite another. A possible, though limited, option is *critical illness insurance*, which pays a lump sum if you are diagnosed with a life-threatening condition such as some cancers or a stroke. However, the cost of cover increases with age and there is usually an age limit above which you cannot get cover – say, 65 or sometimes 70. Pre-existing health conditions will not be covered.

Often a more realistic option is to buy a *care fee annuity* (sometimes known as an 'immediate-needs annuity') if and when the need for care arises. This is a product where you use a lump sum and in return get a regular monthly cash sum for the rest of your life to put towards your care costs. Provided the money is paid direct to a care provider, the income is tax-free. Because someone needing care is likely to have a shorter life expectancy than a person of the same age in good health, the income from this type of annuity is generally higher than the income from the types of annuity described in Chapters 3 and 5. To qualify for this higher income, you will typically need to show that you require help with a specified number of activities of daily living (ADLs), such as being able to bathe, transfer from bed to a chair, and so on. The lump sum to buy the immediate annuity could come from your savings or by releasing equity if you are a homeowner. Prices quoted by different companies to provide exactly the same annual income often differ by many thousands of pounds. You are strongly advised to get advice from a financial adviser (see Chapter 1).

Immediate care annuities and advice about them are regulated by the Financial Conduct Authority. Always check that the companies you are dealing with are authorized by checking their entry on the Financial Services Register, register.fca.org.uk. Provided you deal with an authorized firm, the protection of the Financial Ombudsman Service and Financial Services Compensation Scheme apply should anything go wrong.

Income protection insurance

Income protection insurance, sometimes still called Permanent Health Insurance (PHI), should not be confused with other types of health insurance. It is a replacement-of-earnings policy for people who are still in work and who, because of illness, are unable to continue with their normal occupation for a prolonged period and in consequence suffer loss of earnings. Full policies pay out until retirement (or recovery if earlier); budget policies pay out for a set period of time, such as two or five years. If you are close to retirement, PHI is unlikely to feature on your priority list.

Health screening

Prevention is better than cure, and these days once you are aged between 40 (50 in Wales) and 75 you may be offered a free health check by the NHS (usually this is repeated five-yearly, but more frequent if you have a health condition that needs to be monitored). The NHS may also invite you to take part in other tests, for example, to screen for certain cancers. There are also a variety of private healthcare providers with whom you can pay for check-ups or that come as part of any private medical insurance that you have. Some gyms and health centres carry out routine health tests (similar to the NHS health check) when you first join. In addition to checking your general health (height, weight, blood sugar, cholesterol, blood pressure and heart function), these check-ups also provide advice on diet, drinking and smoking if these are problem areas. For more information, see:

- **BMI Healthcare:** bmihealthcare.co.uk;
- **BUPA:** bupa.co.uk;
- **NHS:** nhs.uk/Conditions/nhs-health-check.

The NHS

You only have to look at the statistics for the United States, where 27 million people have no medical insurance and a quarter of these go without medical care because of cost, to realize that the NHS for all its problems is a great national asset and a socially beneficial way to provide healthcare. However, funding is an issue, and increasingly the NHS does not routinely provide all the treatments that you might expect. Following the Health and Social Care Act 2012, the NHS in England is divided into regions and each region has a Clinical Commissioning Group (CCG) that decides how local NHS funds will be spent. Treatments that are considered low priority – meaning they only change appearance or do not achieve a health gain – will not normally be available on the NHS. However, this will be considered on a case-by-case basis, and your GP can make an Individual Funding Request if he or she considers that your particular circumstances mean that there would be health benefits from receiving the treatment. Similar arrangements apply in the other nations of the UK. So having a GP is important, not just to provide primary medical care but also as a gatekeeper to other treatments should you need them.

Choosing a GP

If you move to a new area, the best way to choose your new GP is to ask for a recommendation. Otherwise your local primary care trust or strategic health authority can assist, or you can search at nhs.uk/Service-Search/GP/LocationSearch/4.

Points you may want to consider include how close the doctor is to your home, whether there is an appointments system, and whether it is a group practice and, if so, how this is organized. All GPs have websites and practice leaflets available at their premises, with details about their service. Having selected a doctor, you should complete a registration form (GMS1) which can be downloaded from the NHS website or obtained from the GP practice. Give the completed form to the receptionist and this will ensure that your medical notes are transferred to your new surgery. You do not have an automatic right to be accepted, as there is a limit to the number of patients any one doctor can accept. Also, some doctors prefer to meet potential patients before accepting them on their list.

Changing your GP

If you want to change your GP, you go about it in exactly the same way. If you know of a doctor whose list you would like to be on, you can simply turn up at his or her surgery and ask to be registered; or you can ask your local primary care trust, or health board in Scotland, to give you a copy of its directory before making a choice. You do not need to give a reason for wanting to change, and you do not need to ask anyone's permission.

When you cannot contact your own GP

If you need medical advice when you are on holiday or at some other time when it may not be possible to contact your own doctor, you can contact any GP surgery and receive treatment for up to 14 days. If you'll need treatment for longer, you'll need to register as a temporary or permanent patient.

If you need urgent but non-emergency medical help out of hours or in other situations when you cannot get to a surgery, you can call the NHS number 111 or complete an online form using 111 Online at 111.nhs.uk. In either case, a trained professional will give you advice, which may include arranging an immediate face-to-face appointment if you need one.

Help with NHS costs

If you or your partner are in receipt of the Pension Credit Guarantee Credit, Universal Credit (or certain benefits that Universal Credit is replacing: Working Tax Credit, Income Support, income-related Employment and Support Allowance, or income-based Jobseeker's Allowance), you will usually both be entitled to free NHS prescriptions, NHS dental treatment, NHS wigs and fabric supports and routine NHS sight tests. You are both equally entitled to the maximum value of an optical voucher to help towards the cost of glasses or contact lenses and payment of travel costs to and from hospital for NHS treatment.

Even if you are not automatically entitled to help with the above costs, you and your partner may be entitled to some help on the grounds of low income. Complete claim form HC1 – available at NHS hospitals, dentists, opticians, GPs and chemists. If you are eligible for help, you will be sent a certificate that is valid for up to 12 months according to your circumstances. Depending on your income, you may receive an HC2 certificate, which entitles you to full help with NHS costs, or alternatively an HC3 certificate, which will entitle you to partial help. See nhsbsa.nhs.uk/nhs-help-health-costs or, if you live in Scotland, gov.scot/publications/hcs-1-entitled-help-health-costs.

The GOV.UK website has an online tool that you can use to check if you are eligible for full or partial help with NHS costs: gov.uk/help-nhs-costs.

Prescriptions

In Scotland, Wales and Northern Ireland, prescriptions are free. England is the only nation of the UK that charges. However, there are a number of exemptions. As described above, you do not pay if you are getting specified means-tested benefits or you've been accepted as having a low income. Men and women aged 60 and over are entitled to free NHS prescriptions, regardless of income. You will also qualify for free prescriptions if you have certain health conditions, such as cancer. You can use the government's online tool to check if you are eligible: gov.uk/help-nhs-costs. Alternatively ask your pharmacist for guidance. If you are not sure if you qualify, you should pay for your prescription and ask the pharmacist for an NHS receipt form FP57, which tells you how to claim a refund. For further information, see leaflet HC11 *Help with health costs*, obtainable from some pharmacies and GP surgeries.

People who do not qualify for free prescriptions but who require a lot of prescriptions could save money by purchasing a prescription prepayment certificate. A prepayment certificate will work out cheaper if you are likely to need more than four prescription items in three months, or more than 14 items in 12 months, as there is no further charge regardless of how many prescription items you require. See nhsbsa.nhs.uk.

Going into hospital

Except in an emergency, your first port of call for medical help is your GP, who will refer you to a hospital if necessary. Many patients are unaware that they can ask their GP to refer them to a consultant at a different NHS hospital from their local one or even, in certain cases, help make arrangements for them to be treated overseas. Before you can become a patient at another hospital, your GP will need to agree to your being referred. A major consideration will be whether the treatment would be as clinically effective as the treatment you would receive locally.

Those likely to need help on leaving hospital should speak to the hospital social worker, who will help make any necessary arrangements. Help is sometimes available to assist patients with their travel costs to and from hospital. If you receive means-tested benefits or your income is low (see *Help with NHS costs* earlier in this chapter), you can ask for repayment of 'necessary travel costs'. If you go into hospital you will continue to receive your State Pension and any bereavement benefits as normal. Means-tested benefits and disability benefits usually continue in full for 28 days, but may be reduced if you are in hospital for longer. Jobseeker's Allowance stops while you are in hospital because you are no longer able to seek work. You will need to tell the government agency that deals with your benefits so that your benefits are adjusted correctly. For further information, see leaflet GL12 *Going into hospital?*, obtainable from your GP, social security or Jobcentre Plus offices and NHS hospitals. There is also useful guidance on the Turn2Us website at turn2us.org.uk, in the section *Hospital and benefits – means-tested benefits when you go into hospital*.

Complaints

The NHS has a complaints procedure if you are unhappy about the treatment you have received. In the first instance, you should speak to someone close to the cause of the problem, such as the doctor, nurse, receptionist or practice manager. If, for whatever reason, you would prefer to speak to someone who was not involved in your care, you can speak to the complaints manager at your local NHS trust or strategic health authority instead; the addresses will be in the telephone directory. In jargon terms, this first stage is known as *local resolution*.

If you are not satisfied with the reply you receive, you can ask the NHS trust or strategic health authority for an *independent review*. The complaints manager will be able to tell you whom to contact about arranging this. If you are still dissatisfied after the independent review, then the Health Service Ombudsman may be able to help. The Ombudsman is independent of both government and the NHS and investigates complaints of failure or maladministration across the whole range of services provided by, or for, the NHS, including pharmacists, opticians and dentists, as well as private hospitals and nursing homes if these are paid for by the NHS. The Ombudsman cannot, however, take up legal causes on a patient's behalf.

Contacts are:

- **Northern Ireland Public Services Ombudsman:** nipso.org.uk;
- **Parliamentary and Health Service Ombudsman** for complaints in England: ombudsman.org.uk;
- **Public Services Ombudsman** for complaints in Wales: ombudsman.wales;
- **Scottish Public Services Ombudsman:** spso.org.uk.

If you wish to make a complaint, there is a time limit. You should register complaints within 12 months of the incident or within 12 months of your realizing that you have reason for complaint. If you need further advice on the complaints procedure, see the independent complaints advisory service, PohWER: pohwer.net.

Rather than proceed through the formal channels described above, an alternative approach is to contact the Patients Association – an independent advice centre that offers guidance to patients in the event of a problem with the health service: patients-association.org.uk.

Alternative medicine

Alternative medicine is dismissed by some doctors out of hand, while many patients claim that it is of great benefit. Here are some of the better-known organizations:

- The **British Acupuncture Council** is the home of traditional acupuncture in the UK. With around 3,000 members, it is the UK's largest body of professional acupuncturists, where excellence in training, safe practice and professional standards are paramount. To find an acupuncturist in your local area, see acupuncture.org.uk.

- **British Chiropractic Association** practitioners specialize in the diagnosis, treatment and overall management of conditions that are due to problems with the joints, ligament, tendons and nerves, especially related to the spine. See chiropractic-uk.co.uk.

- The **British Homeopathic Association** exists to promote homeopathy practised by doctors and other healthcare professionals. For a list of practising GPs and pharmacies that stock homeopathic medicines, see britishhomeopathic.org.

- The **British Hypnotherapy Association** keeps a register of professionally trained practitioners who are able to treat phobias, emotional problems, anxiety, migraine, psoriasis or relationship difficulties. See www.hypnothera py-association.org.

- The **General Osteopathic Council** regulates the practice of osteopathy in the UK with over 5,000 registered practitioners. Osteopathy is a system of diagnosis and treatment of a wide range of medical conditions. See osteopathy.org.uk.

- The **Incorporated Society of Registered Naturopaths**: naturopathy is concerned with the underlying conditions that may cause illness, including, for example, diet, general fitness, posture, stress and the patient's mental outlook on life. See naturecuresociety.co.uk.

- The **National Institute of Medical Herbalists** is the UK's leading professional body representing herbal practitioners. It promotes the benefits, efficacy and safe use of herbal medicine. See nimh.org.uk.

Eyes

Did you know that regular sight tests can pick up conditions such as glaucoma, cataracts, macular degeneration, dry eye and inflammation of the cornea? They can also detect signs of other diseases including diabetes, hypertension (high blood pressure), thyroid toxicosis, auto immune disorders, pituitary tumours, raised cholesterol and shingles. It is advisable to have your sight checked at least every two years.

You will qualify for a free NHS sight test if you are aged 60 and over in England, Wales or Northern Ireland; at any age if you live in Scotland; you or your partner receive means-tested benefits or have a low income; or you have specified eye problems such as glaucoma or a family history that puts you at risk of such conditions. See *Help with NHS costs*, earlier in this chapter, for how to check whether you are eligible.

People with mobility problems who are unable to get to an optician can ask for a domiciliary visit to have their eyes examined at home. This is free for those with an HC2 certificate or who are in receipt of one of the benefits listed in *Help with NHS costs*. People with a (partial help) HC3 certificate can use this towards the cost of a private home visit by their optician. The going rate for private sight tests if you do have to pay is about £25.

You do not need a doctor's referral to have your eyes tested. Whether you have to pay or not, the optician must either give you a prescription identifying what type of glasses you require or give you a statement confirming that you have no need of spectacles. The prescription is valid for two years. If you do not use it straight away, you should keep it safe so that it is handy when you need to use it. When you do decide to buy spectacles or contact lenses, you are under no obligation to obtain them from the optician who tested your eyes, but can buy them where you like.

There is a voucher system for helping with the purchase of glasses or contact lenses. If you or your partner are in receipt of specified means-tested benefits or have a low income as described in the section on *Help with NHS costs*, you will receive an optical voucher, with a cash value. The amount you get will depend on your optical prescription. It might be sufficient to pay for your contact lenses or spectacles outright, or it may make only a small contribution towards the cost. Part of the equation will depend on the frames you choose. You will not be tied to any particular glasses: you can choose spectacles that cost more than the value of the voucher and pay the difference yourself.

People who are registered blind are entitled to a special tax allowance each year. For 2019/20 it is £2,450. For details, see gov.uk/blind-persons-allowance. A great deal of practical help can be obtained from the Royal National Institute of Blind People (RNIB). In addition to giving general advice and information, it can supply a range of special equipment, details of which can be found at rnib.org.uk.

Do you have a family history of glaucoma? Are you short-sighted? Do you have diabetes? Are you of African-Caribbean origin? If the answer to any of these is yes, and you're over 40, then you could be at increased risk of developing glaucoma. There are various types, but the most common is primary open angle glaucoma (POAG). It has no symptoms in the early stages, but slowly and painlessly destroys sight if not detected and treated. For more information, see glaucoma-association.com. Many elderly people with failing sight suffer from macular degeneration, which affects their ability to distinguish detail. Although there is no known cure, individuals can be helped to make the most effective use of their sight by special magnifiers and other aids, such as clip-on lenses that fit over normal spectacles. See partsight.org.uk. British Wireless for the Blind is a national independent charity providing specially modified audio equipment to all UK-registered blind or partially sighted people in receipt of means-tested benefits. See blind.org.uk.

The Equality Act 2010 requires businesses to take reasonable steps to make their services accessible to customers with disabilities. This is nowhere more important than in banking and day-to-day money services. Unfortunately, with the closure of bank branches, it is now more difficult to get face-to-face help. However, there are other options, so do request statements in alternative formats, such as Braille, large print or audio formats; and consider phone banking or online/mobile banking which you can access with the aid of a screen-reader. Some banks also offer talking cash machines.

Feet

Many people forget about their feet until they begin to give trouble. Corns and bunions, if neglected, can become extremely painful, and ideally everyone, especially women who wear high heels, should have podiatry treatment from early middle age or even younger. One of the problems of which podiatrists complain is that because many women wear uncomfortable shoes, they become used to having painful feet and do not notice when something is more seriously wrong. The result can sometimes be ingrowing toenails or infections. Podiatry is available on the NHS without referral from a doctor, but facilities tend to be very oversubscribed, so in many areas it is only the very elderly or those with a real problem who can get appointments.

The College of Podiatry is the professional association for registered chiropodists and podiatrists, and has a searchable directory of its members who are private practitioners across the UK and overseas. See cop.org.uk.

Hearing

In the UK alone there are 10 million people living with a hearing loss, and only 2 million of them are wearing hearing aids, even though many more could benefit from them. Being able to hear properly is important for a number of reasons: for safety and awareness; conversation and interaction; enjoyment and entertainment. Signs to look out for are:

- not hearing the doorbell or a telephone ring;
- turning up the television too loud for the comfort of others;
- failing to hear people come into the room;
- misunderstanding what has been said in conversation;
- not speaking clearly or speaking in a monotonous tone;
- uncertainty about where sounds are coming from;
- difficulty in hearing at a distance or in public gatherings.

If you have noticed any of these, talk to your GP, who may refer you to an audiologist or hearing care professional. They will be able to advise on the best course of action to help your hearing. You can obtain a hearing aid and batteries free on the NHS or buy them privately. There are many other aids on the market that can make life easier. BT, for example, provides guidance on a variety of special features and equipment for when a standard phone becomes too difficult to use. See btplc.com/inclusion.

There are other specialist organizations that can give you a lot of help on hearing aids and on other matters:

- **Action on Hearing Loss** (formerly the Royal National Institute for the Deaf) offers a wide range of services including sign language interpreters and other communication support. See actiononhearingloss.org.uk.

- **Boots Hearingcare** provides a 15-minute free appointment aimed at people who have not had a hearing test before, and are beginning to think they might have an issue. For more information see bootshearingcare.com/hearing-test.

- The **British Deaf Association** works to protect the interests of deaf people and also provides an advice service through its regional offices. See bda.org.uk.

- The **British Tinnitus Association** is a world leader, with a trained team of friendly and experienced advisers for anyone who experiences tinnitus or those simply seeking guidance or information about the condition. See tinnitus.org.uk.

- **Hearing Link** is a voluntary organization providing support and information to people with hearing loss, as well as their families. See hearinglink.org.

Teeth

Everyone knows the importance of having regular dental check-ups. Many adults, however, slip out of the habit, which could result in their having trouble with their teeth as they become older. Dentistry is one of the treatments for which you have to pay under the NHS, unless you have a low income – see *Help with NHS costs*, earlier in this chapter.

Help with the cost is all very well, but for many an even bigger problem than money is actually finding an NHS dentist in their area. You can use the NHS online search tool: nhs.uk/Service-Search/Dentists/LocationSearch/3. This will show you the dentists in your area and indicate whether or not they are taking on NHS patients. However, NHS dentists do not always have the time to give the depth of care and advice that you might be seeking, in which case a private dentist may be a better option. Private dentists tend to focus on prevention as much as treatment, and will spend time explaining and demonstrating good oral hygiene.

Prevention is always better than cure. If you want free, independent and impartial advice on all aspects of oral health and free literature on a wide range of topics, including patients' rights, finding a dentist and dental care for older people, see the Oral Health Foundation website at www.dentalhealth.org.

Personal relationships

Retirement, for couples, involves a major lifestyle change. With it comes fresh opportunities, and, inevitably, a few compromises are needed. Couples can sometimes find it difficult to adjust to spending longer together, while others may feel they have little left in common. There has been a recent increase in the over-60s' divorce rate, so it is important in the early stages of retirement that couples work out the best way of living together in their retirement. Normally, with goodwill and understanding on both sides, difficulties are quickly resolved to allow the relationship to flourish. However, for some couples it does not work out so easily, and it may be helpful to seek skilled guidance:

- **Albany Trust** is a professional therapy service for individuals and couples needing emotional and psychological help. See albanytrust.org.

- **Marriage Care** offers a similar service, plus a confidential telephone helpline, for those who are having problems with their marriage or other close personal relationship. See marriagecare.org.uk.

- **The Spark** is a leading provider of couples counselling and marriage counselling in Scotland. See thespark.org.uk.

- **Relate,** the relationship people, offers advice, relationship counselling, sex therapy, workshops, mediation, consultations and support face to face, by phone and through the website. See relate.org.uk.

Help for grandparents

A sad result of today's divorce statistics is the risk to grandparents of losing contact with their grandchildren. While some divorcing parents lean over backwards to avoid this happening, others – maybe through force of circumstance or hurt feelings – deny grandparents access or even sever the relationship completely. Recourse to the law is never a step to be taken lightly and should obviously be avoided if there is the possibility that a more conciliatory approach could be successful. There are a number of organizations that have experience of advising grandparents and offer practical help and support:

- Grandparents Plus: grandparentsplus.org.uk;

- Gransnet: gransnet.com.

Depression

Depression is a condition that may develop as a result of the lifestyle change from working to having time on your hands. If you find being on your own difficult, or you suffer from loss of self-esteem due to no longer having the status of your job, and the resulting boredom or general lack of purpose, then sometimes, depression can result. If the condition persists for more than a few days, or seems to be more than simply feeling a bit sad or low, then a doctor should always be consulted, as depression can be a debilitating condition. If you find yourself concerned for your mental health or that of a loved one, there are several organizations that may be able to help:

- **Mind**: mind.org.uk;
- **NHS**: nhs.uk/conditions/stress-anxiety-depression;
- **Samaritans**: samaritans.org;
- **Sane**: sane.org.uk.

Some common afflictions

You may be one of the lucky ones and the rest of this chapter will be of no further interest to you. It deals with some of the more common afflictions, such as back pain and heart disease, as well as with disability. However, if you are unfortunate enough to be affected, or have a member of your family who is, then knowing which organizations can provide support could make all the difference in helping you to cope.

Aphasia

This condition makes it hard to speak, read or understand language, and affects individuals who have suffered a stroke, a head injury or other neurological damage. The Stroke Association offers information and support to people with aphasia, their families and their carers. See stroke.org.uk/what-is-aphasia.

Arthritis and rheumatism

You don't have to put up with the pain of arthritis. There are a number of websites to help you:

- **Arthritis Action** is a national charity that promotes ways to increase mobility and lessen the pain of arthritis sufferers. See arthritisaction.org.uk.
- **Versus Arthritis** (formerly Arthritis Care and Arthritis Research UK) exists to support people with arthritis. It encourages self-help and has

local branches and groups offering practical support and social activities. See versusarthritis.org and arthritiscare.org.uk.

Back pain

Four out of five people suffer from back pain at some stage of their lives. While there are many different causes, doctors agree that much of the trouble could be avoided through correct posture, care in lifting heavy articles, a firm mattress, and chairs that provide support in the right places. The following two organizations could be helpful:

- Back in Action established since 1988, offers back care products to help prevent back trouble or provide relief for those who suffer. See backinaction.co.uk.
- BackCare is a national charity that aims to reduce the impact of back pain on society. It acts as a hub between patients, healthcare professionals, employers, policy makers, researchers and all others with an interest in back pain. See backcare.org.uk.

Blood pressure

High blood pressure is the leading cause of strokes in the UK and can lead to heart attack and heart failure. One in three adults has high blood pressure but a third of those will be completely unaware of it. Anyone over the age of 50 should keep a check on their blood pressure as it tends to rise with age. Post-menopausal women also see an increase in their blood pressure. The good news is that blood pressure can be successfully managed with medication and some simple lifestyle changes. In brief:

- watch your salt intake;
- eat at least five portions of fruit and vegetables per day;
- watch your weight;
- cut down on alcohol;
- take regular exercise;
- laugh – watch a funny movie;
- be sociable – lonely people often suffer from high blood pressure.

The Blood Pressure Association offers help and information – see bpassoc. org.uk.

Cancer

Cancer is now a subject that is often discussed openly, and with continuing research and improved treatments more people suffering from cancer make a complete recovery. Early diagnosis can make a vital difference. Doctors recommend that all women should undergo regular screening for cervical cancer, and women over 50 are advised to have a routine mammography to screen for breast cancer at least once every three years. Computerized cervical screening systems for women aged 25 to 64 and breast cancer screening units for women aged 50 to 70 are available nationwide. In both cases, older women can have access to the services on request. It also goes without saying that anyone with a lump or swelling, however small, should waste no time in having it investigated by a doctor. Routine screening for bowel cancer using a home-test kit is now offered by the NHS every two years to people aged 60 to 74.

There is so much work being done to cure cancer that now more than 50 cancer charities exist to research or focus on a particular variant of the disease. To find a list of all of them consult charitychoice.co.uk. There are also many excellent support groups for people affected by cancer, including:

- **Bowel Cancer UK** aims to save lives by raising awareness of bowel cancer, campaigning for best treatment and care, and providing practical support and advice. See bowelcanceruk.org.uk.

- **Breast Cancer Care** offers practical advice, information and emotional support to women who have, or fear they have, breast cancer or benign breast disease. See breastcancercare.org.uk.

- **Macmillan Cancer Support** improves the lives of people affected by cancer, providing practical, medical and financial information and support. See macmillan.org.uk.

- **Marie Curie** offers free, practical information and emotional support for people affected by terminal illness. See mariecurie.org.uk.

Chest and heart diseases

The earlier sections on smoking, diet, drink and exercise list some of the most pertinent 'dos and don'ts' that can help prevent heart disease. The advice should be taken seriously. Statistics reveal that UK death rates from coronary heart disease are among the highest in the world, killing almost 120,000 people a year, and coronary heart disease is responsible for one in five of all deaths. Although people tend to think of heart attacks as particularly affecting men, over four times as many women die from heart disease as from breast cancer.

British Heart Foundation's vision is a world where people do not die prematurely from heart disease. It plays a leading role in the fight against diseases of the heart and circulation. See bhf.org.uk.

Cholesterol

High levels of 'bad cholesterol' in the blood are associated with a raised risk of heart attack, stroke and other cardio-vascular disease. Like raised blood pressure (which sometimes but not always occurs alongside high cholesterol), there are no symptoms and the only way to measure your cholesterol level is to have a blood test. A check on cholesterol is part of the NHS routine health checks offered to people over 40 (50 in Wales).

Good diet (especially avoiding saturated fats), exercise and maintaining a healthy weight may be enough to keep your cholesterol at an acceptable level. However, you may be prescribed a class of drugs called statins. Controversially, some medical experts suggest statins should be prescribed to virtually everyone over 50 as a preventative measure, rather than simply treating people who already have high cholesterol levels. Statins have been associated with side effects in some people, particularly muscle pain and weakness, although the incidence of these effects is low. For more information, see the following websites:

- **British Heart Foundation**: bhf.org.uk;
- **Heart UK**: heartuk.org.uk;
- **NHS**: nhs.uk/conditions/high-cholesterol.

Diabetes

Diabetes occurs when the amount of glucose in the blood is too high for the body to use properly. It can sometimes be treated by diet alone; sometimes pills or insulin may also be needed. Diabetes can be diagnosed at any age, although it is common in the elderly and especially among individuals who are overweight.

- **Diabetes UK** is the charity that aims to improve the lives of people with diabetes. See diabetes.org.uk.

- **Independent Diabetes Trust** (formerly the Insulin Dependent Diabetes Trust) is a small charity offering support and information to people with diabetes and their families on the issues that are important to them. See iddt.org.

Migraine

Migraine affects one in seven people in the UK. It can involve severe head pains, nausea, vomiting, visual disturbances and in some cases temporary paralysis. The leading UK charity that funds and promotes research, holds international symposia and runs an extensive support service is the Migraine Trust – see migrainetrust.org.

Osteoporosis and menopause problems

Healthy bones are important. A diet which is rich in calcium and vitamin D builds and maintains healthy bones. Strong bones help reduce the risk of breaking bones should we fall when we grow older. Around 255,000 emergency admissions to hospital a year relate to falls among the over-65s. Over 3 million people in the UK have osteoporosis, putting them at higher risk of fractures and breaks if they fall. It affects one in two women (and one in five men), and often develops following the menopause, when body levels of oestrogen naturally decrease.

The following websites may be useful:

- **Menopause Exchange** gives independent advice and practical information on a range of topics concerning health issues affecting women in mid-life. See menopause-exchange.co.uk.

- The **Royal Osteoporosis Society** is the only UK-wide charity dedicated to improving the diagnosis, prevention and treatment of osteoporosis. See theros.org.uk.

- **Women's Health Concern** provides an independent service to advise, reassure and educate women about their health concerns, to enable them to work in partnership with their own medical practitioners and health advisers. This is a branch of the British Menopause Society. See womens-health-concern.org.

Stroke

Over 130,000 people suffer a stroke every year in England and Wales. A stroke is a brain injury caused by the sudden interruption of blood flow, which has a greater disability impact than any other medical condition. It is unpredictable in its effects, which may include muscular paralysis or weakness on one side, loss of speech or loss of understanding or language, visual problems or incontinence. Prevention is similar to the prevention of heart disease. The Stroke Association works to prevent strokes and helps stroke patients and their families – see stroke.org.uk.

Disability

Disability is mainly covered in Chapter 13, *Caring for elderly parents*, so if you or someone in your family has a problem you may find the answer you need there. In this section, there are simply one or two points that may be useful for others.

Benefits

If you are on a means-tested benefit, such as the Guarantee Credit part of Pension Credit or Universal Credit, and have a disability, you may be entitled to extra money on top of the standard allowance. Various social security benefits are also available to those with special problems because of health issues, regardless of income and savings (see gov.uk). The aim of these benefits is to help with the additional costs you incur because of disability. They include:

- Attendance Allowance for people over State Pension age. See gov.uk/attendance-allowance.
- Personal Independence Payment (PIP) for people who have not reached State Pension age. See gov.uk/pip.

Local authority services

The adult social care departments of local councils provide many of the services that people with disabilities may need, including:

- Assessments to determine what kind of help you may need.

- Practical help in the home, perhaps with the support of a home help or care worker. This is usually means-tested, so you may have to pay part or all of the cost yourself.

- Adaptations to your home, such as a ramp for a wheelchair or other special equipment for your safety. Again, this may be means-tested.

- Meals on wheels, though this is no longer available in many areas or has been replaced by charitable providers, such as local Age UK schemes or guidance on ordering groceries online.

- Provision of day centres, clubs and similar.

- The issue of badges for cars driven or used by people with a disability. You can apply online and the government will forward your request to your local council: gov.uk/apply-blue-badge.

- Advice about other transport services or concessions that may be available locally.

In most instances, you should speak to a social worker who will either be able to make the arrangements or point you in the right direction. He or she will also be able to tell you of any special facilities or other help provided by the authority. Ten years of austerity and local authority budget cuts have taken their toll and some councils have stripped back their services to the bare minimum that the law requires – so what support is available where you live has become something of a postcode lottery. Supporting people with a disability is part of councils' legal requirement, but they can charge for services unless your income is low.

Healthcare

Services are normally arranged through either a GP or the local authority health centre. Key professional staff include:

- health visitors (who are qualified nurses), who, rather like social workers, will be able to put you in touch with whatever specialized services are required;

- district nurses, who will visit patients in their home;

- physiotherapists, who use exercise and massage to help improve mobility, for example after an operation;

- medical social workers, employed in hospitals, who will help with any arrangements before a patient is discharged;
- occupational therapists, who can advise about special equipment and help teach someone with a disability through training and exercise how best to manage.

Council tax

If someone in your family has a disability, you may be able to claim a reduction on your council tax. If you have a blue badge on your car, you may get a rebate for a garage. You would normally apply to the housing benefits officer, but different councils employ different officers to deal with this. To find your local council, see gov.uk/find-local-council.

12
Holidays

For fit and active older people, there really is no limit when it comes to adventure tourism and far-flung continents. But if you are thinking of your carbon footprint, it isn't necessary to go abroad to try out some exciting activities while on holiday. Mountain climbing, skiing and cycling in England, Wales and Scotland are popular holidays for over-50s. Should you be thinking of camping in the sunshine in Devon and Cornwall, or canoeing through the Norfolk Broads, all are available not too far from home. The beauty of an activity holiday in Britain is that it can take the form of a short break over a weekend. These holidays are also great for meeting and staying in touch with other UK holidaymakers.

Let your imagination roam free when considering the options for an active or adventure holiday. Don't just look at the usual holiday brochures; get on the internet and seek out adventure holiday companies. This year perhaps it's time for you to try something different that will provide unforgettable experiences. The choice is enormous. If you wish to go somewhere exotic, it is likely the prices will be high; but if your budget is limited, with a bit of research you will find some holidays that are extremely reasonable in cost. To help you choose, a couple of the main newspapers publish travel lists, focusing on the best holidays of different types. See theguardian.com/travel/top10 and telegraph.co.uk/travel/lists.

A word of warning: many of the sad tales of holiday woe one hears could have been avoided, or at least softened by compensation. It is essential that holidaymakers check to ensure that their travel agent or tour operator is affiliated to either the Association of British Travel Agents (ABTA) or the Association of Tour Operators (ATO). Both organizations have strict regulations that all member companies must follow, and both run an arbitration scheme in the event of complaints. No one can guarantee you against every mishap, but a recognized travel company plus adequate insurance should go a long way towards giving you at least some measure of protection.

Insurance

Holiday insurance, once you are over the age of 65, is not only more difficult to obtain but also tends to be considerably more expensive, especially if you have health issues. However, were you unfortunate enough to fall ill or experience some other mishap, it would almost certainly cost you very much more than paying a bit extra for decent insurance. Age Co (the commercial arm of Age UK) offers insurance policies for the over-50s and with pre-existing medical conditions – ageco.co.uk/insurance/travel-insurance – as does Saga (saga.co.uk/insurance/travel-insurance). However, there are many other providers catering for older age groups and policies targeted at particular age groups do not necessarily offer the best deal, so it's worth shopping around. The easiest way to do this is using a price comparison website, such as:

- comparethemarket.com;
- confused.com;
- gocompare.com;
- moneysupermarket.com;
- travelsupermarket.com;
- uswitch.com.

Price comparison websites search a wide range of policies, but don't cover the whole market, so it's a good idea to use more than one site before settling on the deal you go for. With travel insurance you will need to disclose any pre-existing medical conditions fully before you can get a quote, and be aware that you will also need to declare the health conditions of anyone close to you that could cause you to cancel your trip. If your circumstances are non-standard, you may want the help of a broker, for example a member of the British Insurance Brokers Association: see biba.org.uk. If you have a pre-existing health condition, these specialist comparison websites may help: medicaltravelcompared.co.uk and allcleartravel.co.uk.

Many tour operators try to insist that, as a condition of booking, you either buy their inclusive insurance package or make private arrangements that are at least as good. While this suggests that they are demanding very high standards, terms and conditions and price vary greatly. Before signing on the dotted line, you should read the small print carefully. Be sure to check that the package you are being offered meets all the eventualities and provides you with adequate cover should you make a claim. It may be convenient to take the cover offered, but you will probably be able to find as good cover more cheaply if you arrange it independently.

You can choose between single-trip insurance policies and annual travel policies. Annual policies often cost very little extra, so, even if you're not quite sure how many trips you will make, it may be worth taking out an annual policy. However, do be aware that you may be required to tell the insurer about any changes, for example, to your health, that occur within the year covered by your annual policy, and this could result in an in-year change in your cover or the cost or even cancellation of your policy.

What cover to look for

Here are some top tips when buying holiday insurance. Your policy should cover you for:

- **Medical expenses,** including hospital treatment and the cost of an ambulance, an air ambulance, flights home (which may require extra space if you are injured or ill) and emergency dental treatment, plus expenses for a companion who may have to remain overseas with you should you become ill. The Money Advice Service suggests you have coverage of £1 million if travelling in Europe, and £2 million for travel elsewhere. Some experts suggest £5 million or even £10 million, especially if you are going to North America because of the high cost of treatment there.

- **Personal liability cover,** should you cause injury to another person or property. The Money Advice Service suggests at least £1 million is the norm.

- **Personal accident** leading to injury or death (check the small print, as some policies have reduced cover for older travellers).

- **Additional hotel and repatriation costs** resulting from injury or illness.

- **Loss of deposit or cancellation** (check what emergencies or contingencies this covers).

- The **cost of having to curtail your holiday,** including extra travel expenses, because of serious illness in the family.

- **Inconvenience** caused by flight cancellations or other travel delays.

- **Baggage and personal effects** and emergency purchases should your baggage be delayed. Money Advice Service notes that most policies include between £1,500 and £3,000 of cover. However, there may be limits per item and there is usually an excess (the first part of a claim that you must bear).

- **Loss of personal money** and documents.

If you are planning to take your car abroad, you will need to check your existing car insurance to ensure that you are properly covered and may need to pay extra to extend your cover. Note that if you have a car provided through Motability, the insurance covers you while driving in the EU, Iceland, Norway, Switzerland and Liechtenstein: motability.co.uk/information-for-customers/taking-your-car-abroad. Alternatively, if you are planning to hire a vehicle overseas, you will be required to take out the cover provided by the hire company.

It is essential that you take copies of the insurance documents with you, as losses or other claims must normally be reported immediately. You will also be required to quote the reference number and/or other details given on the docket. Additionally, there may be particular guidelines laid down by the policy. For instance, you may have to ring a helpline before incurring medical expenses. Failure to report a claim within the specified time limit could nullify your right to compensation. The best advice is to check that you have the 24-hour helpline number and to keep it with you at all times.

Be sure to get a receipt for any special expenses you incur – extra hotel bills, medical treatment, long-distance phone calls and so on. You may not get all the costs reimbursed, but if your insurance covers some or all of these contingencies you will need to produce evidence of your expenditure.

The Association of British Insurers has information on holiday insurance and motoring abroad – see www.abi.org.uk. ABTA operates a code of conduct for all travel agents and tour operators that are ABTA members, and helps holidaymakers seek redress if they are dissatisfied with their travel company. See abta.com.

Medical cover in Europe

For as long as the UK is part of the EU, you can get emergency medical treatment in another EU country plus Iceland, Liechtenstein, Norway and Switzerland on the same basis as local residents if you have a European Health Insurance Card (EHIC). However, do not assume this is a substitute for the medical cover that a travel insurance policy will provide. The EHIC covers only emergency treatment and, in some European countries, even local residents would have to pay for treatment so you will too. Moreover, the EHIC does not cover, for instance, mountain rescue, repatriation to the UK, or paying for a hotel room if you have to extend your stay to look after a sick relative, all of which could quickly rack up substantial costs.

Many travel insurers will require you to have an EHIC if you are travelling in Europe. There is no charge for an EHIC, which lasts for five years, and all UK residents are eligible, though residents of the Channel Islands and Isle of Man are not. Each person, including members of the same family, requires his or her own individual card. If you already have one, check that your card has not expired, because if it has, it can easily be renewed. To obtain a card, or to renew one, go to gov.uk/european-health-insurance-card, or you can phone 0300 330 1350.

If or when the UK leaves the EU, the EHIC is unlikely to be valid, and it will be all the more important that you have bought a suitable travel insurance policy.

Cancelled or overbooked flights

Also useful to know about is the Denied Boarding Regulation, which is European legislation that entitles passengers who cannot travel because their flight is overbooked to some immediate cash payment. This applies even if the airline puts them up in a hotel or books them onto an alternative flight a few hours later. To qualify, passengers must have a confirmed reservation and have checked in on time. Also, the airport where they were 'bumped off' must be in an EU country. (It may sometimes also be possible to get compensation in the United States.)

If, as opposed to being overbooked, your flight is cancelled, you are entitled to get a refund if you decide not to travel. Alternatively, you can request to be re-routed. You may get compensation depending on the length of your journey and how long you are delayed. If the delay is more than two hours, you will also be entitled to meals or refreshments plus two free telephone calls, e-mails or faxes. If it is overnight and you have more than five hours' wait, you will be put up in a hotel and given free transfers. Compensation is not, however, obligatory if the cancellation is due to 'extraordinary circumstances which could not have been avoided'. See the Civil Aviation Authority's consumer guidance at caa.co.uk/consumers.

If you miss your flight or have to cancel your trip, you may be able to get a refund on at least a small part of the ticket cost. Most airlines will reimburse non-fliers for the air passenger duty and overseas government taxes. This applies even to normal non-refundable tickets. However, you have to make a claim, and in most cases there is an administration charge payable. If you booked through a travel agent, there could be a second administration charge. Even so, especially for long-haul travel and family holidays, the savings could be quite considerable.

Travel and other concessions

Buses, coaches, some airline companies and especially the railways offer valuable concessions to people of retirement age.

Trains

Some of the best-value savings that are available to anyone aged 60 and over are provided by train companies. These include:

- **Disabled Persons Railcard:** costs £20 for one year or £54 for three years and entitles the holder and one accompanying adult to reduced train fares. See disabledpersons-railcard.co.uk.

- **Family and Friends Railcard:** costs £30 for a whole year and entitles up to four adults and four children to travel on one card. Adults get one-third off and children get 60 per cent off the normal child fare. See familyandfriends-railcard.co.uk.

- **Network Railcard:** costs £30 and is valid for 12 months, available only in London and the south-east. It gives a one-third reduction on most fares, but on weekdays is restricted to travel starting after 10 am. Up to three adults can travel with you and they will also get a third off their fares, and you can take four children with you and save 60 per cent on their fares. See network-railcard.co.uk.

- **Senior Railcard:** for those aged 60-plus, costs £30 for one year or £70 for three years. It entitles you to a third off a wide range of tickets, including standard and first-class fares, plus discounts on hotels, restaurants and days out. See senior-railcard.co.uk.

- **Two Together Railcard:** for two named adults travelling together. You don't have to be a couple – it could be you and a friend or one of the family. It costs £30 for a year. See twotogether-railcard.co.uk.

Buses and coaches

Over 11 million people over 60 in the UK use buses for free travel around the country. If you live in England, and you are either over State Pension age or have a disability, you can travel free on local buses anywhere in England between 9.30am and 11pm on weekdays and all day weekends and public holidays. However, if you live in London, you can get a free travel pass from age 60 but restricted to London buses, tubes and other public transport. To apply, contact your local council – you can find its website by entering your postcode at gov.uk/apply-for-elderly-person-bus-pass.

If you live in Scotland, over-60s and people with a disability can travel free on local buses and scheduled long-distance coach services in Scotland at any time – no time restrictions. To apply, contact your local authority. For further information, see transport.gov.scot/concessionary-travel/60plus-or-disabled/.

If you live in Wales, over-60s and people with a disability can travel free on local buses in Wales at any time. People living in Wales can also use their passes to travel free on cross-boundary journeys into and out of England, provided the journey starts or finishes in Wales. To apply, contact your local council – you can find its website by entering your postcode at gov.uk/apply-for-elderly-person-bus-pass.

There are often reduced rates for senior citizens and people with disabilities on long-distance buses and coaches. For example, National Express has a Senior Coachcard for people aged 60 and over, and a Disabled Coachcard, both of which offer savings of a third – see nationalexpress.com/en/offers/coachcards. If you are planning to travel by coach, it is worth shopping around to find out what bargains are available.

Airlines

On the whole, airlines do not offer discounts to older travellers, although some do on internal flights within the US. However, it's worth asking your travel agent or the airline at the time of booking what special discounts, if any, are offered.

Overseas

Many countries offer travel and other reductions to older holidaymakers including, for example, discounts for entry to museums and galleries, day excursions, sporting events and other entertainment – so it's always worth asking. As in Britain, provisions are liable to change, and for up-to-date information probably the best source to contact is the national tourist office of the country to which you are travelling.

Many European countries offer discounted rail travel for older travellers who have an appropriate railcard. The railcard you need varies from one country to another. Holders of a Railplus Card can get discounts on many cross-border European trains. The website or operator through which you book your tickets can advise on what cards may be available and how to get them.

Airport meet-and-greet services

If you hate the hassle of parking your car in the long-stay car park and collecting it again on your return after a long journey, BCP offers a better choice for parking – it operates a meet-and-greet service at a variety of airports across the UK. Another option is to stay over the night before your flight in a hotel that allows you to leave your car in its car park until your return. See parkbcp.co.uk.

A number of firms offer a similar meet-and-greet service but, at the time of booking, enquire where your car will be parked. Also, when dropping it off it would be sensible to ask for a 'conditions form' to complete, to avoid disputes if you find any damage on your return.

Health tips for travellers

Remember to pack any regular medicines you require: even familiar branded products can be difficult to obtain in some countries. Also take a mini first-aid kit, including plasters, disinfectant, tummy pills and so on.

If you are going to any developing country, consult your doctor as to what medicines (and any special precautions) you should take. Have any inoculations or vaccinations well in advance of your departure date.

One of the most common ailments among British travellers abroad is too much sun. In some countries it really burns, so take it easy, wear a hat and apply plenty of protective lotion. The other big travellers' woe is 'Delhi belly', which unhappily can occur in most hot countries, even within Europe. Beware the water, ice, salads, seafood, ice cream and any fruit that you do not peel yourself. Always wash your hands before eating or handling food, particularly if you are camping or caravanning.

Travelling is tiring and a sudden change of climate more debilitating than most of us admit. Allow plenty of time during the first couple of days to acclimatize before embarking on any activity programme.

When flying, wear loose clothes and above all comfortable shoes, as feet and ankles tend to swell in the air. To avoid risk of deep vein thrombosis, which can be fatal, medical advice is to do foot exercises and walk around the plane from time to time. For long-haul travel especially, wear compression stockings and, another tip, unless advised otherwise by your doctor, take an aspirin before flying. On long journeys, it helps to drink plenty of water and remember the warning that 'an alcoholic drink in the air is worth two on the ground'. If you have a special diet, inform whoever makes your booking. Most airlines, especially on long-distance journeys, serve vegetarian food.

For more information, specific to the countries you will be visiting, see gov.uk/foreign-travel-advice.

Driving abroad

A number of organizations, including in particular some ferry operators, offer packages for the motorist that include ferry crossings, accommodation and insurance. While these often provide very good value, some people prefer to make all their own arrangements in order to get exactly what they want. Here are some of the major operators:

- The **AA**: for all your motoring needs, at home and abroad, including route planning, maps, AA Five Star Europe Breakdown Assistance and travel service. See theaa.com.
- **Brittany Ferries**: sail and holiday choices, planning your trip, ferry bookings, holiday bookings, routes and timetables. See brittany-ferries.co.uk.
- The **RAC**: for overseas single-trip or annual travel insurance, plus international driving permits and roadside assistance. See rac.co.uk.

Bear in mind that, if Brexit goes ahead, there is likely to be a return of the need to get an international driving permit to drive in Europe as well as a 'green card' to extend your insurance and a GB sticker on the back of your car.

Here are some top tips when motoring abroad, if taking your own vehicle:

- have your car thoroughly serviced before you go;
- make sure your GB sticker is clearly visible;
- check for travel advice at gov.uk/foreign-travel-advice;
- have headlight converters if driving in Europe;
- get insured for medical and travel purposes for the countries you are visiting;
- invest in a good guide book on your destination that advises on local customs and laws;
- check whether you require a green card for the countries you are visiting;
- make sure your passport is valid and you have necessary visas;
- find out about speed limits and if you require any specific equipment;
- check whether your breakdown cover provides roadside assistance while abroad;

- make sure all documentation is easily available, should you need it;
- take the following with you: a tool kit, the manual for your car, spare fuses, a fuel can, a mechanic's light that plugs into the cigarette lighter socket, at least one extra set of keys, and any extras required by local laws such as a reflective tabard and warning triangles;
- always lock your car and park it in a secure place overnight.

Other sources of advice and services are:

- **Association of British Insurers:** abi.org.uk;
- **Europ Assistance:** europ-assistance.com;
- **Green Flag:** greenflag.com.

If instead of taking your own car you plan to hire a vehicle overseas, you will probably have to buy special insurance at the time of hiring the vehicle. Make sure that this is properly comprehensive (check for any excesses or exclusions) or, at the very least, it gives you adequate third-party cover. If in doubt, seek advice from the local motoring organization regarding essential requirements, and do not sign any documents unless you understand them. Typically, you will have to agree to an excess (the first part of any claim that you will pay) unless you buy additional insurance to cover the excess.

If you are not used to driving a left-hand-drive vehicle, consider hiring an automatic. And, if you have not driven an automatic before, you might want to book a lesson in one with a driving school before you set out on your holiday.

How is your driving?

If you've recently travelled in a car and been frightened by a friend's driving, or you think you might be starting to scare others with your driving skills, it is simple enough to get yourself checked. RoSPA Advanced Drivers and Riders offers to a mature driver assessment for anyone wanting to check their driving skills and confidence. It takes about an hour, while you go out with a tactful and helpful examiner who will be a serving or retired police officer. If you pass, you'll receive a certificate and in all cases you receive a written report and practical suggestions for improvement. The assessment costs £55, but it is money well spent to stay safe on the road. See roadar.org.uk/drivers/driving-assessments.htm.

Visa and passport requirements

All too many people get caught out at the airport by not keeping up to date with the visa and other requirements of the country to which they are travelling. These sometimes change without much warning and, at worst if you get it wrong, can result in your being turned away on arrival.

Don't get caught out at customs when you return from a non-EU trip. You can now bring back up to £390 worth of goods for your own use or as gifts (with additional separate limits for alcohol and tobacco) without paying import duties or VAT. But you can't split items – you have to pay the full bill on, say, a £500 camera and not just the balance over £390. And you can't share a high-value item with someone else either. See gov.uk/duty-free-goods/arrivals-from-outside-the-eu. There is, at the time of writing, no duty on goods you bring into the UK from another EU country, but this could change if or when the UK leaves the EU.

Health and safety advice

This sometimes changes and travel agents are not always as good as they should be about keeping customers informed. The best advice, especially if you are travelling out of Europe, including to the United States, is to check the information for the countries you will be visiting at gov.uk/foreign-travel-advice. For the 225 countries listed, this site gives you information about safety and security, terrorism, local laws and customs, entry requirements, health, money and where to get emergency help while abroad. The best plan is to check the site several weeks before departure, to allow time for any inoculations, and again just before you leave.

13
Caring for elderly parents

As anyone who is helping and supporting elderly parents will know, not only is it often difficult and confusing to access care, it is hard to know how good that care is. In addition, it can cost a fortune, and provision varies depending on where you live – a veritable postcode lottery. The undoubted preference for most elderly people is that they remain in their own homes for as long as possible. With a bit of support from friends, relatives or local care organizations, many can and will be able to do this. The main focus of this chapter is on helping aged parents remain as independent as possible, for as long as possible, until a care home or nursing home becomes necessary.

Ways of adapting a home

Many elderly people will not require anything more complicated than a few general improvements. Many of these adaptations are changes you could make yourself if you are up to a bit of DIY, or can be carried out by local contractors. In the case of equipment, such as grab rails, hoists, accessible showers and other aids, there are many suppliers both online and bricks-and-mortar shops where you can buy what you need. It is also possible to borrow equipment. The following organizations may be helpful:

- **Age UK:** local branches can often loan equipment, such as wheelchairs, in the short term and may also be able to advise on local stockists. To find your local branch, see ageuk.org.uk.

- **Boots:** Larger branches of Boots sell a wide range of special items for people with disabilities, including bath aids, wheelchairs and crutches, or visit boots.com/health-pharmacy/livingaids.

- **British Red Cross** local branches make short-term loans of wheelchairs and other equipment, such as toileting aids. Sometimes there is a charge or you may be invited to make a donation. Its online shop also sells a variety of aids. See redcross.org.uk.

- **CAE** (Centre for Accessible Environments) offers a range of access consultancy services customized to the needs of clients. See cae.org.uk.

- **DEMAND** (Design & Manufacture for Disability) is an independent charity that transforms the lives of disabled people through the provision of bespoke equipment. It does not charge clients for its services. See demand.org.uk.

- The **Disabled Living Foundation** is one of the UK's leading health charities, providing impartial advice and information to people of all ages, to help them find equipment to assist with everyday tasks essential to independent living: dlf.org.uk.

- **Disability Wales/Anabledd Cymru** is another helpful source of advice: disabilitywales.org.

- **Hearing and Mobility** has a range of mobility aids and equipment that is available online or through a number of outlet stores nationwide: hearingandmobility.co.uk.

- **Independent Living** has information about equipment and adaptations and a list of suppliers: independentliving.co.uk.

- **Independent Living Centres** (also called Disabled Living Centres or Disabled Resources Centres) is a network of showrooms around the UK where you can get information and advice and also try out equipment. To find your local centre, ask your council or visit focusondisability.org.uk.

- **REMAP** is a special charity working through volunteers who use their ingenuity and skills to enable people with disabilities to achieve much-desired independence. It has panels across the country, and helps thousands of people each year, including through the loan of equipment free of charge. See remap.org.uk.

However, should such arrangements not really be sufficient, you may be able to access advice and possibly financial help from the elderly person's local authority.

Local authority help

The state system in England and Wales is governed by the Care Act 2014 and is designed to support the elderly in their own home for as long as possible. Similar legislation applies in Scotland and Northern Ireland. Regardless of the person's needs or finances, local authorities have a legal duty to assess the support an elderly person may need. Then, depending on what is required and the individual's ability to pay, it may assist with the cost.

To request a care needs assessment, contact the adult social services department of the local authority. There should be a number to call on your local council's website: gov.uk/find-local-council. The request should be made either by the person needing care or, with their permission, you can make the request. If you or somebody else is already providing informal care, they will be included in the assessment. A carer may also request their own assessment to consider what support they need to carry on providing care. You might have to wait up to six months for the assessment to take place, but explain to social services if the request is urgent.

The assessment will determine whether the person's wellbeing is reduced because of a physical or mental condition that means they cannot manage two or more aspects of normal daily living without help. The local authority will then identify what care and support would help, and, while they can ask the local authority to arrange the support, the person receiving help may have to pay for part or all of it. The range of solutions is very wide and can include equipment and adaptations to the home aimed at preventing or reducing the need for care services.

Financial help with home repair and adaptations

Following a needs assessment, even if you could afford to pay, you may find your local authorities will without charge provide equipment such as a raised toilet seat or a hoist, and make minor adaptions to your home, such as grab rails or an access ramp. Equipment may be provided on a long-term loan and will eventually need to be returned. Alternatively, you might be given a prescription for equipment and you then buy it yourself from the suggested suppliers. However, if you need major adaptations to your home, financial help is means-tested.

Disabled facilities grant

This is a local council grant to help towards the cost of adapting a home to enable a disabled or elderly person to live there. It can cover a wide range of improvements to help the occupants manage more independently. This includes work to facilitate access either to the property itself or to the main rooms, like the widening of doors or the installation of ramps or a lift; the provision of suitable bathroom or kitchen facilities; the adaptation of heating or lighting controls; improvement of the heating system, and various other works where these would make a home safe for a disabled person. It is available whether you own or rent your home, but eligibility depends on your income and savings being low. Provided the applicant is eligible, currently a mandatory grant of up to £30,000 in England, £25,000 in Northern Ireland and £36,000 in Wales may be available. See gov.uk/disabled-facilities-grants. Scotland does not have disabled facility grants, but local authorities do have a duty to provide financial assistance for disabled people in adapting their homes in specified circumstances.

Home Improvement Agencies (HIAs)

Foundations is the national body for Home Improvement Agencies in England. HIAs help older and vulnerable people maintain their independence by providing housing-related support. For more information about how home improvement agencies can help, see foundations.uk.com. If your parents live in Wales, see Care and Repair Cymru: careandrepair.org.uk, or, in Scotland, careandrepairscotland.co.uk. For Northern Ireland, contact Housing Advice NI: housingadviceni.org/grants-financial-assistance.

Alarm systems

Alarm systems for the elderly are many and varied, but the knowledge that help can be summoned quickly in the event of an emergency is reassuring in its own right to many elderly or disabled people. Having a personal alarm can enable many people to remain independent far longer than would otherwise be sensible. Some alarm systems allow people living in their own homes to be linked to a central control, or have a telephone link, enabling personal contact to be made. Others simply signal that something is wrong. Sometimes a relative or friend who has been nominated will be alerted.

Your parents' local authority social services department will have information and may even run a community alarm service itself. There will usually be a charge. You can find contact details for your council at gov.uk/find-local-council. You could also try the TEC Services Association – a body representing a wide variety of organizations involved in providing and advising about technology-enabled care, including alarm systems. Its website has a searchable directory of providers: tsa-voice.org.uk/support-at-home. The Disabled Living Foundation also has useful guidance in the section on telecare on its Living Made Easy website: livingmadeeasy.org.uk/telecare.

Some of the many commercial systems you might consider include:

- **Age UK Personal Alarm Service:** ageuk.org.uk;
- **Helpline Limited:** helpline.co.uk;
- **Saga:** saga.co.uk/sos-personal-alarm;
- **Eldercare:** eldercare.co.uk.

Main local authority services

Free social care in Scotland and Northern Ireland

If following a local council needs assessment, your parent requires personal or nursing care in their own home, this will be free in Scotland if your parent is aged 65 or over. It will either be provided directly by the local authority or your parent will receive payments they can use to choose and buy the care themselves.

The services that will be free include, for example, help with personal hygiene, continence, mobility, transferring to and from bed, preparing food, and taking medicines. However, there is normally a charge for other services such as help with housework, laundry and shopping, day centres and providing pre-prepared meals unless your income and savings are low. You can find more information at gov.scot/publications/free-personal-nursing-care-qa/ and careinfoscotland.scot.

In Northern Ireland, if your care needs assessment shows you need social care in your home, this is provided free if you are aged 75 or over or you are getting means-tested benefits. You can, if you prefer, receive payments that enable you to choose and arrange your own support.

Financial help with care services in the rest of the UK

Local authorities have the discretion to charge for most of the social services they can provide, but are bound by the principle that no one should be charged more than they can afford. So, after a needs assessment, and quite separately from that recommendation of the services you require to meet your needs, the local authority will carry out a financial assessment. This could be quite light-touch if it's clear that either you have very few resources or that you are sufficiently well-off that you will not qualify for help. In other cases, it will be a detailed look at your income and capital to determine whether you can receive the services at no charge or should contribute at least something towards the cost. The value of your home is not included in this means test since you will still be living there. Only the income and savings of the person in need of care is taken into account, but includes their share of any joint income and joint savings.

In England, a guiding rule is that, after paying for the services the person should not be left with less than a minimum sum, called the Minimum Income Guarantee. In 2019/20, this is £189 a week for a single person or £144.30 a week if they are part of a couple. You qualify for maximum financial help if your capital is less than £14,250. If you have capital of more than £23,250, you will not get any financial help and will have to bear the full cost yourself.

In Wales, local authorities may not charge more than the cost to the authority of providing the service and there is a maximum collective charge for all services (£90 a week in 2019/20) in addition to being left with a minimum income broadly in line with the Guarantee Credit portion of Pension Credit (£167.25 in 2019/20). However, if you have capital of more than £24,000, you will have to bear the full cost yourself.

Good neighbour schemes

A number of areas of the country have an organized system of good neighbour schemes. In essence, these consist of volunteers agreeing to act as good neighbours to one or several elderly people living close by. Depending on what is required, they may simply pop in on a daily basis to check that everything is all right, or they may give more sustained assistance such as providing help with dressing, bathing, shopping or preparing a light meal. To find out whether such a scheme exists locally, ask social services, your parents' health centre or the Citizens Advice Bureau, or look on the internet.

Key voluntary organizations

Voluntary organizations complement the services provided by statutory health and social services in making life easier for elderly people living at home. The particular organization providing these services depends on where your parents live, but the best organization to advise you is the local Citizens Advice Bureau or your local council. These are the key agencies likely to be acting as providers, but many areas also have their own smaller local charities providing similar services:

- **Age UK**: ageuk.org.uk.
- **Age Scotland**: ageuk.org.uk/scotland.
- **Age Wales**: ageuk.org.uk/cymru.
- **Age Northern Ireland**: ageuk.org.uk/northern-ireland.
- The **British Red Cross** supplies important services to elderly people such as helping sick, disabled or frail people make essential journeys, loaning medical equipment for short-term use, easing the transition of patients to their own home after discharge from hospital, and pointing vulnerable people towards statutory or voluntary services: redcross.org.uk.
- **Centre for Individual Living**, Northern Ireland: cilbelfast.org.
- **Disability Wales**: disabilitywales.org.
- The **Royal Voluntary Service** runs many local projects: books on wheels; social transport; meals on wheels; good neighbour schemes; lunch clubs; a meal delivery service for those not qualifying for meals on wheels: royalvoluntaryservice.org.uk.

Other sources of help and advice include:

- The **Civil Service Retirement Fellowship** is a charity dedicated to helping former civil servants, their partners, widows, widowers and dependents. See csrf.org.uk.
- **Disability Rights UK** is a national registered charity that provides help and information including the *Disability Rights Handbook*, which is a mine of information on benefits and rights for the disabled. See disabilityrightsuk.org.
- **Independent Age** (including the former Counsel and Care) is a national charity working with older people, their families and carers to get the best care and support. It provides personalized, in-depth help and advice. See independentage.org.
- **Jewish Care** provides services for elderly Jewish people, including those who are mentally ill, in London and the south-east of England. Principal facilities include special day-care centres, residential and nursing homes, community centres, a home care service for the housebound and short-term respite care. See jewishcare.org.

- The **National Centre for Independent Living** is run by disabled people for disabled people and recommends reliable local people including 'support brokers'. It can give you details of independent living schemes in your county. See ncil.org.

- The **National Brokerage Network** helps you find a support broker to make the most of using your direct payments for care. See nationalbrokeragenetwork.org.uk.

Transport

Difficulty in getting around is often a major problem for elderly and disabled people. In addition to the facilities run by voluntary organizations already mentioned, including local councils and small local charities running their own community accessible transport (CAT) schemes, there are several other very useful services:

- The **Forum of Mobility Centres** is a network of independent organizations throughout the UK helping individuals who have a medical condition that may affect their ability to drive. For a list of centres see gov.uk/government/publications/appendix-2-forum-of-mobility-centres.

- **London Taxicard** provides subsidized door-to-door transport in taxis and private-hire vehicles for people who have serious mobility or visual impairment. See taxicard.org.uk.

- **Motability** is a registered charity set up to assist recipients of the mobility allowance part of state disability benefits to use their allowance to lease or buy a car or a powered wheelchair or scooter. See motability.co.uk.

Driving licence renewal at age 70

All drivers aged 70 are sent a licence renewal form to have their driving licence renewed. The entitlement to drive will need to be renewed by the DVLA; the new licence will normally be valid for three years. See gov.uk/renew-driving-licence-at-70.

Power of Attorney

Giving another person Power of Attorney authorizes someone else to take business and other financial decisions on the donor's behalf. This can be a temporary arrangement – for example, while your parent is in hospital – or set up in advance so that someone can take over in the event that your parent loses their mental capacity. This second type of power has different names in the different nations of the UK. In England and Wales, it is called a Lasting Power of Attorney (LPA) and there are two types – one to cover property financial affairs and the other regarding health and welfare decisions. In Scotland, there are similarly a Continuing Power of Attorney to cover property and financial matters and a Welfare Power of Attorney for health and welfare – although they can be combined. In Northern Ireland, there is just an Enduring Power of Attorney for both property and financial matters.

A Lasting Power of Attorney (and its equivalents) can only be made while the donor is still of sound mind, and then comes into effect if they cease to be able to make their own decisions. It then continues, if necessary, throughout the remainder of the individual's life. To protect the donor and the nominated attorney, the law clearly lays down certain principles that must be observed, with both sides signing a declaration that they understand the various rights and duties involved. The law furthermore calls for the power to be formally registered with the relevant public office, which can also provide information and the forms you need:

- England and Wales – the Office of the Public Guardian: gov.uk/power-of-attorney;
- Office of the Public Guardian in Scotland: publicguardian-scotland.gov.uk;
- Northern Ireland, High Court (Office of Care and Protection) – justice-ni.gov.uk.

For the Lasting Power of Attorney to be valid, the donor must be capable of understanding what he or she is agreeing to at the time of making the power. To ensure this is clear, if your parents are considering setting up an LPA, it may be advisable that they consult their GP and the family solicitor.

If your parent has not made a Lasting Power of Attorney but becomes unable to make decisions for him or herself, you can apply to the Court of Protection for a similar power to act, called being a deputy, guardian or controller. For England and Wales, there is more information at gov.uk/become-deputy/apply-deputy. For Scotland, see mygov.scot/guardianship. For Northern Ireland, visit justice-ni.gov.uk/articles/how-apply-become-controller.

Living-in help

Temporary

Elderly people living alone can be more vulnerable to flu and other winter ailments; they may have a fall; or, for no apparent reason, they may go through a period of being forgetful and neglecting themselves. Equally, as they become older, they may not be able to cope as well with managing their homes or caring for themselves. In the event of an emergency or if you have reason for concern – perhaps because you are going on holiday and will not be around to keep a watchful eye on them – engaging living-in help can be a godsend. Most agencies tend inevitably to be on the expensive side, although in the event of a real problem they often represent excellent value for money. A more unusual and interesting longer-term possibility is to recruit the help of a volunteer with Volunteering Matters.

Volunteering Matters

Volunteering Matters, formerly Community Service Volunteers, is the UK's leading training and volunteering charity. It engages 20,000 volunteers a year to work with 85,000 beneficiaries through 100 programmes across the UK, providing practical assistance in the home and also offering companionship. Usually a care scheme is set up through a social worker, who supervises how the arrangement is working out. For more information contact your parents' local social services department, or see volunteeringmatters.org.uk.

Agencies

The agencies listed specialize in providing temporary help, rather than permanent staff. Charges vary, but in addition to the weekly payment to helpers there is normally an agency booking fee:

- **Consultus Care & Nursing Agency Ltd:** consultuscare.com;
- **Country Cousins:** www.country-cousins.co.uk;
- **Universal Aunts Ltd:** universalaunts.co.uk.

For a further list of agencies, see *The Lady* magazine, or search the internet under the heading 'Nursing agencies' or 'Care agencies': lady.co.uk.

Nursing care

If one of your parents needs regular nursing care, the GP may be able to arrange for a community or district nurse to visit him or her at home. This will not be a sleeping-in arrangement, but simply involves a qualified nurse calling round when necessary. If they need more concentrated home nursing, you will have to go through a private agency. Some of the agencies listed above can sometimes supply trained nurses. Additionally, there are many specialist agencies that can arrange hourly, daily or live-in nurses on a temporary or longer-term basis.

Fees and services vary considerably. Some nurses undertake nursing duties only – and nothing else – and may even expect to have their meals provided. Others will do light housework and act as nurse-companions. Costs vary throughout the country, with London inevitably being most expensive. Private health insurance can sometimes be claimed against part of the cost, but this is generally only in respect of qualified nurses. Your local health centre or social services department should be able to give you names and addresses of local agencies, or search the internet for 'nursing agencies'.

Permanent

There may come a time when you feel that it is no longer safe to allow one of your parents to live entirely on his or her own. One possibility is to engage a companion or housekeeper on a permanent basis; such arrangements are normally very expensive. However, if you want to investigate the idea further, many domestic agencies supply housekeeper-companions. Alternatively, you might consider advertising in *The Lady* magazine, which is probably the most widely read publication for these kinds of posts: lady.co.uk.

Permanent help can also sometimes be provided by agencies, which will supply continuous four-weekly placements. This is an expensive option, and the lack of continuity can at times be distressing for elderly people, particularly at the changeover point. The three agencies listed above may be worth contacting.

An alternative solution for some families is to engage a reliable daily help who, in the event of illness or other problems, would be prepared to stay overnight.

Flexible care arrangements

One of the problems for many elderly people is that the amount of care they need is liable to vary according to the state of their health. There are other relevant factors including, for example, the availability of neighbours and family. Whereas after an operation the requirement may be for someone with basic nursing skills, a few weeks later the only need may be for someone to act as a companion. Under normal circumstances it may be as little as simply popping in for the odd hour during the day to cook a hot meal and check all is well. Few agencies cater for all the complex permutations that may be necessary in caring for an elderly person in his or her own home, but here are some that offer a flexible service:

- **Christies Care** is the largest independent specialist provider of live-in care, providing a professional and dedicated service tailored to clients' individual requirements. See christiescare.com.
- **Corinium Care** (including the former Cura Domi) is a specialist organization able to provide care and support seven days a week, 52 weeks of the year, as much or as little as required. See coriniumcare.com.
- **Miracle Workers** offers both long- and short-term care. It looks after clients in all sorts of situations. Live-in carers provide practical assistance, support and companionship. See miracle-workers.co.uk.
- The **United Kingdom Home Care Association** is the professional association for home care providers, which may include specialist nursing care to elderly and/or disabled people in their own home. See ukhca.co.uk.

Although any of these suggestions can work extremely well for a while, with many families it may sooner or later come down to a choice between residential care and inviting a parent to live with you. Sometimes, particularly in the case of an unmarried son or daughter or other relative, it is more practical to move into the parent's (or relative's) home if the accommodation is more suitable.

Emergency care for pets

For many elderly people a pet is a very important part of their lives. It provides companionship and fun as well as stimulating them into taking regular outdoor exercise. But in the event of the owner having to go into hospital or through some other emergency being temporarily unable to care for the pet, there can be real problems. Two organizations that can help under these circumstances are listed here:

- The **Cinnamon Trust** offers permanent care for pets whose owners have died, as well as respite care while the owners are in hospital. Animals either stay at the Trust's havens in Cornwall and Devon or are found alternative loving homes with a new owner. See cinnamon.org.uk.

- **Pet Fostering Service Scotland** focuses on temporary care. The only charges are the cost of the pet's food, litter (in the case of cats) and any veterinary fees that may be incurred during fostering. See pfss.org.uk.

Practical help for carers

If your parent is still fairly active – visits friends, does his or her own shopping, or enjoys some hobby that gets him or her out and about – the strains and difficulties may be fairly minimal. This applies particularly if your parent is moving in with you and your home lends itself to creating a granny flat, so everyone can retain some privacy and your parent can continue to enjoy maximum independence. However, this is not always possible, and in the case of an ill or very frail person far more intensive care may be required. It is important to know what help is available and how to obtain it. The many services provided by local authorities and voluntary agencies, described earlier in the chapter, apply as much to an elderly person living with a family as to one living alone. If there is nothing there that solves a particular problem you may have, it could be that one of the following organizations could help or provide useful information:

- **Age UK**: ageuk.org.uk;
- **British Red Cross**: redcross.org.uk;
- **Carers Trust**: carers.org;
- **Carers UK**: carersuk.org;
- **Royal Voluntary Service**: royalvoluntaryservice.org.uk.

Most areas have respite care facilities to enable carers to take a break from their dependents from time to time. Depending on the circumstances, this could be for just the odd day or possibly for a week or two to enable carers who need it to have a real rest. A particularly welcome aspect of respite care is that many schemes specially cater for, among others, elderly people with dementia.

Holiday breaks for carers

There are various schemes to enable those with an elderly relative to go on holiday alone or simply to enjoy a respite from their caring responsibilities. A number of local authorities run fostering schemes, on similar lines to child fostering. Elderly people are invited to stay in a neighbour's home and live in the household as an ordinary family member. Lasting relationships often develop. There may be a charge, or the service may be run on a voluntary basis (or be paid for by the local authority). Some voluntary organizations arrange holidays for older people to give relatives a break. Different charities take responsibility according to where you live: the Citizens Advice Bureau, volunteer centre or social services department should know whom you should approach.

Another solution is a short-stay home, which is residential accommodation variously run by local authorities, voluntary organizations or private individuals, catering specifically for elderly people. The different types of home are described under *Residential care homes* later in this chapter. For information about local authority provision, ask the social services department. If, as opposed to general care, proper medical attention is necessary, you should consult your parent's GP. Many hospitals and nursing homes offer short-stay care arrangements as a means of relieving relatives, and a doctor should be able to help organize this for you.

Carers UK was set up to support and campaign for those caring for an ill, frail or disabled relative at home. It has around 80 self-help branches that are run for and by carers. See carersuk.org. Alternatively, **Jewish Care** runs a number of carers' groups, mostly in London. See jewishcare.org.

Benefits and allowances

There are a number of benefits or allowances available to those with responsibility for the care of an elderly person and/or to elderly people themselves. If you are caring for someone, GOV.UK is a good place to start for the latest and widest range of online public information. There is a menu bringing together links to information relevant to carers and those with a disability. See gov.uk/browse/benefits/disability.

Entitlements for carers

Carer's Allowance

If you spend at least 35 hours a week caring for someone who is getting Attendance Allowance or the daily living component of Personal Independence Payment (PIP), you may be able to claim Carer's Allowance. This is a cash payment (£66.15 a week in 2019/20) but, unlike many benefits, it is taxable. You cannot get this if you are already getting the State Pension or work and earn over £123 per week. See gov.uk/carers-allowance.

Carer's Credit

This is a means of protecting your State Pension if you are unable to work because of the need to care for an elderly person for at least 20 hours a week. For further details, see Chapter 3. If you're claiming Carer's Allowance, you will get this credit automatically. Otherwise, you'll need to claim. You can do this by calling the Carer's Allowance Unit on 0800 731 0297 or downloading the form from gov.uk/government/publications/carers-credit-application-form.

Entitlements for elderly or disabled people

Attendance Allowance

This is paid to people who are State Pension age or over, are severely disabled, either mentally or physically, and have needed almost constant care for at least six months. (They may be able to get the allowance even if no one has actually given them that help.) An exception to the six months' qualifying period is made in the case of those who are terminally ill, who can receive the allowance without having to wait.

There are two rates of allowance: £87.65 a week for those needing 24-hour care, and £58.70 for those needing intensive day- or night-time care. It is intended to help with the extra costs of living with a disability, although there are no actual restrictions on how it is spent. The allowance is tax free and is generally paid regardless of income (although payment might be affected by entering residential care). See gov.uk/attendance-allowance.

Personal Independence Payment (PIP)

This benefit is paid to adults who are under State Pension age and have a disability. To qualify, a person must have a disability or health condition that has affected their daily living or ability to get around for at least three months and is expected to continue for at least a further nine months. The amount depends on the extent to which the person is affected and is determined after a medical assessment. It has two components: a daily living component (£58.70 a week or £87.56 in 2019/20); and a mobility component (£23.20 a week or £61.20 in 2019/20). A person can be entitled either to one or to both components. PIP is tax-free and is generally paid regardless of income (although payment may be affected by entering residential care). See gov.uk/pip.

Extra Pension Credit

Pension Credit is the main means-tested benefit for people who have reached State Pension age and are on a low income. Someone with a severe disability who is getting the highest rate of Attendance Allowance may qualify for extra Pension Credit as well. Similarly, a carer on a low income and in receipt of Carer's Allowance may qualify for extra Pension Credit.

Winter Fuel Payment

This is a special annual tax-free payment of between £125 to £300, given to all households with a resident over State Pension age. You will not be eligible if you live in a care home and you are getting Pension Credit. See gov.uk/winter-fuel-payment.

Financial assistance

The main financial assistance with care costs comes from your local authority. You can find details in the sections of this chapter on *Ways of adapting your home*, *Main local authority services* and *Care homes*. People with disabilities and their carers may also be entitled to the state benefits described in the section earlier in this chapter on *Benefits and allowances*.

In addition, a number of charities give financial assistance to elderly people in need. For many people, one of the main barriers to getting help is knowing which of the many thousands of charities to approach. A good place to start is Turn2Us, which has an online grants finder: grants-search.turn2us.org.uk. A few examples of organizations that offer grants include the following:

- The **Royal Agricultural Benevolent Institution** is a grant-making charity that supports members of the farming community and their families facing need, hardship or distress. See rabi.org.uk.

- **SSAFA Forces Help** is restricted to those who have served in the armed forces (including reservists and those who have done National Service) and their families. See ssafa.org.uk.

- **Wavelength** loans TVs and radios on a permanent basis to elderly housebound people who cannot afford sets. Application should be made through a health visitor, social worker or officer of a recognized organization. See wavelength.org.uk.

For other sources of financial help, you could ask at your library if it has a subscription to Funds Online which is a searchable directory of grant-making organizations: fundsonline.org.uk.

Useful reading

Independent Age is a unique and growing charity, a support community for thousands of older people across the UK and the Republic of Ireland. It offers a 'helping hand from a trusted friend', tackling older people's poverty and loneliness by offering information, advice and friendship. Their helpful publication, *Wise Guide – Life-improving advice for the over-65s* is the practical pensioners' handbook. See independentage.org.

Special accommodation

Elderly parents who no longer feel able to maintain a family home may decide that the time has come to move into accommodation that is smaller, easier and more economic to maintain. Purpose-designed retirement housing, with a high degree of independence and with the option to have a range of support resources as and when required, is a solution that suits increasing numbers of people. There is a wide choice available to meet individual requirements, budgets and tastes.

Sheltered housing

Sheltered housing is usually a development of independent, purpose-designed bungalows or flats within easy access of shops and public transport. It generally has a house manager and an alarm system for emergencies, and often some common facilities. These could include a garden, possibly a launderette, a sitting room and a dining room, with meals provided for residents, on an optional basis, either once a day or several days a week.

Residents normally have access to all the usual range of services – home helps, meals on wheels and so on – in the same way as any other elderly people. Sheltered housing is available for sale or rent through private developers, housing associations or local authorities. It is occasionally provided through gifted housing schemes, or on a shared ownership basis.

Good developments are always sought after, and can require you to join a waiting list. Although this is emphatically not a reason for rushing into a decision you might regret, if you were hoping to move in the fairly near future it could be as well to start looking sooner rather than later.

Sheltered housing for sale

The following organizations can provide information about sheltered housing for sale:

- **Elderly Accommodation Counsel** is a nationwide charity that aims to help older people make informed choices about meeting their housing and care needs. See eac.org.uk.
- **Retirement Homesearch** has an extensive nationwide portfolio of over 2,000 retirement properties, including flats, houses and bungalows, in all price ranges. See retirementhomesearch.co.uk.

New developments are constantly under construction. Properties tend to be sold quickly soon after completion, so it pays to find out about future developments and to get on any waiting lists well in advance of a prospective purchase. Firms specializing in this type of property include the following:

- **Churchill Retirement Living**: churchillretirement.co.uk;
- **Cognatum** (the merger of Beechcroft and the English Courtyard Association): cognatum.co.uk;
- **McCarthy & Stone Retirement Living**: mccarthyandstone.co.uk;
- **Pegasus Life**: pegasuslife.co.uk;
- **Richmond Villages**: richmond-villages.com.

Housing associations build sheltered housing for sale and also manage sheltered housing developments on behalf of private construction companies; see Anchor Hanover: anchor.org.uk.

Rented sheltered housing

This is normally provided by local authorities, housing associations and certain benevolent societies. As with accommodation to buy, quality varies.

Local authority housing is usually only available to people who have resided in the area for some time. There is often an upper and lower age limit for admission, and prospective tenants may have to undergo a medical examination, since as a rule only those who are physically fit are accepted. Should a resident become infirm or frail, alternative accommodation will be found. Apply to the local housing or social services department or via a housing advice centre.

Housing associations supply much of the newly built sheltered housing. Both rent and service charges vary around the country. In case of need, Income Support or Housing Benefit may be obtained to help with the cost. Citizens Advice Bureau and housing departments often keep a list of local housing associations. There are hundreds to choose from; here are just a few:

- **Abbeyfield**: abbeyfield.com;
- **Anchor Hanover Group**: anchor.org.uk and www.hanover.org.uk;
- **Girlings**: girlings.co.uk;
- **Habinteg Housing Association**: habinteg.org.uk;
- **Southern Housing Group**: shgroup.org.uk.

Benevolent societies

These all cater for specific professional and other groups:

- **Housing 21** is a major national provider of housing, care and support services for older people. See housing21.org.uk.
- **Royal Alfred Seafarers' Society** provides quality long-term care for elderly seafarers, their widows and dependents. See royalalfredseafarers.co.uk.
- **SSAFA Forces Help** is restricted to those who have served in the armed forces (including reservists and those who did National Service) and their families. See ssafa.org.uk.

Alternative ways of buying sheltered accommodation

For those who cannot afford to buy into sheltered housing either outright or through a mortgage, there is a variety of alternative payment methods.

Shared ownership and 'Sundowner' schemes

Part-ownership schemes are now offered by a number of developers. Would-be residents, who must be over 55 years, part-buy or part-rent with the amount of rent varying according to the size of the initial lump sum. Residents can sell at any time, but they only recoup that percentage of the sale price that is proportionate to their original capital investment, with no allowance for any rental payments made over the intervening period.

'Investment' and gifted housing schemes

Some charities and housing associations operate these schemes, for which a capital sum is required, to obtain sheltered accommodation. 'Investment' schemes work as follows. The buyer puts in the larger share of the capital, usually 50 to 80 per cent, and the housing association puts in the remainder. The buyer pays rent on the housing association's share of the accommodation and also service charges for the communal facilities.

Gifted housing schemes differ in that an individual donates his or her property to a registered charity, in return for being housed and cared for in his or her own home. The attraction is that the owner can remain in his or her own property with none of the burden of its upkeep. However, it is advisable to consult a solicitor before signing anything, because such schemes have the big negative of reducing the value of the owner's estate, with consequent loss for any beneficiaries.

Age UK offers a free advice and information service about community or residential care and housing options. See ageuk.org.uk.

Almshouses

Most almshouses are endowed by a charity for the benefit of older people of reduced means who live locally or have a connection with a particular trade. There are now over 2,000 groups of almshouses, providing about 35,000 dwellings. Although many are of considerable age, most of them have been modernized and new ones are being built. Rents are not charged, but there will be a maintenance contribution towards upkeep and heating.

A point you should be aware of is that almshouses do not provide the same security of tenure as some other tenancies. You would be well advised to have the proposed letter of appointment checked by a lawyer or other expert to ensure you understand exactly what the beneficiary's rights are. There is no standard way to apply for an almshouse, since each charity has its own qualifications for residence. Some housing departments and advice centres keep lists of local almshouses. An organization that could help is the Almshouse Association, which supplies information on almshouses and contact details in the county in which you are interested: almshouses.org.

Granny flats

A granny flat or annexe is a self-contained unit attached to a family house. A large house can be converted or extended for this purpose, but planning permission is needed. Enquire at your local authority planning department. Some councils, particularly new towns, have houses to rent with granny flats.

Salvation Army homes

The Salvation Army has a limited number of homes for elderly people in various parts of the UK, offering residential care for men and women unable to manage in their own homes. Christian caring is given within a family atmosphere, in pleasant surroundings, but the homes are not nursing homes. See saha.org.uk.

Extra-care schemes

A number of organizations that provide sheltered accommodation also have extra-care sheltered housing, designed for those who can no longer look after themselves without assistance. Although expensive, it is cheaper than most private care homes and often more appropriate than full-scale nursing care. A possible problem is that tenants of some of these schemes do not have security of tenure and, should they become frail, could be asked to leave if more intensive care were required. Among the housing associations that provide these facilities are Housing 21, Anchor Hanover Housing Association and Abbeyfield (see the details listed earlier in this chapter).

Care homes

While a person has a right to a care needs assessment, there is no compulsion to have one and you may in any case come to the conclusion that your parent would be better off moving into a home. This is a major decision, not just because of the emotional trauma it may cause, but because of the high cost and, as discussed at the start of this chapter, the difficulty in some regions of finding a care home place. Here are some suggestions before taking the decision:

- Is a care home really needed? Get advice on the housing options.
- What type of care home is wanted? Some offer accommodation and help with personal care; other care homes offer nursing care as well as the

basic help. (This is the crucial difference between residential homes and nursing homes, though they are no longer classed as such.)

- How to find a care home? Think of it like buying a house: you need to get a feel for what is out there before making a decision. Personal recommendations are important.

- How much will it cost? There is a lot of variation in care home fees. If the local council is paying, it will set a maximum cost that it will contribute. If the costs are higher, a relative or friend will need to top up that amount. If your parents are self-funding, make sure they can afford the fees. The Competition and Markets Authority market study of care homes published in 2017 found that the average self-funder paid £846 a week, which is nearly £44,000 a year.

Financial help with care home costs

If moving into a nursing home is a continuation of NHS treatment that your parents have been having for an illness – for example, he or she is discharged from hospital direct to a home – this should be paid for by the NHS. However, this is a grey area and you may have to be persistent to get their costs met in this way.

If they do not qualify for NHS continuing care, assuming the recommendation to move into a home is the result of a local authority needs assessment, they may still qualify for some state help with care home fees, provided their assessment found this was the best option for them and the subsequent financial assessment finds that their income and capital are low enough. The rules around this means assessments are complicated and vary from one nation of the UK to another.

In England and Northern Ireland, you will get maximum help if your income is low and your capital comes to no more than £14,250. If your capital exceeds £23,250, you will have to pay the full cost of care (called self-funding) until your capital drops below that limit. For capital between those limits, you are treated as if each £250 of capital above the lower £14,250 threshold produces £1 a week of income and this is added to the rest of your income for the purpose of working out what you can afford to pay. You will be allowed to keep a small amount of income (£24.90 a week in 2019/20 in England and £26.33 in Northern Ireland) as a personal expenses allowance.

Wales has the most generous means-test of all the UK nations. In 2019/20 you will have to self-fund if your capital is above £50,000. Below that, the help you get is based just on your income, with up to £50,000 of capital being disregarded. You are allowed to keep £29.50 a week for personal expenses.

In Scotland, you will get maximum help if your income is low and your capital comes to no more than £17,500. If your capital exceeds £28,000, you will have to pay the full cost of care (self-funding) until your capital drops below that limit. For capital between those limits, you are treated as if each £250 of capital above the lower £17,500 threshold produces £1 a week of income and this is added to the rest of your income for the purpose of working out what you can afford to pay. You will be allowed to keep a small amount of income (£27.75 a week in 2019/20) as a personal expenses allowance.

For the purpose of these means tests, a home you own does not count as capital if your partner or another dependent still lives there. But, in other cases, it will be counted, which means your home may have to be sold or the local authority can put a charge against the home so that it can recover the cost of care fees it has paid once the home is sold. Another option could be to rent out the home and put the rental income towards paying the care home fees. Be aware that, if your parent gives away some or all of their wealth, this may be treated as 'deprivation of capital' and the means test can be carried out as if they still own the assets.

Residential care homes

In a residential care home, sometimes known as a 'rest home', the accommodation usually consists of a bedroom plus communal dining rooms, lounges and gardens. All meals are provided, rooms are cleaned, and staff are at hand to give whatever help is needed. Most homes are fully furnished, though it is usually possible to take small items of furniture. Except in some of the more expensive private homes, bathrooms are normally shared. Intensive nursing care is not usually included.

Homes are run by private individuals (or companies), voluntary organizations and local authorities. All homes must be registered with the public body responsible for ensuring minimum standards (the Care Quality Commission in England). An unregistered home should not be considered. It is very important that the individual should have a proper chance to visit it and ask any questions. Before reaching a final decision, it is a good idea to arrange a short stay to see whether the facilities are suitable and pleasant.

It could also be sensible to enquire what long-term plans there are for the home. Moving to a new care home can be a highly distressing experience for an elderly person who has become attached to the staff and made friends among the other residents. Though a move can never be totally ruled out, awareness of whether the home is likely to remain a going concern could be a deciding factor when making a choice. Possible clues could include whether the place is short-staffed or in need of decoration. If it is run by a company or charity, you could request to see the latest accounts.

Nursing homes

Nursing homes provide medical supervision and fully qualified nurses, 24 hours a day. Most are privately run, with the remainder being supported by voluntary organizations. All nursing homes in England must be registered with the Care Quality Commission, which keeps a list of what homes are available in the area. There are equivalent bodies in the other nations of the UK. Nursing homes are significantly more expensive than residential homes.

Finding a care home

For information about residential and nursing homes in the UK, contact the following:

- The **Care Quality Commission** maintains a register of the homes it regulates across England. You can search for care homes and check their inspection reports and ratings. See cqc.org.uk.
- The **Elderly Accommodation Counsel** maintains a nationwide database of all types of specialist accommodation for elderly people and gives advice and detailed information to help enquirers choose the support and care most suited to their needs. See eac.org.uk and housingcare.org.
- The **Registered Nursing Home Association** (RNHA) is an organization that provides support for nursing homeowners, requiring its members to meet high levels of standards and service. Patients in nursing homes that are members of the RNHA can expect to receive some of the best standards of service available. See rnha.co.uk.

Voluntary organizations that run care homes include:

- **Friends of the Elderly**: fote.org.uk;
- **Jewish Care**: jewishcare.org.

Useful reading

Read *Care Home Accommodation: Finding, choosing and paying for a care home*, a free fact sheet downloadable from ageuk.org.uk.

Some special problems

A minority of people, as they become older, suffer from special problems that can cause great distress. Because families do not like to talk about these problems, they may be unaware of what services are available and so may be missing out on practical help and sometimes also on financial assistance.

Hypothermia

Elderly people tend to be more vulnerable to the cold. If the body drops below a certain temperature, this can be dangerous, because one of the symptoms of hypothermia is that sufferers no longer actually feel cold. Instead, they may lose their appetite and vitality and may become mentally confused. Instead of doing sensible things like getting a hot drink and putting on an extra sweater, they are liable to neglect themselves further and can put themselves at real risk. Although heating costs are often blamed, quite wealthy people can also be victims by allowing their home to become too cold or not wearing sufficient clothing. For this reason, during a cold snap it is very important to check up regularly on an elderly person living alone.

Energy companies and the Solid Fuel Association (solidfuel.co.uk) are all willing to give advice on how heating systems can be used more efficiently and economically. It is also worth checking that elderly parents are on the correct tariff when it comes to utility bills. Some utility providers have reduced charges for elderly, vulnerable people who are in receipt of certain benefits. It could make the difference between them staying warm and feeling obliged to turn off their heating. Insulation can also play a very large part in keeping a home warmer and cheaper to heat. It may be possible to obtain a grant from the local authority, although normally this would only be likely on grounds of real need.

Elderly and disabled people in receipt of Pension Credit or other means-tested benefits may receive a Cold Weather Payment to help with heating costs during a particularly cold spell – that is, when the temperature is forecast to drop to zero degrees Celsius (or below) for seven consecutive days.

Those eligible should receive the money automatically. In an emergency, such as a power cut, contact your parent's energy provider or Citizens Advice Bureau or Age UK for advice.

Finally, every household with someone over State Pension age will get an annual tax-free Winter Fuel Payment of between £100 and £300. This is usually paid automatically but, if not, your parent will need to make a claim. See gov.uk/winter-fuel-payment.

Incontinence

Bladder or bowel problems can cause deep embarrassment to sufferers as well as inconvenience to relatives. The problem can occur in an elderly person for all sorts of reasons, and a doctor should always be consulted, as it can often be cured or at least alleviated by proper treatment. To assist with the practical problems, some local authorities operate a laundry service that collects soiled linen, sometimes several times a week. Talk to the health visitor or district nurse (at their local health centre), who will be able to advise about this and other facilities.

B&B (Bladder and Bowel Community) is the charity for people with bladder and bowel dysfunction. The charity offers advice from its specially trained nurses. See bladderandbowel.org.

Dementia

Sometimes an elderly person can become confused or forgetful, suffer severe loss of memory or have violent mood swings and at times be abnormally aggressive. It is important to consult a doctor as soon as possible, as the cause may be depression, stress or even vitamin deficiency. All of these can be treated and often completely cured. If dementia is diagnosed, there are ways of helping a sufferer to cope better with acute forgetfulness and other symptoms. Arguably the hardest aspect is the thought that there is no cure for a progressive disease that gradually erodes the personality of the person one loves. But there is ongoing research into finding a cure and there are some treatments that can delay the progression of some forms of dementia. Meanwhile there are many ways to make life for people with dementia more manageable and enjoyable.

The most common type of dementia is Alzheimer's disease, which is usually found in people aged over 65. Approximately 50 million people worldwide have dementia, according to Alzheimer's Disease International, of which the majority of cases (over 60 per cent) are due to Alzheimer's. Clinical signs are characterized by progressive cognitive deterioration, together with a decline in the ability to carry out common daily tasks, and behavioural changes. The first readily identifiable symptoms of Alzheimer's disease are usually short-term memory loss and visual-spatial confusion. These initial symptoms progress from seemingly simple and fluctuating to a more pervasive loss of memory, including difficulty navigating familiar areas such as the local neighbourhood. This advances to loss of other familiar and well known skills, as well as recognition of objects and people.

Since family members are often the first to notice changes that might indicate the onset of Alzheimer's (or other forms of dementia), they should learn the early warning signs. They should serve as informants during initial clinical evaluation of patients. It is important to consult your doctor as soon as you have concerns. It is also a good idea to talk to the health visitor, as he or she will know about any helpful facilities that may be available locally. The health visitor is also able to arrange appointments with other professionals, such as the community psychiatric nurse and the occupational therapist.

It is important to remember that people with dementia are still people. The Alzheimer's Society recommends the following tips: always treat the person with respect and dignity, be a good listener, be a good communicator, and remember that little things mean a lot. Staying in touch shows that you care, offer practical help, organize a treat, and find out more about the condition so that you understand and feel comfortable spending time with the person with dementia.

Sources of help and support for people with dementia and their carers are:

- **Alzheimer Scotland:** alzscot.org;
- **Alzheimer's Society:** alzheimers.org.uk;
- **Mind:** mind.org.uk.

Useful reading

Read *Caring for the Person with Dementia* on the Alzheimer's Society website: alzheimers.org.uk.

14
No-one is immortal

Before we get too old, it is important to think for a moment about the practicalities of dying. We all know that we should write a will, but it is one of those things that many of us never seem to get around to. A great deal of heartbreak and real financial worry could be avoided if people were more open about the subject. At the earliest and most appropriate moment, if you can bring yourself and your relatives to have an honest and open discussion about mortality, it could potentially save huge amounts of trouble later on.

Wills

Planning what will happen to your money and possessions after your death helps ensure your survivors are financially secure, and that the people you want to inherit from you do so. When you retire, there are often big changes to your finances as well as to the rest of your life. It is at this stage that it is important to review how your survivors would manage financially if you were to die. Would, in fact, your money and possessions (your 'estate') be passed on as you would wish? (Your estate is everything you own at the time you die, including your share of any joint possessions, less everything you owe.)

There are five rules of will making:

1 The person making the will must be of sound mind.
2 The will must be properly signed.
3 The will must be correctly witnessed.
4 Be clear about what or how much you want to leave and to whom.
5 Remember to update your will as your life circumstances change.

Having a will is especially important if you live with an unmarried partner, have remarried, need to provide for someone with a disability, own a business, own property abroad, or your estate is large (ie over the inheritance tax (IHT) threshold). A will is a legal document that needs to be drawn up precisely and set out your wishes clearly and unambiguously. Although you can write your own will, it is safer to get a solicitor to do it.

Laws of intestacy

Dying without having made a will is called dying 'intestate'. The laws of intestacy are different in the different nations of the UK. However, they all follow the same basic principles:

- your husband, wife or civil partner and your own children are favoured; this includes a former partner if you are only separated rather than divorced;
- an unmarried partner and stepchildren have no automatic rights;
- your husband, wife or civil partner does not automatically get the whole of your estate;
- possessions, including your home, may have to be sold to split the proceeds between your heirs;
- if children are among your heirs, their inheritance may have to be held in a trust until they reach adulthood;
- if you have no partner or children, more distant relatives inherit;
- if you have no relatives, the state gets the lot.

Making a will

You have four choices: you can do it yourself, you can ask your bank to help you, hire a solicitor or use a will-writing service.

Doing it yourself

Home-made wills are not generally recommended. People often use ambiguous wording which, while perfectly clear to the individual who has written it, may be less obvious to others. This could result in the donor's wishes being misinterpreted, and could also cause considerable delay in settling the estate.

The wording of a will is important, including a formal revocation of any earlier wills. It's also important to think beyond your basic wishes and address questions such as what if a beneficiary dies before you, what if you and your partner (if you have one) die together or within a short space of time of each other? Few people would start writing a will from scratch – templates are available from stationers and can be downloaded from the internet. They are not perfect, however, and still leave considerable margin for error, especially if your circumstances or your estate are complicated.

Two witnesses are needed, and an essential point to remember is that witnesses and their spouses cannot be beneficiaries of a will, so if they do witness it they will be automatically disinherited. In certain circumstances, a will can be rendered invalid. There will also be confusion if part of a will seems to be missing, so, if you do need to change your will, it's best to start from scratch with a new one rather than staple an amendment (called a codicil) that might become detached.

A sensible precaution for those doing it themselves is to have it checked by a solicitor, in which case it will usually be simpler and cheaper to use a solicitor from the start.

Banks

Advice on wills and the administration of estates is given by the trustee companies of most of the major high street banks. In particular, the services they offer are to provide general guidance, to act as executor and to administer the estate. They will introduce clients to a solicitor and can arrange other related advice on tax planning and financial advice.

As with using a solicitor (see below), an advantage of using a bank is that they can keep a copy of the will – plus other important documents – in their safe, avoiding the risk of these documents being mislaid or lost in, say, a house fire. However, the contract for services is between you and the bank, so after you have died, your heirs have very little leverage to get the bank to speed up if it is taking a long time administering the estate or to control what the bank charges.

Solicitors

Solicitors are the traditional professional to use to draw up a will. You can also appoint them to act as executors and administer the estate, though as with banks this is not necessarily a good idea since your heirs will have no control over the speed or cost of the solicitor's services in this capacity. Like banks, solicitors will also retain a copy of your will in safekeeping and most will not charge for this.

If you do not have a solicitor, friends or family may be able to recommend one, or you can find a member of one of the legal professional bodies:

- the **Law Society:** use its Find a Solicitor service to find legal advice in England, Wales and Scotland, solicitors.lawsociety.org.uk;

- **Law Society of Northern Ireland:** lawsoc-ni.org/solicitors.aspx.

A simple will could normally start at about £150. Couples sometimes make 'mirror wills' leaving everything on broadly the same terms, and there may be a discount for doing both at the same time. However, many solicitors take part in special schemes where they partner with charities and offer free writing of simple wills. The schemes include:

- **Free Wills Month.** During the campaign months (March and October), people aged 55 and over can have a will written by a solicitor for free. Participating charities hope you will leave them a legacy in your will although you cannot be forced to do so. See freewillsmonth.org.uk.

- **Make a Will Week.** Participating solicitors write your will for free in return for you making a suggested donation to a partner charity. The week has been in May in recent years, and the charities involved advertise if they are taking part.

- **National Free Wills Network** is a partnership where participating charities pay for solicitors to write free wills for their supporters. Again, the hope is that you will leave a legacy to the charity, but that is up to you. See nationalfreewills.net.

- **Will Aid** is a partnership between solicitors and nine charities. The solicitors write your will for free, but suggest a voluntary donation to Will Aid which then supports the work of the charities. See willaid.org.uk/will-makers/find-a-solicitor.

The schemes work because solicitors earn extra where it turns out you need more than just a simple will or decide to buy other services. For the charities, the schemes bring in donations and legacies that exceed their outlay to the solicitors. If you make an immediate donation, you might not be saving money, but what you do spend goes to the charity you want to support. If you leave a legacy, you are in effect paying later for the will you have drawn up today, but again through a donation to the charity of your choice.

Many charities rely heavily on legacies to fund their work, and to support this they provide guidance on their websites and can put you in touch with solicitors who may draw up a will for you at a reduced cost. Charities do this in the hope that you will include a legacy to them in your will, but they cannot make it a requirement of using their services, they do not have access to the will that you have written, and the solicitor involved is working for you not the charity.

For individuals with sight problems, the Royal National Institute of Blind People (RNIB) has produced a comprehensive guide to making or changing a will and offers a number of options, including free will writing through the National Free Wills Network. RNIB also offers a free service to transcribe your will into large print size, Braille or audio. See rnib.org.uk (the section on *Help writing or amending a will*). Age UK is a partner in the Will Aid scheme and its website has a lot of useful information about writing a will: ageuk.org.uk.

Will-writing services

A will-writing service is a sort of halfway house that is generally more reliable than a DIY will, but cheaper than a solicitor. Will-writers take you through a questionnaire to find out your needs and are trained to be able to draw up simple wills. But they are not professionally trained in the law as solicitors are and they are not regulated to the same degree, so do not use a will-writing service if your affairs are at all complex. Do make sure that any will-writer you use belongs to one of the following self-regulating bodies which requires members to abide by a code of conduct including having a formal complaints procedure and professional indemnity insurance:

- **Institute of Professional Willwriters**: ipw.org.uk/directory;
- **The Society of Will Writers**: willwriters.com/members/.

Executors

If you die without making a will, usually your next of kin will be expected to sort out your estate. This might not be the best person for the job, and writing a will gives you the chance to say who you want to finalize your affairs when you're gone. Appointing an executor is not a decision to be made without some serious consideration and agreeing to be an executor should not be made lightly.

The duties of an executor are many, including dealing with the financial wishes made by the testator. An executor may have to settle debts, create trusts and distribute the testator's assets among nominated individuals. Executors may also have to inform the next of kin of the death, register the death, deal with house sales and tax if required. The testator, when appointing an executor, should be sure of the intended person's ability to carry out these duties when making their choice.

It is possible for a bank, solicitor or accountant to take on this responsibility, but note the warnings above about the fact that there is very little your beneficiaries can do if the executor that you (not they) contracted with during your lifetime turns out to take a long time executing the estate and charges a lot. Make sure you understand what the charges will be – for example, based on time taken or a percentage of the value of your estate – and that you are happy with these.

When choosing an executor of a will, the following points are worth bearing in mind:

- A spouse as a sole executor is not the best choice, especially if both husband and wife are elderly.
- It might be advisable not to appoint one or two out of several beneficiaries as executors in case others claim there is a conflict of interests.
- The chosen people should be asked in advance to agree to the role.
- Legally, an executor must be over 18, of sound mind and not in prison when the executor decision is made.
- If conflicts within the family are likely to be a factor, it may be worthwhile appointing more than one executor, or even hiring a professional executor.
- If family members are chosen, they should have the time and capability to carry out all the duties. This can be difficult if an executor does not live in the same part of the country.

Other points

Wills should always be kept in a safe place – and their whereabouts known. The most sensible arrangement is for a solicitor to keep the original and for both you and each executor to have a copy.

A helpful initiative devised by the Law Society is a mini-form, known as a personal assets log. This is for individuals drawing up a will to give to their executor or close relatives. It is, quite simply, a four-sided leaflet with space to record essential information: name and address of solicitor, where the will and other important documents (for example, share certificates and insurance policies) are kept, the date of any codicils, and so on. Logs should be obtainable from most solicitors. Alternatively, create your own log and keep it with your copy of the will. This will help your executors locate all your assets and liabilities when the time comes.

Wills may need updating in the event of an important change of circumstances, for example a divorce, a remarriage or the birth of a grandchild. An existing will normally becomes invalid in the event of marriage or remarriage and should be replaced. An exception is where the will is made in anticipation of the marriage. A will is not invalidated by divorce or dissolution of a civil partnership, but bequests to your ex-partner are automatically invalidated, – however, this does not apply if you merely separate. Any changes to your will must be by codicil (for minor alterations) or by a new will, and must be properly witnessed. The witnesses of a codicil do not have to be the same people who witnessed the will.

Another reason why you may need, or wish, to change your will is in consequence of changes in the IHT rules. For example, prior to 9 October 2007, it was quite common for husbands and wives to write wills that created a trust on death to receive some of the deceased's assets in order to prevent their IHT nil-rate band (see Chapter 4) being wasted. However, since then, it has been possible for a surviving spouse or civil partner to inherit the deceased person's unused nil-rate band, reducing the need to create these so-called will trusts.

If you have views about your funeral, it is sensible to write a letter to your executors explaining your wishes and to lodge it with your will. If you have any pets, you may equally wish to leave a letter filed with your will explaining what arrangements you have made for their immediate and long-term welfare.

Some related documents are best communicated with family and executors rather than stored with your will, since they are important while you are still living. Over the years there has been increased interest in advance decision making, sometimes called an 'advance directive' or 'living will'. These set out what you would like to happen in the event that you are still alive but unable to communicate your wishes, for example, because you are in a persistent vegetative state. It lets your family and medical practitioners know if you want treatment to be withheld. For those who would like more information, there is basic guidance at nhs.uk/conditions/end-of-life-care/advance-decision-to-refuse-treatment.

Assisted dying is a troubled issue in the UK, but Dignity in Dying is very helpful and can supply you with forms and advice. See dignityindying.org.uk. You may want to think about organ donation. Wales has an 'opt-out' system where you are deemed to be a willing donor unless you register that you do not want this to happen. From 2020, England and Scotland will also change to opt-out, but in Northern Ireland you will still need to 'opt in'. To register your decision either way, visit https://www.organdonation.nhs.uk/register-your-decision/.

IHT points

IHT is a tax on money or possessions you leave behind when you die, and on some gifts you make during your lifetime (see Chapter 4, *Tax*). There are two main aims to planning inheritance: to make sure your estate is divided as you wish, and to minimize the amount of tax paid on the estate. The particular inheritance planning strategies you adopt will depend largely on your personal intentions and circumstances.

One way of reducing IHT is to make tax-free gifts in your will. Whatever you leave to your spouse or civil partner is tax-free, as are bequests to charity. Some 75 per cent of people in England give to charity during their lifetime, according to a 2018 survey, but only 7 per cent include a charitable legacy in their will (despite 35 per cent saying they intend to). Obviously whatever you leave to charity reduces the amount your family and friends inherit from you, but provided a charity is among the list of the beneficiaries you want to leave money to, such gifts could save your family tax as well. This is because, since 2012, if you leave 10 per cent or more of your taxable estate to charity, the rate of IHT on the rest is reduced from 40 per cent to 36 per cent. This benefits larger estates – if your estate is less than the nil rate band (£325,000 in 2019/20 or up to £475,000 if your estate includes a home), there is no tax to pay anyway.

For more information about IHT, including using lifetime gifts to reduce tax on your estate, see Chapter 4.

Provision for dependent adult children

A particular concern for parents with a physically or mentally dependent son or daughter is what plans they can make to ensure his or her care when they are no longer in a position to manage. There is no easy answer, as each case varies according to the severity of the disability or illness, the range of helpful voluntary or statutory facilities locally, and the extent to which they, as parents, can provide for their child's financial security long-term.

While social services may be able to advise, parents thinking ahead might do better to consult a specialist organization experienced in helping carers in this situation to explore the possible options available to them. Useful addresses are:

- Carers UK: carersuk.org;
- Carers Trust: carers.org.

Parents concerned about financial matters such as setting up a trust or making alternative provision in their will would also be advised to consult a solicitor or accountant.

Money and other worries – and how to minimize them

Many people say that the first time they really think about death, in terms of what would happen to their nearest and dearest, is after the birth of their first child. As children grow up, requirements change, but key points that anyone with a family should consider – and review from time to time – include life insurance, survivor pensions and mortgage protection.

During their working lives, both partners in a relationship (married or not) should have life insurance cover if anyone, such as children, is dependent on them or they are co-dependent on each other (for example, sharing household bills). If either were to die, not only would the partner lose the financial benefit of the other's earnings, but the survivor would lose the value of any unpaid work done by the deceased, such as childcare, laundry and home maintenance. A very common motive for life insurance is where a couple or single parents have a mortgage; this ensures the mortgage would be paid off in full in the event of death, helping to ensure the survivor has a secure home. People without dependents, such as single people without children, do not normally need life insurance, since no one's financial security is at risk.

Later in life, the need for insurance should be re-examined. By this stage, any mortgage is commonly paid off and children financially independent. Where couples each have their own pension income, they might be financially independent and still secure in the event of their partner's death. However, due largely to caring responsibilities, many women have much smaller pensions than their partner. In that case, the couple should consider what the financial position of a survivor would be. It may be that the pension schemes of the deceased person would pay out a survivor pension or continuing annuity income or the survivor might inherit a remaining fund of pension savings. If that's not the case or the amounts involved would not be sufficient, there may be a need for life insurance to plug the gap. However, be aware that the cost of life cover rises steeply at older ages.

A note about debts, since this can be a cause of confusion. Where a debt is jointly held, it is invariably on a 'joint and several basis' which means that each person is responsible for the whole debt. In that case, if one person dies, the remaining borrower takes over the whole debt and responsibility for continuing the repayments. Where a debt is in the name of just one person, if they die, then the debt is repaid out of that person's estate. If the estate is too small to pay off the debt in full, the remainder of the debt is written off. So these debts, while they reduce the amount of the estate left to be passed on, do not become the debts of anyone else.

Life insurance is also sometimes used for IHT planning. At its simplest, life insurance can cover a potential tax bill either on lifetime gifts that become taxable due to death within seven years (failed PETs – see Chapter 4) or on the estate. Life insurance may also form part of more complex tax avoidance schemes – be aware that complicated schemes could be challenged by HM Revenue & Customs (HMRC) and might in the end not save tax at all.

Funeral plans

Many people worry about funeral costs. Burial service costs can vary, according to different parts of the country. The costs tend to rise faster than inflation, not just because of funeral directors' fees but more because disbursements – payments to third parties including church, grave or crematorium – which have soared in the past few years. Since January 2002, prepaid funeral plans have been regulated, although companies can avoid being regulated directly by the Financial Conduct Authority if they keep clients' money in either a trust or a life insurance policy. Then they can choose to be regulated by the voluntary Funeral Planning Authority (funeralplanningauthority. co.uk), although not all have done so.

Before handing over any money, make sure the company has signed up with the Funeral Planning Authority. Prepaid schemes are usually linked to a particular funeral director, which you might, or might not, be able to choose. The funeral director must then carry out your funeral with whatever money is available in the trust or insurance policy. If that is less than they are charging at the time, that is their loss.

However, do check what is covered in the package you buy – there are usually exclusions. For example, the cost of cremation might be covered, but not burial. Because of the large increases in fees being charged by some cemeteries and crematoria, as well as the rising cost of other disbursements, a number of funeral plan providers are now restricting their guarantee on price to those services within the control of the funeral director. This does not necessarily mean that there would be an excess to pay. If you are considering this type of scheme, as with any other important purchase it is sensible to compare the different plans on the market to ensure that you are choosing the one that best suits your requirements.

If you are interested in taking out a funeral plan, you might check out these providers:

- **Age UK Funeral Plan**: ageco.co.uk;
- **Co-operative Funeralcare**: co-operativefuneralcare.co.uk;
- **Dignity Caring Funeral Services**: dignityfunerals.co.uk/funeral-plans;
- **Golden Charter**: goldencharter.co.uk.

Before making any advance payment, you would be wise to investigate the following points:

- whether your money will be put into an insurance policy or trust fund or, if not, whether the plan provider is authorized by the Financial Conduct Authority;
- what fees are deducted from the investment;
- what exact expenses the plan covers;
- what freedom you have if you subsequently want to change any of the details of the plan;
- if you cancel the plan, whether you can get all your money back – or only a part.

Before paying, you should receive a letter confirming the terms and conditions, together with full details of the arrangements you have specified. It is important to check this carefully and inform your next of kin where the letter is filed.

For further information see:

- the **Funeral Planning Authority**: funeralplanningauthority.com;
- the **National Association of Funeral Directors**: nafd.org.uk;
- the **National Society of Allied and Independent Funeral Directors**: saif. org.uk.

An alternative, but less satisfactory arrangement, is to buy a small-premium life insurance policy designed to pay out when you die. These are targeted at the over-50s and are sometimes marketed as funeral plans, although the money can be used for any purpose and there's no guarantee it will be enough to pay for a funeral. (And your relatives will still have to make your funeral arrangements.) These are whole-of-life policies, which means you have to continue paying premiums until you die – and quite possibly will pay much more in premiums than the pay-out they promise. If you stop paying premiums, the cover stops immediately and you don't get any money back.

You do not need to have a dedicated funeral plan at all. You could simply put what you would have paid for one into a savings account, for example an Individual Savings Account (ISA) where your money grows tax-free. You could either tell your family that this is earmarked as your funeral fund, or let them sort out drawing money from your estate when the time comes. You can still, if you like, leave instructions alongside your will about the sort of funeral you want.

Survivors in receipt of Pension Credit or other means-tested benefits might qualify for a payment from the Social Fund to help with funeral costs, if there is not enough money in your estate. For details of eligibility and how you claim, see gov.uk/funeral-payments.

Dealing with a death

A very real crisis for some families is the need for immediate money while waiting for the estate to be settled. At least part of the problem can be overcome by couples having a joint bank account, with both partners having drawing rights without the signature of the other being required. Sole-name bank accounts and joint accounts requiring both signatures are frozen. For the same reason, it may also be a good idea for any savings or investments to be held in the joint name of the couple. However, some accounts – such as ISAs – can only be held in a single name.

Additionally, an essential practical point for all couples is that any financial and other important documents should be discussed together and understood by both parties. Even today, an all-too-common situation is for bereaved spouses to come across insurance policies and other papers that they have never seen before and do not understand, often causing quite unnecessary anxiety. A further common-sense 'must' is for both partners to know where important papers are kept. The best idea is either to lock them, filed together, in a home safe, or to give them to the bank to look after.

When someone dies, the bank manager should be notified as soon as possible so he or she can assist with the problems of unpaid bills and help work out a solution until the estate is settled. The same goes for the suppliers of essential services: gas, electricity, telephone and so on. Unless they know the situation, there is a risk of services being cut off if there is a delay in paying the bill. Add, too, any credit card companies, where if bills lie neglected the additional interest could mount up alarmingly.

Normally, you must register the death within the first five days (eight in Scotland). Your local registrar can be found at gov.uk. You will need to take to the registrar's office the medical certificate issued by the doctor who attended the death, and if possible, the deceased's medical card, birth certificate and any marriage or civil partnership certificate. The registrar will give you:

- A certificate allowing cremation or burial to go ahead; give this to the funeral director you appoint.

- A certificate to give to the Jobcentre Plus or the Pension Service, if the deceased had been getting state benefits or pensions.

- A leaflet with details of bereavement benefits you may be able to claim.

- One or more death certificates, for which there is a fee. You normally need to send a death certificate to each provider of pensions, life insurance, savings and investments that the deceased had. It is cheaper to buy extra certificates straight away than later.

Registering a death is upsetting, and dealing with a death involves more paperwork and phone calls than a family wants to deal with at such a time. With exceptional common sense, the government operates a simple scheme in most areas called Tell Us Once. It means people need to make just one appointment with their local registrar, who can then advise a whole range of different government services of the changed circumstances, including State Pension and benefits through the Department for Work and Pensions, and HMRC, passports, driving licences, council tax, local library, Blue Badge and social services.

Another organization that may be able to help you after a loved one has died is the Bereavement Register. This organization has one aim: to reduce the amount of direct mail to those who are deceased. Coming to terms with the loss of a loved one takes time; receiving direct mail bearing the name of the deceased is often painful and unnecessary. The Bereavement Register puts an end to such occurrences. See thebereavementregister.org.uk.

For step-by-step guidance on what to do when someone dies, see:

- England and Wales: gov.uk/when-someone-dies;

- Northern Ireland: nidirect.gov.uk/articles/what-do-when-someone-dies-checklist;

- Scotland: www2.gov.scot/Publications/2012/05/4929.

State benefits and tax

The state provides an extra financial benefit for widowed people. However, this is restricted to those whose husband, wife or civil partner has died. It is not available to unmarried partners. Similarly, there are some aspects of the tax system that favour married couples and civil partners, but not unmarried couples, in the event of death.

Benefits and bereavement

What help you can get from the state differs depending on whether you were under or over State Pension age at the time of death.

Under State Pension age

Where death occurs on or after 6 April 2017, a widowed person under State Pension age may be entitled to Bereavement Support Payment. This benefit is not means-tested and depends on your late partner (not you) having paid or been credited with sufficient National Insurance contributions or their death being work-related. You cannot get this payment if you and your late partner were divorced or you are living in a relationship with someone else. Find out more at gov.uk/bereavement-support-payment.

Bereavement Support Payment has two parts, which are both tax-free: a lump sum plus a monthly payment paid for a maximum of 18 months. There is a standard rate paid to people without children and a higher rate for people who are bringing up children. In 2019/20, the standard rate is a lump sum of £2,500 and monthly payments of £100. The higher rate is a lump sum of £3,500 and £350 a month. To claim this benefit, get the bereavement pack (form BSP1) either from gov.uk, or by phoning your local Jobcentre Plus (England, Wales and Scotland). In Northern Ireland, download an application form from nidirect.gov.uk, or contact the Bereavement Service on 0800 085 2463. To get the full amount, you must claim within three months of your partner's death.

Whether or not you get Bereavement Support Payment, if your income and savings are low, you may qualify for means-tested benefits, such as Universal Credit and Council Tax Reduction – and, if you have a mortgage, you might be eligible for the government's equity release loan, Support for Mortgage Interest. Chapters 3 and 6 have more information.

Over State Pension age

If you are over State Pension age at the time your partner dies, you do not get state bereavement benefits. If you reached State Pension age before 6 April 2016, you might instead be able to get a higher state basic pension based on your late husband's, wife's or civil partner's National Insurance record, and you might inherit up to half their state additional pension. These arrangements do not usually apply if you reached State Pension age on or after 6 April 2016 because the rules for the new State Pension that started then are different. However, under transitional rules, you might inherit half of your late partner's 'protected payment' if they had one. Chapter 3 has more details.

In either case, if your income is low, you might be able to claim means-tested benefits, such as Pension Credit, Housing Benefit and Council Tax Reduction – and, if you have a mortgage, you might be eligible for the government's equity release loan, Support for Mortgage Interest. Chapters 3 and 6 have more information.

Tax and bereavement

The UK has a system of independent taxation, which means that broadly speaking, the tax you pay depends only on your particular circumstances, not those of a partner or anyone else. However, there are some exceptions and some work to the advantage of married couples and civil partners in the event of one of them dying.

ISAs

ISAs are often described as 'tax-free', but this description has been challenged by people who point out that ISAs nevertheless count as part of someone's estate, and so may be subject to IHT on death. Moreover, the protective 'tax wrapper' (see Chapter 2) disappears on death. Since ISAs cannot be held in joint names, this is a problem for couples who have been forced to take out ISAs independently, but view their ISA savings as being on behalf of them both.

This latter problem has been solved for married couples and civil partners, but not unmarried couples. For deaths occurring on or after 3 December 2014, a surviving husband, wife or civil partner can inherit an ISA allowance equal to the value of the ISA savings and investments their late-partner owned. This is an extra allowance on top of your own normal annual allowance. The extra allowance is available for three years from the date of death or 180 days after the administration of the estate has been completed, whichever is later. You get this allowance even if the actual savings and investments left in your late partner's ISAs are inherited by someone else. However, the extra allowance means that you can continue to get the freedom from income tax and CGT if you do inherit those assets or if you choose to invest money of an equivalent value. Inheriting the ISA allowance does not affect IHT, though. Your late partner's ISAs will still count as part of their estate, and there could be IHT to pay.

The IHT nil-rate band

IHT is mostly a tax on the estate you leave when you die (but can affect some lifetime gifts too) – see Chapter 4 for how this tax works. However, the tax bites only if your estate (and any taxable gifts in the seven years before death) come to more than your nil-rate band. In 2019/20, the standard nil-rate band is £325,000, but increased to as much as £475,000 if your estate includes a home, in which case you may qualify for a main-residence nil-rate band too.

It's common for couples to leave the bulk of their estate to each other so that the survivor will be financially secure. Since gifts in lifetime and on death between married couples and civil partners are IHT-free, this used to mean that many spouses and civil partners wasted their nil-rate band. This changed from 9 October 2007 onwards. Since then, a surviving husband, wife or civil partner can inherit any nil-rate band their late partner did not use.

Gifts and bequests between unmarried partners are not tax-free, so whatever they leave to each other uses up some or all of their nil-rate band. Moreover any unused part cannot be inherited, but is simply lost for good. Particularly for couples who have a valuable home (maybe in London where house prices are especially high), this can mean that assets, such as the family home, have to be sold on the first death in order to release enough money to pay the IHT due and any tax on the second death will typically be higher than a married couple would pay. This affects other people who live together too, such as siblings.

Organizations that can help

Problems vary. For some, the hardest thing to bear is the loneliness of returning to an empty house. For others, money problems seem to dominate everything else. For many older women, in particular, who have not got a job, widowhood creates a great gulf where for a while there is no real sense of purpose. Many widowed men and women go through a spell of feeling enraged at their partner for dying. Most are baffled and hurt by the seeming indifference of friends, who appear more embarrassed than sympathetic.

In time, problems diminish and individuals are able to recapture some of their joy for living with all its many pleasures. Talking to other people who know the difficulties from their own experience can be a tremendous help. The following organizations not only offer opportunities for companionship but also provide an advisory and support service:

- **Cruse Bereavement Care** offers free help to anyone who has been bereaved by providing both one-to-one and group support through its local branches throughout the UK. See cruse.org.uk.

- The **National Association of Widows** is a national voluntary organization. Its many branches provide a supportive social network for widows and – despite the name – widowers throughout the UK. See nawidows.org.uk.

Many professional and other groups offer a range of services for widows and widowers associated with them. These include:

- the **Civil Service Retirement Fellowship**: csrf.org.uk;
- the **War Widows Association**: warwidows.org.uk.

Many local Age UK groups offer a counselling service. Trade unions are often particularly supportive, as are Rotary Clubs, all the armed forces organizations and most benevolent societies.

INDEX

CPSIA information can be obtained
at www.ICGtesting.com
Printed in the USA
LVHW071710211219
641357LV00010B/156/P